"It seems that every decade or so, the institutional form of the church reinvents itself. It is no wonder if members of congregations weary of proposals to adopt the next 'new' approach to congregational life and ministry. This is not a how-to-have-a-successful-church manual. The authors set the church in a biblical context, reminding us that it might be the past that is the key to its future. The church's rationale is the gospel; its character is derived from the historic practices of the Christian church and the clear descriptions of what God expects of the people of God. The authors' specializations include theology, multiculturalism, the nature of learning and spirituality. As a result, this book reflects a holistic perspective and practicality that is not always evident in books about the church."

Linda Cannell, dean of academic life, North Park Theological Seminary

"After reading *Teaching the Faith, Forming the Faithful* I concluded, 'This text is perfect for my Foundations for Educational Ministry course.' Grounded in Scripture, conversant with theory, spanning the globe and the centuries of Christian tradition, Parrett and Kang have produced a comprehensive study of the church's teaching ministry. It will ignite passion in its readers and equip them with a clear, compelling vision for educational ministry."

Robert Drovdahl, professor of educational ministry, Seattle Pacific University

"Although Parrett and Kang seem to misread my priorities in my first book on worship, still I heartily recommend their work! In this book's massive thoroughness, they skillfully explore all the major questions for a congregation's educational ministry. This volume's comprehensive view of spiritual formation is critically necessary—and intensively beneficial!—reading for everyone who serves to teach the faith, from the preschool Sunday school teacher to the senior pastor!"

Marva J. Dawn, teaching fellow in spiritual theology, Regent College, Vancouver, British Columbia, and author of *Keeping the Sabbath Wholly, Is It a Lost Cause?* and *In the Beginning, GOD*

"This book moves almost seamlessly between Bible, theology and education to provide foundational insights into how the church must educate its members toward Christian maturity. In a time when serious education of believers has been neglected, this work offers an important and helpful corrective by using sound theology and the best of educational theory to guide the practice of the church."

Perry G. Downs, professor of educational ministries, Trinity Evangelical Divinity School, author of *Teaching for Spiritual Growth*

"*Teaching the Faith, Forming the Faithful* is a fairly comprehensive orientation and guidebook for pastors and church leaders regarding the essential educational ministry of the church. The overall organization of the book is clear (aims, essential content of the gospel, participants, and processes and practices), and the last two chapters offer a macroframework for conceptualizing and guiding overall educational ministry practice. The authors' 'pastoral insider' perspective yields useful lists and suggestions that can easily be contextualized in any local church, especially those with a liturgical tradition. The book is biblically grounded throughout and offers a wide range of notes and resources from church history, making it a rich resource for the seminary classroom and on the pastor's shelf."

Klaus Issler, Ph.D., professor of Christian education and theology, Talbot School of Theology, Biola University, and author of *Wasting Time with God*

"Well-grounded in Scripture, committed to the church and the gospel of Christ, *Teaching the Faith, Forming the Faithful* describes and explains the essential elements for a teaching that truly aims to form the believer and the church community unto a more faithful living of the gospel. This is a book well worth reading by those who teach and share the goal of promoting a lifestyle that daily lives the story of the good news of Jesus Christ. I look forward to engaging my students with this well-rounded text on teaching as they too seek to learn to teach and form the faithful in the way of the gospel."

Jackie L. Smallbones, Th.D., professor of religion and Christian education, Northwestern College, Iowa, and author of *Keeping Company with Jesus*

"This is the kind of book on the teaching ministry of the church that we have needed for some time! Parrett and Kang provide a solid biblical grounding for the purpose and practices of educational ministry, connecting it with the broader life and ministry of the church. Their 'take and bake' approach makes this a thought-provoking read, challenging church leaders to look more deeply into the nature of the church, its calling in the world, and the ways educational ministry can better strengthen the faith and faithfulness of God's people. This is a must-read for everyone in vocational ministry who desires to see the church grow into a more faithful image of Christ in this world."

Kevin E. Lawson, director, Ph.D. and Ed.D. programs in educational studies, and editor, *Christian Education Journal,* Talbot School of Theology, Biola University

TEACHING THE FAITH, FORMING THE FAITHFUL

A BIBLICAL VISION FOR
EDUCATION IN THE CHURCH

▼

GARY A. PARRETT AND S. STEVE KANG

Foreword by J. I. PACKER

IVP Academic
An imprint of InterVarsity Press
Downers Grove, Illinois

InterVarsity Press
P.O. Box 1400, Downers Grove, IL 60515-1426
World Wide Web: www.ivpress.com
E-mail: email@ivpress.com

InterVarsity Press® is the book-publishing division of InterVarsity Christian Fellowship/USA®, a movement of students and faculty active on campus at hundreds of universities, colleges and schools of nursing in the United States of America, and a member movement of the International Fellowship of Evangelical Students. For information about local and regional activities, write Public Relations Dept., InterVarsity Christian Fellowship/USA, 6400 Schroeder Rd., P.O. Box 7895, Madison, WI 53707-7895, or visit the IVCF website at <www.intervarsity.org>.

Design: Cindy Kiple

Images: 5 multicultural friends: iStockphoto
       open book: Tim Starkey/iStockphoto

ISBN 978-0-8308-2587-5

Printed in the United States of America ∞

Library of Congress Cataloging-in-Publication Data

Parrett, Gary A., 1957-
  Teaching the faith, forming the faithful: a biblical vision for
  education in the church / Gary A. Parrett and S. Steve Kang.
     p. cm.
  Includes bibliographical references and indexes.
  ISBN 978-0-8308-2587-5 (pbk.: alk. paper)
  1. Christian education—Study and teaching. 2. Spiritual
formation—Study and teaching. I. Kang, S. Steve. II. Title.
BV1471.3.P37 2009
268—dc22

                                                            2009026593

P	18	17	16	15	14	13	12	11	10	9	8	7	6	5	4
Y	24	23	22	21	20	19	18	17	16	15	14	13			

Contents

Foreword

The following facts are surely beyond dispute.

First, the Christian church is presented in the New Testament as a multi-congregational community that is called to a life of worship, work and witness according to God's will, and of constant teaching and learning as a means to these ends. As trainers impress upon athletes that they must never stop training, so Jesus and his apostles make it clear that the church must never stop learning, for only so will it move generation by generation into true maturity in Christ. So the teaching ministry of the church must be continuous.

Second, genuine Christian education changes people significantly, leading them into obedience to God the Father and the Lord Jesus Christ that would not otherwise take place at all.

Third, the teaching and learning of biblical faith, church doctrine and Christian theology (three realities that ideally will always be one) is not the acknowledged priority in the patterns of church life that prevail throughout the Christian world today. Certainly in the West, smatterings of Scripture knowledge and occasional dippings into matters of doctrine are regularly treated as sufficient for spiritual health and discipleship. By comparison with our evangelical Protestant predecessors, we are falling woefully short here, and it shows.

The present wide-ranging volume is a wake-up call to us all on these matters. Recognizing that the well-being and upbuilding of congregations depends in the first instance on a really educative pattern of Christian education being integral to their ongoing life, Parrett and Kang lay out in detail, with good judgment, firm grasp and many lively proposals, the authentic elements of what is needed. Much wisdom that has been broached in bits and pieces in recent years is brought together here. Rich in its pastoral discernment, this is emphatically a book for our times, and I commend it with enthusiasm.

J. I. Packer
Vancouver, B.C.

Tables

Figures

Preface

For we know in part and we prophesy in part.

1 CORINTHIANS 13:9

This is a book about teaching and formation in the church. It is the collaborative effort of two friends and colleagues who have been learning, studying, laboring and teaching in these areas of ministry for decades. It has been written with a view to serving pastors and church leaders, as well as others whose primary ministry as followers of Jesus Christ is to teach, mentor, direct or form fellow believers.

Many wonderfully helpful books have been written on these subjects, including several volumes recently written by friends of ours.[1] What then motivates us to add to these significant works?

Our hope is to contribute to the ongoing discussion and especially to speak to areas that sometimes seem to be overlooked. Like the rest of our colleagues in the field, "we know in part and we prophesy in part." God, in infinite wisdom, has chosen not to invest in any *one* of us all the possible insights about this or any other subject. The apostle Paul understood his own knowledge to be partial, and thus what he preached and taught was also "in part." He therefore forbade others from seeing him as somehow competitive with Apollos or Peter or anyone else. "So then," he admonished the Corinthians, "no more boasting about men! All things are yours, whether Paul or Apollos or Cephas" (1 Cor 3:21-22).

He was a fellow laborer with those other servants of God. We offer this book in such a spirit. We write as fellow laborers with the many others who have written, and shall write, about these issues of such great import for the life of the church.

---

[1]For example, Jim Wilhoit, *Spiritual Formation as If the Church Mattered* (Grand Rapids: Baker, 2008); Ron Habermas, *Introducing Christian Education and Formation* (Grand Rapids: Zondervan, 2008); and Richard Osmer, *Practical Theology: An Introduction* (Grand Rapids: Eerdmans, 2008), and *The Teaching Ministry of Congregations* (Louisville, Ky.: Westminster/John Knox Press, 2007).

Many have approached educational ministry[2] by organizing their thoughts around some basic questions, questions like *why* and *what, how,* and *who.* There have been many ways of enumerating and organizing such questions.[3] We prefer to think of seven questions in all: *Why* do we teach? *What* do we teach? *When* do we teach what? *Whom* are we teaching (and what difference does that make)? *How* shall we teach? *Where* shall we teach? And, finally, *who* are the teachers?[4]

Among these seven questions, it seems to us, there are several that have not been given the attention they deserve in recent decades, at least in evangelical Protestant circles. While many books have been written with emphasis on matters of *how* and *where,* it seems that less has been written about the questions of *who, whom* and *when.* More striking is the absence of attention to the questions of *why* and, especially, of *what.*

In an earlier work, *A Many Colored Kingdom,*[5] we joined with another dear friend and colleague, Elizabeth Conde-Frazier, in touching upon most or all of the seven questions. However, our emphasis was primarily on the *whom* question—and *how* that affects our approach to all the others. Books have been written on the *who* question, but we believe there is still much that needs saying about this critical topic. "*When* shall we teach *what?*" is a question that has been addressed in many volumes, but mostly with a view to issues of natural development.[6] We address it here with an additional emphasis on spiritual development.

We open this book with two chapters addressing the question of *why* the church must teach. This question is, we believe, the most foundational of all, and yet many church leaders seem to assume that there is already widespread clarity about how to answer it. This does not seem to us to be the case at all. Finally, we spend a great deal of space addressing the question of *what* the church should teach—speaking to what may be the most neglected question of all in our day.

---

[2]Terminology can be troublesome in this field. "Christian education" is used by one, "educational ministry" by another, "spiritual formation" by some, "Christian formation" by others. Some would emphasize learning, while others emphasize teaching, and so on. Throughout the course of this book we will make reference to many of these terms and the questions they raise.

[3]See Thomas Groome, *Christian Religious Education* (San Francisco: HarperSanFrancisco, 1982).

[4]We formally introduce these questions in chapter five.

[5]Elizabeth Conde-Frazier, S. Steve Kang and Gary A. Parrett, *A Many Colored Kingdom: Multicultural Dynamics in Spiritual Formation* (Grand Rapids: Baker, 2004).

[6]See Perry Downs, *Teaching for Spiritual Growth* (Grand Rapids: Zondervan, 1994); and James Wilhoit and John Detonni, *Nurture That Is Christian: Developmental Perspectives on Christian Education* (Grand Rapids: Baker, 1995).

The other key feature of the contribution we hope to make by means of this book is that we attempt here to cast a vision for teaching and formation that is biblically driven, from first to last. Of course, we dare not suggest that our friends and colleagues have done anything less in what they have written. We simply mean that it has been a very intentional decision on our part to try to filter all these questions and concerns through a biblical grid and from a biblical worldview. We know that, in spite of our efforts, we will be found to have fallen short at many points. After all, as we have said, *we know in part.*

TAKE AND BAKE

Years ago, our colleague at Gordon-Conwell Theological Seminary, New Testament scholar Sean McDonough, told the faculty about one of his favorite teaching strategies. From time to time he shares with his students what he calls "half-baked ideas." That is, he lets the students peer into his biblical and theological works in progress, then updates them occasionally on the progress he has been making as he wrestles with a particular question or topic.

As I (Gary) heard Sean describe this strategy, I thought to myself, *"All* the ideas I share in class are 'half-baked'!" Then, upon further reflection, I realized that this was not quite right. Actually, my ideas are usually offered more on the order of "take and bake"—like hand-made pizzas prepared and sold to be baked at home.

In this book, many of the ideas presented are either half-baked or, to say it more accurately, of the "take and bake" variety. That is, we offer here many principles that are, we believe, biblically and practically sound. But we fully expect that how these principles might be worked out in practice will vary widely from context to context. Therefore, we boldly encourage our readers to "take and bake" any of concepts they find here that strike them as faithful and wise, and do so in ways that will best serve the congregations they serve.

WIDE AND DEEP: THE NATURE OF THE COLLABORATION

The broad shape of this book is Gary's work, based on materials from several classes he has taught at Gordon-Conwell over the past decade. Thus whenever words like *I* or *my* occur, this is—unless otherwise noted—Gary speaking. The key exception to the above is found in chapters eight and nine. There Steve takes the wheel for a time to help steer us through the difficult terrain of theoretical insights on learning and development. In those two chapters, all references to "I" are from Steve.

If the breadth is largely Gary's doing, Steve is largely responsible for helping to deepen the discussion. Steve has worked through every part of this text with a fine-tooth comb, correcting where necessary, adding nuance throughout and helping to fill out the picture. Aside from the two chapters on learning and development, Steve's voice can be found primarily in the footnotes and in the "Questions for Planning and Practice" and the "Resources for Further Study" sections at the conclusion of each chapter. This approach to the collaboration reflects, in part, our passions and our giftings, and the way we often work together. Gary delights in framing things; Steve delights in details. Gary studies the Bible and reads selected works from historical theology, biblical theology and practical theology; Steve studies the Bible—and reads pretty much everything in print! Gary thinks in hymns, acronyms and acrostics; Steve thinks in very big words. Gary loves baseball; Steve loves international soccer. This is our second book project together, and we are very grateful to God for enabling us to partner with one another once again.

SPECIAL RESOURCES

Each chapter closes with three special resources. The first is "Hymn for Contemplation and Worship." Gary wrote most of these texts over the years, and they are intended to be sung to familiar hymn tunes. The hymns have been selected to provide an opportunity for doxology following the theological and practical material presented in the chapter. We invite the reader to read or sing these texts, to personally consider their words as a sort of poetic echo to the material they have just read in prose. Please feel free, as well, to use these hymns in small-group settings or in congregational worship.[7]

We have also designed a set of questions for each chapter to invite the readers to pause and reflect deeply as to what God might have them ponder after reading the chapter, especially with a view to concrete planning and practice in present or future ministry contexts. When we decided to list a carefully selected set of books for further study at the end of each chapter, we happily assumed that those who are concerned about growing as teachers will definitely want to read more deeply in the various topics we address.

---

[7]Most of the hymns, and many others, can be found in a collection titled *Psalms, Hymns and Spiritual Songs* by Gary Parrett and Julie Tennent, due to be released in 2009 by Morgen-Books.

MANY THANKS . . .

We are very grateful to our good friends at InterVarsity Press for their support in this effort, and we especially want to thank Al Hsu for his patience, support and many excellent suggestions and questions. We also thank our many colleagues and students throughout the years at Gordon-Conwell, as well as at Gordon College (where Gary previously taught) and at Wheaton College (where Steve previously taught).

We also give thanks for the friends and colleagues who have read all or portions of this book, including the "anonymous" readers who read the first draft and offered very thoughtful advice. Our Gordon-Conwell colleague John Jefferson Davis also made a number of helpful suggestions—and we have heeded all of them. We want to express our gratitude to Gina Bellofatto, our research assistant, who gladly took part in helping us with formulating the questions for planning and practice at the end of each chapter and aided in the writing of an initial draft of chapters eight and nine.

We are grateful as well for the learning, fellowship and worship we have experienced in our church homes through the decades of our respective faith journeys. The impact of these congregations on our lives is surely more significant than we can begin to realize.

To God we give great thanks for our loving families: Gary's wife, Holly, and daughter, Alisa, and Steve's wife, Chris, and children, Ashley and Andrew.

Above all, thanks be to God for the unfathomable and indescribable gift of his Son Jesus Christ and the life that is ours through his grace. To God be all the glory in the church and in Christ Jesus forever!

PART 1

PURPOSE

A Mission to Fulfill

"Tell me a story, and put me in it!"

▼

SOME YEARS BACK, NEW TESTAMENT SCHOLAR GORDON FEE was sitting with other attendees at a workshop about the power of story. The speaker was Eugene Peterson, his faculty colleague. Peterson mentioned an episode in which his four-year-old grandson jumped onto his lap and demanded, "Grandpa, tell me a story, and put me in it." Upon hearing this account, Fee began to weep, overwhelmed by the fact that this is precisely what God has done for all of us.[1] God is unfolding the great Story, and he has invited us to take our places in that story.

In this first section of the book, we consider this great Story into which God has invited us. It is a grand drama of redemption and reconciliation. Growing in our understanding of the Story, and of our places in it, is critical for teaching and formation in the church. In chapter one, we overview the Story itself, drawing heavily on Paul's writing in the letter to the Ephesians to catch a glimpse of God's intended instrument for his ongoing work of reconciliation—the church of Jesus Christ. In chapter two, we consider how the Story and our place in it can help us answer the important question of *why* the church must ever engage in faithful ministries of teaching and formation. Some of the themes introduced in these first two chapters will be revisited throughout the remainder of the book.

---

[1] Fee told this story during a pastors' forum titled "Paul, the Spirit, and the People of God," hosted by the Ockenga Institute's Shoemaker Center for Church Renewal at Gordon-Conwell Theological Seminary in South Hamilton, Massachusetts, Fall 1998.

The *Poiēma* of God

For we are God's workmanship, created in Christ Jesus
to do good works, which God prepared in advance for us to do.

EPHESIANS 2:10

▼

As THE FAMILIAR TALE HAS IT, THE PROFESSOR of a Philosophy 101 class enters the classroom to administer the final exam. Stepping silently to the blackboard, he writes there the one-word question "Why?" Turning to the class, he says, "Here is your exam question. Write."[1]

There is, as well, the persistent image of the toddler, curious about everything but limited by experience, exposure, knowledge and vocabulary. And so it is that she begins to ask her parents, "Why?" No matter what answer they offer, the child's response is invariably a follow-up question: "Why?"

Tragically, many of us in positions of ministry leadership seem less wise than either the philosophy professor or the toddler. "Why?" is nearly always the most critical of questions, yet it often remains unasked. We are impatient. We prefer to dive in with other questions, questions that strike us as being more relevant. "How?" typically tops the list. The tyranny of the "urgent" needs and demands of those we serve presses us to swift response. We feel a need to act and to do so now. It is not surprising then that books with titles or subtitles promising how-to solutions for pastors, teachers and other servants typically top the charts of best-selling Christian books, just as is the case in other publishing markets. Perhaps it is a sign of the times.

---

[1]The urban legend continues by noting that the only student to score an A on the exam was one whose answer read, simply, "Why not?"

How is certainly a critical question. We would be unwise to neglect it. In this book, we will try to tackle it head-on. But critical as it is, it is not the first question. It *must not be* the first question. *Why* is the proper question with which to begin our exploration of the church's teaching ministry. Constantly asking this question, and answering it faithfully, will guide us toward an understanding of which questions we will need to ask further as we journey on. "He knows the 'why' for his existence, and will be able to bear almost any 'how.'"[2]

The first question before us, given the topic of the book, is "Why teach?" Why does the church of Jesus Christ engage in a ministry of teaching? In asking this, we are seeking both a rationale and a *telos*.[3] Both aspects of the *why* query are important. Concerning a rationale, we seek to set forth a foundation, a starting point for our endeavor. What is it that prompts us to act? Concerning a *telos,* we are probing the issue of the "ends" toward which we teach—our aims, goals, objectives and so on. We will address both of these aspects in some detail in chapter two.

GOD'S PURPOSES FOR THE CHURCH

However, the question "Why does the church teach?" actually evokes other, even more primary questions. In this chapter, we will examine two such questions before addressing the "Why teach?" inquiry in the chapter that follows. These questions are *Why does the church exist?* And, *Why does the church exist* on earth—*in space and in time?* To run ahead to the question of why the church teaches, without first probing more fundamental issues such as these would be presumptuous or, at the very least, premature. On the other hand, attending to these two questions will take us a long way toward understanding why the church must engage in a ministry of teaching.

The Westminster catechisms famously framed the most primary of all our questions: "What is the chief end of man?" The Larger Catechism answers, "The chief end of man is to glorify God and fully to enjoy Him forever."[4] Surely the catechism gets it right at this most fundamental of points. All things, including especially humans, exist ultimately for the glory of God.

---

[2]Viktor Frankl, *Man's Search for Meaning: An Introduction to Logotherapy,* 4th ed. (Boston: Beacon Press, 1992), p. 88.

[3]*Telos* refers to an ultimate goal, final cause or result; related to teleology, the study of design, purpose and intent.

[4]*The Westminster Larger Catechism,* Question 1 and Answer.

This is our *telos,* as the Scriptures consistently affirm.[5] The question "Why does the church exist?" therefore has an obvious answer that also readily affirms that which is true of every human being and indeed of all things in heaven and on earth. We, the church of Jesus Christ, exist to give glory to our sovereign King.

With this in mind, we turn to our second essential question: Why does the church exist in space and in time? Why must the church endure this precarious and often painful, time-locked sojourn on earth? Why do we have to speak not only of the church triumphant but also of the church militant and, indeed, of the suffering church? If our ultimate end is to bring glory to God and fully to enjoy him forever, why does God not simply take us to be with him—face to face—upon conversion?

WHY DID JESUS COME TO EARTH?

One way to approach these concerns is to ask a similar question about Jesus Christ. Why did the eternal Son of God leave the glory and splendor of unbroken fellowship with the Father and the Holy Spirit in heaven to sojourn among us for a few decades? Answering the question about *his* earthly sojourn will perhaps prove helpful toward helping us understand our own. Thankfully, Jesus and the New Testament writers have much to say concerning the motives for the incarnation of God's Son. Here are some pieces of the puzzle:

- The Son of Man did not come to be served, but to serve, and to give his life as a ransom for many. (Mk 10:45)

- The Son of Man came to seek and to save what was lost. (Lk 19:10)

- God so loved the world that he gave his one and only Son, that whoever believes in him shall not perish but have eternal life. (Jn 3:16)

- I have come that they may have life, and have it to the full. (Jn 10:10)

- For this reason I was born, and for this I came into the world, to testify to the truth. (Jn 18:37)

- But when the time had fully come, God sent his Son, born of a woman, born under law, to redeem those under law, that we might receive the full rights of sons. (Gal 4:4-5)

---

[5]See, for example, Isaiah 43:7; Romans 11:36; 1 Corinthians 10:31; Ephesians 1:3-14; 3:21; Revelation 4:11.

- Here is a trustworthy saying that deserves full acceptance: Christ Jesus came into the world to save sinners—of whom I am the worst. (1 Tim 1:15)

- Since the children have flesh and blood, he too shared in their humanity so that by his death he might destroy him who holds the power of death—that is, the devil—and free those who all their lives were held in slavery by their fear of death. (Heb 2:14-15)

- The reason the Son of God appeared was to destroy the devil's work. (1 Jn 3:8)

From such texts as the above we can begin to understand some of the principle motives for the incarnation. Simply put, God the Son became human to redeem humans, to reconcile them to God and to one another, and in so doing, to crush the evil one and destroy his works.

These emphases are clearly in view in what may be the most important passage regarding the mission of Jesus—Luke 4:14 and following. The story is situated near the beginning of Jesus' ministry. He has been baptized by John and tested by the devil. He now returns to his hometown of Nazareth "in the power of the Spirit" and goes where he had always gone on the Sabbath, to the synagogue (Lk 4:14, 16). It was given to him to read from a passage in Isaiah. We know the text he read as Isaiah 61:1-2: "The Spirit of the Lord is on me, because he has anointed me to preach good news to the poor. He has sent me to proclaim freedom for the prisoners and recovery of sight for the blind, to release the oppressed, to proclaim the year of the Lord's favor" (Lk 4:18-19). All of these things became dramatically manifest in the subsequent earthly ministry of Jesus.

As significant as what Jesus *did* read from Isaiah's scroll is what he *did not* read on that occasion. He stopped his reading abruptly, in midsentence. Isaiah 61:2 goes onto say, "and the day of vengeance of our God, to comfort all who mourn." Before reaching these words, however, Luke records that Jesus "rolled up the scroll, gave it back to the attendant and sat down," and went on to say, with all eyes fixed on him, "Today this scripture is fulfilled in your hearing" (Lk 4:20-21). The word of God that Jesus had come to fulfill was a word of good news, a proclamation of an extended time of God's favor. He had not come in this, his *first* advent, to execute God's vengeance. Nor had he come to bring a final comfort to all who mourn. For fulfillment of *these* things, we eagerly await the *second* coming of the Lord.

The Bible portrays that coming Day as one of both horror and hope. For those on whom the wrath of God falls, it is the "great and dreadful day of the LORD" (Joel 2:31). For those whose names are written in God's book, it is the "blessed hope" (Tit 2:13). In either case, it is not *this* day. We who live between the first and the second advents of our Lord are living still in the "year of the Lord's favor" (see also 2 Pet 3:8-14).

The implications of this for the ministry of the church are profound. The believer or congregation that misses these, and believes that it is our duty to execute God's vengeance, can only perpetrate evil. Sadly, many have done precisely that over the course of the two millennia of the church's history. As well, churches that promise members or visitors that all their hurts and imperfections can or will be healed in the here-and-now of this life are offering false hopes.

The term that the apostle Paul typically uses to describe the great mission of Jesus, with a view to both his first and his second comings, is *reconciliation*. His teaching in this area is an affirmation of, and expansion on, all that we have discussed above. Before exploring Paul's vision of reconciliation, we must do a bit of background work. And so, in yet another variation on the *why* question, we ask, "Why reconciliation?"

FROM HARMONY TO ENMITY

The first two chapters of the Bible record God's creation of the heavens and the earth, and all their hosts (see Gen 2:1). All that God created, we are told, was good, very good (see Gen 1:31). God—who is within his triune self the ultimately relational One[6]—created humans to be in his image and likeness (see Gen 1:27). Humans, too, were relational beings from the start. And all the human relations were good, characterized by an essential harmony. The first man and woman were in harmony with each other, at peace with creation and the other creatures, at peace with themselves and in a wonderfully harmonious relationship with the living God.

However, Genesis 3 records the tragic turn of events that would change the course of our history. Through the willful rebellion of Adam and Eve, sin, suffering, death and condemnation enter the human narrative. All the relationships that had been characterized by harmony are now marked instead by

---

[6]John Zizioulas, *Being as Communion: Studies in Personhood and Communion* (Crestwood, N.Y.: St. Vladimir's Seminary Press, 1985); Catherine LaCugna, *God for Us: The Trinity and Christian Life* (San Francisco: HarperSanFrancisco, 1991).

bitter enmity. The man suggests that the woman is responsible for their plight (see Gen 3:12), and this first interhuman hostility soon spreads to affect all human relationships adversely (see Gen 4:8 and following). The first man and woman are also now at enmity with both the animals and the creation as a whole (see Gen 3:17-19). There is also the first appearance of turmoil and conflict within their own hearts—a kind of internal enmity. The man and woman had formerly been described as "naked, and they felt no shame" (Gen 2:25). But now they are troubled by their nakedness, and they take steps to clothe themselves (see Gen 3:7). Most significantly, their relationship with God is now radically altered. They are afraid of him with a new and unhealthy fear, and they hide from his presence (see Gen 3:8). Deep indeed is the so-called Fall of man.

A few years ago, I was ministering—and learning much—in Sri Lanka. I was teaching a group of pastors about aspects of the Fall and its implications for our present ministries. At one point, saying it as markedly as I could, I exclaimed, "Everything fell apart," my words accompanied by the gesture of spreading my hands outward and downward. My translator—a dear friend and key church leader in Sri Lanka[7]—did his part well, matching me not only in word but also in gesture. As he spread his own hands outward and downward, his right hand struck a glass full of water on the table in front of us. The glass flew onto the concrete floor and shattered, water flowing everywhere. After a moment's pause, I remarked, "Perfect!" and, following the translation, we all laughed at having witnessed, accidentally, the ideal illustration for my point.

The laughter died down quickly as we returned to the very sober truths we were discussing. The glass was broken, no longer able to do what it had been designed to do. Indeed, it was no longer even recognizable. No sooner had I resumed my teaching than one of the group members quickly stepped out of the room and returned with a broom and dustpan. Quietly, he swept up the pieces of the shattered glass and discarded them.

So might God also have done with all of us.

But this is not how the story of Genesis 3 proceeds. Instead, God begins a new and great work, the work of reconciling all things to himself. He himself provides suitable (and costly[8]) covering for the nakedness of the humans. He

---

[7]Rev. Adrian DeVisser, founding pastor and leader of the Kithu Sevana church-planting network.

[8]God covered the man and the woman with animal skins, which cost the lives and blood of some of his creatures.

pronounces consequences for their actions on each of them. God also addresses the one who had deceived and tempted them toward their sinful choices. It is to the serpent (that is, the devil; see Rev 20:2) that God most plainly announces his plan for redemption. The offspring of the woman would be in perpetual enmity with the serpent and his "offspring." And, at some point in the future, the seed of the woman would crush the head of that serpent (see Gen 3:15).

Historically, Christians have seen in this word a first glimpse of the Gospel. Thus the verse has been called the *protoevangelion*[9]—a text and a truth to which New Testament writers will later make numerous references and allusions (for example, Rom 16:20; 1 Cor 15:25; Gal 4:4: Heb 2:14-15; 1 Jn 3:8).

The story of Genesis 3 points to one additional relationship of enmity. Even as God foretold, there exists to this day an enmity between the devil (and his offspring) and the children born to woman. Humans are, in fact, actively opposed by Satan. He is our "adversary" (1 Pet 5:8 NASB), and the "accuser of our brothers" (Rev 12:10). He is a "murderer from the beginning" (Jn 8:44). Like a thief, he comes "to steal and kill and destroy" (Jn 10:10). Many have regarded the serpent's "offspring" mentioned in Genesis 3 as referring to the whole demonic realm and to that realm identified by mysterious titles such as "powers," "principalities," "rulers" and "authorities."[10] There has been significant discussion concerning the identities of these entities, but suffice it to say that there are many "fallen powers"[11] aligned against God and against his purposes and creatures, especially humans—and, among humans, especially against the church.

FROM ENMITY TO RECONCILIATION

It is in the face of all this enmity and hostility that God begins the great work of reconciling all things to himself. God had ceased from the work of creation (see Gen 2:1), but by Genesis 3, he begins this new work, the work of restoring, redeeming, reconciling all things. To this end, God raises up for himself a

---

[9]For instance, see James Hamilton, "The Skull Crushing Seed of the Woman: Inner-Biblical Interpretation of Genesis 3:15," *The Southern Baptist Journal of Theology* 10, no. 2 (Summer 2006): 30-55.

[10]See, for example, Marva Dawn, *Powers, Weakness, and the Tabernacling of God* (Grand Rapids: Eerdmans, 2001). For other biblical references to these "fallen powers," see 1 Corinthians 15:24; Ephesians 1:21; 3:10; 6:12; Colossians 1:16; 2:10, 15.

[11]Christopher Forbes, "Pauline Demonology and/or Cosmology? Principalities, Powers, and the Elements of the World in Their Context," *Journal for the Study of the New Testament* 85 (March 2002): 51-73.

people of his own—Israel—to be a light to the nations (see Is 43:21). Within Israel, he raises up prophets and other teachers to declare his will in and through this people (see Deut 18:14-22). To Israel, he commits his Torah—a record of both his saving deeds and his righteous will for his people (see Deut 4:8; Rom 3:2). And from Israel, in the fullness of time, he brings forth his own Son to fully effect the reconciliation of all things to himself (see Gal 4:4-5).

Jesus' incarnation, as we implied above, was largely motivated by this ministry of reconciliation. In John 5, Jesus heals a man who had been lame for thirty-eight years. Questioned by the religious authorities about having done this work on the Sabbath, Jesus answered, "My Father is always at his work to this very day, and I, too, am working" (Jn 5:17). The context of John 5 plainly suggests that the work that now "always" engages God is this great work of reconciliation. It was for such work that Jesus had come, at the bidding of his Father (see Jn 4:34).[12]

Jesus' earthly life was devoted to works of love, healing, deliverance and mercy, as we have seen. The climactic work of reconciliation that he performed, however, was in his death. Dying on the cross for us, Jesus bore our sins away forever (see Is 53:4; Heb 9:28; 1 Pet 2:24) and reconciled us both to God (see Col 1:19-23) and to one another (see Eph 2:11-21). Through his powerful resurrection from the dead, we are assured that Jesus has conquered sin, death and the devil forever (see Is 53:11-12; Rom 4:25).

As we have already suggested, Paul's principle term for all this wondrous work is *reconciliation*.[13] "God was reconciling the world to himself in Christ," he writes, "not counting men's sins against them" (2 Cor 5:19). In Colossians 1 he puts it this way: "For God was pleased to have all his fullness dwell in [Christ], and through him to reconcile to himself all things, whether things on earth or things in heaven, by making peace through his blood, shed on the cross" (Col 1:19-20).

ALREADY . . . NOT YET

In his writings, Paul often presents the work of reconciliation as having al-

---

[12]See also John 9:4; 14:10-14; 17:4; 19:30; Hebrews 10:5-7; compare Psalm 40:6-8.

[13]In the Greek, *katallagē,* which denotes "the state between God and us and therewith of our own state, for by it we become new creatures, no longer ungodly or sinners, but justified, with God's love shed abroad in our hearts. God has not changed; the change is in our relation to him and consequently in our whole lives. Reconciliation is through the death of Jesus. He was made sin for us and we are made God's righteousness in him." Geoffrey Bromiley, *Theological Dictionary of the New Testament, Abridged in One Volume,* ed. Gerhard Kittel and Gerhard Friedrich (Grand Rapids: Eerdmans, 1985), pp. 40-41.

ready been accomplished (see, for example, Rom 5:10; 2 Cor 5:19; Col 1:20-22). We also hear this implied in the "It is finished!" of Jesus on the cross. On the other hand, it is obvious that reconciliation has not been worked out, fully and practically, in either earthly or heavenly experience. All the points of enmity that we discussed from Genesis 3 are still obviously in place.[14] Paul teaches that Christ "must reign until he has put all his enemies under his feet," the last of which is death (1 Cor 15:25-26). It is clear from our daily experience that these enemies have not yet been fully subdued. For the final "day of vengeance" and the comforting "of all who mourn," as we noted before, we await the return of Christ.

Putting these apparently contradictory strands of biblical data together, we are faced with the fact that reconciliation is one of those biblical doctrines that we often describe with the language of "already . . . not yet." The cross and resurrection of Christ have accomplished and fully guaranteed the final outcome, but we have not yet fully experienced that outcome. Such an idea is perhaps more easily seen in the more particular wonder of salvation. As Paul wrote to the Ephesians, "Having believed, you were marked in [Christ] with a seal, the promised Holy Spirit, who is a deposit guaranteeing our inheritance until the redemption of those who are God's possession—to the praise of his glory" (Eph 1:13-14). That is, although we "have been saved" (Eph 2:5, 8), our present experience of that salvation is but the down payment on the whole. How great then is the glory that awaits us! So great a prospect becomes for us the impetus on our pilgrimage toward full salvation. As it is with our personal and corporate experience of salvation, so it is with our personal, corporate and cosmic experience of reconciliation.[15]

We return then to the question that led us to this entire line of inquiry: Why does the church exist *on earth,* in this time and space? The answer emerging is that just as there is an *already* and a *not yet* of reconciliation, there is also an *even now.* We have received and experienced the foretaste of God's recon-

---

[14]Including human vs. human, human vs. creation, human vs. powers, powers vs. God and humans vs. God. "Sin is . . . *hyperrelational,* or 'multi'-relational. It is active corruption in all directions . . . Godward, selfward, otherward, and worldward. . . . Sin is the hyperrelational distortion and corruption of the Eikon's relationship with God and therefore with self, with others, and with the world." Scot McKnight, *A Community Called Atonement* (Nashville: Abingdon, 2007), pp. 22-23.

[15]The implication of this language, of course, is that *reconciliation* is taken here to describe a work even more grand in scale than our *salvation.* Or, said otherwise, we see our salvation as a major aspect of God's "reconciling all things to himself" in and through Christ. We do not see these terms as being identical.

ciliation accomplished through Christ's life, death and resurrection. We anticipate the full inheritance of our salvation and await both the day of God's vengeance and his promised comforting of all who mourn. Between these, the church is called to fully participate in God's ongoing ministry of reconciliation. We read earlier that "God was reconciling the world to himself in Christ." That passage continues with these words: "And he has committed to us the ministry of reconciliation" (2 Cor 5:19). Like Jesus, we have reason to conclude that the "Father is always at his work to this very day," and so we also must work.

Jesus had come to do his Father's work, that is, good works of reconciliation. These he did in life and in death by means of his physical body. With that body he spoke good news to the poor, touched and healed the leper and the blind, cast out demons and raised the dead. With that same body he suffered and died in our place, "reconciling the world" to God, "not counting men's sin against them," but, rather, becoming "sin for us, so that in him we might become the righteousness of God" (2 Cor 5:19, 21). His death and subsequent resurrection and ascension guarantee the final outcome of perfect reconciliation of all things to God, and we now await that certain outcome. But, in the meantime—by God's gracious invitation to us—we have work to do. Jesus continues his great reconciling work in the *even now,* through his spiritual body—the church. The church exists in *this* time and in *this* space because of the *even now* commission to Christ's ministry of reconciliation.

THE CHURCH AS GOD'S *POIĒMA*

To further explore this notion of the church as the agent of God's ongoing work of reconciliation, we now look to Paul's letter to the Ephesians as a kind of lodestar to guide our thinking. Ephesians seems an appropriate choice for such a guiding light. The great concern of the epistle is, in fact, the church. Here we find a grand vision of God's plan for the body of Christ, a vision full with implications both for eternity and for the here and now. Unlike some of Paul's other letters to churches, Ephesians does not address particular questions, issues or problems that had arisen specific to the context. Instead, Paul focused attention on the nature and purposes of the church in broad and bold strokes, and in ways that can easily be applied in a wide variety of settings.

The church is, as Paul put it, the "workmanship" of God (Eph 2:10). Other English versions of the Bible render this word "handiwork." The

Greek word translated here is *poiēma*.[16] When we refer in this book—from this point onward—to the *poiēma* of God, we intend to communicate a lofty view of the church that Jesus told us he himself would build (see Mt 16:18), the church that has historically been called "one, holy, catholic and apostolic."[17]

In unpacking the grand vision of God's plan for the body of Christ that is found in Paul's letter to the Ephesians, we will be making use of the word *poiēma* in an additional way—as an acronym to outline the contents of the letter, as follows:

> **P**raise for God's glorious grace (1:1—2:10)
> **O**ne body in Christ (2:11-22)
> **I**ntercession toward knowledge of God's unknowable love (3:1-21)
> **E**xhortation, equipping and edification of the body (4:1—5:2)
> **M**aturity through Spirit-fullness (5:3—6:9)
> **A**rmor for spiritual warfare (6:10-24)

PRAISE FOR GOD'S GLORIOUS GRACE

Paul's letter to the Ephesians begins with an explosion of praise. Paul makes God's glory preeminent in this letter. In the Greek, Ephesians 1:3-14 is one effusive sentence, filled with a vision of the "praise of [God's] glory," "the praise of his glorious grace" and so on. God does all things according to his own good pleasure (see Eph 1:9) and works out all things in accordance with his own will (see Eph 1:11). God is himself the "Father of glory" (Eph 1:17 RSV) and is, as Paul goes on to say later in the letter, to be glorified "in the church and in Christ Jesus throughout all generations" (Eph 3:21). All of this is clear affirmation of our earlier assertion that the church exists, ultimately, for the glory of our great God.

---

[16] *Poiēma* means "something made." It may well seem a stretch to arrive at, as some commentators suggest, a rendering like masterpiece. But in the context, the church is something made by God, the "Master of the universe." Hence, even if *masterpiece* may be a bit too extravagant a rendering, it certainly captures an aspect of the truth of the matter.

[17] This language is found in the Nicene Creed and elsewhere. The holiness of the church is grounded not in itself but in the life, death, resurrection of Jesus Christ. The oneness of the church is interrelated to the unity of God and the fellowship that believers have with God. The church is catholic in that it is present in all parts of the world and in all periods of history. There are indeed individual churches, but these churches do not exist independently. Rather, they exist as a part of a greater, unified whole. The apostolic character of the church is to be exhibited in what the church proclaims and how the church lives in service and ministry. The church is to commit itself to the constant judgment and correction of the Gospel and the Scriptures as a whole.

What is it that spurs Paul toward such rapturous praise in Ephesians? It is this very truth that we have been exploring thus far: the fact that God, in Christ, is reconciling all things to himself. Here, however, Paul describes this work by means of a different expression. He writes that God has revealed a great, mysterious intention purposed in Christ "to be put into effect when the times will have reached their fulfillment—to bring all things in heaven and on earth together under one head, even Christ" (Eph 1:10). "To bring . . . together under one head" translates another Greek term,[18] one which has also been rendered in English "to sum up." An ancient use of the term referred to totaling a column of numbers and writing the sum atop the column.[19] Everything in heaven and on earth will ultimately be put back together under the headship of Christ.[20]

God is, of course, eminently worthy of our praise simply because of who he is. But the praise Paul renders and calls for in Ephesians is particularly focused on the fact that God is unfolding this great work and that *we* have become the objects of his reconciling grace. We have been chosen in Christ to be holy, blameless and adopted as God's children. We have been given "every spiritual blessing in Christ" (Eph 1:3) because we have been "included in Christ" (Eph 1:13). We were dead in our trespasses and sins and had become "by nature objects of wrath" (Eph 2:1-3). "But God," as many English versions begin verse four, "because of his great love for us . . . made us alive with Christ. . . . It is by grace" that we "have been saved" (Eph 2:4-5).

Although these wonders of reconciliation certainly apply to each individual believer, Paul is here writing with the church in mind—in both its local and its universal expressions. Later in Ephesians, he will go on to identify the church corporately as the temple of the Holy Spirit, as the body of Christ and the bride of Christ. Or, as he puts it in 2:10, *we* are God's *poiēma*. While we can speak of each human as being, in a very real sense, a *poiēma* of God, that notion is a Psalm 139 testimony. There the psalmist writes, "I praise you be-

---

[18]The Greek term used here is *anakephalaioō*. While the NIV translates the word as "bring together under one head," "whether the word involves any connotation of 'head' or 'headship' is doubtful. The word means 'sum up' or 'recapitulate.' The whole universe is to be brought together in Christ. He is the focal point that gives all creation coherence. One day every knee will bow (Phil 2:10) and God's creation will be unified around Christ. Both troublesome words then focus on Christ as Lord of all." Klyne Snodgrass, *Ephesians: The NIV Application Commentary* (Grand Rapids: Zondervan, 1996), p. 53. See also Colossians 1:20.

[19]Markus Barth, *Ephesians 1-3: The Anchor Bible* Commentary (Garden City, N.Y.: Doubleday, 1974), pp. 89-92.

[20]And Christ, in turn, will hand it all over to the Father (see 1 Cor 15:24).

cause I am fearfully and wonderfully made" (Ps 139:14). But in Ephesians 2:10, we observe that the emphasis is on the *corporate* masterpiece—the one body, *the church* as the beautiful creation of God.

Paul's speech concerning the church in this letter is praise nearly as lavish as his praise of God. Or, better, it is *part of* his praise for God—a key reason for the doxology. Some features of the church's lofty reality and call are as follows:

- It is "his body, the fullness of him who fills everything in every way" (Eph 1:23).

- It "rises to become a holy temple in the Lord . . . a dwelling in which God lives by his Spirit" (Eph 2:21-22).

- Through it "the manifold wisdom of God should [now] be made known to the rulers and authorities in the heavenly realms" (Eph 3:10).

- It is an arena for God's glory "throughout all generations" (Eph 3:21).

- It is the bride of Christ, whom he died for and whom he glorifies (Eph 5:25-32).

No wonder Paul makes an appeal to his readers to "live a life worthy of the calling you have received" (Eph 4:1). What a lofty calling it is!

Our key text, again, says that "we are God's workmanship, created in Christ Jesus to do good works, which God prepared in advance for us to do" (Eph 2:10). As Christian leaders, many of us have emphasized Ephesians 2:8-9 and the wonderful truths therein—that we are saved by grace, through faith, apart from any works of our own—but have stopped our reading of the passage too abruptly. For if we read only verses 8 and 9, without continuing on to verse 10, we may in fact be guilty of inadvertently promoting a very serious error: the notion that good works have no place in the Christian life. Nothing could be further from the truth! We may think our way through Ephesians 2:1-10 by means of several questions:

1. What are we saved *from?* Clearly, in light of verses 1 to 3, we are saved from sin, spiritual death and the coming wrath of God.

2. What are we saved *by?* We are saved by the "but God" of verse 4—that is, by his great love for us and the riches of his mercy. And, as Paul puts it plainly in verses 5 and 8, it is "by grace" that we are saved.

3. What are we saved *through?* We are saved through faith, says Paul. That is, we are saved by believing the Gospel of Jesus Christ—that he died

for our sins, was buried, was raised on the third day and appeared to many (see 1 Cor 15:3-8)—and by trusting this One who saves. It is faith in the perfect work of a perfect Savior that saves us, and not any works of our own.

While many of us have typically been good at asking (and suggesting answers for) the first three questions, there is a critical fourth question that we have not often asked:

4. What are we saved *for*?

If we stop after Ephesians 2:9, we will miss the answer to this fourth question. But verse 10 illuminates: We are "created in Christ Jesus to do good works, which God has prepared in advance for us to do."

Our salvation is entirely by grace alone, through faith alone, in Christ alone. But we are "created in Christ Jesus" (a reference not to the original creation but to our re-creation as believers; see 2 Cor 5:17) "to do good works, which God prepared in advance for us to do" (literally, "to walk in"). In other words, we are saved entirely *apart from* any works of our own, but we are saved *in order to* walk in good works. Good works both testify to the reality of our faith and of our identity as God's children (see, for example, Jas 2:17, 26; Jn 14:15; 1 Jn 3:7) and are the intended outcome of our faith, as Ephesians 2:10 reveals. Paul says essentially the same thing in Titus 2:14, where we read that Christ "gave himself for us to redeem us from all wickedness and to purify for himself a people that are his very own, eager to do what is good." Good works surely have a part in a full-orbed doctrine of salvation. But we must remember the old saying that pertains to keeping a tidy home: "A place for everything and everything in its place."[21] Good works are not peripheral to, or even antithetical to, our doctrine of salvation; they are actually vital to it. Good works do have their *proper place*—that of flowing out from our salvation, not of contributing to it.[22]

We note once again that Paul has primarily a corporate vision in view in this letter to the Ephesians. It is not individuals who are the *poiēma* of God; it is the

---

[21]This saying is much better exemplified by Steve's office than it is by Gary's.

[22]Of course, important theological nuance is called for here. If we choose more specific terms, like *justification* and *sanctification,* we might say that good works have no place in our "justification," but do have a place in our "sanctification." This is a classic Reformed approach, though some scholars have recently called it into question. For now, we are simply using the language as Paul does in Ephesians 2:8-10: We are saved by grace, through faith and not by works. We are created anew to do good works. We will have a good deal more to say about all this in chapter two.

church, the body of Christ. While many contemporary English versions of the Bible translate the end of Ephesians 2:10 to say that good works have been prepared for us "to do," a more literal translation would be "to walk in." For Paul is setting forth a powerful metaphor in this letter. We are to see the church as the body of Christ. walking in good works in the midst of the still-broken world.

We have been musing about the reasons for the church's existence. As we have seen thus far, we exist for the praise of God's glorious grace. We glorify God because he is worthy to be praised. Further, we glorify him for reconciling us and all things to himself in Christ. And to the further praise of his glory we, as the one body of Christ, are privileged to join ourselves to this great reconciling work.

ONE BODY IN CHRIST

Another crucial point to glean from the letter to the Ephesians is that the *telos* of believers must not be thought of exclusively in terms of the individual. Paul's focus in the letter is on the body of Christ. We are not helped in this matter by the fact that in contemporary English it is not possible to distinguish between singular and plural when we see the word *you*.[23] In the vast majority of cases, when the New Testament letters address the readers as "you," the address is plural in the Greek. But many Western readers—already deeply influenced by a radically individualized view of things—will likely assume the address to be singular.

Thus in our reading of the New Testament, many English readers will miss a crucial biblical emphasis. If, when I read *you*, I take it as addressed singularly to *me*, I may not consider the corporate implications of the word. If, on the other hand, I read *you* as applying, first of all, to the body of believers to which I belong, I will begin with the corporate implications and yet still be very likely to consider the personal implications of God's word for me as a part of that body.

So then, we, *as the church* of Jesus Christ, exist ultimately for the glory of God. This is our *telos*, both corporately and individually. In reconciling all things to himself, God forms us into one body in Christ. Indeed, it is only as we are joined to the body of Christ that we are reconciled to God. This may surprise, even offend, the sensibilities of many evangelical ears, at least in the West. We may hear echoes of St. Cyprian's famous dictum "there is no salva-

---

[23]Older English sometimes used *ye* when a plural audience was in view. In many Southern states, *y'all* continues to capture the plural *you* very effectively. But in most of our English translations of the Bible, the fact that we are nearly always reading plural *you* throughout the New Testament letters is noted only in footnotes, if at all.

tion apart from the Church,"[24] a notion that, for many, rings more Catholic than Protestant. In fact, however, the same notion was essentially articulated by both Luther and Calvin.[25]

Of even greater weight than the testimony of any historical figure from the church is the testimony of Scripture itself. In Ephesians, we find Paul making the case that no one can be connected to Christ, the Head of the body, without being connected to the body. For many evangelical Protestants, what is deemed *essential* is that we be reconciled to God through Christ; perhaps seen as important, but *not as essential,* is that we also be reconciled to one another in Christ.

Paul, however, puts the matter far differently in Ephesians 2:11 and following. Addressing a primarily Gentile audience, he assures his readers that though they had once been separated from God and his covenants, they who were once "far away" have now been "brought near through the blood of Christ" (Eph 2:13). For Christ has made peace through the cross, uniting in himself those who had long been at enmity with one another—Jews and Gentiles (see Eph 2:14-15). Then he continues: "His purpose was to create in himself one new man out of the two, thus making peace, and in this one body to reconcile both of them to God through the cross, by which he put to death their hostility" (Eph 2:15-16). There is, in other words, no reconciliation to God that does not also include a reconciling to one another in the one body of Christ. God unites Jews and Gentiles as "one new man"[26] in Christ (Eph 2:15) to walk in the good works, which God has prepared in advance for us.

The one body is the new creation, the *poiēma,* newly "created in Christ

---

[24]Cyprian *On the Unity of the Church* 6. Quoted in Otto W. Heick, *A History of Christian Thought* (Philadelphia: Fortress, 1965), 1:104. Cyprian also said, "If someone has not the church for his mother, he has not God for his father." Ibid.

[25]See, for example, Calvin's *Institutes of the Christian Religion* 4.1. Among other claims along the same line of thought, Calvin refers to Cyprian's image of the church as our "mother": "For there is no other way to enter into life unless this mother conceive us in her womb, give us birth, nourish us at her breast, and lastly, unless she keep us under her care and guidance until. . . . Furthermore, away from her bosom one cannot hope for any forgiveness of sins or any salvation" (4.1.4).

[26]While some English translations soften the original to a more gender-sensitive "one new humanity," it is actually critical that we retain Paul's intended metaphor here of a singular individual. For it is the one body, the "one new man" or "one new person," newly formed by God, who will grow into maturity, be filled with the Spirit and be clothed with spiritual armor. Thus we, the "one new man," will walk in the good works that God has prepared for us. Later, of course, Paul uses a different communal identity, envisioning the church as the bride of Christ (Eph 5). Thus both masculine and feminine images are appropriated for describing aspects of the church's identity.

Jesus." D. Martin Lloyd-Jones put it thus: *"The Church is something absolutely new* that has been brought into being, something that was not there before. It is comparable to what happened in the very beginning when God created the heavens and the earth. There was nothing there before God created."[27] The life of this new spiritual body owes its existence to the death, resurrection and ascension of Christ's physical body (see Eph 2:6-16).

In the one body, then, we are reconciled to God. Thus there can be no vision of being reconciled to God that does not include being reconciled to one another in and through the church. Any such vision is opposed to the plain teaching of Scripture. We think, for example, of the oft-repeated double commandment of love: "'The most important one,' answered Jesus, 'is this: "Hear, O Israel, the Lord our God, the Lord is one. Love the Lord your God with all your heart and with all your soul and with all your mind and with all your strength." The second is this: "Love your neighbor as yourself"'" (Mk 12:28-31; see Deut 6:4-5; Lev 19:18). This dual love is affirmed by numerous passages in the writings of the apostles (for example, 1 Jn 4:8, 20).

These vital aspects of reconciliation cannot be separated, except in the minds, hearts and practices of ill-formed Christians. Furthermore, it simply will not do to have believers bearing a message of reconciliation to others while unconcerned themselves with living in reconciled relationships with one another. Jesus told us as much when he said, "By this all men will know that you are my disciples, if you love one another" (Jn 13:35). He also prayed toward this end: "Father, . . . may they also be [one] in us so that the world may believe that you have sent me" (Jn 17:21).

It is essential that we acknowledge all these truths about the one body of Christ because it is in and through the one body of Christ that God's reconciling work continues in the *even now*. This is implied in what has already been said, but we make this point more explicitly in what follows.

A BODY YOU PREPARED FOR ME

God's grand design to unite all things under one Head, even Christ, as we have seen, has "already," "not yet" and "even now" aspects to it. Now, here is a wonder for contemplation: the entirety of this reconciling work is achieved—always and only—through the body of Christ. The author of Hebrews makes it clear that without having a truly human body—and its ac-

---

[27]D. Martin Lloyd-Jones, *God's Way of Reconciliation: Studies in Ephesians 2* (Grand Rapids: Baker, 1972), p. 214.

companying fully human experience—Christ could neither have atoned for our sins nor become for us a merciful high priest (see Heb 2:10-18). So it is that "when Christ came into the world, he said: 'Sacrifice and offering you did not desire, but a body you prepared for me. . . . Then I said, "Here I am—it is written about me in the scroll—I have come to do your will, O God"'" (Heb 10:5-7; compare Ps 40:6-8).

In the "already" of reconciliation, Christ, in his physical body, touched and healed the sick, spoke good news to the poor, commanded freedom for the demonically oppressed, looked on and wept for the shepherdless sheep of Israel and much more. In that same physical body, he "suffered under Pontius Pilate, was crucified dead, and buried."[28] By means of this suffering, he bore our sins away and became the once-for-all atoning sacrifice for sin. It was with a glorified, yet still material, body (see Lk 24:39) that he rose from the dead "for our justification" (Rom 4:25) and has now ascended to heaven, where he ever lives to make intercession for us, thus assuring our complete salvation (see Heb 7:25). In this glorious body he will return to execute all matters pertaining to the "not yet" of reconciliation.

And what shall we say about the "even now" of God's reconciling work? This work, too, continues only by means of the body of Christ. But now this work continues on earth through the church, the spiritual body of Christ, with Christ himself as our Head. The God who was "reconciling the world to himself in Christ," has now extended to us "the message of reconciliation" and the ministry of reconciliation (2 Cor 5:19-20). We are to join ourselves to the very work of God, as God's "fellow workers" (1 Cor 3:9; 2 Cor 6:1; 1 Thess 3:2). Jesus had earlier invited his followers to join themselves to this work (see, for example, Jn 4:34-38; 9:4) and even promised that they would do both the same works and even "greater works" than he himself had done (Jn 14:12 rsv) because of his ascension and the subsequent outpouring of the Holy Spirit that was to come.

What are the works of reconciliation that are to concern us, as the body of Christ, in the here and now? They include *bearing* the Gospel in bold proclamation and constant instruction, and *obeying* the Gospel (that is, living "in line with the truth of the Gospel," Gal 2:14). We are also to obey the so-called Great Commission texts (see Mt 28:18-20; Mk 16:15; Lk 24:48; Jn 20:21-23; Acts 1:8) and the Great Commandments of loving God and loving neighbor. These things we are called to attend to as the body of Christ, for the following reasons:

---

[28]This is, of course, language from the Apostles' Creed.

- Although "God was reconciling the world to himself in Christ, not counting men's sins against them" (2 Cor 5:19), most of the world remains unaware of God's reconciling work. Thus God has given to us the "message of reconciliation."

- Although God's righteous wrath has been propitiated at the cross (see Rom 3:25; 2 Cor 5:21; 1 Jn 2:2), it is still essential that people turn and "be reconciled to God." Thus we are appointed "Christ's ambassadors, as though God were making his appeal through us" (2 Cor 5:20).

- Although the cross of Christ tore down the wall of hostility between Jew and Gentile, and ended the enmity between male and female, slave and free—and whatsoever other historic or contemporary human enmity there may be—most have not heard or have not obeyed this aspect of God's reconciling work (even Peter, Barnabas and other leading believers stumbled at this point in Antioch; see Gal 2:11-14).[29] It is critical that we acknowledge, and repent of, our own active and passive participation in these enmities.

- The love of Christ compels us to act as ministers of reconciliation, for the world in which we live is still broken. In spite of what God has accomplished at the cross, the full experience of our reconciliation eludes us all. Some seem to be far greater victims of the present brokenness than others. In this extended "year of the Lord's favor," Christ continues, in and through his body, to preach good news to the poor, to proclaim freedom for the prisoners and recovery of sight for the blind, and to release the oppressed (see Lk 4:18-19).

- Mysteriously, when we minister *as* Christ in such acts of love, justice and mercy, we are simultaneously ministering *to* Christ. For he receives such acts—done to "the least of these"—as though "you did [it] for me" (Mt 25:31-40).

To reiterate, we engage in the ministry of reconciliation as the one body of Christ. Thus it is imperative that the church safeguard, and function in, its unity. A fragmented and dysfunctional body will be less effective than it must be, and its witness to the watching world will be suspect.

---

[29]For more on this, see Gary A. Parrett, "The Wondrous Cross and the Broken Wall," in Elizabeth Conde-Frazier, S. Steve Kang and Gary A. Parrett, *A Many Colored Kingdom* (Grand Rapids: Baker, 2004), pp. 63-78.

INTERCESSION TOWARD KNOWLEDGE OF GOD'S UNKNOWABLE LOVE

We have seen that Paul offered and called for praise to God for his great work of reconciling all things to himself and including us in this great redemptive Story. A critical part of that reconciling work is the role of the church as the one body of Christ. *In* this one body, we are reconciled to God and to one another. *As* this one body, we engage in the ministry of reconciliation until the return of Christ. But this body, though created by the power of God, is still in the process of being fully formed in the likeness of Christ. There is much still to be done if we are to become the fully functioning body of Christ in this still-broken world. In light of the enormity of this task, Paul turns next, in his letter to the Ephesians, to intercession for the body.

God *has* reconciled us to himself and to one another through his Son, Jesus Christ. This is deep theology that evokes and demands rich doxology. But there is often, in our experience, a disconnect between the theology we affirm and the manner in which we conduct our daily affairs. Therefore, Paul prays. Ephesians 3 begins with, "For this reason I, Paul, the prisoner of Christ Jesus for the sake of you Gentiles . . ." Whatever he is about to say is to be understood in light of what he has just said. Thus we return to the theology of the wondrous cross and the broken wall of hostility, the wonder of the one body of Christ, which is also (after a different metaphor) one new temple rising by God's grace as the dwelling place of God (see Eph 2:20-22).

However, Paul interrupts his own train of thought to offer an explanation of his apostleship to the Gentiles. In this extended parenthetical passage, he returns to the fact that God's enfolding of the Gentiles into his covenant family is a wondrous mystery that has now been revealed. So great is this wondrous reconciling work of the cross that God boasts over and against the powers and principalities concerning what he has accomplished in the church (see Eph 3:10).

Only at Ephesians 3:14 does Paul return to his original thought, taking up again the language of verse 1. "For this reason," he resumes, "I kneel before the Father." The great intercessory prayer that follows, surely one of the most cherished and beautiful prayers in the Scriptures, must be understood in its context. Paul prays that his readers will, by the power of God, come to truly understand the love of God that has been revealed at the cross.

The horizontal dimensions of reconciliation (concerning our relations with one another) are displayed in his prayer as fully as the vertical (concerning our relationship with God). The prayer is addressed to the Father, "from whom his whole family in heaven and on earth derives its name" (Eph 3:15). He prays that his believing readers may have power, "together with all the saints" (Eph 3:18), to grasp the width, length, height and depth of God's love. He proclaims that God is to be glorified "in the church" and in Christ Jesus for all generations (Eph 3:21).

Again, the *you* is plural throughout. Paul is praying that the believing community might come to truly "know"—in the Hebrew sense of *yada,* that is, a deep experiential knowledge[30]—the wondrous theology of the cross that they have already affirmed. This prayer echoes and expands on his earlier prayer, in Ephesians 1:15-19. Filling up the all-too-common gap between affirmation and action requires the powerful work of the Holy Spirit. For the body to be more fully formed, this work of the Spirit is essential. For all this, Paul intercedes. And so should we intercede on behalf of the congregations we serve, and on behalf of the body of Christ dispersed throughout the world today.

EXHORTATION, EQUIPPING AND EDIFICATION OF THE BODY

As we are called to pray without ceasing that the wonderful realities of the cross will fill our hearts, we are also exhorted to live out this reality in our experience as the body of Christ. Ephesians 4 thus begins with Paul urging believers to "live [here again, the word is, literally, *walk*] a life worthy of the calling you have received" as God's *poiēma.* The apostle pleads, in particular, that we make every effort "to keep the unity of the Spirit through the bond of peace." Reminding the church of the theological verities already implied, he hammers home the theme of the oneness of the church: "There is one body and one Spirit . . . one hope . . . one Lord, one faith, one baptism; one God and Father of all, who is over all and through all and in all" (Eph 4:4-6). This oneness must be acknowledged, safeguarded and obeyed.

However, the one body is made up of a diversity of parts, a diversity of gifts having been distributed by Christ to the church. Here, four (or five)[31] types of

---

[30]In Hebrew, *yada* means "more than the possession of abstract concepts. Knowledge compasses inner appropriation, feeling, a reception into the soul. It involves both an intellectual and an emotional act. . . . [It] denotes an act involving concern, inner engagement, dedication, or attachment to a person. It also means to have sympathy, pity, or affection for someone." Abraham Heschel, *The Prophets: An Introduction* (New York: Harper & Row, 1962), 1:57.

[31]Charles Talbert identifies two broad categories of gifts for ministry in word and deed, which he further divides into three subcategories each: (1) Endowments for Ministry in Word: A. Gifts of Gospel proclamation—apostles, evangelists; B. Gifts of inspired utterance—prophets,

gifted leaders are identified: apostles, prophets, evangelists, pastors and teachers (see Eph 4:11). These have been given to the church to aid in its formation.
The specific tasks to which these leaders are called have been the subject of
some debate through the years, based on the translation and interpretation of
Ephesians 4:12. There are two common understandings of this verse and its
implications for the function of the aforementioned gifted leaders, and these
understandings are reflected in differing approaches to English translations of
the verse.

In the first approach, traditional English renderings of the text, such as the
King James Version, the verse reads as follows: "For the perfecting of the saints,
for the work of the ministry, for the edifying of the body of Christ." Rendered
thus, with a comma following *saints,* the verse appears to indicate that the gifted
leaders, including pastors and teachers, have a threefold task: (1) perfecting the
saints, (2) doing the work of the ministry and (3) edifying the body.

In the original Greek, however, there are no punctuation marks; these
must be determined by the English translators in their efforts to best capture
the intended meaning of the text. This leads to the second common approach
to the text: some have argued that the traditional renderings missed the mark
by including the first comma.[32] Thus the New International Version renders
Ephesians 4:12 "to prepare God's people for works of service, so that the body
of Christ may be built up." Similarly, the Revised Standard Version has "to
equip the saints for the work of ministry, for the building up of the body of
Christ." In both of these more recent renderings, the primary work of pastors
and teachers is either singular or a twofold work. First, they commit to *preparing (or equipping) God's people* so that they (that is, God's people) can do works
of service or ministry. Therefore, the work of *building up the body* can be taken
either as a second task of the pastor-teacher or as the consequence of fulfilling
the singular task of equipping the saints.

---

discernments of spirits, tongues, interpretation of tongues, utterances of knowledge; and C.
Gifts of didactic speech—teachers/pastors, exhortation, utterances of wisdom; and (2) Equip-
ment for Ministry of Deed: A. Gifts of supernatural power—miracles, healing, faith; B. Gifts
of administrative leadership—administrators, pastors; and C. Gifts of practical assistance—
helping, serving, sharing, caring, showing mercy. *Ephesians and Colossians: Paideia Commentaries on the New Testament* (Grand Rapids: Baker, 2007), pp. 118-19.

[32]For example, in *Liberating the Laity,* Paul Stevens refers to the first comma as "the fatal comma"
(Vancouver: Regent College Publishing, 1977). J. I. Packer, referring to a sixteenth-century
edition of the Bible in which the word *not* had been omitted from the seventh commandment
and which became known as the "Wicked Bible," suggests that we name this comma that the
King James Version placed after *saints* the "Wicked Comma." *Keep in Step with the Spirit,* rev.
ed. (Grand Rapids: Baker, 2005).

John Jefferson Davis has argued that the traditional rendering is probably correct, but that the revised versions point to important realities about how the body should actually function. In other words, Davis intimates that those who insist on "every member ministry" from Ephesians 4:12 have perhaps gotten the right doctrine from the wrong text. He would direct them elsewhere for such teaching, including Ephesians 4:16, where we read that the body grows "as each part does its work."[33]

Regardless of whether or not we opt for the "traditional" or the "revised" rendering of verse 12, taken as a whole, Ephesians 4:12-16 leaves us with this clear message: while every member of the body of Christ has work to do, God has given leaders to the church who are specifically charged with and gifted for equipping those members to do that appointed work. Said otherwise, the gifted leaders have a vitally formative task to fulfill in helping the body mature and function properly, a goal that requires that each member of the body be able and willing to do its uniquely appointed part. This "preparing" or "equipping" work of the leaders must continue until "we all reach"

- "unity in the faith"
- "and in the knowledge of the Son of God"
- "and become mature, attaining to the whole measure of the fullness of Christ" (Eph 4:13)[34]

MATURITY THROUGH SPIRIT-FULLNESS

Paul's vision of the mature, fully functioning body of Christ is sketched in some detail from the middle of Ephesians 4 and onward through the beginning verses of chapter 6. Here is a vision of what a well-instructed, well-formed community may come to look like, by God's grace. The mature body is stable, truthful, loving, laboring and united (see Eph 4:14-16). It grows "up into him who is the Head, that is, Christ." Perhaps we can envision here a newborn baby whose body, after years of loving care and proper nourishment, "grows up" in proportion to *its* head.

The manner of life lived by God's people is easily distinguished from that of the surrounding world (see Eph 4:17-21), and the new lives of its individual

---

[33] John J. Davis, "Ephesians 4:12 Once More: 'Equipping the Saints for the Work of Ministry?'" *Evangelical Review of Theology* 24, no. 2 (April 2000): 167-76.

[34] We examine these three elements in some detail in the next chapter.

members are significantly different from their former patterns. Each of them has "put off [the] old self" and "put on the new" (Eph 4:22-24). They are devoted to edifying and truthful speech, and to following Christ's example of sacrificial love (see Eph 4:25—5:2).

The mature body of Christ empties itself of all that is impure and unsuitable for the people of God (see Eph 5:3-14). Understanding the Lord's will, it refuses to be under the sway of drunkenness (see Eph 5:15-18). Instead, the body of Christ is to be perpetually filled with the Holy Spirit. The body that God has formed by his own handiwork—his *poiēma*—must be filled by his Spirit, just as the first man, formed by God from the dust of the earth, received the breath of God and so became a living soul (see Gen 2:7). Without this Spirit-filling, the body of Christ cannot attain its proper form, achieve genuine maturity or function as God intended it to function.

The body cannot fill itself with the Holy Spirit, but by means of four postures or practices, it can position itself to be filled by the Spirit by observing the instruction of Ephesians 5:18-21. The command here is that we "be [continually] filled with the Spirit." The participial phrases that follow explain that this occurs when we are

- speaking to one another in psalms, hymns and spiritual songs (Eph 5:19)

- singing and making music in our hearts to the Lord (Eph 5:19)

- always giving thanks to God the Father for everything (Eph 5:20)

- submitting to one another out of reverence for Christ (Eph 5:21—6:9)

Paul then unpacks this vision of mutual submission for the sake of Christ by applying it to a variety of relationships: spouse and spouse, child and parent, servant and master. It is by means of these four practices—speaking to one another, singing in our hearts, always giving thanks and submitting to one another—that the body experiences the fullness of God's Spirit and so matures, becoming more fit to fulfill our God-ordained purposes.

ARMOR FOR SPIRITUAL WARFARE

The body of Christ—the "one new man" God forms from members of every nation, tongue and tribe—once built up and filled up, is ready to be arrayed for battle. Paul's description of the panoply in Ephesians 6:10-17 continues the imagery that he has been working with all along. We may be missing his main point if we envision the armor as that which each individual Christian is to put on. It is *the body* that is to be properly outfitted for its work and warfare, just as it is the body that is to grow up into the Head and the body that is to be filled with the Spirit. Of course, the body can only be as strong as its weakest members "permit" it to be, for "if one part suffers, every part suffers with it" (1 Cor 12:26). Thus it is not inappropriate to speak of the individual believer's need to be Spirit-filled and Spirit-arrayed with armor. But it seems clear from the flow of Paul's argument in Ephesians that this is not his main point here. From first to last, Paul has the glorious church in view, the body and bride of Christ, the *poiēma* of God.

Why is the armor—of truth, righteousness, Gospel centrism, faith, salvation covering and the mighty sword of God's Word—necessary? Because the good works of reconciliation to which the body is called involve serious spiritual warfare. Paul refers again to the fallen powers, calling them "the rulers . . . the authorities . . . the powers of this dark world and . . . the spiritual forces of evil in the heavenly realms" (Eph 6:12), against whom the body wrestles. These forces are actively opposed to God's plan to reconcile all things to himself, and they fight the church at every turn. But they cannot, by any means, prevail against it (see Mt 16:18). Their dismal destiny was assured at the cross (see Col 2:15). Christ "must reign" until each of them is utterly defeated (see 1 Cor 15:25), until finally, as promised long ago, the serpent's head is crushed beneath the feet of the seed of the woman (see Gen 3:15).

That time draws nearer every day. As Paul tells the believers in Rome, "the God of peace will soon crush Satan under your feet" (Rom 16:20). Under *your* feet (again, *your* is plural in the Greek), did Paul say? Is it not under the feet of Jesus that Satan is crushed? Indeed, that is the case. But Christ is one with his people, the Head over his own body, "one flesh" with his glorious bride. Without diminishing his deity in any way and without compromising his unique place as second person of the Holy Trinity, Christ, who—for us and for our salvation, as the Nicene Creed puts it—was *made flesh* (see Jn 1:14), has become *one flesh* with the church. Surely this is, as Paul terms it, a most "profound mystery" (Eph 5:32).

Concerning this "profound mystery," we return to a phrase that has been mentioned three times, in various forms, during Paul's progressive argument in the letter to the Ephesians: the church as the "fullness of Christ." First, Paul declares this as a theological reality in Ephesians 1:23. He calls the church "his body, the fullness of him who fills everything in every way." Next, in Paul's intercessory prayer of Ephesians 3, he prays "that you may be filled to the measure of all the fullness of God" (Eph 3:19). Finally, in Paul's exhortatory section, he speaks of the body living out this fullness by becoming mature, "attaining to the whole measure of the fullness of Christ" (Eph 4:13). Just as the Head is completed by the body, and the bride-groom becomes "one flesh" with the bride, so the church is, in some utterly inscrutable way, the "fullness of Christ" in this world. Such an idea is, of course, breathtaking, humbling and convicting.

CONCLUSION

We exist, when all is said and done, wholly for the glory of God. We exist now, on earth—in time and space—to glorify God by participating in the grand Story he is unfolding, that of reconciling all things to himself. Toward this end, we have been reconciled to God through faith in Jesus Christ and are declared to be the wonderful *poiēma* of God—his handiwork, the church, the body of Christ. It is as the body of Christ that we engage in the "even now" of Christ's ministry of reconciliation.

But the body is not fully formed and thus is not fully functional. It stands in need of equipping and edification, of Spirit filling and Spirit armoring. Toward these ends, God has given gifted leaders to the church to foster formation of God's people in the image of Jesus Christ. One of the most vital of the formative tasks for the sake of the body is that of teaching. What role does the ministry of teaching play in the grand scheme of things? How does it relate to the other, equally vital formative tasks of the church? To such questions as these we are now ready to turn our attention.

HYMN FOR CONTEMPLATION AND WORSHIP

The Spirit of the Lord Is on Me

The Spirit of the Lord is on me, is on me.
I come to preach good news to the poor,
to call the captives free and cause the blind to see,
to speak the favored year of the Lord, of the Lord,
proclaim the favored year of the Lord.
(Is 61:1-2; Lk 4:18-19)

The Father has sent me; I send you, I send you.
The works that I have done, you shall do.
Within your lives receive the Spirit as I breathe.
Go forth and bear much fruit. I send you, I send you.

The Father has sent me; I send you.
(Jn 20:21-22; 14:12; 15:1-17)

And in the final days, says the Lord, says the Lord,
my Spirit on all flesh, I will pour:
on daughters and on sons, on old men and the young,
on men and women both, I will pour, I will pour.
My Spirit on all flesh, I will pour.
(Joel 2:28-29; Acts 2:17-18)

Full with the Spirit now, we are one, we are one,
one body called to labor and pray.
Who labors in the Lord shall find a good reward
and enter perfect joy on that Day, on that Day,
shall enter perfect joy on that Day.
(1 Cor 12:13; Gal 3:26-28; Eph 4:1-16; Mt 25:21; 2 Tim 4:7-8)

Text: Gary A. Parrett (2005)
Tune: Wondrous Love
Familiar use of the tune: "What Wondrous Love Is This?"

QUESTIONS FOR PLANNING AND PRACTICE

1. The church is the workmanship (that is, *poiēma*) of God. In your life as a believer, how have you seen the church adequately reflect this reality? How have you seen the church fall short of this vision? Where and how have you seen ministries of education and formation playing a positive role in the church being the *poiēma* of God?

2. Which aspect of our *poiēma* outline have you especially seen as missing in churches? How does this affect the world in which the church has been placed? How does this affect the progress of God's story being told to every tribe, tongue and nation on earth?

3. Although frequently interpreted and applied to individuals, the book of Ephesians is in most cases referring to a collective *you* (that is, the household of God), though implications for individual Christians are clear. How does this rendering of Scripture change your outlook on the educational formation ministry of the church? Does it prompt you to consider reexamining your perspective or your life as a part of the story of God?

4. With a group or a partner, we invite you to read aloud the book of Ephesians. As you do so, focus on the perspective that Paul is speaking to the

body of Christ corporately as God's chosen people in Jesus Christ, rather than to a mere congregation of like-minded individuals. Does this give you a different picture of the workmanship, the *poiēma,* of God? Why or why not? After discussing this together, create a list of Scriptures that are particularly important as you begin to reenvision the educational ministry of the church.

5. This chapter has basically described the crux of the Gospel and the purpose of the Christian life. With a group or partner, using *poiēma* as a foundation, rehearse the points made in this chapter, keeping in mind the goal of creating a three-minute Gospel presentation for yourself and for others. What are the salient issues, Scriptures and points? How can this view of the Story of God lead someone to salvation, as well as nourish your own soul every day as you preach the Gospel to yourself?

RESOURCES FOR FURTHER STUDY

Adams, Peter. *Hearing God's Words: Exploring Biblical Spirituality.* Downers Grove, Ill.: InterVarsity Press, 2004.

Choung, James. *True Story: A Christianity Worth Believing In.* Downers Grove, Ill.: InterVarsity Press, 2008.

Conde-Frazier, Elizabeth, S. Steve Kang and Gary A. Parrett. *A Many Colored Kingdom: Multicultural Dynamics for Spiritual Formation.* Grand Rapids: Baker Academic, 2004.

Dawn, Marva. *Powers, Weakness and the Tabernacling of God.* Grand Rapids: Eerdmans, 2001.

DeVisser, Adrian, and David Sprowl. *Ministry in the Balance: A Scriptural Guide to Holistic Ministry.* Otsego, Mich.: PageFree Publishing, 2008.

Habermas, Ron. *Introduction to Christian Education and Formation: A Lifelong Plan for Christ-Centered Restoration.* Grand Rapids: Zondervan, 2009.

Lloyd-Jones, D. Martin. *God's Way of Reconciliation: Studies in Ephesians 2.* Grand Rapids: Baker, 1974.

Snodgrass, Klyne. *Ephesians.* Grand Rapids: Zondervan, 1996.

Stott, John. *The Message of Ephesians.* Leicester, U.K.: Inter-Varsity Press, 1979.

———. *The Contemporary Christian: Applying God's Word to Today's World.* Downers Grove, Ill.: InterVarsity Press, 1992.

———. *The Living Church: Convictions of a Lifelong Pastor.* Downers Grove, Ill.: InterVarsity Press, 2007.

Webber, Robert. *Ancient-Future Faith: Rethinking Evangelicalism for a Postmodern World*. Grand Rapids: Baker, 1999.

Wells, David. *The Courage to Be Protestant: Truth-Lovers, Marketers, and Emergents in the Postmodern World*. Grand Rapids: Eerdmans, 2008.

Wilhoit, James. *Spiritual Formation as If the Church Mattered*. Grand Rapids: Baker, 2008.

2

Building Up the Body

. . . to prepare God's people for works of service, so that the body of Christ may be
built up until we reach unity in the faith and in the knowledge of the Son of God and
become mature, attaining to the whole measure of the fullness of Christ.

EPHESIANS 4:12-13

▼

SOME DECADES AGO, MY WIFE and I were part of a small but growing congregation. The church featured a number of older, long-time members and was now enjoying an influx of younger congregants like us. As the numbers increased, a good deal of the church's energy was diverted—as so often seems to be the case—by visions of adding on to the building that the church occupied on Sundays. And so began work on a new "education wing."

Even as this building was going forward through a great expenditure of time and money, another, more critical aspect of building the church became increasingly neglected. Probably for a host of reasons, most of which I do not recall, the congregation seemed to shrink in stature, both spiritually and numerically. Many of my fellow, younger worshipers became disgruntled when the Sunday sermon was replaced with brief "meditations" by the pastor— often meditations on a Christian book he was reading at the time. A number of older members were dissatisfied when the pastor seemed to push for "a plurality of leadership" as his own role grew less and less visible. Regrettably, I was not privy to the struggles the pastor himself was facing at the time, but I can imagine that there were plenty.

After many months of construction, the education wing was finally finished. By that time, however, there seemed to be little need for the extra space because a very sizable portion of the congregation had left the church, my wife and I among them. Members of the congregation had built on to "the church"—that is, to the building owned by the church. The real church, however—that is, the body of Christ that gathered in that building—had suffered significant losses. By God's grace, a season of restoration and revitalization would follow in subsequent years.

In this chapter, as we continue our explorations of how the church of Jesus moves forward in fulfilling its God-ordained purposes for existence, we seek to gain a vision of how the body of Christ is to be built up and equipped for its labors. We have in mind the building up neither of the physical structures that congregations use nor simply of the programs they undertake. Neither are we concerned with the numerical growth of congregations. Instead, our focus is on the sort of upbuilding that Paul urged in Ephesians 4 and that we considered in the previous chapter: edification that leads believers to more deeply experience unity in the faith, knowledge of the Son of God and maturity as the body of Christ. Of course, there are countless ways we might answer the question of why the church must engage in a ministry of teaching. We make no claim that the five suggestions set forth in this chapter represent the only way to approach the question or that the list is in any way comprehensive. We do believe, though, that these aims comport well with the models and mandates of Scripture. We teach

- *out of* and *unto* **obedience**
- *unto* **conformity** to Christ
- *unto* **salvation,** holistically understood
- *unto* **faith, hope** and **love**
- *unto* **edification** of the body

The first four of these aims can be applied at the level of both individuals and the community as a whole. The fifth aim—that of edification—specifically focuses on the building up of the body of Christ, and thus calls our attention back to the explicitly communal emphases we considered in chapter one.

TEACHING OUT OF AND UNTO OBEDIENCE

Perhaps the most basic of ways to answer the "Why teach?" question is to do so thus: We teach *from* obedience and *unto* obedience. That is, we teach because we have been commanded to do so. And the teaching we have been commanded to perform is a teaching unto obedience. Both sides of this notion are very evident in the so-called Great Commission of Matthew 28:18-20.

Before his ascension into heaven, Jesus "commissioned" his disciples to participate fully in the great reconciling work of God. This commission takes various forms throughout the New Testament, including passages at the end of all four Gospel accounts and at the beginning of the book of Acts. The most familiar of these passages is Matthew's account. The commissioning of the disciples begins there with a declaration of authorization: "All authority in heaven and on earth has been given to me." Authority had been granted to Jesus by his Father. In turn, he now grants that authority to his followers (see also Jn 20:21). The "commission" concludes with a wonderful word of promise: "And surely I am with you always, to the very end of the age."[1] Between these potent opening and closing words, we find this command: "Therefore go and make disciples of all nations, baptizing them in the name of the Father and of the Son and of the Holy Spirit, and teaching them to obey everything I have commanded you."

The imperative is that the followers of Jesus are to "disciple the nations" or "disciple the peoples."[2] What does this task involve? This is revealed by the three participles in this section: *going, baptizing* and *teaching.* The first of these—*going*—is linked to the imperative in such a way as to make it clear that it, too, is commanded.[3] Going is essential, since it is *all nations* that are to be reached with the Gospel. In Luke, the idea is expressed thus: "repentance and forgiveness of sins will be preached in [Christ's] name to all nations, beginning at Jerusalem. You are witnesses of these things" (Lk 24:47-48). In Acts, Jesus indicates that the *going* of the apostles would proceed from Jerusalem and Judea to Samaria "and to the ends of the earth" (Acts 1:8). Recalling our earlier emphasis on the church being the body of Christ corporately, we may here envision a body that is actively engaged in the world. The church is moving against the forces of darkness, and the gates of hell cannot prevail against it (see Mt 16:18).

The second of the three participles in Matthew 28:19 is *baptizing.* As the church goes forth with the Gospel, by the sovereign grace of God, all who are "appointed for eternal life" shall believe the good news (Acts 13:48) and are

---

[1] In Acts 1:8, where there is another form of Jesus' commissioning his apostles, there is likewise a great promise: "You will receive power when the Holy Spirit comes on you." Thus in both passages we find the clear promise of God's empowering presence as the disciples fulfill their calling.

[2] D. A. Carson, *Matthew,* The Expositor's Bible Commentary, vol. 8, ed. Frank Gaebelein (Grand Rapids: Zondervan, 1984), pp. 596-97.

[3] Ibid., p. 596.

to be baptized into the name of the triune God as the sign and seal of their inclusion in Christ and in his body, the church. This baptism is a rite of initiation into both the public and the inner life of discipleship. But it must not be treated as the culmination.

Thus we come to the third participle, *teaching*. Newly baptized believers are to be nurtured toward maturity through teaching. We see this at work in Acts 2, when three thousand are baptized in Jerusalem on the day of Pentecost and then devote themselves to "the apostles' teaching" (Acts 2:42), among other things. The Great Commission, this call to disciple nations, cannot be fulfilled without the church's unwavering commitment to going forth, baptizing new believers and teaching them to obey all that Jesus has commanded.

It is not surprising that those engaged in many different tasks of the church's ministry have turned to this text in Matthew for a fundamental starting point. For in the Great Commission we find ourselves commanded by our Lord to engage in missionary endeavor, evangelism and teaching. It is this third point that is our particular concern here. As we have seen, to fulfill our mandate to disciple the nations, we must engage in a ministry of teaching. Thus we conclude that a reasonable answer to the question "Why teach?" is this: we teach out of obedience to our Lord Jesus Christ. We teach because we have been plainly commanded to do so. We teach because it is integral to the making of disciples, which is integral to the ministry of reconciliation, which is integral to our glorifying God.

Matthew's Great Commission text makes it clear that we teach not only *out of* a sense of obedience. We teach also *unto* obedience. Jesus says, "[Teach] them to obey everything I have commanded you" (28:20). But it is not sufficient to teach merely all that Jesus taught or commanded, though this would be a challenging task in and of itself. The task is actually far more daunting: to make real disciples—people who actually *follow* Jesus. Dallas Willard has charged (in many of his works over many years) that evangelicals have woefully missed the point here. Willard labels our failure to actually *teach obedience* to all that Jesus commanded (and thus to foster the notion that one could be a Christian forever yet never become an actual disciple) "the Great Omission."[4]

Our omission is even more pronounced when we note that Jesus' emphasis

---

[4]Dallas Willard, *The Great Omission: Reclaiming Jesus's Essential Teachings on Discipleship* (New York: HarperOne, 2006), pp. xi, xii. We return to this focus on teaching unto obedience in chapter ten, "Visions of Christian Teaching."

in this text on actually obeying his teaching is nothing novel. *Doing* what he said was, in fact, his constant concern throughout the Gospel accounts. A few examples illustrate this well.

- In Matthew 7, near the close of the so-called Sermon on the Mount, Jesus says, "Not everyone who says to me, 'Lord, Lord,' will enter the kingdom of heaven, but only he who does the will of my Father who is in heaven" (Mt 7:21). A few verses later we find him saying, "Therefore everyone who hears these words of mine and *puts them into practice* is like a wise man who built his house on the rock" (Mt 7:24, emphasis added).

- In Luke 10, we read of Jesus' conversation with a scribe—an expert in the Torah—who plainly knew that the Torah requires love of God and neighbor. But to demonstrate that mere knowledge of what is required is insufficient, Jesus told a shocking tale (which we have come to call "the parable of the good Samaritan") and asked a critical question. When the scribe answered, correctly again, that it was "the one who showed mercy," who had actually done what the Torah required, Jesus said to him, *"Go and do likewise"* (Lk 10:37 RSV, emphasis added).

- A third example of the principle is found in John 13. There Jesus stuns the Twelve by stooping to wash their feet. Afterward, he asks them if they understand what he has done for them, and he tells them that he has given them an example that they are to follow. He concludes with these words: "Now that you know these things, you will be blessed *if you do them*" (Jn 13:17, emphasis added).

These few examples point to what is plainly the norm, not the exception, in Jesus' emphasis. And his emphasis is in keeping with the overall teaching of the Scriptures. Israel was to be "careful to obey" all that God commanded them (Deut 6:3; see also, for example, Ps 78:7). New Testament believers are likewise called "to obey his commands" (1 Jn 5:3), to "not merely listen to the word" but to "do what it says" (Jas 1:22).

Why, then, do we teach? The first and simplest answer is, We teach *from* obedience and *unto* obedience.

TEACHING UNTO CONFORMITY TO CHRIST

As we saw in our survey of Ephesians in the previous chapter, it is necessary that the body of Christ be properly formed if it is to function as intended in the world. Therefore, it should not surprise us that *formation* is a critical aspect of the *telos* of the church's teaching ministry. The word *formation* derives from the Greek root *morphē*. Paul uses variations of the word in several places, often in verbal forms and making use of a prefix appropriate to the sense of the term he has in mind.

For example, we find Paul teaching that God's great purpose for all those whom he has foreknown as his own is that they be "conformed *[symmorphous]* to the likeness of his Son" (Rom 8:29). For this end, Paul says, every believer is predestined. The context makes it clear that this is (at least part of) "the good" toward which God causes "all things" to work together for those "who love him, who have been called according to his purpose" (Rom 8:28). This intention of God shall surely be accomplished, for the text goes on to say that as many as were foreknown and predestined, God "also called; those he called, he also justified; those he justified, he also glorified" (Rom 8:30). This points to the final and perfect fulfillment of being conformed to the likeness of God's Son. As Paul says, "The one who calls you is faithful and he will do it" (1 Thess 5:24). God will accomplish his purposes in our lives.

At present, however, none of us is fully conformed to the likeness of Christ. Many years into his apostolic ministry, Paul himself made it clear that he had not yet "obtained all this" and was still pressing on (Phil 3:12-14). It is necessary that all believers—individually and corporately be *trans*formed *(metamorphousthe)*. This occurs through having our minds renewed (see Rom 12:2) and by means of the liberating presence of the Holy Spirit (see 2 Cor 3:17-18). Here is a reminder of Jesus' earlier promises that it would be by the Spirit's power that his followers would fulfill their mission.

Paul puts the matter a bit differently to the Galatian churches. Concerning these believers, who were being tempted to abandon the Gospel, Paul finds his soul in anguish. He writes, "My dear children, for whom I am again in the pains of childbirth until Christ is formed in you" (Gal 4:19). Here "formed" is offered without a prefix, and the image is somewhat altered. Rather than believers being conformed or transformed toward the likeness of Christ, here we see that Christ is to be formed *(mōrphothē)* in the believing community. Paul speaks as though he thought this had already occurred, but the present crisis in the Galatian churches has made him question this.

The language of formation in each of the above references reminds us of the great call of the church to "grow up into him who is the Head, that is, Christ" (Eph 4:15) and to "become mature, attaining to the whole measure of the fullness of Christ" (Eph 4:13). It is clear that Paul had made, as one of his chief goals in working with the churches, the very goal that God has established for his people: conformity to the likeness of Jesus Christ. All who engage in the teaching ministry of the church can aspire to nothing less for their labors.

The goal of conformity to the likeness of Christ then is a second and clear answer to the question "Why teach?" But we need to recognize that such a process does not begin with persons who are simply *un*formed. It begins, rather, with persons who are *de*formed or *mal*formed.[5] Therefore, the ministry of formation must involve serious attention to these deformities, the tragic malformation in the lives of those we serve (and in our own selves as ministers of the Gospel).

We further note that issues of formation must be applied to both the community as a whole and to individuals within the community. There is a critical and inescapable interconnection at work here. On the one hand, it takes a strong and healthy body to help individual believers toward healthy formation. On the other hand, the body cannot be properly formed if the individual members are not growing toward health and each doing their appointed part. In the final section of the book, we will turn our attention to practices for both congregational and personal formation.

TEACHING UNTO SALVATION

Another important answer to the "Why teach?" question is that we teach unto salvation. This may seem a bit surprising to some readers. Is this not, after all, the proper goal of evangelism rather than of education? We reply that it is a worthy goal of both. The key to what we intend here, however, is in properly understanding the biblical concept of salvation.

Salvation is often used by evangelical Christians as a synonym for being "born again." Thus it is regarded as something believers have already experienced in full. It is seen as an experience that is now in our past. And many are confident that this is the way to view things, since they have been nurtured in an understanding of salvation based largely on Ephesians 2:8-9: "It is by grace you have been saved, through faith—and this not from yourselves, it is the gift of God—not by works, so that no one can boast." Paul plainly speaks of salvation as something *already* experienced by believers: we "have been saved." Many have committed these verses to memory, typically to emphasize not the finality of our salvation, but its origins: it is by grace alone, through faith alone and apart from any works of our own that we have been saved. As a result, it is locked into our consciousness that we "*have* been saved," that our salvation is complete, already experienced in full.

---

[5]For more on this, see the introduction to part four of this book.

But thinking like this is to mistake the part for the whole. If salvation were simply a matter of being "born again," then perhaps we would need only the ministry of evangelism in our churches. Any form of Christian education might actually be regarded as superfluous. What could possibly matter beyond "getting people saved" we might reason? In fact, many church leaders do seem to reason along these lines. To do so, however, is to miss both the emphases of the Great Commission and the biblical meaning of our salvation. The Great Commission is a mandate to *disciple* the nations. And, as we have seen, this requires both evangelism and "teaching them to obey" all that Christ commanded. Likewise, careful reflection on the biblical teaching regarding salvation will disavow us of any reduction in the church's task to evangelism alone.

The New Testament doctrine of salvation is more rich and profound than most of us nurtured in evangelical communities have understood. This is somewhat surprising, not only because of the clear witness of the Scriptures but also because evangelical theologians have consistently written and taught about the fact that our salvation is experienced in a sort of progressive manner. The notion of an *ordo salutis,* that is, an order or progress of salvation, is standard fare in volumes on soteriology. Regarding this *ordo,* theologians offer presentations of various complexities. In simplest form, we may speak of salvation as having three "tenses": past, present and future. That is, the Bible invites the believer to say, "I have been saved; I am being saved; I shall be saved." When we speak of "teaching unto salvation," we are referring to all three aspects. (See table 2.1 on p. 56.)

Regarding the "past" tense of salvation, believers recall that "in his great mercy [God] has given us new birth" (1 Pet 1:3). This is the new birth that Jesus told Nicodemus must occur before one can see the kingdom of God (see Jn 3:3). The language of new birth, however, should immediately point us toward what ought to come next—that is, growth and maturing. Peter exhorts his readers, "Like newborn babies, crave pure spiritual milk, so that by it you may grow up in your salvation" (1 Pet 2:2). Sadly, many Christians seem to regard being "born again" not as a beginning of their salvation experience but as the totality of it.

The apostle John puts new birth in the past tense of the believer's experience (with powerful implications for the present) when he testifies of the Father's great love that has been lavished on us, making us God's children (see 1 Jn 3:1). What a wondrous work of grace was wrought in our hearts

Table 2.1. Aspects of Salvation[a]

Past	*Present*		*Future*
We *have been* saved	We *are being* saved		We *shall be* saved
From sin's *penalty*	From sin's *power* over us		From sin's very *presence*
Saved by the *finished work* of Christ—his death and resurrection	*Working out* our salvation with fear and trembling as God works in us by his Spirit	Saved in order to walk in the *good works* God has prepared for us	Saved completely by the One who *works all things* according to his purposes
FAITH	LOVE *of God*	LOVE *of neighbor*	HOPE
Rom 5	Rom 6:1–8:17	Rom 12–16	Rom 8:18-39
Eph 2:1-9	Phil 2:12-13	Eph 2:10	Col 3:1-4
Tit 2:11	Tit 2:12	Tit 2:14	Tit 2:13
1 Pet 1:3	1 Pet 1:6-9	1 Pet 2:12	1 Pet 1:4-5
1 Jn 3:1	1 Jn 3:3-10	1 Jn 3:11-17	1 Jn 3:2
Justification	Sanctification and Vocation		Glorification

[a]Although some of the particulars on this table are original—especially the inclusion of vocation and the place of work(s) in a full-orbed doctrine of salvation—the overall concept of salvation in three tenses is a familiar one. Variations of this table can thus be readily found elsewhere.

when, having heard the Gospel of Jesus Christ, we believed this good news and were "included in Christ" and sealed as God's own with "the promised Holy Spirit" (Eph 1:13)! But the presence of the Spirit—the marvelous gift of God promised to all who believe (see Acts 2:38-39)—is "a deposit guaranteeing our inheritance until the redemption" that is yet to come (Eph 1:14). There is much more to come in our experience of salvation. We praise God that by grace we "have been saved, through faith" (Eph 2:8), that we "have been justified through faith" and now "have peace with God through our Lord Jesus Christ, through whom we have gained access by faith into this grace in which we now stand" (Rom 5:1-2). But the Spirit witnesses to our hearts that this is but a foretaste of the fullness of our salvation.

Indeed, in several of the key passages referenced in the previous paragraph, there is an immediate movement from what *has* happened to what *shall* happen. In 1 John 3, immediately after speaking of God's lavish love having made us his children, John declares that "what we will be has not yet been made known.

But we know that when he appears, we shall be like him, for we shall see him as he is" (1 Jn 3:2). Paul writes to the Ephesians that the indwelling Spirit is the earnest payment on the full inheritance to come, "the redemption of those who are God's possession—to the praise of his glory" (Eph 1:14; see also Rom 8:23 on the future "redemption of our bodies"). And, having declared to the Roman church that we have come to stand in grace through faith in Christ, Paul writes, "And we rejoice in the hope of the glory of God" (Rom 5:2).

All of these testify to the "future tense" of our salvation experience. As Paul writes later to the Romans, "our salvation is nearer now than when we first believed," because the "night is nearly over; the day is almost here" (Rom 13:11-12). Or, as Peter puts it, our new birth has brought us into a "living hope" and "into an inheritance that can never perish, spoil or fade— kept in heaven for you, who through faith are shielded by God's power until the coming of the salvation that is ready to be revealed in the last time" (1 Pet 1:3-5).

In light of both the past and the future aspects of our salvation, the New Testament authors speak also of its present reality and power in our lives. Having spoken of our destiny to be like Jesus forever, John writes, "Everyone who has this hope in him purifies himself, just as [Jesus Christ] is pure" (1 Jn 3:3)—a "present tense" response. Paul speaks of our rejoicing in the hope of the glory of God, then adds, "Not only so, but we also rejoice in our sufferings," knowing that our "suffering produces perseverance" (Rom 5:3). Paul writes elsewhere about the need for believers to "work out" their salvation "with fear and trembling, for it is God who works in you" (Phil 2:12-13). After writing of the "salvation . . . ready to be revealed in the last time," the apostle Peter goes on to say that through their present hardships, believers "are receiving the goal of your faith, the salvation of your souls" (1 Pet 1:5, 9). How rich, multifaceted and wondrous is God's saving work in our lives! No wonder the prophets were consumed with it and "angels long to look into these things" (1 Pet 1:12; see 1 Pet 1:10-11).

Returning to the text from Ephesians 2, we note that Paul links what has already happened in our hearts to what ought to be happening now and in the future. We *have* been saved—by grace through faith, apart from any works of our own. In other words, we have been created anew in Christ Jesus, and that work was God's alone. But all that has happened to the end that, now and henceforth, we would walk in the good works God has prepared for us (see Eph 2:8-10).

In Titus 2:11-14 Paul marvelously captures the full breadth of the doctrine of salvation in the space of a few verses:

> For the grace of God that brings salvation has appeared to all men. It teaches us to say "No" to ungodliness and worldly passions, and to live self-controlled, upright and godly lives in this present age, while we wait for the blessed hope—the glorious appearing of our great God and Savior, Jesus Christ, who gave himself for us to redeem us from all wickedness and to purify for himself a people that are his very own, eager to do what is good.

We see, in verse 11, that God's saving grace has already been revealed to us (a past-tense reality). Verse 12 reminds us that this saving grace teaches us that we ought to live in an upright, godly and patient manner (present-tense realities). All the while, as verse 13 makes clear, we look longingly to our blessed hope—the imminent return of our glorious Lord (a future-tense anticipation). In verse 14, we see that we have been saved not only that God might make us a people of his very own but also that we might eagerly do what is good.

In theological terms, the *ordo salutis,* with reference to these three tenses, is often explained further by reference to the terms *justification, sanctification* and *glorification,* corresponding to past, present and future tenses. However, the biblical approach often invites us to think of these wonders in a different order: past, future and present. For it is when we lay hold of the reality of our justification and are filled with the hope of glorification that the power of sanctification grips our hearts and transforms us in the present, spurring us onward toward love and good deeds.

In our teaching and preaching, we must exhort God's people to the joyous call of holy living and good works. Yet it is not the continual reminder of those things that will actually bring forth holiness and good works in our lives. Instead, it is as we are overwhelmed by the grace of God, by his lavish love for us and by the certain hope that the Gospel fixes in our hearts, that we are freed to live full and well in the present (see 1 Jn 3:1-3). It is in view of God's incomparable mercies that we are compelled to "offer [our] bodies as living sacrifices" (Rom 12:1). It is the love of Christ that constrains us and draws us into the ministry of reconciliation (see 2 Cor 5:14-21).

Although we suggested that the word *justification* corresponds to our past-tense experience, glorification to the future and sanctification to the present, we must not use these terms too rigidly with regard to tense, for matters are far too complex for such a simple classification. Justification,[6] for example, though primarily

---

[6]Bromiley, *Theological Dictionary,* pp. 172-75.

referred to in the New Testament as something already experienced by the believer, is occasionally spoken of with reference to the future (see, for example, Rom 2:13). Glorification[7] is indeed the great and ultimately unfathomable doctrine of the believer's blessed hope. Yet there is a sense in which the believer already possesses the glory that is to come and experiences this in ever-increasing measure (see, for example, 2 Cor 3:7-18). And sanctification[8] cannot be consid-

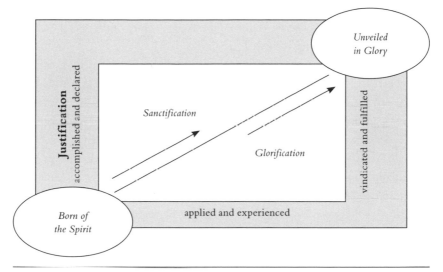

Figure 2.1. Justification, sanctification and glorification

ered as referring to only the present tense of the believer. Indeed, it may well be argued that the term is *primarily* used to describe another aspect of what has already happened to those who have believed, namely that they have been "possessed by God," as David Peterson puts it in his helpful survey of the doctrine.[9] In figure 2.1, we have attempted to illustrate some of these relationships.

TEACHING UNTO FAITH, HOPE AND LOVE

The implications of all these truths for the teaching ministry of the church are profound. To speak of teaching unto salvation includes, at the very least,

---

[7]David Wright, "Edinburgh Dogmatics Conference Sermon: *The Lamb That Was Slain,*" in *Engaging the Doctrine of God: Contemporary Protestant Perspectives,* ed. Bruce McCormack (Grand Rapids: Baker, 2008), p. 18.

[8]See "Deification, Union, and Sanctification in Later Protestant Theologies," chapter five in Veli-Matti Kärkkäinen, *One with God: Salvation as Deification and Justification* (Collegeville, Minn.: Liturgical Press, 2004).

[9]David Peterson, *Possessed by God: A New Testament Theology of Sanctification and Holiness* (Downers Grove, Ill.: InterVarsity Press, 2001).

teaching unto justification, unto glorification and unto sanctification. Put otherwise, we may speak of teaching to nurture faith, hope and love. Justification is experienced by *faith*. We here affirm the great reformation notion of *sola fide:* we are justified through *faith alone* in Christ alone, by grace alone. This is the overwhelming testimony of the New Testament witnesses (see, for example, Rom 3:24-28; 4:5; 5:1; Gal 2:16; 3:8, 11, 24). The biblical notion of faith is deep and complex, to be sure. With regard to justifying faith, we describe (rather than attempt to define exhaustively) faith as a *depending on, trusting in* and *clinging to* Christ alone.[10]

It is in light of such saving faith that Paul writes, "For it is by grace you have been saved, through faith—and this not from yourselves, it is the gift of God—not by works, so that no one can boast" (Eph 2:8-9). The teaching ministry of the church then must seek to promote genuine saving faith in Christ Jesus by means of a clear proclamation of the glorious Gospel of the blessed God. With Paul, we must resolve to know nothing "except Jesus Christ and him crucified" (1 Cor 2:2), explaining that "God was reconciling the world to himself in Christ, not counting men's sins against them" and pleading with people, on behalf of Christ, to "be reconciled to God" (2 Cor 5:19-20). We must proclaim that God scandalously "justifies *the wicked*" (Rom 4:5, emphasis added); that is to say, God justifies people like us.

By means of this same Gospel[11]—"that Christ died for our sins according to the Scriptures . . . was buried . . . was raised on the third day . . . and . . . he appeared" (1 Cor 15:3-8)—we teach unto *hope*. With regard to the experience of justification, the essential response of the human heart is faith. With regard to glorification, the believer's response is *hope*. Tragically, this word has been greatly devalued in contemporary English usage, having become little more than a synonym for *wish*. But the biblical notion of hope is stronger by far. We may define it as "confident expectation."[12] Paul speaks of the biblical "hope of glory" that is given to the community of faith. Far from an impotent wish, the Christian hope is the confident expectation of the glory that is to come, "the blessed hope—the glorious appearing of our great God and Savior, Jesus Christ" (Tit 2:13). Just as we must teach that we are put right with God through faith in Christ, so we must also teach that we shall be with him

---

[10]See "Faith Formed by Christ," chapter two in Tuomo Mannermaa, *Christ Present in Faith: Luther's View of Justification* (Minneapolis: Fortress, 2005).

[11]For a fuller consideration of the essence and implications of the Gospel, please see chapter four.

[12]Bromiley, *Theological Dictionary,* p. 231.

and like him forever. His glory shall be revealed not only *to* us but even *in* us (see Rom 8:18[13]). That is, when he returns in glory, we shall appear with him in glory (see Col 3:4; 1 Jn 3:2). For this glorious unveiling of the "sons of God," all of creation now waits in eager expectation (Rom 8:19-21).

In the "present tense," we teach unto *love*. The entire law of God is summed up by the two greatest commandments: We are to love the Lord our God with all our heart, soul, mind and strength, and to love our neighbors as ourselves. To fulfill the requirements of God's law, we make our appeal once again to the Gospel of Jesus Christ. For the Gospel has sanctifying and regenerating power to change our lives. The Spirit who indwells all those who belong to Christ (see Rom 8:9) liberates us from the bondage to sin, and we are transformed from glory to glory into the likeness of the Savior (see 2 Cor 3:17-18). The result is that we grow in love of God and neighbor. A sound doctrine of sanctification will give proper emphases to both these objects of our love.

Many centuries ago, Augustine argued that love was the proper aim of faithful catechetical work and, indeed, of all Christian ministry. He wrote,

> Christ came chiefly for this reason: that we might learn how much God loves us, and might learn this to the end that we begin to glow with love of him by whom we were first loved, and so might love our neighbor at the bidding and after the example of him who made himself our neighbor by loving us.[14]

Sadly, however, it has become common in some Christian circles to reduce the idea of sanctification to a matter of personal piety, to a vision of "loving God" that does not necessarily evoke a corresponding love of all our neighbors. According to overwhelming biblical testimony, such a proposition is simply untenable.

On the other hand, many younger evangelicals (or "post-evangelicals," as some prefer to call themselves) have reacted against this emphasis on personal piety by advocating a vigorous social ethic. While this emphasis is right and

---

[13]The Greek preposition in Romans 8:18 is *eis*. In many English versions of the New Testament, it is rendered *to* in this verse: "the glory that will be revealed to us." In the NIV and some other versions, it is rendered *in:* "the glory that will be revealed in us." Though rules of grammar may well argue for "to us" in this sentence, the context seems to argue for "in us." In fact, the very next verse elaborates by saying that all creation is waiting for the unveiling of the "sons of God." The fact is that both aspects are true: glory shall be revealed *to* us and, as the result of that, it shall be revealed *in* us. Paul seems to argue along these lines in Colossians 3:4. John surely does so in 1 John 3:2: "When he appears, we shall be like him, for we shall see him as he is."

[14]Quoted in William J. Harmless, *Augustine and the Catechumenate* (Collegeville, Minn.: Liturgical Press, 1995), pp. 381-82.

proper, it seems sometimes to be accompanied by a new laxity in terms of personal holiness. Whereas many evangelicals of a generation ago may have measured holiness in terms of "Do not handle! Do not taste! Do not touch!" (Col 2:21), some younger evangelicals seem to have concluded that, because of grace, "Everything is permissible for me" (1 Cor 6:12).

The fact is, we need to emphasize both a genuine personal piety and an active participation in good works. In other words, we are called to love both God and neighbor. Loving God, if not accompanied by sincere and active love of neighbor, is spurious (see 1 Jn 4:20). However, loving one's neighbor cannot be taken as fulfilling, by itself, the command to love God. We may seek to *do justly* and *love mercy.* But if these things are not accompanied by a *humble walk with God,* then we still fall short of what God has required of us (see Mic 6:8; Hos 6:6).

While we have suggested that faith is essential to our experience of justification, hope to our future experience of glory and love to our present experience of sanctification, we dare not press the distinctions too hard. For it is clear that all three of these graces are essential in the present experience of believers and that the lines between them are fuzzy, at best. We may think of faith in the saving grace of God as that which gives birth to hope. Paul seems to argue along these lines in Romans 5. Through faith we have come to peace with God through Christ (see Rom 5:1), and "we have gained access by faith into this grace in which we now stand"; and so it is that "we rejoice in the hope of the glory of God" (Rom 5:2).

Elsewhere, Paul arranges these puzzle pieces a bit differently, as in these three examples:

- Faith and love spring from the hope that is stored up for us in heaven (see Col 1:5).

- Faith produces work, love leads us to labor and hope leads to perseverance (see 1 Thess 1:3).

- By faith we wait for the righteousness for which we hope, and that same faith expresses itself in love (see Gal 5:5-6).

Faith, hope and love are gifts to us to sustain us in this present age (see 1 Cor 13:13). Paul writes that love is the greatest of these. Why is this so? There may be many reasons, but we suggest the following clues. First, love is greatest because it endures forever; it never fails (see 1 Cor 13:8). One day, our precious faith will give way to sight (see 2 Cor 5:7; Heb 11). One day, too, our hope will no longer be needed, for we will have what we always hoped for (see Rom 8:24-25).

But love endures forever. We love imperfectly this side of glory. But on "the other side," we will perfectly love both God and neighbor. Furthermore, love is the greatest because to love is to imitate God. We cannot say that God exercises either faith or hope—at least not as we do. But God does exercise love and calls us, in and through his love, to live in imitation of him (see Eph 5:1-2). And, while we do not say that "God is faith" or "God is hope," we most certainly do proclaim that "God is love" (1 Jn 4:8). We teach, then, unto faith, unto hope and unto love. Especially, we teach unto love—the ultimate sign of our true communion with God.

TEACHING UNTO EDIFICATION

Terms like *obedience, conformity, salvation, faith, hope* and *love* can certainly be applied both to individuals and to churches as a whole. Attention to the spiritual nurture of individuals is certainly appropriate, for we long to see "everyone perfect in Christ" (Col 1:28). No member of the body of Christ is to be left behind. We dare not focus so much on the community as a whole that we neglect to care for its individual members. Though we may tend a flock of a hundred, attention to the particular needs of even one sheep is always imperative.

Now, however, we remind ourselves that though we ought to pay due attention to each individual member, we need also to address the body as a whole. Ephesians again offers a special reminder of this critical truth. We return to chapter 4 of that epistle and to that critically important section, Ephesians 4:11-16. We recall that verse 11 mentioned that Christ gave to the church apostles, prophets, evangelists, pastors and teachers. Verse 12 reminds us that these servant leaders are to equip the saints—the body of Christ—for the work of the ministry. This leads us to a consideration of verse 13. Here we find the desired outcome of such equipping and such ministry. The body is to be edified—that is, built up—"until we all reach unity in the faith and in the knowledge of the Son of God and become mature, attaining to the whole measure of the fullness of Christ" (Eph 4:13).

There are numerous ways that this verse might be exposited. For example, it could be taken that the verse has three ends in view: unity in the faith, knowledge of the Son of God and maturity. Or it could be understood that there is one end in view: a maturity that requires unity in the faith and knowledge of the Son of God. Furthermore, one could see the verse as applying to the body as a whole, or believe that a church united in the faith and in the knowledge of the Son of God will lead each individual believer to genuine maturity.[15] Our approach is to focus on the ultimate aim of maturity for the body as a whole. However, this requires that we also consider the supporting aims of unity in the faith and knowledge of the Son of God.

UNITY IN THE FAITH

It may strike the attentive reader of Ephesians as odd that Paul speaks of a need for attaining unity in the faith. After all, has not Paul been emphatically clear in making the point that the body is already one? Indeed he has. He has spoken of the wall of hostility that was abolished by the death of Christ, creating "in himself one new man" out of Jew and Gentile (Eph 2:15). It is "in this one body" that God reconciles both Jew and Gentile to himself (Eph 2:16). And, earlier in chapter 4, Paul has underscored the critical importance of this unity, declaring, "There is one body and one Spirit—just as you were called to one hope when you were called—one Lord, one faith, one baptism; one God and Father of all, who is over all and through all and in all" (Eph 4:4-6). Thus he speaks of our "unity of the Spirit" (Eph 4:3) not as something to be attained but as something to be preserved. We are *already* one, whether we like it or not, whether we accept this reality or not.

What then can Paul possibly mean by saying that church communities will require equipping ministries "until we all reach unity in the faith"? It may simply be that Paul intends the readers to understand that unity—like so many other features of Christian truth—is an *already . . . not yet* reality. That is, we *are* one, *are becoming* one and *shall be* perfectly one in Christ. We have already applied this line of thinking to the concepts of reconciliation and salvation. It is entirely reasonable to understand our spiritual unity in the same way. Jesus had prayed to the Father, regarding his own, "that they may be one as we are one" (Jn 17:22). Surely such an experience of unity is attained only by degree.

Another possible interpretation of this passage is to highlight the distinction between "unity of the Spirit" in verse 3 and "unity in the faith" here, in verse 13. While the phrase "unity in the faith" has been variously understood

---

[15]This seems to be the interpretation of John Stott in *The Message of Ephesians,* The Bible Speaks Today (Downers Grove, Ill.: InterVarsity Press, 1979), pp. 169-73.

by interpreters,[16] the view adopted here is that Paul is using the expression "the faith" in a technical sense of the term. As we will seek to demonstrate in chapter three, "the faith" includes the Gospel and all its implications for life and doctrine. This faith "was once for all entrusted to the saints" (Jude 3).

If we take this view, Paul is arguing that, while the church has an unbreakable and essential "unity in the Spirit," the matter of "unity in the faith" is not a given, is not automatically possessed by the church and is actually something we must labor toward. Jude declares that we must "contend for the faith" (Jude 3). In Ephesians 4:13, Paul affirms much the same concern. To take such a view of the passage does not mean a rejection of the idea presented in the previous paragraph—that our unity in the Spirit is an *already . . . not yet* reality. These may well be complementary truths. That is, our "unity of the Spirit" is experienced in deeper ways as we move ever closer to true "unity in the faith."

Throughout the history of the church, innumerable counterfeit Gospels and perversions of the faith have been competing for the hearts, souls and minds of believers. It has always been essential that believers "not believe every spirit, but test the spirits to see whether they are from God, because many false prophets have gone out into the world" (1 Jn 4:1). Those in the church must "test everything. Hold on to the good" (1 Thess 5:21).

The goal of "unity in the faith," then, concerns unity in *the Truth as disclosed in Jesus Christ.* In chapter four, we will further explore this notion of "the Truth," contending that it is one of the critical aspects of the Gospel, linking it to matters of "sound doctrine" (Tit 1:9) and of "the apostles' teaching" (Acts 2:42). We are thus now concerned with a convergence regarding the *why* of our teaching and the *what* of our teaching. That is, we must faithfully and diligently teach the faith that was once for all delivered to the saints until the church is unified in that faith.

As we have said, such a unity in the faith is not the automatic possession of any given church. A quick turn of our gaze to both historic and contemporary Christian experience illumines the matter. Historically, we can easily identify the fracturing of the church along various lines, including theological divisions. The Center for the Study of Global Christianity estimates that by the year 1800, there were approximately five hundred Christian denominations in the world. By June of 2008, that estimate was forty thousand![17] Of course,

---

[16]See "The Creed: One God and One Church" comment 4.B in Markus Barth, *Ephesians 4-6,* Anchor Bible Commentary (Garden City, N.Y.: Doubleday, 1974), pp. 464-67.

[17]See <http://www.gets.edu/sites/default/files/1BMR2009.pdf>. Accessed on July 30, 2009.

most of this manifold division concerns Protestant communities. We can also see how wide the divides continue to be both *within* Catholic and Orthodox communions and *between* these communions, as well as between each of these and Protestant Christianity. While the cause for these divisions is multiform— contributing factors including the sociocultural, political, ethnic, racial, generational, national and more—one of the obvious sources of much division concerns theology. That is, the universal body of Christ is not currently experiencing the full measure of "unity in the faith."

Turning our gaze to the global expansion of the church today, we see another illustration of the challenge. As has been well documented by a number of recent authors,[18] the church has been experiencing amazingly rapid growth throughout the world, especially in the global South and East. Evangelistic efforts have been explosively successful in numerous countries in South America, Africa and Asia. But alongside the rapid expansion has come an obvious and deepening need for sound teaching to ground and unite these believers. Where the number of new believers vastly outnumbers the availability of sound teaching, schisms often seem inevitable, as do the rise of cults and other perversions of the faith. In many of the countries where the church is growing most rapidly, leaders have begun to establish effective training ministries, and the needs are being increasingly met. In other cases, however, church leaders are scrambling for answers and not yet finding many that are sufficient.

There is also the plight of the evangelical movement here in the West. In spite of many centuries of vibrant church history, we face in North America today a tragically splintered evangelical movement (not to mention the deep divides between conservative and liberal wings of the Protestant movement). Indeed, many have already decided that the word *evangelical* is no longer particularly helpful. One of the reasons for such a view is that the term now seems to mean whatever one wishes it to mean.

The sense of a widely acknowledged list of essentials of the faith is largely absent in our day. Today we find nontrinitarian ministries, preachers of an unfettered health-and-wealth gospel, hardline political conservatives and

---

[18]For example, Philip Jenkins, *The Next Christendom: The Coming of Global Christianity* (New York: Oxford University Press, 2002), and *The New Faces of Christianity: Believing the Bible in the Global South* (New York: Oxford University Press, 2006); Lamin Sanneh, *Whose Religion Is Christianity? The Gospel Beyond the West* (Grand Rapids: Eerdmans, 2003), and *Disciples of All Nations: Pillars of World Christianity* (New York: Oxford University Press, 2008); and Andrew Walls, *The Missionary Movement in Christian History: Studies in the Transmission of Faith* (Maryknoll, N.Y.: Orbis, 1996).

even groups that have historically been regarded as "Christian" cults all claiming the label "evangelical" as their own. As surely as the newly emerging Christian communities in the world need to labor toward "unity in the faith," we in the West must also work for this with a new resolve. This calls us to a new spirit of humble cooperation as Christians from the North and South, East and West learn to listen to and speak truth to one another.

The knowledge of the Son of God. The second key phrase of Ephesians 4:13 is "in the knowledge of the Son of God." Some interpreters see the clause as simply an extension and qualification of the preceding one. In this view, the "unity in the faith" that we must pursue is "faith toward Jesus." A somewhat different view would speak of "unity in the faith" that results in the "knowledge of the Son of God." However, we join numerous commentators in highlighting the importance of the conjunction *kai*—"and." The ministry of the church moves toward both "unity in the faith" *and* "the knowledge of the Son of God." But what kind of knowledge does Paul have in view here?

The word here translated *knowledge* bespeaks "recognition" or "understanding."[19] It is clear that the knowledge Paul envisions is not merely cognitive apprehension of certain facts relating to Jesus. Indeed, it may be helpful to view Paul's understanding of "knowledge" as rooted in the Hebrew concept of *yada*. *Yada*—the most basic Hebrew word for knowing—implies a deep, intimate, experiential knowledge.[20] As has often been said, it is one thing to *know about God;* it is quite another to *know God*.[21] Paul plainly seems to have the latter sense in view here—that the church must come to recognize and understand Jesus in his fullness and to know him experientially.

Such knowledge is to be understood as an *already . . . not yet* matter. Upon coming to faith, believers can claim to "know God" or, better, to be "known by God" (Gal 4:9). But surely our knowledge is profoundly limited and always in need of growth. Thus we find Paul himself, many years into his own walk with Jesus, speaking of one enduring goal: "I want to know Christ" (Phil 3:10).

For Paul to speak of ministry continuing until the whole church attains to knowledge of the Son of God is best understood in the same spirit as his personal reference in Philippians 3:10. Surely we would understand that

---

[19]Snodgrass, *Ephesians*, p. 205.
[20]See footnote 30 in chapter 1.
[21]Such language is found, for example, in J. I. Packer's classic work *Knowing God* (Downers Grove, Ill.: InterVarsity Press, 1993).

Paul already had a knowledge of the Son of God, and yet he professed to be pressing on to achieve this very thing. Our knowledge of the Son of God can never be deemed sufficient. The believer who thinks she has no further need to know Jesus more deeply has tragically misunderstood the nature and calling of our faith.

Paul explains his holy ambition to know Jesus further by saying that he longed to know Christ "and the power of his resurrection and the fellowship of sharing in his sufferings, becoming like him in his death, and so, somehow, to attain to the resurrection from the dead" (Phil 3:10-11). In the next breath, he confesses that he has not yet "obtained all this," nor has he "been made perfect" (Phil 3:12). But toward this prize he earnestly presses on (see Phil 3:14), and "all of us who are mature should take such a view of things" (Phil 3:15). The mature believer, in other words, is not one who has come as far as possible into an intimate knowledge of Christ. He is, rather, the one who knows he must ever pursue this goal. The same can and should be said of mature congregations.

And become mature. The third phrase in Ephesians 4:13 speaks of becoming "mature." The Greek word translated here is *teleios*. Once again, Paul's meaning can be understood in several different ways. Some believe that he is urging each *individual* to become mature, complete, perfect in Christ. In Colossians 1:28, where Paul uses the same word, it seems clear that he intends as much. There, Paul identifies this as the goal of all his labor. He writes, "We proclaim [Christ], admonishing and teaching everyone with all wisdom, so that we may present everyone perfect in Christ."

For Paul to assert that each of the believers in Colosse must and can become *teleion* was especially significant, as the Colossians were apparently under the influence of a heresy with Gnostic elements. Significant among those elements, apparently, was the notion that only an elite few could ever attain such "completeness." Paul utterly rejects such a view and affirms that every Christian is, in fact, called and graced toward this lofty goal.

In Ephesians 4:13, however, we understand the body *as a whole* to be the focus of concern. It is the church as a whole—not just individual believers—that must grow into maturity, "attaining to the whole measure of the fullness of Christ" (Eph 4:13). Paul has already declared the church to be "the fullness of him who fills everything in every way" (Eph 1:23). This is already reality in the spiritual realm and is how God sees his *poiēma*. But in our lived experience, this is a goal for us to pursue. It is another of those glorious *already . . . not yet* doctrines. Thus Paul prays that, through the experience of God's love, the church will move toward this (see Eph 3:19). And here in Ephesians 4 he exhorts the church to labor in ministry until such maturity is attained.

In the verses that follow, Paul speaks of a church that is mature in several respects. First, it is stable, not quickly moved by faulty doctrines and deceitful schemes that may assault it (see Eph 4:14). Second, it is mature in how the members of the body relate to one another. They speak the truth in love to one another, and thereby the body grows up into the Head (see Eph 4:15). And third, it is mature in the sense that it is able to function properly as each part of the body does its appointed work (see Eph 4:16). Why do we teach and labor in ministry? Our answer must include this vision of maturity, of helping the body to be all that it is designed to be—a stable, loving, fully functioning body. This is critical to our aims, since it is for good works that the body was created in Christ (see Eph 2:10).

To enhance our understanding of what Paul intends by *teleios,* it is helpful to consider the use of a similar word by another New Testament writer. The author of the letter to the Hebrews uses a verb from the same root in a way that may well startle readers. We read concerning Jesus Christ that "in bringing many sons to glory, it was fitting that God, for whom and through whom everything exists, should make the author of their salvation perfect through suffering" (Heb 2:10). The Greek word rendered here as "make . . . perfect" is *teleioō.* The author repeats the claim a few chapters later: "Although he was a son, [Jesus] learned obedience from what he suffered and, once *made perfect,* he became the source of eternal salvation for all who obey him" (Heb 5:8-9, emphasis added).

We may well wonder in what sense the ever-perfect Son of God had to be made perfect! But the context of the two passages provides answers to the mystery. We read that Jesus had "to be made like his brothers in every way, in order that he might become a merciful and faithful high priest in service to God, and that he might make atonement for the sins of the people" (Heb 2:17). To be our fully sufficient Savior, to be the one and only sacrifice for our sins, to be our faithful and merciful high priest, Jesus needed to experience true humanity, including the suffering involved in his incarnation, temptation and passion. Apart from all this, he would not be *teleios.* That is, though he was perfectly divine from all eternity, he needed also to be fully human to assume his appointed roles and complete his appointed tasks.

In other words, he needed to be *fully equipped* for the roles and tasks to which he was called. In John 5, we see yet another role that Jesus will play in the future that is linked to his human experience. We read that "the Father judges no one, but has entrusted all judgment to the Son. . . . And he has given him authority to judge because he is the Son of Man" (Jn 5:22, 27). For all these roles—atoning sacrifice, merciful high priest, author of eternal salvation, great and coming judge—Jesus needed to be "made perfect" through the experience of full humanity.[22]

What insight does this offer us concerning our own ministries of edification toward the maturity of the body? We learn from this that the church, Christ's body, is to be built up until it also is fully equipped to operate in its appointed roles and to engage the ministry of reconciliation to which it is called. This will surely involve a ministry of teaching and other formative ministries we may design for our churches. It will also involve all the informal interconnections within the body, the relationships of mutual edification, in which each member does its unique part and all the members speak truth in love to one another (see Eph 4:14-16). And, as surely as Jesus had to experience suffering in preparation for fulfilling his ministries, we must suffer if we will be fully equipped to perform ours. As Paul told the Philippians, "It has been granted to you . . . not only to believe on [Jesus], but also to suffer for him" (Phil 1:29). Such a calling Paul himself did not disdain. Indeed, he longed to know Jesus in "the fellowship of sharing in his suffering, becoming like him in his death" (Phil 3:10).[23]

The hardships that believers must experience as part of their journey toward maturity may sometimes seem like a harsh rod of discipline. But God performs such, or permits such, because he is a loving Father (see Heb 12:4-11). He uses such things to refine our faith (see 1 Pet 1:7) and to help us to be even more fruitful in serving him (see Jn 15:2). The suffering we experience equips us for helping others in their suffering (see 2 Cor 1:3-7). In light of all this, how tragic are the triumphalism and the "prosperity gospel" that are found in so many

---

[22]"Jesus became *fully qualified* as pioneer of man's salvation by undergoing the experience of human sufferings, inasmuch as through suffering is the way to salvation. Although Christ was morally perfect and sinless, his life and work were brought by suffering to a form of perfection or completion which cannot have been possible without them." Raymond Brown, *The Message of Hebrews,* The Bible Speaks Today (Downers Grove, Ill.: InterVarsity Press), pp. 61-62.

[23]The participation in Christ's suffering "partly follows upon and partly precedes the power of His resurrection. It follows, as the practical result on our life; it precedes, as leading up to the full and final appreciation of this power." J. B. Lightfoot, *St. Paul's Epistle to the Philippians* (1868; reprint, Peabody, Mass.: Hendrickson, 1987), p. 150.

ministries identifying themselves as evangelical.[24] Many churches choose to ignore suffering, to deny its reality or, worse, to teach that all our suffering is the devil's doing and therefore can never be God's will for us.

CONCLUSION

In this chapter we have spoken of becoming more obedient disciples of Christ, of being more fully conformed to his likeness, of growing up in our salvation, of learning to love God and neighbor, of equipping the saints for ministry so that the body of Christ is edified and thus may faithfully and effectively walk in the good works of reconciliation God has prepared for us. All of these things are essential aspects of forming the faithful.

As discussed in chapter one, the church exists ultimately for the glory of God. We could then justly summarize all that we have said in this chapter thus: we teach unto worship of the living God. Abraham Joshua Heschel—the famed twentieth-century rabbi, philosopher and activist—argued that worship was the proper goal of education from the perspective of Jews. Drawing a contrast with other cultures, he wrote, "The Greeks learned in order to comprehend. The Hebrews learned in order to revere. The modern man learns in order to use."[25]

We do well to borrow this notion and say that we teach in order to revere the living God and help others do the same. The Father is still seeking worshipers who will worship him in spirit and truth (see Jn 4:23). John Piper wrote that "missions exist because worship doesn't."[26] Along these same lines, we can say that "teaching exists because worship must."

The church of Jesus Christ exists to glory in and to glorify the living God. We exist *here and now,* on earth—in time and in space—to glorify God *by means of* walking in good works of reconciliation. To walk that walk, the body must be built up. In pursuit of these aims, we engage in a variety of ministries of teaching and formation. These ministries are sometimes formal, sometimes not; sometimes preemptive, sometimes responsive; sometimes engaging large groups, other times engaging small groups; always attentive to the needs of

---

[24]This is surely a misuse of the term *evangelical,* since that word—built from the Greek word for "gospel"—ought to evoke not only the power of the risen Lord but also his profound suffering and death for us.

[25]Abraham Joshua Heschel, *God in Search of Man: A Philosophy of Judaism* (New York: Farrar, Strauss & Giroux, 1976), p. 34.

[26]John Piper, *Let the Nations Be Glad! The Supremacy of God in Missions,* 2nd ed. (Grand Rapids: Baker, 1993), p. 17.

individuals, but never losing sight of the church as a whole.

Having devoted our first two chapters to a discussion of our *mission* as the people of God, we next turn attention to consideration of our *message*. What is it that we must proclaim and teach both *to* the church and *as* the church? In chapters three through five, we propose answers to these questions.

HYMN FOR CONTEMPLATION AND WORSHIP

How Great the Father's Love
(1 Jn 3:1-3; Tit 2:11-14)

How great the Father's love,
so lavished upon us
that we should be one family
in Christ Jesus!
We have been saved!
Christ crucified has justified us.
God be praised!

When Jesus comes again
what will our glory be?
For by his grace, the Savior's face
our eyes shall see.
We shall be saved!
A glorified and spotless bride—
O, God be praised!

The Holy Spirit fills
our thirsting souls today.
He intercedes for us and leads us
in God's Way.
We are now saved—
his sanctifying pow'r applying.
God be praised!

The grace of God appeared:
salvation from above!
In this faith and this hope we stand,
ablaze with love.
The God who saves—
the Father, Son and Spirit,
One in Three—be praised!

Text: Gary A. Parrett (2001)
Tune: Darwall
Familiar use of the tune: "Rejoice, the Lord Is King!"

QUESTIONS FOR PLANNING AND PRACTICE

1. Before reading this chapter, what would your answer have been to the question Why does the church teach? Had you assumed that this is something the church simply *does?* How has this chapter challenged your view of the purpose of teaching ministry in the church? Specifically, how would it potentially change your role in or your approach to your own congregation's teaching ministry?

2. What are the five elements chiefly discussed in the chapter regarding the purpose of formation ministries in the church? How do these components correspond to the goals of your own educational formation ministry?

3. "We teach *from* obedience and *unto* obedience." From what Scripture passages do we primarily derive this notion, and why is it so crucial in educational formation ministry? What are some other salient concepts or commands in those passages concerning educational ministry?

4. In this chapter, the notion of salvation is discussed at some length. Thinking back on your own evangelistic efforts in the past, how have you presented salvation in Jesus Christ to an unbeliever? Which tense or aspects of salvation did you stress—past, present or future? Using table 2.1 on page 56 and the discussion of salvation, we invite you, with a partner in ministry, to consider how to better reflect the various aspects of salvation when teaching about the glorious Gospel of Jesus Christ.

5. Reflecting on Ephesians 4:13 ("until we all reach unity in the faith and in the knowledge of the Son of God and become mature, attaining to the whole measure of the fullness of Christ"), what is the desired outcome of equipping the body of Christ for ministry? Try to restate these aims in your own words. How would you evaluate your congregation's efforts to date, relative to such aims?

6. Hebrews 2:10 tells us that even Jesus had to be "made perfect" to fulfill his purpose here on Earth. In what ways did the Son of God have to be made perfect? What does this teach us about our ministries of preparing the body of Christ now for perfection and total maturity?

7. This chapter concludes with the idea of teaching unto reverence. When you teach, do you approach it as an act of worship to God? Do you encourage fellow teachers to do the same? Reflect on Rabbi Heschel's statement "The Greeks learned in order to comprehend. The Hebrews learned in order to revere. The modern man learns in order to use." Which of these three aims best describes your own teaching to date? Why do you personally desire to be a lifelong learner?

RESOURCES FOR FURTHER STUDY

Dykstra, Craig. *Growing in the Life of Faith: Education and Christian Practices.* Louisville, Ky.: Geneva, 1999.

Newbigin, Lesslie. *Proper Confidence: Faith, Doubt and Certainty in Christian Discipleship.* Grand Rapids: Eerdmans, 1995.

Osmer, Richard. *The Teaching Ministry of Congregations.* Louisville, Ky.: Westminster/John Knox Press, 2007.

Packer, J. I. *Knowing God.* Downers Grove, Ill.: InterVarsity Press, 1993.

————. *The Quest for Godliness: A Puritan Vision of the Christian Life.* Wheaton: Crossway Books. 1994.

Pazmiño, Robert. *Foundational Issues in Christian Education: An Introduction in Evangelical Perspective.* 3rd edition. Grand Rapids: Baker, 2008.

Penner, Myron, ed. *Christianity and the Postmodern Turn.* Grand Rapids: Brazos, 2005.

Peterson, David. *Possessed by God: A New Testament Theology of Sanctification and Holiness.* Downers Grove, Ill.: InterVarsity Press, 2001.

Ryle, J. C. *Holiness: Its Nature, Difficulty, Hindrances and Roots.* Peabody, Mass.: Hendrickson, 2007.

Stevens, Paul. *Liberating the Laity.* Vancouver: Regent College Publishing, 1977.

Stott, John. *The Cross of Christ.* Downers Grove, Ill.: InterVarsity Press, 1986.

————. *The Incomparable Christ.* Downers Grove, Ill.: InterVarsity Press, 2001.

Wilhoit, James, and John Detonni. *Nurture That Is Christian: Developmental Perspectives on Christian Education.* Grand Rapids: Baker, 1995.

Willard, Dallas. *The Great Omission: Reclaiming Jesus's Essential Teachings on Discipleship.* New York: HarperOne, 2006.

PART 2

PROCLAMATION

A Message to Obey and Teach

"If we don't want to see our future generations abandon the faith, we won't abandon
schooling as an aspect of ministry in our churches."

RICHARD OSMER

▼

Richard Osmer of Princeton Theological Seminary was the guest speaker for a large gathering of evangelical professors of Christian education. During a question-and-answer session, one of the conference participants had raised his voice against the "schooling paradigm"[1] in Christian education. In reply, Osmer uttered the words quoted above, admonishing his audience that to entirely re-move the concept of schooling our children and new members in the basic truths of the Christian faith is to profoundly imperil the future health of our churches. Later, in personal correspondence with me, Osmer expanded: "I am concerned that too much focus on relational approaches to discipling and spiritual forma-tion will undercut the strong evangelical emphasis on biblical content—simply knowing the story scripture tells in depth."

Osmer's remark that day echoes Walter Brueggemann's statement that "every community that wants to last more than one generation must be concerned with

---

[1]Sometimes this critique is aimed at ministries in local churches; other times it is aimed at seminary education. The concern is that education and formation is often reduced to sitting folks down in desks and chairs, where they are made passive recipients of certain content. If this is all or most that a church (or a seminary) does, then the concerns are certainly valid.

education."[2] Faithful education must take many forms, to be sure. But one of those forms must be, as Osmer puts it, a proper emphasis on biblical content. For decades now, it seems to us, this emphasis has been wanting in many evangelical circles, as attention has shifted toward effective processes. Without wishing in any way to diminish the critical role of faithful practices in forming believers and congregations, it is our intention in this second section of the book to call for a wholehearted and intentional commitment to substantive content in the teaching ministries of our churches.

This commitment to substantive content is critical in light of the mission that we—the *poiēma* of God—have been called to fulfill. To us has been given "the ministry of reconciliation" (2 Cor 5:18). Central to this ministry is "the message of reconciliation" (1 Cor 5:19). This message is the proclamation of what God has done and is doing in and through his Son, Jesus Christ. The content of our teaching ministry, when all is said and done, is a clear and multifaceted proclamation of Christ (see Col 1:28).

God creates and forms by means of his word. By his word he created the heavens and the earth. By his word he sanctifies his people (Jn 17:17). And by his word he furnishes the church and its members with all that is needed for salvation, maturity and the good works God requires (see 2 Tim 3:15-17). If we would see God's people formed for life and ministry, we must faithfully teach God's Word in substantive ways.

In chapter three, we examine the notion of teaching "the Faith" that was "once for all entrusted to the saints" (Jude 3). Chapter four is an examination of the glorious Gospel of the blessed God, including its implications for faith and life. We conclude the section, in chapter five, with a proposal for a CORE[3] content for a congregational curriculum.

---

[2]Walter Brueggemann, *The Creative Word: Canon as a Model for Biblical Education* (Philadelphia: Fortress, 1982), p. 1.
[3]CORE is used here as an acronym indicating our concern to teach Comprehensive, Orthodox, Renewing Essentials.

3

The Faith Once Delivered

So then, just as you received Christ Jesus as Lord,

continue to live in him, rooted and built up in him,

strengthened in the faith as you were taught,

and overflowing with thankfulness.

COLOSSIANS 2:6-7

▼

THERE ARE VERY FEW SPHERES IN WHICH an approach to education is as random and haphazard as that practiced in many of our churches today. If someone wanted to study toward a degree in economics, for example, it would be most unlikely that the college would let her choose all her own courses or choose simply not to take classes at all. If we wish our child to learn to play an instrument, we would certainly hope to find an instructor who has some idea and plan about what particular things really must be learned and when and how. When we look at the medical school diploma on the walls of our doctors' offices, we probably assume—and gratefully so—that our doctors actually attended (in the full sense of the term) all the required classes in the curriculum and not only those that suited their fancies at the time. How strange it is that, in this matter of Christian education and formation, we have come to adopt so very different a scheme.[1]

In these next three chapters, we focus on the *content* of our teaching.[2] We

---

[1]Dallas Willard has long argued along such lines when addressing the challenge of helping people become like Jesus. See, for example, *The Spirit of the Disciplines: Understanding How God Changes Lives* (New York: HarperOne, 1990).

[2]The issue of educational content is complex. One witness to the issues involved is Harold W. Burgess, in his *Models of Religious Education* (Grand Rapids: BridgePoint Books, 1996). Burgess

will consider the issue of *what* the church must proclaim and teach. We use the word *proclamation,* in a general sense here, to include that which is preached and taught by, in, for and through the church. But we do not intend to limit proclamation to that which is verbally declared in the form of a sermon or a lecture. Our proclamation takes many forms—verbal and nonverbal, formal and nonformal—and must include both traditional pedagogical strategies and faithful community practices.

Of course, to attend to faithful and substantive content does not, in and of itself, equal good education. Both the history of religious education and the current experience of the church bear this out. However, some who lead and labor in evangelical Christian education seem to have erred in the opposite direction, largely neglecting any significant transmission of content. We submit that *little* transmission of content is not an advance over what is often dismissed as *mere* transmission of content. Indeed, we must reject the unhelpful warring that is frequent in educational circles, pitting content over against process. Careful attention to both is essential for faithful and effective Christian education. While the focus in these next three chapters is content, we address issues of educational process throughout this book.

Our approach to the issue of content is not to ask what *might* be taught or what *could* be taught. We ask, rather, what *must* be taught?[3] In other words, is there anything that the church should consider *essential content* for its members? If the question seems a bit strange to us, it is not because the question is unreasonable. Rather, it is strange to us simply because, for quite some time, too few evangelicals have been asking this question. This puts us at odds with our own history, since for most of church history there was broad consensus on what

---

summarizes five different "models" of religious education, which he labels the Historic Prototype, Classical Liberal, Mid-century Mainline, Evangelical/Kerygmatic and Social-Science. Burgess outlines his approach to each model using five familiar categories: aim, subject-matter content, teacher, learner and environment. As the survey progresses, it becomes clear that the notion of content is handled quite differently in the various approaches to religious education. The approach adopted here contains elements of what Burgess calls the Historic Prototype and the Evangelical/Kerygmatic models. With the latter in view, Burgess writes, "The faithful transmission, or impartation, of an intact salvific message is the heart of effective education" (p. 170). While we may not say things quite as Burgess has here, we do approach the issue of content with concern for the actual substance of what is proclaimed and taught in the church. The Social-Science of James Michael Lee, as presented by Burgess, distinguishes between structural content and substantive content. In our discussion of content, or of the *what* question, we are concerned with the latter. We take up matters of structure elsewhere in this book, under various titles.

[3]We will deal throughout the remainder of this book with issues of further content that can complement and supplement the essential content of the teaching ministry.

represented "the minimum of knowledge required of a Christian,"[4] a consensus that included, among other things, instruction in the Apostles' Creed, the Decalogue (that is, the Ten Commandments) and the Lord's Prayer.[5]

To help illuminate the issues in view here, it may be helpful to consider the following scenario. What might happen if a person who had visited a local evangelical church for a few weeks approached the pastor and announced, "Pastor, I'd like to become a Christian"? How would the pastor respond? He might engage in a brief interview to discern the spiritual state and religious background of the inquirer. At some point, he would probably offer a summary of the Gospel, perhaps in the form of the "four spiritual laws" or something similar.

But where might the pastor go from there? Would there be any sense that there are some things that *must* be studied in the process of becoming a Christian? There may well be a session or two required in advance of baptism. There may also be some sort of membership class. But even if there were (and there are many evangelical churches where such things simply are neither offered nor expected), we would likely find a wide divergence from congregation to congregation, with each church establishing its own guidelines regarding what makes one a Christian and what a would-be Christian or new believer *must* learn.

TASKS OF THE CHURCH AND FAITHFUL PRACTICES

It is not easy to find evangelical educators who have engaged the What must we teach? question in a serious and sustained manner in recent decades.[6] In many recent books in the field of Christian education, the issue seems not even to be raised at all. Some, however, have at least entertained the question and offered proposals. Among the more commonly offered suggestions, one has been to link the essential content of our teaching ministry to the tasks of the church. This is usually based on Acts 2:42 and following. In that passage we read of the newly baptized thousands in Jerusalem who "devoted themselves to the apostles' teaching, and to the fellowship, to the breaking of bread and to prayer." In the verses that follow, we read the wonderful description of

---

[4]This language is from Luther's shorter preface to the Large Catechism, in *The Book of Concord: The Confessions of the Evangelical Lutheran Church* (Philadelphia: Fortress Press, 1959), p. 362.

[5]We will discuss these three "summaries of the faith" at some length in chapter five.

[6]However, Robert Pazmiño has a fine discussion of this in his *Principles and Practices of Christian Education: An Evangelical Perspective* (Grand Rapids: Baker, 1992). In the following discussion, we consider some of his suggestions, as well as those of several other authors.

that nascent community, who shared meals with one another, devoted themselves to service of others, experienced the favor of all their neighbors, witnessed the miraculous power of God and welcomed new believers daily into their numbers. When we hear believers today say that they would love to be a truly "New Testament church," it is usually this Jerusalem community they have in mind (rather than some of those other New Testament churches—the communities in Corinth or Galatia, for example).

How did this beautiful and blessed community emerge in Jerusalem? The text points us to three things. First, there is the outpouring of the Spirit on the disciples. Second, there is a potent proclamation of the Gospel by the apostle Peter, who points his hearers toward Jesus the crucified and risen Lord. And, third, there are the four commitments noted in verse 42. The new believers, we are told, steadfastly devoted themselves to

1. *the apostles' teaching*—this undoubtedly centered on the Person and saving work of Jesus Christ.

2. *the fellowship*—the Greek word here is *koinōnia* and gives the sense that the believers had devoted themselves to sharing all things "in common" with one another, as verse 44 reiterates.

3. *the breaking of the bread*—the Greek has the definite article before bread, unlike the reference to breaking bread together in verse 46. Many scholars believe that this breaking of "the bread" refers to the celebration of the Lord's Supper in the gathered worship of the community.[7]

4. *the prayers*—many of the common English renderings miss both the definite article here and the fact of the plural; this is not a commitment to prayer in a general sense but to "the prayers," which has a more communal and (likely, at least) a more liturgical sense.

Attention to a passage like this makes good sense, to be sure. The foundational practices of the first Christian community provide us with an important glimpse of how a church can live together the life of worship. We see here something like an early catechumenate. In this case, however, the instruction comes primarily after baptism, not before it, as would be the case in many catechetical efforts of the post–New Testament church. In the Greek, the term for "devoted themselves" is very strong and suggests that this was a

---

[7]I. Howard Marshall, *The Acts of the Apostle: An Introduction and Commentary* (Leicester, U.K.: Inter-Varsity Press, 1980), p. 83; F. F. Bruce, *The Book of the Acts,* rev. ed. (Grand Rapids: Eerdmans, 1988), p. 73.

wholehearted commitment of the new believers.[8] Wisdom plainly suggests
that we pay serious attention to this passage in our own efforts. So it is that a
number of authors have taken this as a principle text for giving shape to the
content of our educational and formational ministries today.[9]

Taking their lead from this passage (sometimes noting Acts 2:42, sometimes not), several authors have suggested an outline of formational content
that includes some or all of the following elements:[10]

- *didachē*—the teaching of the apostles

- *kerygma*—the proclamation of the Gospel, implied in Acts 2:47

- *koinōnia*—the fellowship

- *leitourgia*—a reference to worship and to prayer, the two latter commitments we find in Acts 2:42

- *diakonia*—service or ministry, implied in Acts 2:45

- *propheteia*—prophetic ministries of justice and mercy, also implied in
  2:45

While all of the above indeed represent valuable educational commitments
to which the church really should pay heed, certain features of this list seem a
bit problematic if it is intended to be representative of the commitments in
Acts 2. The grammatical construction of Acts 2:42 suggests that there were
four practices to which the new believers devoted themselves. What follows,
in verses 43 through 47, is better taken as a description of the fruit of those
commitments or as an example of how these were being expressed, rather
than as a further enumerating of them.

Furthermore, if we are to understand that verses 43 through 47 are taken
as extending the list of commitments, we have to wonder why these authors
include in their lists service and prophetic (in the sense of justice and mercy)
ministry but have not included other features in the passage, including meeting daily in the temple courts, holding all things in common, selling of possessions and the regular experience of many wonders and miraculous signs.

---

[8]*Proskartereō* connotes "a steadfast and singleminded fidelity to a certain course of action."
Richard Longenecker, *The Expositor's Bible Commentary: Acts,* ed. Frank Gaebelein (Grand
Rapids: Zondervan, 1981), p. 289.
[9]See, for example, Maria Harris, *Fashion Me a People* (Louisville, Ky.: Westminster/John Knox
Press, 1989), pp. 15-72; and Marva Dawn, *Powers, Weakness, and the Tabernacling of God* (Grand
Rapids: Eerdmans, 2001), pp. 78-117.
[10]See again Harris, *Fashion Me a People.* See also Pazmiño, *Principles and Practices of Christian
Education,* pp. 45-57.

In summary, we find the appeal to Acts 2:42 to be compelling in terms of helping us to generate a list of essentials for teaching and formation today. From what precedes that list—the narrative of Acts 2:1-41—we are reminded of both the primacy of the Gospel and the fact that apart from the Spirit's ministry there is no church at all. From what follows, in verses 43 through 47, we see an expression of the fruit manifested in its particular cultural context and social arrangements, fruit that was borne by the convergence of the Spirit's sovereign power, the proclamation of the Gospel and the steadfast commitment of the believers to the four commitments of Acts 2:42.

FIRST PRINCIPLES, ELEMENTARY TEACHINGS OR BASIC ELEMENTS

Another important New Testament passage to which we might well turn our attention is Hebrews 5:11—6:3. In this passage, the author to the Hebrews rebukes his readers for their lack of maturity. By this time, he tells them, they ought to be teaching others. But, as it is, "you need someone to teach you the elementary truths of God's word all over again. You need milk, not solid food!" (Heb 5:12). A few verses later, he exhorts the readers to "leave the elementary teachings about Christ and go on to maturity" (6:1).

What the NIV renders in these two verses as "elementary truths" or "elementary teachings" has elsewhere been rendered "first principles," "basic elements" and so on. The idea seems to be that which is rudimentary. The author says that this may be a suitable foundation, but it is time to move on from the "milk" to the "meat," from infancy to maturity. The "first principles" or "elementary teachings" of Christ referred to in Hebrews 6:1 stand in stark contrast to those of this world (see Col 2:8; Gal 4:3, 9).

Six items are mentioned in Hebrews 6:1-2 as representing a foundation that should not be laid yet again. These are evidently in three pairs, as follows:

(1)"repentance from acts that lead to death" and (2) "faith in God"
(3) "instruction about baptisms," and (4) "the laying on of hands"
(5) "the resurrection of the dead," and (6) and "eternal judgment"[11]

Over the centuries, New Testament commentators have offered a wide variety of interpretations about what these six elements or three pairs actually mean. The list as a whole is often taken to represent something of an early

---

[11]David H. Stern, in his *Jewish New Testament Commentary* (Clarksville, Md.: Messianic Jewish Resources International, 1992), renders these six elements as repentance, trust, purification, ordination, resurrection and judgment.

catechetical outline, which was useful especially for believers of Jewish back-ground.[12] The first pair represents the basic commitments of repenting from acts that lead to death and placing faith in the living God (as in Acts 20:21). The second pair is the most controversial among interpreters. "Baptisms" may refer either to various Jewish ritual washings, including the immersion of proselytes, or to the need to distinguish between these baptisms and Christian baptism. The laying on of hands was a feature of both Jewish and early Christian practice. The third pair is clearly of great theological import for many Jews (Christian or not) and Christians (whether Jewish or Gentile).[13]

As with Acts 2:42, this is clearly an important passage for our consideration of educational content today. If Hebrews 6:1-2 is indeed an early catechetical outline, we should surely consider its merits, especially since it is biblical material. As with the four commitments of Acts 2:42, we see here a comprehensiveness of concern. The six items (or three pairs of items) mentioned here would help us once again be attentive to ethical, liturgical and theological elements. This list also has the advantage of reminding us of the Jewish roots of the Christian faith—something that is all too often forgotten (to our great shame and loss) by Gentile believers today. Finally, if the list truly represents the "elementary teachings about Christ" (Heb 6:1), then we should be anxious to understand and teach these things.

On the other hand, the list presents us with a few problems or limitations for contemporary application. In the first place, as we have noted, there is no clear consensus on the actual meaning of these six elements, especially "baptisms" and "the laying on of hands." Commentators have ranged widely when discussing these two items in particular. Second, it is very notable that this entire passage is set in the context and tone of rebuke. This makes it very unlike other passages we find in both Testaments, where believers are commanded to adhere to and pass on to others that which they have received.

Third, it is not clear that, even if this list represented the outline of an early catechism for Jewish believers, it should be understood to be prescriptive for believers in all ages and in all contexts. Thus while instruction about "baptisms," "ablutions" or "ritual washings" may have been part of an important starting point for Jewish believers in the first century, it may not be so for

---

[12]See, for example, the comments by F. F. Bruce in his *The Epistle to the Hebrews* (Grand Rapids: Eerdmans, 1964), pp. 111-17.

[13]By speaking like this, we do not intend to suggest a dichotomy between "Jews" and "Christians." Rather, we acknowledge the reality of two emerging communities in the first century.

believers in many settings today. We know from Acts 15 and elsewhere that even in the first century the apostles had decided not to impose on Gentile believers some of the practices that Jewish believers were adhering to. It seems the Gospel must always be permitted to grow in distinctive cultural soils and to take the appropriate cultural shape of a given people. Likewise, faithful and effective catechesis must always be culturally appropriate.

A final hindrance to simply adopting the elements of Hebrews 6:1-2 for teaching ministries today concerns questions about the place of this passage in the overall context of the letter. Most commentators have read the book as a warning that its readers—understood by most to be Jewish believers who are now being persecuted because of their adherence to Christ—must not retreat under trial to a Christless Judaism. It is significant that none of the six items listed in the passage is distinctively Christian at all.[14] Indeed,

> the writer probably chooses these items as the "basics" because they were the basic sort of instructions about Jewish belief given to converts to Judaism, which all the author's readers would have understood before becoming followers of Jesus. These items represented Jewish teachings still useful for followers of Christ.[15]

Could it have been the case that these elements were being championed in this believing community precisely because they may have made a "retreat" from distinctively Christian faith more palatable?[16]

To summarize, we find much in this passage that calls for our attention. In particular, we are reminded of the need for comprehensiveness of concern in our teaching content. It is noteworthy, as well, that all believers are called onward to maturity in our faith. The idea of spiritual growth or progress that is pronounced so loudly in this passage is echoed in many other New Testament passages (see, for example, 1 Cor 3:1-15; 1 Pet 2:2; 2 Pet 1:5-21).

We are reminded also of the fact that the Christian faith is indeed Jewish in its roots. After all, nearly three quarters of our Bible is made up of the Hebrew scriptures. There is little, if anything, that is truly "new" about the theological or ethical principles found in the New Testament writings. But, just as it is a grave mistake for Gentile Christians to shun our Jewish roots or

---

[14]Bruce writes in *Epistle to the Hebrews*, "When we consider the 'rudiments' one by one, it is remarkable how little in the list is distinctive of Christianity, for practically every item could have its place in a fairly orthodox Jewish community" (p. 112).

[15]Craig S. Keener, *The IVP Bible Background Commentary: New Testament* (Downers Grove, Ill.: InterVarsity Press, 1993), pp. 659-60.

[16]Bruce wonders about this possibility. See *Epistle to the Hebrews*, pp. 117-18.

underplay the many points of continuity between the Testaments, it is also a mistake to ignore points of discontinuity between the Testaments. Nor, when forming the outlines of our instructional content, can we ignore the fact that the Gospel must take on appropriate cultural forms wherever it is planted and nurtured. Thus it seems wise to us to take Hebrews 6:1-2 as descriptive, rather than as a prescriptive list of essential teaching elements for all churches in all times and places.

OUR FAITH AND *THE* FAITH

To further help us engage the conversation about the question of what we must teach, it is important for us to deal with the matter of two aspects of faith that we find in the New Testament. A good deal of effort in contemporary Christian education is devoted to nurturing faith in individual believers or in the community. This first aspect (as we have called it) of biblical faith is altogether proper and essential. Numerous resources are available to help in this critical area, with emphases on teaching for faith, developing practices of faith and so on. Much of the work in what is called "spiritual formation" is also devoted to similar themes.

The vision of faith here is that described in biblical passages like Hebrews 11. There we read of the countless heroes of faith who trusted God and walked with him through often perilous circumstances. Faith is there defined as "being sure of what we hope for and certain of what we do not see" (Heb 11:1). Without such faith, we are told, "it is impossible to please God, because anyone who comes to him must believe that he exists and that he rewards those who earnestly seek him" (Heb 11:6). Faith of this sort is a constant theme in Scripture, as Hebrews 11 makes clear with its appeals to the faithful characters of the Old Testament. We may describe such faith as the proper response to the God who proves himself to be ever faithful or as our response to the gracious revelation of God. Such faith is subjective and personal, and thus it can be strong or weak; it waxes and wanes.

Critical as this dimension of faith is, there is another essential vision of faith in the Scriptures that is often neglected in evangelical Christian education in our times. It is the notion of *the* faith. The definite article, placed before the Greek word *pistis,* normally points the reader of the New Testament toward a vision of faith that is not about our response to what God has revealed but rather about that revelation itself. This use of "the faith" is striking in a verse like Jude 3. The author there urges his readers to "contend for the faith that was once for all entrusted to the saints." It is clear that "the faith" here is objective, not subjective; it is about God's revelation rather than about our response to it; it is perdurable; it has been given once for all (time) and is catholic in nature—for it has been delivered to all (the saints).

There are many references in the New Testament to the expression "the faith" in this sense. However, determining which uses of the phrase are referring to the once-for-all-delivered-to-the-saints faith and which are referring to our response of faith toward God is not always easy to do. In some cases, the presence of the definite article is necessary for other reasons. When we read of "the faith of Abraham" in Romans 4, for example, the definite article simply points us to the type of faith response that Abraham demonstrated.

Some of the references to "the faith" could be seen as referring to either the objective or the subjective senses of the word. When Paul testifies, "I have fought the good fight, I have finished the race, I have kept the faith" (2 Tim 4:7-8), and when he instructs the Corinthians to "examine yourselves to see whether you are in the faith" (2 Cor 13:5), the sense could be taken either, or both, ways.

Nevertheless, there are a great many references that seem clearly to speak of "the faith" in the objective sense outlined above. When citing such references in this book, we will capitalize in this manner—the Faith—to highlight that we are dealing with this objective use of the term. Examining these, it becomes apparent that there are numerous ways in which people can, should and should not respond to the Faith, as the textbox on page 87 indicates.

That which is intended by "the Faith" in the Bible is sometimes communicated by means of other, related terms. These include "the teaching," "sound doctrine" and "the tradition(s)."[17] The notion of "the tradition(s)" (*paradosis*[18] in the Greek) is also brought out by use of the verbal expression "to pass on" or "to deliver" or "to teach" (*paradidōmi* in the Greek). There are numerous examples of the use of such terms in the New Testament.[19]

To summarize, while educational ministers must be committed to nurturing personal faith in the lives of those they minister to, they are also obligated

---

[17]See D. H. Williams, *Evangelicals and Tradition: The Formative Influence of the Early Church* (Grand Rapids: Baker, 2005) for a helpful and provocative (at least for many evangelicals) overview of the notion of tradition and its place in Christian doctrine.

[18]"Tradition" can be either positive or negative, and this is clear in New Testament teaching. In most cases, the noun *paradosis* is actually used to refer to traditions that are not of God, while the verbal form, *paradidōmi,* is usually used in a clearly positive sense.

[19]See, for example, Acts 2:42; Romans 16:17; 1 Corinthians 11:2, 23-24; 15:3-4; 2 Thessalonians 2:15; 3:6; 1 Timothy 1:3; 6:1, 3-4; 2 Timothy 4:3; Titus 1:5; 2:10; 2 Peter 2:21.

Guidelines for Responding to the Faith

The Faith is to be believed, professed (Heb 4:14).

We are to stand firm in, hold firmly to, remain true to and keep the Faith (Acts 14:22; 1 Cor 16:13; 2 Tim 4:7; Heb 4:14; 1 Pet 5:9).

We are to be grounded in and strengthened in the Faith (Acts 16:5; Col 2:7).

We are to be nourished on the words of the Faith (1 Tim 4:6).

We are to become obedient to the Faith (Acts 6:7).

We are to love others who are in the Faith (Gal 6:10; Tit 3:15).

We are to fight the good fight of and contend earnestly for the Faith (1 Tim 6:12; Jude 3).

We are to hold to the deep truths of and be sound in the Faith (1 Tim 3:9; Tit 1:13).

We are to preach the Faith (Gal 1:23).

We are to teach the Faith and its implications (1 Tim 4:6-11).

We are to minister until the church reaches unity in the Faith (Eph 4:13).

We are to prophesy in agreement with the Faith (Rom 12:6).[a]

Some wander from or are tempted to turn from the Faith (Acts 13:8; 1 Tim 6:10, 21).

By their actions, some deny the Faith (1 Tim 5:8).

Some, as far as the Faith goes, are rejected (2 Tim 3:8).

Some turn away from, abandon or fall away from the Faith (Mt 24:10-11; 1 Tim 4:1).

---

[a]In the NIV, the translation note b for Rom 12:6 has "Or *in agreement with the*."

to pass on the Faith faithfully, to defend it against the threat of encroaching heresy and perversion, to proclaim it and teach it with diligence, and to teach the kind of life that properly adorns it. Sadly, we have often failed to pay adequate attention to this vital duty of our teaching ministries. The evidence of our collective failure is frightfully clear as we survey the widespread biblical illiteracy and "life illiteracy" in much of the evangelical world today.[20]

THE MINISTRY OF CATECHESIS

To speak of passing on the Faith and to refer to the concept of practices associated with *paradidōmi* is to enter the realm of catechesis. Catechesis—although a practice not widely known by contemporary evangelicals—is an ancient Christian practice that still thrives in certain quarters of Christianity today.[21] The term "catechesis" comes from the Greek word *katēcheō.* That word means, literally, "to echo," "to resound," "to sound from above." It is one of many New Testament words for teaching. In the New Testament itself, the term often seems simply to refer to instruction. But, very early in the life of the church, it came to mean instruction of a particular sort in terms of both form and substance. In terms of form, catechesis generally was verbal instruction that involved a good deal of repetition and memorization. In terms of substance, catechesis came to refer to instruction in the basics or essentials of the Faith.

Several important terms arise from *katēcheō,* and these may be taken as representing the following:

- catechesis—the general term that describes this overall form of ministry

- catechize—the process of teaching in this manner

- catechism—the content of that instruction; often used to describe a printed catechism, such as the Heidelberg Catechism; sometimes used as a catchword to embrace the entire ministry of catechesis

- catechetics—the "study of catechesis," as homiletics is the study of preaching and liturgics is the study of worship

- catechist—the instructor

- catechumen—the learner

- catechumenate—the ancient "school of the Faith" (with varying degrees

---

[20]"Life illiteracy" is a phrase often repeated by our colleague Walter C. Kaiser. Decrying the sad plight of our evangelical illiteracies in matters of Scripture itself, of theology and of life in recent years are the voices of numerous authors, including Gary M. Burge, "The Greatest Story Never Read: Recovering Biblical Literacy in the Church" <www.christianitytoday .com/ct/9t9/9t9045.html>.

[21]Many Catholics, Orthodox, Anglicans, Lutherans and Presbyterians will be familiar with catechesis. Actual practice of catechesis may be found in these communities in varying degrees of seriousness.

of both duration and formality), which prepared candidates for baptism

The ministry of catechesis was the cornerstone of educational practices in the church during the first several centuries following the New Testament era and again from the Reformation period and on through the times of the Puritans both in England and in America. Although it was thus a priority for most of church history, it has been largely abandoned by most evangelical Protestants over the past two centuries—quite tragically, we believe.[22]

As we noted above, catechesis is a ministry largely associated with grounding believers in the essentials of the Faith. It has historically been linked especially to preparing candidates for baptism. By interacting with the content of historic catechisms and of the ancient catechism (singular) on which the great majority of particular catechisms[23] have been based, we gain insight into what the church has historically considered to be the content of the Faith, at least in outline. We consider this further in chapters four and five.

A sound ministry of catechesis has several essential features. It is *relational,* involving dynamic interaction between catechist and catechumen, all in the context of the entire faith community. It is *liturgical,* occurring chiefly in the worship of the gathered community. It is *holistic,* engaging the full humanity of catechumens—their minds, hearts and bodies. It is *culturally responsive,* paying careful attention to the backdrop in which catechumens are living and against which they receive this vital instruction. It *pedagogically strategic,* featuring sound educational processes and practices. And it is *content rich,* focused properly, as we have said, on the essentials of the Faith.

While a church that is committed to the ministry of catechesis may seek to be innovative in terms of pedagogical strategies or cultural relevance, novelty is the last thing it ought to seek when it comes to content. Of course, we should and do come to newer understandings of the Faith, and we gain new insights from the Scriptures as God enables us. Such blessings often lead us to see that our earlier perspectives and articulations of the Faith may well have been inadequate in critically important ways. But in terms of the essential

---

[22]For a consideration of some factors contributing to this decline, please see chapter 3, "The Waxing and Waning of Catechesis," of *Grounded in the Gospel: Building Believers the Old-Fashioned Way* by J. I. Packer and Gary A. Parrett, scheduled for publication in 2010 by Baker.

[23]As noted above, while the word *catechism* is most often used today to refer to a printed summary of the faith—the Heidelberg Catechism, Luther's Small Catechism and so on—the idea of a catechism is ancient and need not be linked to something that is actually printed. Rather, catechism can refer to that content in which one is catechized, whether that catechesis is formal or informal and whether the content is printed or not.

components of the Faith, the catechist retains the notion of *paradidōmi* that we considered above. Like Paul, the catechist says, "What I received, I pass on to you." It is the ancient Faith that comprises the content of catechesis, not the new or the trendy. When we engage this ancient Faith in deep and faithful ways, we will be better able to apply it creatively and appropriately to the varied contexts in which we live and minister today.

WHAT CONSTITUTES THE FAITH?

It is, we believe, absolutely essential that churches engage in some sort of rigorous catechetical work today. By doing so, we will help believers become well rooted in the Faith and poised to grow in grace and in the knowledge of the Lord Jesus Christ. But what constitutes the Faith? In the ancient church, "the Faith" soon came to be the term that was used to describe the creedal confessions of the church or, said otherwise, that which was thought to be succinctly summed up by the creedal confessions. Church fathers Irenaeus, Tertullian and others sometimes referred to "the Rule of Faith" with this intent.[24]

It is common to speak of the Christian church as consisting of three major bodies or communions: Catholic, Orthodox and Protestant. Members of these three communities regard one another with widely varying levels of acceptance and affirmation. At some point or at many, however, members in each tradition finally regard those in the others as being off the mark in certain respects. Still, there are many truths that Christians in all three traditions have commonly affirmed through the ages. With this understanding in view, some evangelical Protestants have been actively engaged in efforts to celebrate common ground with Catholic and Orthodox Christians.[25] In this spirit, participants search for that which C. S. Lewis (drawing on the earlier work of Richard Baxter[26]) called "mere Christianity."

Along this line of thinking, Charles Colson and Harold Fickett have recently authored *The Faith: What Christians Believe, Why They Believe It, and Why It Matters.*[27] The authors cite a familiar quotation from the fifth-century monk St. Vincent of Lerins: "Hold fast that which has been believed everywhere, always

---

[24]See Williams, *Evangelicals and Tradition,* for a helpful summary.

[25]See, for example, the journals *Common Ground* and *First Things* and the publications of Evangelicals and Catholics Together. In recent years, key evangelical leaders in such efforts have included J. I. Packer, Timothy George, Thomas Oden and Charles Colson.

[26]See Paul Lim, "A Pen in God's Hand: Richard Baxter Wrote, Preached, Taught, and Visited His Way to Become the Model Pastor" <http://www.ctlibrary.com/ch/2006/issue89/4.17.html>.

[27]Charles Colson and Harold Fickett, *The Faith: What Christians Believe, Why They Believe It, and Why It Matters* (Grand Rapids: Zondervan, 2008).

and by all."[28] Combining biblical teaching, historical references and contemporary illustrations, Colson and Fickett offer an engaging survey of what they believe meets these criteria. At the close of their book, they offer the following list of "the essential doctrines that constitute the Christian faith":

- God Is
- He Has Spoken
- The Fall/Original Sin
- The Incarnation
- The Cross and the Atoning Death of Christ
- The Bodily Resurrection
- The Nature of God/His Sovereignty
- The Trinity
- Justification by Faith/Conversion
- Forgiveness and Reconciliation
- The Church
- Sanctification/Holiness
- Dignity of Human Life
- The Return of Jesus and the End of History[29]

They also suggest the Nicene Creed as an example of a suitable summary of that which has been believed everywhere, always and by all.

Helpful as the work of Colson and Fickett is, it does not fully address some of the significant challenges that present themselves to those who would seek to understand and articulate for others what really constitutes the Faith. The quote from St. Vincent, for example, appears to have been prompted, at least in part, because of his concern over the "novel" teachings of Augustine on predestination. These teachings St. Vincent "regarded as unwise and hasty improvisations."[30] Thus we find that Augustine can be, on the one hand, a theological champion to both Catholics and evangelical Protestants and yet, on the other hand, an early source of theological division between different Christian constituancies. Furthermore, while the topics that Colson and Fick-

---

[28]Ibid., p. 30.
[29]Ibid., p. 238.
[30]Alister McGrath, *The Christian Theology Reader* (Malden, Mass.: Blackwell, 2006), p. 90.

ett offer can certainly be listed with widespread agreement, the actual unpacking of those topics is another matter.

Protestants, Catholics and Orthodox believers have had great difficulty arriving at consensus on many of those issues, including original sin, the atoning
death of Christ, justification by faith/conversion, the church and sanctification/
holiness. Even the reference to the Nicene Creed points out the divide that has
existed between Catholics and Orthodox Christians for more than a millen-
nium. Colson and Fickett have used the Western version of the creed, with the
inclusion of the *filioque* clause that prompts believers to confess faith in the Holy
Spirit as "the Lord and giver of life, who proceeds from the Father *and the Son*"
(emphasis added). This inclusion is rejected by the Orthodox churches.

What actually constitutes the Faith, then, remains a matter of both agreement and disagreement. We can point to some consensus, but must honestly
admit where and when we fall short of this. For evangelical Protestants, the
challenge may be greatest of all. For many Catholics, the Faith is that faith
which the Church of Rome teaches and practices.[31] For many Orthodox believers, the Faith is that faith which the Orthodox churches teach and practice.
For evangelical Protestants, however, arriving at an answer to this question is
more complicated. With nearly forty thousand denominations, it can prove
difficult for Protestants to point to those things that have been believed
everywhere, always and by all. This difficulty should lead us not to despair
but to humility. The humility we speak of includes the acknowledgment that
our reading of both Holy Scripture and sacred tradition is limited and biased,
for we are all—both individually and corporately—finite, sinful and contex-
tually situated persons.

A PROPOSAL

In light of what we have just said, we make no claim that what follows in the
next two chapters is the definitive answer to the crucial question of what
constitutes the Faith. But we are bold to propose (we hope in a properly
humble spirit) a broad outline of some essential ingredients for faithful teaching of the Faith.

Our proposal centers around the Gospel. This is consonant with the historic emphasis of the church and is actually demanded by the Scriptures themselves. Our forebears, in tending to equate the Rule of Faith with the ancient

---

[31]This is not to deny that many church leaders and academicians in the Catholic Church do not
align themselves with the official teaching of the church.

creeds, plainly understood these creeds to be faithful summaries of the Gospel. It is clear that the Reformers—Luther, Calvin and many others—thought along these lines. Thus they used expositions of the Apostles' Creed in their published catechisms as a means of proclaiming the Gospel.

In brief, our Gospel-centric outline of the Faith is as follows. We will unpack this outline in the following chapter.

Outline of the Faith

1. The Gospel, as of first importance (1 Cor 15:1-5)
2. The sound doctrine that conforms to the Gospel (1 Tim 1:10-11)
3. The life-giving benefits that flow from the Gospel (2 Tim 1:10)
4. The way of living that conforms to sound doctrine (Tit 2:1-15)

CONCLUSION

Over the course of the next two chapters, we will be interacting further with the question of what the essential content of our teaching ministries should comprise. In chapter four, we make our case that the Gospel must be the foundation for all our proclamation, and then we look at further dimensions of the Faith that derive from the Gospel. We conclude this part of the book in chapter five by suggesting content for a congregational curriculum for teaching and forming the people of God.

HYMN FOR CONTEMPLATION AND WORSHIP

There Is None Good but God Alone

There is none good but *God alone*.
Not one of us is righteous.
We spurned God's Way
and sought our own,
and so have become worthless.
What hope then can we see?
Christ Jesus: only he
the path of life has trod,
to love both man and God.
Yes he alone is worthy.
(Mk 10:18; Rom 3:9-23; Is 53:6; 1 Jn 2:1; Rev 5)

Scripture alone reveals these things;
thus do the Fathers witness.
Good news of life and light it brings
to those now lost in darkness.
For from this sacred Word,
what wonders we have heard:
God's grace in Christ revealed.
By his stripes we are healed.
We glory in the Gospel!
(2 Tim 3:15-17; 2 Pet 1:19-21; Lk 24:25-27, 45-47;
Tit 2:11; Is 9:2; 53:5; 1 Tim 1:11)

In *Christ alone* is all our trust
for full and free salvation.
With his own blood he ransomed us
from ev'ry tribe and nation.
For us he lived and died.
Now at the Father's side,
full knowing all our needs,
our High Priest intercedes.
He lives to make us holy.
(1 Tim 2:5-6; Acts 4:12; 1 Pet 1:19; Rev 5:9;
Heb 2:11; 7:25; Rom 8:28-39)

And now by *faith alone* we stand
in Christ, our risen Savior,
who has fulfilled each just command
and made us just forever.
In him is all our peace
and life that cannot cease.
By no work of our own,
but all of *grace alone,*
have we become God's people.
(Rom 3:28; 5:1-2, 15-19; Eph 1:4-5; 2:5-10; 1 Pet 2:9-10)

Above all pow'rs abides the Word,
God's mighty Word that frees us.
Through prophets and apostles heard,
for us made flesh in Jesus.
No other word we speak,
nor human glory seek.
All earthly schemes must fail.

God's kingdom shall prevail.
To God alone be glory!
(Jn 1:1, 14; Heb 1:1-2; 2:1-4; 1 Pet 1:23-25;
Rev 4:11; 11:15; Ps 145:13; Rom 11:36; Is 42:8)

Text: Gary A. Parrett (2008)
Tune: Ein' Feste Burg
Familiar use of the tune: "A Mighty Fortress"

QUESTIONS FOR PLANNING AND PRACTICE

1. "Every community that wants to last more than one generation must be concerned with education." How does this statement by Walter Brueggemann, quoted earlier, affect how you "pass the torch" of educational ministry in your local church? Do you observe that the younger generations are concerned with their own education (that is, formation unto the image of Jesus Christ) and have a desire to continue it? If not, how might you come alongside them to achieve this goal or yearning?

2. Describe how Acts 2:42 ("They devoted themselves to the apostles' teaching and to the fellowship, to the breaking of bread and to prayer") illustrates the entirety of the church's holistic curriculum that the church is called to educate and form its people.

3. We invite you to compare Acts 2:42 and Hebrews 5:11—6:3. In terms of the holistic content of educational formation ministry, how are these two passages similar, and how are they different? How might deeper attention to either or both of these passages reshape your view of what the church should be teaching?

4. Imagine that someone came to you in a church setting and asked what is involved in becoming a Christian. What would be your response? What essential things would you have them consider and do? What would be the next steps for the person to take as you invite him or her to become a follower of Jesus Christ? How does Jesus' response to this question in Matthew 19:21 (Jesus answered, "If you want to be perfect, go, sell your possessions and give to the poor, and you will have treasure in heaven. Then come, follow me") illuminate your view of discipleship?

5. This chapter states that it is the obligation of the church to teach the Faith. Has this been a clear goal of your own church's educational formation ministry? How does your church's curriculum reflect (or not reflect) the

outline in this chapter of what the Faith is and how to teach it?

6. We want to invite you to reflect on the idea of catechesis as presented in this chapter. Do you come from a tradition with some form of catechetical ministry? Do you feel that your church should adopt—in whole or in part—aspects of catechesis? Why or why not?

7. With a group of other teachers in the church, we invite you to reflect together on your own description of what constitutes the Faith. Using key scriptural passages to support your description, compare and contrast your descriptions with the proposal of the present authors. Where are there similarities and differences? Where you see differences, do you see the divergence more as a healthy, positive thing or as a negative and potentially dangerous thing? Explain your response.

RESOURCES FOR FURTHER STUDY

Colson, Charles, and Harold Fickett. *The Faith: What Christians Believe, Why They Believe It, and Why It Matters.* Grand Rapids: Zondervan, 2008.

Edwards, O. C., Jr., and John Westerhoff III, eds. *A Faithful Church: Issues in the History of Catechesis.* Eugene, Ore.: Wipf and Stock, 2003.

Harmless, William. *Augustine and the Catechumenate.* Collegeville, Minn.: Liturgical Press, 1995.

Horton, Michael. *We Believe: Recovering the Essentials of the Apostles' Creed.* Nashville: Word, 1998.

Marshall, I. Howard. *New Testament Theology: Many Witnesses, One Gospel.* Downers Grove, Ill.: InterVarsity Press, 2004.

Migliore, Daniel. *Faith Seeking Understanding: An Introduction to Christian Theology.* Grand Rapids: Eerdmans, 1991.

Olson, Roger. *The Mosaic of Christian Belief: Twenty Centuries of Unity and Diversity.* Downers Grove, Ill.: InterVarsity Press, 2002.

Packer, J. I., and Gary A. Parrett. *Grounded in the Gospel: Building Believers the Old-Fashioned Way.* Grand Rapids: Baker, forthcoming.

Pazmiño, Robert. *Principles and Practices of Christian Education: An Evangelical Perspective.* Grand Rapids: Baker, 1992.

Stott, John. *The Message of Acts.* The Bible Speaks Today. Downers Grove, Ill.: InterVarsity Press, 1990.

Wengert, Timothy J. *Martin Luther's Catechism: Forming the Faith.* Minneapolis: Fortress, 2009.

Williams, D. H. *Evangelicals and Tradition: The Formative Influence of the Early Church*. Grand Rapids: Baker, 2005.

Wilson, Jonathan. *God So Loved the World: A Christology for Disciples*. Grand Rapids: Baker, 2001.

CATECHISMS

The Catechism of the Catholic Church. 2nd edition. Liguori, Mo.: Liguori Publications, 1994.

The Heidelberg Catechism: A New Translation for the 21st Century. Translated by Lee Barrett III. Cleveland: Pilgrim Press, 2007.

The Living God: A Catechism for the Christian Faith. 2 vols. Translated by Olga Dunlop. Crestwood, N.Y.: St. Vladimir's Seminary Press, 1989.

Luther, Martin. *The Large Catechism of Martin Luther*. Minneapolis: Augsburg Fortress, 1963.

———. *Luther's Small Catechism*. Minneapolis: Augsburg Fortress, 2001.

Torrance, T. F. *The School of Faith: The Catechisms of the Reformed Church*. Eugene, Ore.: Wipf and Stock, 1996.

4

The Glorious Gospel
and Its Implications

" . . . the sound doctrine that conforms to the glorious gospel
of the blessed God, which he entrusted to me."

1 TIMOTHY 1:10-11

▼

W<small>E ARGUED IN THE PREVIOUS CHAPTER</small> that the essential content of our teaching ministry is the Faith that was once-for-all delivered to the saints. In simple outline, we suggested that the Faith includes

1. the Gospel, as of first importance (1 Cor 15:1-5)
2. the sound doctrine that conforms to the Gospel (1 Tim 1:10-11)
3. the life-giving benefits that flow from the Gospel (2 Tim 1:10)
4. the way of living that conforms to sound doctrine (Tit 2:1-15)

In this chapter, we examine each of these four components as elements of essential content for our teaching ministries. We begin with a consideration of the Gospel, then turn attention to the other three components that derive from and respond to the Gospel.

THE GOSPEL, AS OF FIRST IMPORTANCE

The first element constituting the Faith that was "once for all delivered to the saints" is "the glorious gospel of the blessed God" (1 Tim 1:11).[1] The Gospel[2]

---

[1]This phrase could also be rendered as "the gospel of the glorious and blessed God."
[2]We capitalize *Gospel* throughout the book as befitting its God-ordained glory and foundational position in the life of the church.

is the message of God's great reconciling work, the mission of God that we explored in chapter one. It is the summary and the apex of the great redemptive Story into which God graciously invites us. Because it is so central to the work that God is engaged in and into which he has called us, the Gospel must be at the center of our ministries. It is the fundamental message we proclaim, to believer and unbeliever alike.

In proclaiming the Gospel, we are proclaiming Christ himself (see Col 1:28). The Gospel is, after all, the good news *about* Jesus Christ (see Mk 1:1), who came into the world "to seek and to save what was lost" (Lk 19:10). In this Gospel resides power for the saving of all who believe (see Rom 1:16). For many Christians, it is axiomatic that the Gospel is the message we must proclaim to unbelievers. We are confident it is *they* who need to be saved. Thus the Gospel, especially among evangelical Protestants, is seen as the proper content for our ministries of evangelism. With this conclusion, we could not agree more.

Yet what we often fail to see is that the same Gospel is also the essential content for our ministries of teaching, nurturing and forming believers. We should not see the Gospel as the "milk" from which we must move on to more "meaty" things. We do not move on *from* the Gospel. Instead, we move on *in* the Gospel, for its depths are unfathomable and its implications for life and teaching are innumerable. In other words, the Gospel is to be both the center of our *kerygma* (proclamation) and the heart of our *didachē* (teaching).[3]

The apostle Paul declared to the Corinthians that he had passed on to them "as of first importance" what he had also received (1 Cor 15:3). He then outlined the Gospel in simple terms: "Christ died for our sins, according to the Scriptures . . . he was buried . . . he was raised on the third day according to the Scriptures, and . . . he appeared . . ." (1 Cor 15:4-6). This, he declares, is the Gospel that he preached to them, which they had received and on which they had taken their stand (see 1 Cor 15:1). Furthermore, during his eighteen months of ministry in Corinth, Paul had resolved to know nothing among

---

[3]The *kerygma* concerns certain realities about Christ, namely, the "proclamation of the death, resurrection, and exaltation of Jesus that led to evaluation of His person as both Lord and Christ, confronted man with the necessity of repentance and promised the forgiveness of sins." Robert H. Mounce, *The Essential Nature of New Testament Preaching* (Grand Rapids: Eerdmans, 1960), p. 84. *Didachē* is the noun form of the most common New Testament word for teaching *(didaskō)*. It is used, for example, in Acts 2:42, in reference to the four commitments of the three thousand newly baptized believers in Jerusalem: "They devoted themselves to the apostles' teaching."

Table 4.1. The Glorious Gospel

The Gospel of . . . / about . . .	The Gospel is . . . / does . . .
• Jesus Christ (Mk 1:1) • promised beforehand through the prophets in the Holy Scriptures (Rom 1:2) • God's Son (Rom 1:9) • the glory of Christ (2 Cor 4:4) • announced in advance to Abraham (Gal 3:8) • your salvation (Eph 1:13) • peace (Eph 6:15) • God (1 Thess 2:9) • Christ (1 Thess 3:2) • our Lord Jesus Christ (2 Thess 1:8) • the glorious gospel of the blessed God (1 Tim 1:11) • the eternal gospel (Rev 14:6) • good news of the kingdom (Mt 4:23; 9:35) • good news of God (Mk 1:14) • good news of the kingdom of God (Lk 8:1; 16:16) • good news that Jesus is the Christ (Acts 5:42) • good news of the kingdom of God and the name of Jesus Christ (Acts 8:12) • good news about Jesus (Acts 8:35) • good news of peace through Jesus Christ, who is Lord of all (Acts 10:36) • good news about the Lord Jesus (Acts 11:20) • good news about Jesus and the resurrection (Acts 17:18)	• the power of God for salvation of believers (Rom 1:16) • reveals a righteousness from God that is by faith from first to last (Rom 1:17) • declares that judgment is coming (Rom 2:16) • produces enmity between Jews and Gentiles (Rom 11:28) • establishes believers (Rom 16:25) • gives birth (1 Cor 4:15) • saves us (1 Cor 15:2) • is veiled to those who are perishing (2 Cor 4:3) • makes Gentiles heirs with Israel (Eph 3:6) • is filled with mystery (Eph 6:19) • is the word of truth (Col 1:5) • bears fruit all over the world (Col 1:6) • holds out hope (Col 1:23) • calls us to salvation, sanctification and belief in the truth (2 Thess 2:13-14) • destroyed death and brought life and immortality to light (2 Tim 1:10) • is Jesus Christ, risen from the dead, descended from David (2 Tim 2:8) • what God promised to the fathers, this he has fulfilled to us by raising Jesus (Acts 13:32-33) • good news, telling you to turn from these worthless things to the living God (Acts 14:15)
The Gospel must be . . .	**Other right responses to the Gospel**
• preached / proclaimed / taught – in the whole world, among all peoples (Mt 24:14; 26:13; Mk 13:10; 14:9; 16:15; Lk 4:43; Acts 8:25, 40; 11:20; 14:6-7, 21; 15:7; 16:10; 2 Cor 2:12; 10:16; Gal 2:2, 7) – to the poor (Is 61:1; Lk 4:18; 7:22) – together with healing (Lk 9:6) – together with teaching (Lk 20:1) – to believers as well (Rom 1:15) – as a priestly duty (Rom 15:16) – fully proclaimed (Rom 15:19) – where Christ is not known (Rom 15:20) – not with human wisdom (1 Cor 1:17) – fearlessly (Eph 6:19)	• must lose our lives, all things, for it (Mk 8:35; 10:29) • (Paul was) set apart for the gospel (Rom 1:1) • must not let anything hinder it (1 Cor 9:12; 1 Thess 2:9) • must be its servants (Rom 1:9; Eph 3:7; Phil 2:22; 4:3) • those who preach it should receive their living from it (1 Cor 9:14) • woe to me (Paul) if it I do not preach it (1 Cor 9:16) • blessing (for Paul) in preaching it free of charge (1 Cor 9:18; 2 Cor 11:7) • (Paul) becomes all things to all people for its sake (1 Cor 9:22)

Table 4.1. The Glorious Gospel continued

– with power, with the Holy Spirit, with deep conviction (1 Thess 1:5) – in spite of opposition (1 Thess 2:2) – giving our lives as well (1 Thess 2:8) – by the Holy Spirit (1 Pet 1:12) – for the sake of judgment and life (1 Pet 4:6) • testified to (Acts 20:24) • not to be perverted (Gal 1:7) • not to be made up by men (Gal 1:11) • defended in all its truth (Gal 2:5) • defended and confirmed (Phil 1:7, 16) • advanced at all cost (Phil 1:12) • heard (Col 1:6, 23) • obeyed (2 Thess 1:8; Heb 4:6; 1 Pet 4:17) • suffered for (2 Tim 1:8; Philem 13) • heard with faith (Heb 4:2) • believed, with repentance (Mk 1:15) • accepted (Rom 10:16)	• must receive it; take our stand on it (1 Cor 15:1) • offer our service for it (2 Cor 8:18) • obedience must accompany our confession of it (2 Cor 9:13) • must never accept a different, or perverted Gospel (2 Cor 11:4; Gal 1:6-9) • must act in line with the truth of it (Gal 2:14) • must fit our feet with readiness that comes from it (Eph 6:15) • must partner with others for its sake (Phil 1:5) • must unite, act as "one man," for its sake (Phil 1:27) • must grow in our acquaintance with it (Phil 4:15) • must speak as those entrusted with it (1 Thess 2:4) • must conform our doctrines and our lives to it (1 Tim 1:11) • (Paul) appointed a herald and an apostle and a teacher of it (2 Tim 1:11) • makes beautiful the feet of those who bring good news (Is 52:7; Nahum 1:15; Rom 10:15)

them "except Jesus Christ and him crucified" (1 Cor 2:2). Paul describes himself as one who had been "set apart for the gospel" (Rom 1:1) He had been appointed by God as "a herald and an apostle and a teacher" of the Gospel (2 Tim 1:11). Thus the Gospel was evidently his central message throughout all aspects and phases of his ministry.

That the Gospel should have such a central place in Christian ministry should not surprise us. For "the glorious gospel of the blessed God" (1 Tim 1:11) is infinite in its depth and power and application. See table 4.1 for a glimpse of its remarkable width, length, height and depth.

ESSENCE AND IMPLICATIONS OF THE GOSPEL

Despite its amazing depths, the Gospel can be quite simply summarized. In fact, Scripture itself presents many brief, clear and concise summaries of the Gospel.

In light of these summaries, the *essence* of the Gospel seems clear: God has intervened on behalf of fallen humanity to reconcile sinners to himself through his Son Jesus Christ. Central to that reconciling work—as the refer-

Some Biblical Summaries of the Gospel

"He was pierced for our transgressions, he was crushed for our iniquities; the punishment that brought us peace was upon him, and by his wounds we are healed" (Is 53:5).[a]

"All the prophets testify about him that everyone who believes in him receives forgiveness of sins through his name" (Acts 10:43).

"Through Jesus the forgiveness of sins is proclaimed to you. Through him everyone who believes is justified from everything you could not be justified from by the law of Moses" (Acts 13:38-39).

"Christ died for our sins according to the Scripture . . . he was buried . . . he was raised the third day according to the Scriptures, and . . . he appeared" (1 Cor 15:3-5). Paul writes that this is the Gospel "I preached to you, which you received and on which you have taken your stand. By this gospel you are saved" (1 Cor 15:1-2). In outlining it here, Paul asserts that "what I received I passed on to you as of first importance" (1 Cor 15:3).

"But God demonstrates his own love for us in this: While we were still sinners, Christ died for us" (Rom 5:8).

"God was reconciling the world to himself in Christ, not counting men's sins against them" (2 Cor 5:19).

"God made him who had no sin to be sin for us, so that in him we might become the righteousness of God" (2 Cor 5:21).

"Remember Jesus Christ, raised from the dead, descended from David. This is my gospel" (2 Tim 2:8).

". . . Jesus Christ, who gave himself for us to redeem us from all wickedness and to purify for himself a people that are his very own, eager to do what is good" (Tit 2:13-14).

"So Christ was sacrificed once to take away the sins of many people; and he will appear a second time, not to bear sin, but to bring salvation to those who are waiting for him" (Heb 9:28).

"He himself bore our sins in his body on the tree, so that we might die to sins and live for righteousness; by his wounds you have been healed" (1 Pet 2:24).

"Christ died for sins once for all, the righteous for the unrighteous, to bring you to God" (1 Pet 3:18).

"This is love: not that we loved God but that he loved us and sent his Son as an atoning sacrifice for our sins" (1 Jn 4:10).

"God so loved the world that he gave his one and only Son, that whoever believes in him shall not perish but have eternal life" (Jn 3:16).

[a]That the apostles believed Isaiah 53 to be a pivotal Gospel passage is clear from the numerous uses of that passage they employed in their Gospel proclamation. For example, Philip uses this text as the starting point in explaining the Gospel to the Ethiopian eunuch (see Acts 8:31-35). See also, for example, 1 Peter 2:24-25; Romans 10:16; John 12:38.

ences in figure 4.1 make abundantly clear—is the atoning sacrifice of Christ on the cross and his glorious resurrection from the dead. The Gospel is the *good news* about the God who has acted in history to save us. It answers the very bad news about the fallen state of humanity, our alienation from God and from one another.

J. I. Packer has suggested that the truths of the biblical Gospel can be summed up in three words: "God Saves Sinners." He writes,

> *God*—the Triune Jehovah, Father, Son and Spirit; three Persons working together in sovereign wisdom, power and love to achieve the salvation of a chosen people, the Father electing, the Son fulfilling the Father's will by redeeming, the Spirit executing the purpose of Father and Son by renewing. *Saves*—does everything, first to last, that is involved in bringing man from death in sin to life in glory: plans, achieves and communicates redemption, calls and keeps, justifies, sanctifies, glorifies. *Sinners*—men as God finds them, guilty, vile, helpless, powerless, unable to lift a finger to do God's will or better their spiritual lot.[4]

Packer's words reveal much about the nature of both our salvation and the Gospel message. His explanation of what it means that God *saves* us makes it clear that salvation is—as we sought to demonstrate in chapter two—far more than what many evangelicals have taken it to be. It involves God's transforming work of the whole person, a work that began in the

[4]"Saved by His Precious Blood," in J. I. Packer and Mark Dever, *In My Place Condemned He Stood: Celebrating the Glory of the Atonement* (Wheaton, Ill.: Crossway, 2007), p. 118. This piece was originally written as an introductory essay for John Owen's masterful work on the atonement, *The Death of Death in the Death of Christ: A Treatise in Which the Whole Controversy About Universal Redemption Is Fully Discussed* (Carlisle, Penn.: Banner of Truth, 1959).

eternal past and reaches to the eternal future. It is not simply a matter of being born again.

Therefore, when Paul writes to the Roman believers that the Gospel is the power of God for the salvation of all believers (see Rom 1:16), he means that the Gospel is the power that accomplishes the whole matter of salvation. It should be clear then that we cannot—we dare not—ever move "beyond" the Gospel if we would see ourselves and those we minister to become transformed into Christ's likeness. Apart from the Gospel and its power, no such transformation can possibly occur.

If the essence of the Gospel is profoundly simple, its implications and applications are manifold, so much so that aspects of the Gospel are missed, even by its most faithful adherents and advocates. For example, it seems clear that many North American evangelicals in the past century have been guilty of thinking that the Gospel is concerned almost exclusively with our *personal* reconciliation to God, having our sins forgiven and thus being assured of eternal life.[5]

With such a view dominant in their thinking, evangelicals have sometimes ignored or diminished the importance of critical implications and applications of the Gospel. Among those that we often seem to miss are the following:

- a concern for reconciliation on the horizontal dimension, that is, human to human

- a concern for growing up into salvation (see 1 Pet 2:2) and working out one's salvation in fear and trembling (see Phil 2:12)

- a concern for social justice, acts of mercy and so on

- proper attention to communitarian concerns—missed because of the inordinate emphasis on the individual's reconciliation to God, possibly leading to failure to address issues like poverty, racism, environmental concerns and so on[6]

---

[5]The inordinate emphasis in the West on personal or individual reconciliation has inevitably hindered God's people from realizing the necessity to be reconciled from the cosmic nature— that is, social and systemic and so on—of sins. Moreover, focusing on only eternal life or after life, the church has yet to capture the fullness or the holistic nature of salvation available in Jesus Christ. In the process, the notion of "eternal life" has diminished to a mere individual sentiment rather than the *telos* of God's people through which they realize the fullness of God's reconciling work here and now and beyond.

[6]In *A Community Called Atonement* (Nashville: Abingdon, 2007), Scot McKnight sets out to deconstruct simplistic, individualistic theories of the atonement by reminding us that atonement in Jesus Christ is the "at-one-ment" par excellence, where all the separated are now at one (p. 15).

In some instances, it is not that evangelicals have completely ignored issues like the above, but that these have been seen as unrelated to Gospel ministry. In this view, the Gospel is seen as focused on things "spiritual," whereas these other concerns are "social" in nature. This unhealthy and unwarranted bifurcation has led evangelicals to reason that "what really matters is getting people saved—everything else is secondary at best" (note that the word *saved* has been greatly diminished in its meaning here).

A faithful ministry of the Gospel will attend both to the *essence* of the Gospel and to its *implications* for doctrine, devotion and duty.[7] As our proposed outline for teaching the Faith suggests, these include an array of "sound doctrines" that conform to the Gospel; the transformative power that springs forth from the Gospel; and the manner of godly living (that is, love of God and neighbor), which is in line with the Gospel. To present the Gospel without proper attention to these implications and applications of it is to set the Gospel before our hearers without all its clothes on, as it were. Sound doctrine, godly living and the deep experience of God all serve to adorn the Gospel, to "make the teaching about God our Savior attractive" to the watching world (Tit 2:10). Without these, the Gospel we present may be correct in and of itself, but it will not likely be attractive to many unbelievers. In such instances, we cannot excuse our ineffectiveness in reaching unbelievers as simply a consequence of "the offense of the Gospel." Rather, it may be our offensive teaching and living—speech and conduct that are unbecoming of the Gospel—that are really to blame.[8]

It should not surprise us that there have been, from within our own Bible-believing Christian communities, strong reactions against this unhealthy state of affairs. The so-called emerging church movement, for example, has strongly emphasized such Gospel implications as social justice.[9] This is altogether

---

He maintains that "the atonement—from beginning to end—is designed to resolve the macroscopic problem of evil and sin" (p. 61). While we affirm the "traditional" understanding of the atonement, with its emphasis on the centrality of substitutionary nature of Christ's death, we appreciate McKnight's insights in highlighting further dimensions of Christ's atoning work.

[7]This language is unpacked in *Grounded in the Gospel* by J. I. Packer and Gary A. Parrett, scheduled for publication in 2010 by Baker. They add the notion of "delight" at the end of their formula, defining catechesis as "grounding and growing God's people in the Gospel and its implications for doctrine, devotion, duty and delight."

[8]For a glimpse into how all this can play out, see David Kinnaman and Gabe Lyons, *unChristian: What a New Generation Really Thinks About Christianity . . . and Why It Matters* (Grand Rapids: Baker, 2007).

[9]For a helpful survey of the thinking of many leaders within this movement, see Eddie Gibbs and Ryan K. Bolger, *Emerging Churches* (Grand Rapids: Baker, 2005).

proper, but there is cause for concern. As this has played out over the past decade or so, it seems that some emerging church leaders may have confused the implications of the Gospel with its essence. Some have suggested that we need to move from "the Gospel of Paul" to "the Gospel of Jesus," setting the apostle against his Lord, and urge that we preach not "the Gospel of salvation," but rather "the Gospel of the kingdom." "The good news is not that [Christ] died," one leader in the movement explains, "but that the kingdom has come."[10]

Here may be an example of what J. I. Packer and Mark Dever identify as a trend in our day toward what they call "anti-redemptionism"—a minimizing or underplaying of the centrality of Christ's atoning work on the cross in favor of emphasizing Jesus as our teacher, model, pioneer and so on.[11] Packer suggests further potential implications of all this when he notes that "liberalism keeps reinventing itself and luring evangelicals away from the heritage."[12] Could it be that some who now identify themselves as "postevangelical" are laying the foundations for the next generation of theological liberals?[13]

PROPOSALS FOR A BETTER COURSE

Certainly, we would be unwise to reject some of the truly important questions and the responsive engagements of emerging church leaders, even if we find some of their answers to those questions unsatisfying. We propose that evangelical churches would respond well to the critique outlined above by pursuing a course something like the following:

1. We must retain and indeed fully *return to* the Gospel in its essence. Such a return will, we believe, reveal that the biblical summaries mentioned above are fully accurate descriptions of the Gospel. But it will also reveal that the depths of the Gospel, the power of the Gospel, the reach of the Gospel, the

---

[10]Anonymous quote in Gibbs and Bolger, *Emerging Churches,* p. 54. Such a statement puts one at odds with the apostle Paul, who clearly summarized the essence of the Gospel in these very words: "Christ died for our sins according to the Scriptures" (1 Cor 15:3; see also the other biblical references noted above).

[11]Packer and Dever, *In My Place,* p. 18.

[12]Ibid., p. 21.

[13]It would seem that some who formerly identified themselves with the movement have such fears. Mark Driscoll, for example, became quite critical of aspects of the movement and has since affiliated himself with such efforts as Together for the Gospel. See Mark Driscoll, "The Emerging Church and Biblicist Theology," in *Listening to the Beliefs of Emerging Churches: Five Perspectives,* ed. Robert Webber (Grand Rapids: Zondervan, 2007), pp. 19-35.

implications of the Gospel and the applications of the Gospel are greater than we can imagine.

2. We must repent of thinking, teaching and acting as though the implications and applications of the Gospel are negotiable or nonessential. For, in fact

   • The Gospel is a message of God's reconciling to himself *all things* in heaven and on earth (see Col 1:19-23), a comprehensive reconciliation that flows from the peace that was effected by Jesus and the blood of his cross.

   • The reconciling work of the cross plainly includes reconciliation on the "horizontal plane," making us one not only with God but also with our neighbors who come to faith in Christ (see Eph 2:14-16; Gal 3:28).

   • Thus any failure to love as we have been loved, any failure to act "in line with the truth of the gospel" (Gal 2:14), must be treated as serious sin.

   • Indeed, we must treat as sin all behavior that is "contrary to the sound doctrine that conforms to the glorious gospel of the blessed God" (1 Tim 1:11). And we should think twice before assigning to one set of sins (for example, sins of personal morality) more weight than we assign to another set (for example, sins of social morality).

3. We must resist the call to set Jesus over against Paul or the Gospel of the kingdom over against the Gospel of salvation. Such an approach represents an unfaithful reading of Scripture if indeed we believe that all Scripture has been inspired by the Holy Spirit. A survey of the New Testament references to the Gospel, as listed in figure 4.1 above, reveals that arguing for such a division between Jesus and Paul in their approaches to the Gospel really cannot be sustained based on the biblical evidence itself.

4. We must not turn from the one, true Gospel to any other supposed gospel (see Gal 1:6-9). Any "gospel" that does not focus on the person and saving work of Jesus Christ on the cross *for us* is no gospel at all.

5. By all means, we should continually strive to hear from one another within the body of Christ, to mutually sharpen our understanding of the Gospel in terms of its essence, its implications and its application.

The Gospel is clearly and unequivocally the first and most fundamental word of our Christ-proclamation. It is critical not only in evangelism but also in ministries of edification and, indeed, in all aspects of the church's life. This message of reconciliation is God's power to save us who believe and to form us more fully as the body we are called to be in this broken world.

The idea that the Gospel should be the center of contemporary efforts in Christian education is not a novel one. In the twentieth century, passionate advocates for this approach could be found in both Catholic (for example, Josef Andreas Jungmann[14]) and Protestant (for example, D. Campbell Wyckoff[15]) communities. Wyckoff's argument for this Gospel-centrality in educational ministry is based on the following points:

- Revelation—the Word of God—is central in Christian education theory.

- The Gospel—God's redeeming activity in Jesus Christ—is the very heart and point of the word he has spoken to men in their self-centered helplessness throughout the ages, and the very heart and point of the word he speaks to men today.

- The Gospel is the clue to the meaning of history.

- The Gospel is the clue to the meaning of existence.

- The Gospel is the reason for the church's existence: it brings the church into existence; it sustains the church; it informs, directs and corrects the church.[16]

In his book *Spiritual Formation as If the Church Mattered,* evangelical educator Jim Wilhoit seeks to remind evangelical educators about this essential emphasis. He writes, "The Gospel is the power of God for the beginning, middle, and end of salvation. It is not merely what we need to proclaim to unbelievers; the Gospel also needs to permeate our entire Christian experience."[17] Numerous recent authors have argued that the Gospel must drive all our ministries, not just those of Christian education.[18]

---

[14]See Josef Andreas Jungmann, *The Good News Yesterday and Today,* trans. and ed. William A. Huesman (New York: Sadlier, 1962).

[15]See his *The Gospel and Christian Education: A Theory of Christian Education for Our Times* (Philadelphia: Westminster Press, 1959). Wyckoff was profoundly influenced by Karl Barth's sustained analysis of how the truncated, liberal Gospel has bankrupted the identity and vision of the modern Protestant church. See D. Campbell Wyckoff, "From Practice to Theory—and Back Again," in *Modern Masters of Religious Education,* ed. Marlene Mayr (Birmingham, Ala.: Religious Education Press, 1983), p. 96.

[16]Ibid., p. 98.

[17]James C. Wilhoit, *Spiritual Formation as If the Church Mattered: Growing in Christ Through Community* (Grand Rapids: Baker, 2008), p. 27.

[18]See, for example, D. A. Carson, *The Cross and Christian Ministry* (Grand Rapids: Baker Books,

THE IMPLICATIONS OF THE GOSPEL (1 TIM 1:10-11)

Having settled on the Gospel in essence as foundational for all our ministries, we turn our attention to what we have suggested are three vital dimensions of the Faith that both derive from the Gospel and represent critical implications of it.

In 1 Timothy 1:10-11, Paul refers to "the sound doctrines that conforms to the glorious gospel of the blessed God." The word translated *doctrine* here simply means "teaching," and thus could refer to any sort of teaching from Paul or one of the other apostles. In context, Paul is rebuking lifestyles and behaviors that fail to accord with the sound doctrine which, in turn, is to be in accord with the glorious Gospel. This suggests to us a relationship something like the following.

From the Gospel, we derive a host of doctrinal affirmations—truths that follow from the truth of the Gospel. For example, we learn from the Gospel that God is righteous and that God is love. We learn that humans are dead in their trespasses and sin and in desperate need of a Savior. We learn that God gave Jesus, his only begotten Son, for our sakes, to be an atoning sacrifice for our sins. We learn that Christ actually became sin for us, that we might become the righteousness of God in him. Christ died for us even while we were enemies of God. And, of course, we learn much, much more. The truths that flow from the Gospel and conform to it are more numerous than we can calculate. We can summarize all this profound theology as the truth(s) of the Gospel.

Each of these truths—which together constitute "sound doctrine"—has implications for what we could call "sound living." For example, if God so loved us, we ought also to love one another (see 1 Jn 4:10-11). If God is righteous and loving, so must we be. If God was merciful toward us when we were his enemies, how dare we be less so toward others. And on it goes. The truth of the Gospel, in other words, requires that we walk according to a certain way, the Way of Christ. That is, we are to conduct ourselves in such a manner as to "make the teaching about God our Savior attractive" (Tit 2:10).

This being the case, it is necessary that teachers of the Faith not only expound on sound doctrine itself but also "teach what is in accord with sound doctrine" (Tit 2:1). Concerning these things, Paul tells Titus that he must teach about godly living to the members of his Christian communities in Crete (see Tit 2:1-10). Such living derives from the glorious doctrines of grace

---

2004); and C. J. Mahaney, *Living the Cross Centered Life* (Sisters, Ore.: Multnomah, 2006).

that Paul then rehearses: of the blessed hope of the believer, of redemption and more (see Tit 2:11-14). Taken together, the great truths and their implications for daily living constitute "the things you should teach" (Tit 2:15).

In Galatians, Paul recounts his encounter with the apostle Peter at Antioch. On that occasion, Paul states, Peter and others were "not acting in line with the truth of the gospel" (Gal 2:14). From the Gospel we learn that God has destroyed—through the death of Jesus Christ—the barrier of hostility that had long separated Jew from Gentile (Eph 2:11-22). But by withdrawing from table fellowship with Gentile believers for fear of offending a delegation of Jewish church authorities who had come from Jerusalem, Peter, Barnabas and others were acting in violation of that truth.

Elsewhere, Paul rebuked some of the believers in Rome for missing the mark by becoming unduly proud of their privileges as God's elect people, recipients of profound kindness and grace. Though they had been greatly favored, they were passing judgment on others. They failed to realize that God's kindness was calling them to repentance (see Rom 2:1-4). Apparently focusing on some of the Jewish believers in Rome, Paul applied a rebuke from Isaiah 52:5: because of their careless living, God's name was being blasphemed

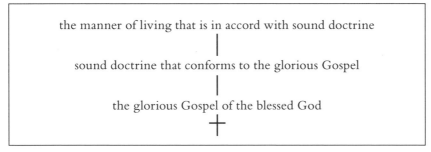

Figure 4.1. The Gospel as plumb line

among the Gentiles on their account (see Rom 2:24).

We might say then that the Gospel is to function as a sort of plumb line by which we measure our faith and our conduct, our belief and our behavior. If we are careless in either direction, we can easily fall out of plumb with the Gospel. In other words, the Gospel points us to certain doctrines as essential truths that are in keeping with the Gospel. These truths call for a certain manner of living. Perhaps we could illustrate these relationships as in figure 4.1.

So then, in teaching the Faith we proclaim the Gospel, as of first importance. We also teach the sound doctrine that derives from and conforms to that Gospel. And we draw attention to the way of living that is in accord with sound doctrine. Most of us know all too well, however, from both observation and personal experience, that the gulf between belief and behavior can be great. Paul urged the Philippians, "Only let us live up to what we have already attained" (Phil 3:16). The mere fact that he had to utter such words points to the unhappy reality that living by the Gospel does not automatically follow from our profession of the Gospel.

Where then shall we find the power to translate Gospel convictions into Gospel living? This power, too, is found in the Gospel that we proclaim! Paul declares that the Gospel "is the power of God for the salvation of everyone who believes" (Rom 1:16). As we saw in chapter two, the biblical vision of salvation refers to the entire process of our being transformed into the likeness of Jesus Christ. The Gospel's power for salvation therefore includes the power for such transformation.

In other words, the Gospel not only reveals God's gracious truths and his righteous requirements. It also invites us into communion with the living God through Jesus Christ. One of the most precious truths of the Gospel is that we who believe are now "in Christ."[19] This is not only a marvelous doctrine to be affirmed. It is a truth to be experienced. In Christ, there is a new creation (see 2 Cor 5:17), and we have become the righteousness of God (see 2 Cor 5:21). In him we have been raised with Christ and seated in heavenly places (see Eph 2:6). In Christ dwells the fullness of the deity, and we are given fullness in him (see Col 2:9-10).

Because of this relationship with God that we have in Christ, we are enabled to begin living as we ought to live but never could before. Apart from a vital relationship with Jesus Christ, we can do nothing at all (see Jn 15:5). But living in such a relationship, we can do all things through him who gives us strength (see Phil 4:13). For the same Gospel that illumines gracious truth and demands a righteous response also provides what is needed for godly living. It not only teaches us to live godly lives in this present age (see Tit 2:12), it actually empowers us to do so, by destroying death and bringing life and immortality to light (see 2 Tim 1:10).

---

[19]"In Christ" is a critical expression in the New Testament. See, for example, that potent doxological passage of Ephesians 1:3-14.

A HISTORIC PATTERN FOR TEACHING

In sum, what we have been arguing is that there are three aspects or dimensions of the Faith, each of which derives from and represents implications of the Gospel. The first concerns matters of Christian belief. The second concerns Christian behavior. And the third concerns the vital relationship with God that helps us bridge the all-too-common gulf between belief and behavior. In the history of the church, we discover what we may call "historic witnesses" to this threefold pattern.

For the first of these "witnesses," we turn to the catechisms that were produced by the Reformers and their successors. Even a cursory examination of the majority of the Reformation-era catechisms reveals that the content of the catechisms was quite standardized. Luther's small and large catechisms, Calvin's earlier and later Geneva catechisms, and the Heidelberg Catechism, all feature the same basic "ingredients." Each centers on instruction in three great summaries[20] of the Faith: the Apostles' Creed, the Ten Commandments and the Lord's Prayer. Alongside these three, there is typically some instruction in the sacraments of baptism and the Lord's Supper, though these are not generally afforded quite the same status as the three summaries.

The Puritan era—both in England and in the United States—was also marked by the publication, distribution of and instruction in catechisms. With few exceptions, exposition in the three great summaries continued to make up the bulk of the content.[21] Puritan pastors like Richard Baxter and John Owen utilized available catechisms "as is," modified them as deemed appropriate for reasons of conviction or simply wrote their own.

It may surprise some evangelical Protestants to discover that the catechisms printed and widely distributed by the Roman Catholics have followed much the same pattern. There are great differences, to be sure, between the catechisms of the early Protestants and those of the Church of Rome, but the three formulae are the principle content on both sides of this divide. Indeed, the counterreformation attention to printing and distributing catechisms was actually spurred by the successes that Protestants were having with their catechetical efforts. It was the Protestants—Luther, Calvin and others—who championed the recovery of a rigorous catechesis, something that had been largely lost in the Western church since around the time of Augustine. How

---

[20]J. I. Packer calls these "the three formulae which have always been central in Christian teaching." *Growing in Christ* (Wheaton: Tyndale House, 1994), p. xi.
[21]The Westminster Catechisms do not include line-by-line instruction in the Creed.

ironic that in the eyes of many contemporary evangelicals, catechesis is seen as a thoroughly Roman Catholic idea and practice.

Although the Reformers were the first to seize upon the educational opportunity afforded them by the printing press to publish and distribute printed catechisms, they hardly thought of their teaching as novel. Indeed, the notions of catechesis and novelty of content are simply incompatible, as we discussed earlier. To the contrary, Luther, Calvin and all who took catechesis seriously in both Protestant and Catholic circles believed that they were teaching essentially what the church had always taught.

This conviction is evident in the prefaces to Luther's catechisms. In the preface to the Large Catechism, Luther refers to this triad as "the three parts which have been the heritage of Christendom from ancient times."[22] It is fair to ask whether or not Luther and others were right in their assertion that the church has always catechized its members via the three summaries: the Creed, the Decalogue and the Lord's Prayer. We will not fully explore the historical case for and against this claim here, as it would prove to be a rather lengthy excursion and diversion from the aims of this chapter.[23] We will simply state that Luther seems to have been essentially, if not precisely, correct. From the earliest days of catechetical work, the instruction involved training in the Lord's Prayer, some sort of creedal instruction and some form of moral instruction. There was also instruction in that fourth area of concern: the sacraments of baptism and the Lord's Supper. But it would be going too far to say that the particular forms of instruction *always* included an exposition of the Apostles' Creed. That creed, in the form that we now know it, was developed over several centuries, though its basic outline and content are ancient.

The catechesis of Augustine in the fifth century, Cyril of Jerusalem in the fourth centuries and even earlier catechists included instruction in creeds that were very similar to the Apostles' Creed that the Reformers utilized.[24] These creedal statements seem to have developed along with baptismal rites as a

---

[22]Martin Luther, "Preface to the Small Catechism," in *The Book of Concord,* ed. Theodore Tappert (Philadelphia: Fortress, 1959), p. 362. In his twentieth-century work on catechetical renewal in the Catholic Church, Josef Andreas Jungman refers to "the *old traditional formulation of Creed,* Our Father, Ten Commandments, Sacraments" and argues that this pattern "must determine the plan in some way" (emphasis in the original). *The Good News Yesterday and Today* (New York: Sadlier, 1962), p. 102.

[23]For a more thorough survey, see the previously mentioned forthcoming book on catechesis by Packer and Parrett, *Grounded in the Gospel.*

[24]Such as the Jerusalem Creed and the Old Roman Creed.

means for the candidates to articulate the Faith in which, and into which, they were being baptized. Almost always, the language of such confessions of faith was determined to a greater or lesser extent in response to competing truth claims and particular heresies that were current in the age and culture. Such things were already happening in the New Testament era, as we will see below.

The last of the three summaries to appear regularly in Christian catechetical efforts was the Ten Commandments. We do not see these appearing as a consistent feature in catechisms until medieval times. However, the heart and emphases of the Decalogue appears, in various catechetical documents, much earlier. In his fifth-century *Enchiridion,* Augustine has three major sections, which he labels *Faith, Hope* and *Love.* The first of these is an exposition of the creed; the second is a briefer exposition of the Lord's Prayer; and the third is an even briefer exposition of the double command of love—love of God and love of neighbor—which both Jews and Christians have long regarded as a summary of the Decalogue. Concern for such ethical instruction was found even in the earliest of catechetical works, the *Didachē,* by means of instruction around the "Two Ways": "There are two ways, one of life and one of death, and there is a great difference between the two ways. The way of life is this. First of all, thou shalt love the God that made thee; secondly, thy neighbour as thyself."[25]

Besides the pattern evidenced in catechesis, there are additional historical witnesses to the notion of a threefold pattern for formation. There is, for example, the threefold function of the synagogue as a house of prayer, a house of study and a house of assembly. These three functions correspond to what Abraham Heschel refers to as the main aspects of religious existence: worship, learning and action.[26]

There is also a twofold and sometimes threefold formula to be found in the historic church that emphasizes the interrelationship between the various dimensions of our spiritual lives. This has been expressed by the Latin phrases *lex orandi, lex credendi* (the law of prayer is the law of belief, or "as we pray, so we believe"). Some have added a third expression, *lex vivendi* (law of life),

---

[25]The opening lines of *The Didache of the Apostles,* according to the translation of J. B. Lightfoot. Available at <www.earlychristianwritings.com/text/didache-lightfoot.html>.

[26]Heschel earlier identified these as (1) the way of sensing the presence of God in the world, in things; (2) the way of sensing his presence in the Bible, and (3) the way of sensing his presence in sacred deeds. *God in Search of Man: A Philosophy of Judaism* (New York: Farrar, Strauss & Giroux, 1976), p. 31.

which reminds us that as we believe, so shall we live.[27] A pattern of this sort was, and remains, "made flesh," as it were, in the three-part day of the Benedictine monks. Theirs was a rhythm of life that included manual labor, sacred study, and their most important task—the *opus Dei* (work of God)—prayer in and as community.

BIBLICAL BASIS FOR THE PATTERN

This pattern that we have illustrated from the history of church teaching has biblical witnesses as well. To begin with, it is clear from Scripture that God is concerned with the formation of all aspects of our humanity. We are to love the Lord with all our heart, soul, mind and strength (see Deut 6:5; Lev 19:18; Mk 12:29-31). It is evident that simply loving God with our minds, for example, will not do. It is not enough to believe, confess or teach correctly about God. We must align our affections and our behavior with our convictions. Scripture continually affirms this. Indeed, the command to love the Lord is an imperative response to Israel's most basic confession, the *shema* of Deuteronomy 6:4: "Hear, O Israel: the LORD our God, the LORD is one." Because of the truth of this confession, the response of loving the Lord above all, and with one's all, must follow.

A comprehensive concern for ministries of teaching and formation is affirmed by numerous other biblical passages. Indeed, the very structure of the Hebrew Scriptures appears to argue for this. Jews refer to their Bible as the Tanakh. This title is actually an acronym representing the three parts of the Hebrew Bible, as follows:

1. **T**orah—the five books of Moses

2. **N**evi'im—the prophetic books

3. **Kh**etuvim—the writings (the first and largest of these books being the Psalms)

This three-part division of the Scriptures is affirmed by Jesus himself in Luke 24, when, in a postresurrection appearance to his disciples, he said, "Everything must be fulfilled that is written about me in the Law of Moses, the Prophets and the Psalms" (Lk 24:44). Old Testament scholar Walter Brueggemann has argued that these three parts each represented different kinds of education for the people of God. The Torah was taught by the priests and

---

[27]Geoffrey Wainwright has offered an extensive treatment of these "laws" in his book *Doxology: The Praise of God in Worship, Doctrine, and Life* (New York: Oxford University Press, 1980).

concerned Israel's fundamental precepts. The words of the Prophets came like lightening bolts to the people, jarring them from complacency and calling them to action. The writings represented the contemplation of the sages, calling Israel to ponder the profound mysteries of life and submit to God's way of wisdom.[28] While agreeing with Brueggemann's broad suggestions, our own view of the role of the Prophets is somewhat different. Rather than a sort of alien, unexpected word from outside the Torah of the priests, we take the prophetic call as a return to the Torah, indeed as a demand that the precepts of the Torah actually be obeyed and practiced. In any case, we find Brueggemann's work very insightful and helpful in pointing out this biblical witness to holistic spiritual formation.

In the New Testament, we find further examples of a comprehensive pattern for essential teaching. Texts such as Acts 2:42 and Hebrews 6:1-2—both of which we considered in chapter three—point to such comprehensiveness. Further New Testament witnesses are found especially in the Pastoral Epistles and in the first letter of John. In the pastorals, for example, we see an emphasis on teaching and exhorting toward "sound doctrine" (Tit 1:10; 2 Tim 4:3), "the pattern of sound teaching" and "the good deposit" (2 Tim 1:13-14), "the deep truths of the faith" (1 Tim 3:9; 4:6), and so on.

Alongside all this, Paul also insists on teaching the manner of living that "is in accord with sound doctrine" (Tit 2:1), that makes "the teaching about God our Savior attractive" (Tit 2:10). Such a lifestyle is in stark contrast to all the godlessness that "is contrary to the sound doctrine that conforms to the glorious gospel of the blessed God" (1 Tim 1:10-11). It is not only in teaching others that this balance of concerns must be made clear. Paul tells Timothy that he must watch his own life and doctrine closely and persevere in them, "because if you do, you will save both yourself and your hearers" (1 Tim 4:16).

In the first epistle of John, we see that the beloved apostle also draws attention to multiple dimensions of the Faith. A key concern of the letter is the true knowledge of God. Evidence for such knowledge is multifaceted. There is a doctrinal test to be employed concerning what we believe and confess about Jesus Christ (see 1 Jn 4:1-6, 15; 5:1, 10, 13). There is also as a moral test: the one who does what is right knows God (see 1 Jn 2:3-6, 29; 3:7-10, 18-20; 5:2-3, 18). Chief among these moral concerns seems to be the sincere love of fellow believers (see 1 Jn 2:9-10; 3:10-18; 4:7-12, 16, 19-21). And John offers one

---

[28]Walter Brueggemann, *The Creative Word: Canon as Model for Biblical Education* (Philadelphia: Fortress, 1982).

other witness to the true knowledge of God. God has given us his Spirit (see 1 Jn 3:24; 4:13), who supplies a testimony within our own hearts that we belong to God (see 1 Jn 5:6-12).

The point we are trying to demonstrate, again, is that our biblically mandated teaching is comprehensive in nature. This should not surprise us, of course, since our humanity is complex and multifaceted (more on this later, especially in chapters eight through ten). So, too, our knowledge of God and loving response to God require the engagement of our whole being (see Deut 6:5). Thus Scripture calls us to believe in Jesus and his words, to receive and abide in him, to obey and follow him, and more. Faithful teaching of the Faith requires attention to the Gospel and its implications for doctrine, devotion and duty.

FORMATIONAL WISDOM OF THE PATTERN

Those who have been engaged in ministries of Christian education and formation will recognize the value of the pattern emerging from the Scriptures and affirmed throughout church history. Educators have long recognized a similar triad of concerns in their labors. This has sometimes been referred to as the triad of "head, heart and hands." In formal language, three domains of learning are acknowledged: cognitive, affective and behavioral (or psychomotor).[29]

Such patterns correspond, finally, to certain realities of our humanness. We are made for communion with God, but we find ourselves alienated from God. This creates a longing for God deep within us—sometimes acknowledged, sometimes not. Augustine wrote beautifully of this in his confessions: "For Thou hast made us for Thyself, and our hearts know no rest until they rest in Thee."[30] C. S. Lewis referred to this sort of longing by use of the German word *Sehnsucht*: "And every day there were what we called 'the Green Hills' that is, the low line of the Castlereagh Hills which we saw from the nursery windows. They were not very far off but they were, to children, quite unattainable. They taught me longing—*Sehnsucht*."[31]

Our human longings are reflected in one of the most traditional approaches to the major categories of philosophy: epistemology, ontology and axiology.

---

[29]We examine these things further in chapters eight through ten.

[30]Augustine, *The Confessions of St. Augustine,* trans. John Ryan (Garden City, N.Y.: Doubleday, 1960), p. 43.

[31]C. S. Lewis, *Surprised by Joy: The Shape of My Early Life* (New York: Harcourt, 1956), p. 5. See also Marva Dawn, *Is It a Lost Cause? Having the Heart of God for the Church's Children* (Grand Rapids: Eerdmans, 1997), pp. 18-19.

John Stott has written of "three quests" that engage all humans in every age and in every culture: the quest for significance, the quest for transcendence and the quest for community.[32] God, in his infinite grace, has provided the answers to these quests in his church, Stott argues. Through the ministries of teaching, worship and fellowship, respectively, we are to speak to these great quests. Tragically, the church all too often muddles the message we are to teach, offers little or no true experience of God in our worship and functions more like a pseudo-community than a truly loving community of fellowship.

In answer to these deep human longings, the church proclaims Jesus Christ, who is the Truth, the Life and the Way.

THE TRUTH, THE LIFE AND THE WAY

We have considered briefly the historical, biblical and formational value of what we have called three *implications* of the Gospel—implications for doctrine, devotion and duty. In his *Enchiridion,* Augustine labeled these three areas of concern Faith, Hope and Love, utilizing that very familiar biblical triad.[33] Helpful as such language is, we see those three terms as better representing the aims toward which we teach (as we explored in chapter two). Thus we teach *unto* faith, unto hope and unto love. In terms of labeling our fundamental content, however, we prefer the language of another biblical triad: the Way, the Truth, and the Life. This language occurs in John 14:6. There Jesus has told his disciples that he is about to leave them but that they know the way to where he is going. After Thomas's protest to the contrary, Jesus declares, "I am the way and the truth and the life. No one comes to the Father except through me."

He goes on to remind his followers that he is the full revelation of the unseen God. "Anyone who has seen me has seen the Father," he assures them (Jn 14:9). It is through Jesus alone then that one comes to truly know God. And our knowledge of God is multifaceted. Jesus communicates this here by use of three important biblical concepts: the Way and the Truth and the Life. These three terms correspond to the threefold pattern we have been considering in this chapter. To make that correspondence clearer, we take up the three in this order: the Truth, the Life and the Way.

The Truth refers to all that God has revealed concerning himself and the many doctrines that accompany that revelation. This Truth must be be-

---

[32]John Stott, *Between Two Worlds: The Challenge of Preaching Today* (Grand Rapids: Eerdmans, 1994), p. 151.

[33]See, for example, 1 Corinthians 13:13; Romans 5:2-5; Galatians 5:5-6; Ephesians 4:2-5; Colossians 1:4-5; 1 Thessalonians 1:3; 5:8; Hebrews 6:10-12; 1 Peter 1:21-22.

lieved, adhered to and loved. Many, however, reject the truth and so are lost (see 2 Thess 2:10-12). The essence of the Truth is proclaimed in the Gospel (see Gal 2:5; Eph 1:13). Jesus himself is the Truth incarnate (see Eph 4:21), the totality of God's revelation concerning himself (see Jn 1:1, 14, 18; Col 1:15; 2:9; Heb 1:1-3).

The Life, especially in John's writings, refers to a vital and eternal relationship with the living God (see Jn 17:3). Jesus came to offer this Life to others (see Jn 3:16; 4:10; 5:21; 10:10; 11:25-26; 20:31; 1 Jn 5:11-13). Jesus is this Life incarnate. Through the ministry of the Holy Spirit (see Jn 7:37-39), he extends this Life to all who believe him and receive him, thus making them children of God (see Jn 1:12).

The Way is a critical concept in the Hebrew Scriptures and describes the manner of living that God requires and desires (for example, Ps 1:6; 32:8; Is 30:21). It is the Way of the Lord, the Way of the righteous, the Way of life, and is distinguished from the way of the world, the way of the wicked and the way of death. It is the Way of wisdom as opposed to the way of folly (as, especially, in Proverbs and Ecclesiastes). Jesus takes up this teaching of two distinct ways in the Sermon on the Mount (see Mt 7:13-14), and Christians were early known as followers of "the Way" (see Acts 9:2; 19:9, 23; 22:4; 24:14, 22).

The Way that God requires is this: we must love the Lord with all that is within us and love our neighbors as ourselves. Jesus incarnated this Way and, by living this Way faithfully—when all others had departed from it—he becomes for all who believe in him a new and living Way into the Holy of holies (see Heb 10:20). That is, through his obedience in life and in death, we are enabled to know the Father and to be in right relationship with him.

It should be clear that our understanding of teaching such content as we have been describing cannot be confined to narrow visions of teaching. We will explore this more fully in chapter ten. For now, we summarize simply by saying that in our ministries of teaching and formation:

> We proclaim to one another the Truth of the Gospel.
> We experience with one another the Life of the Gospel.
> We practice, corporately and individually, the Way of the Gospel.

In table 4.2, we bring together various "witnesses" to the threefold pattern we have been discussing throughout this chapter.

Table 4.2. The Three Facets of the Faith

The Jewish religious experience (Heschel)	Learning	Worship	Action
Three purposes of the synagogue	House of Study	House of Prayer	House of Assembly
The Christian life experience	*Lex Credendi*	*Lex Orandi*	*Lex Vivendi*
Augustine's "Enchiridion"	Faith—concerning the Creed	Hope—concerning the Our Father	Love—of God and neighbor
Benedictine rhythm in monastic life	Sacred study	Opus Dei	Labor in service of the community
The Reformation catechisms	Exposition of the Creed	Exposition of the Lord's Prayer	Exposition of the Decalogue
The Tanakh	Torah—Torah shapes Israel	Khetuvim—Torah contemplated	Nevi'im—Torah obeyed
Threefold office of Christ	Prophet, proclaiming truth	Priest, mediating life	King, declaring, enforcing law
John's tests of the believer	Believes the truth about Jesus Christ	God's Spirit witnesses within	Obeys God, loves brothers and sisters
Paul's commands to Timothy	Watch your doctrine		Watch your life
Paul's commands to Titus	Teach sound doctrine		Teach what accords with sound doctrine
Four commitments of Acts 2:42	The apostles' teaching	The breaking of the bread; prayers	The fellowship
The three theological virtues	Faith	Hope	Love
Our deep longings (Lewis)	*Sehnsucht*		
expressed in three quests (Stott)	Significance	Transcendence	Community
which are reflected in philosophy as	Epistemology	Ontology	Axiology
In answer to the above . . .	. . . we proclaim Christ! (Col. 1:28)		
By preaching and teaching . . .	. . . the glorious Gospel of the blessed God (1 Tim 1:11)		
three dimensions of the one Faith	sound doctrine that conforms to the Gospel	the life-giving benefits that flow from the Gospel	the way of living that accords with the sound doctrine
In other words, we teach Christ who is	**The Truth**	**The Life**	**The Way**

CONCLUSION

In proclaiming Christ, the church sets forth the Gospel as its primary message. This "message of reconciliation" is the centerpiece of the "ministry of reconciliation" to which we have been called (2 Cor 5:18-20). Believing and receiving this good news, we discover that, in Christ, there is a new creation (see 2 Cor 5:17). Henceforth, we live no longer for ourselves, but for the One who loves us and gave his life for us (see 2 Cor 5:15). This is what it means to live as those who have been reconciled to God. As we contemplate the Gospel and its implications, we come to see what such a manner of life looks like. The Gospel itself, with all its promised benefits, empowers us to begin walking in that way.

Having worked through the various elements we consider vital for faithful proclamation, we attempt in the following chapter to illustrate how such a vision of essential content may be worked out practically in the teaching of local church ministries of teaching and formation.

HYMN FOR CONTEMPLATION AND WORSHIP
We Will Not Cease the Gospel to Proclaim
(Rom 1:16-17)

We will not cease the Gospel to proclaim.
Nor dare we ever turn from it in shame.
It is God's pow'r to save in Jesus' name.
Hallelujah! Hallelujah!
(1 Cor 1:18-25; 9:16; 15:1-8; Gal 1:6-9)

Both Jew and Greek, and all those who believe,
by faith alone the gift of life receive.
By grace alone, to Christ alone we cleave.
Hallelujah! Hallelujah!
(Ps 32:7-8; Gal 3:21-28; 6:14; Eph 2:1-22; Acts 4:12)

God's righteousness is in the Gospel shown.
Christ Jesus died for sinners to atone.
God is both just and justifies his own!
Hallelujah! Hallelujah!
(Rom 3:21-26; Gal 2:15-21; Heb 4:10; 9:11—10:14)

From faith to faith, this righteousness proceeds.
The child of God the Gospel ever heeds
as, in new life, the Holy Spirit leads.
Hallelujah! Hallelujah!
(Rom 4; Gal 2:20; Heb 11:1—12:2; Phil 3:7-16)

At peace with God, by faith let us be bold.
Of his great pow'r for living we lay hold.
"The just by faith shall live!" It was foretold.
Hallelujah! Hallelujah!
(Rom 5:1—8:17; Gal 3:11; 5:1, 22-25; Hab 2:4)

Text: Gary A. Parrett, 2007
Tune: Sine Nomine
Familiar use of the tune: "For All the Saints"

QUESTIONS FOR PLANNING AND PRACTICE

1. In this chapter, the authors argue that the Gospel must be at the center of our educational and formation ministries. Do you agree? Why or why not?

2. Figure 4.1 illustrates "the glorious Gospel." Choose one Scripture verse from each section and reflect on how your own Christian education ministry is (or is not) fulfilling that particular aspect of the Gospel. Reflect especially on the "The Gospel must be . . . " section.

3. How would you respond to the alleged overemphasis on the implications of the Gospel vis-à-vis the essence of the Gospel? In what ways do you sympathize with so-called emerging believers (or post-evangelical believers) on these points? In what ways do their emphases concern you? How might you consider redirecting your church's educational formation ministries in light of this important discussion?

4. Using D. Campbell Wyckoff's outline on page 108, expound how each point is played out in your own educational formation ministry. What are some areas that you wish to address or bolster in your own ministry?

5. Would you say that the three facets of essential Christian teaching—the Truth, the Life and the Way—are apparent in your own teaching? In what ways is this so?

6. Many churches today aim toward "relevance" and adapt "modern" thinking or practices. Do you believe it's possible to be relevant to modern society while drawing on the history of the church? How do you try to strike a balance in this regard in your own educational ministry?

7. Reflect on the notion of *Sehnsucht* as introduced in this chapter. Do you see a similar "deep longing" in your heart and the hearts of those to whom you minister? What are some manifestations of this?

8. In this chapter, the authors point out that the church historically grounded believers in the Faith, in part by utilizing the Apostles' Creed, the Decalogue and the Lord's Prayer. Are these summaries of the Faith introduced in your own congregation's ministry? If so, what place do they have forming the believers in your congregation? If not, do you believe they should be?

9. With a partner or group, reflect on the Way of the Lord as discussed in the chapter. How do you understand the role of educational formation ministry in inviting God's people to follow Jesus on so precious a pilgrimage?

RESOURCES FOR FURTHER STUDY

Brueggemann, Walter. *The Creative Word: Canon as a Model for Biblical Education*. Philadelphia: Fortress, 1982.

Carson, D. A. *The Cross and Christian Ministry: The Leadership Lessons from 1 Corinthians*. Grand Rapids: Baker, 2004.

Dawn, Marva. *Is It a Lost Cause? Having the Heart of God for the Church's Children*. Grand Rapids: Eerdmans, 1997.

Gibbs, Eddie, and Ryan Bolger. *Emerging Churches: Creating Christian Communities in Postmodern Cultures*. Grand Rapids: Baker, 2005.

Jones, E. Stanley. *The Way: 364 Adventures in Daily Living*. Nashville: Abingdon, 1946.

McGrath, Alister, ed. *The Christian Theology Reader*. 3rd edition. Malden, Mass.: Blackwell, 2007.

McKnight, Scot. *A Community Called Atonement*. Nashville: Abingdon, 2007.

Oden, Thomas. *The Justification Reader*. Grand Rapids: Eerdmans, 2002.

Packer, J. I. *Growing in Christ*. Wheaton: Tyndale House, 1994.

Packer, J. I., and Gary A. Parrett. *Grounded in the Gospel: Building Believers the Old-Fashioned Way*. Grand Rapids: Baker, forthcoming.

Packer, J. I., and Mark Dever. *In My Place Condemned He Stood: Celebrating the Glory of the Atonement*. Wheaton: Crossway, 2007.

Peterson, Eugene. *The Jesus Way: A Conversation on the Ways That Jesus Is the Way*. Grand Rapids: Eerdmans, 2007.

Sanneh, Lamin. *Whose Religion Is Christianity? The Gospel Beyond the West*. Grand Rapids: Eerdmans, 2003.

Willard, Dallas. *The Divine Conspiracy: Rediscovering Our Hidden Life in God*. New York, HarperCollins, 1998.

5

CORE Content
for a Congregational Curriculum

We proclaim him, admonishing and teaching everyone with all wisdom,

so that we may present everyone perfect in Christ.

COLOSSIANS 1:28

▼

IN THIS SECOND SECTION OF THE BOOK, we have discussed at length issues of essential content for teaching ministries. We have identified several components that should be part of a faithful and effective teaching ministry in congregations. These include

- *the glorious Gospel* of the blessed God
- three dimensions of *the Faith,* which we have called *the Truth, the Life* and *the Way*

In chapter one, we gave our full attention to what should be regarded as another, overreaching component of our teaching ministry, namely *the Story* of God's reconciling all things to himself in Christ.

The Gospel is the good news of God's reconciling work in Christ. Its essence is that God has intervened on our behalf to save us sinners from our sin and all its consequences. "God so loved the world that he gave his one and only Son" (Jn 3:16) to be "an atoning sacrifice [a propitiation] for our sins" (1 Jn 4:10). God "made him who had no sin to be sin for us, so that in him we might become the righteousness of God" (2 Cor 5:21). "Christ died for our sins according to the Scriptures . . . he was buried . . . he was raised on the third day according to the Scriptures" (1 Cor 15:3-5). Therefore, we preach and teach Christ crucified and risen from the dead.

The Gospel is the summary and centerpiece of what may be called *the Story,* the biblical drama that has been unfolding throughout history. God is working all things according to his good purposes (see Eph 1:11). God has included us in this Story, "to the praise of his glorious grace" (Eph 1:6) by reconciling us to himself (see Col 1:22) and to one another in the one body of Christ (see Eph 2:11-22). The church, as the body of Christ, has been called by God to a further level of engagement in the Story: God continues his reconciling work in and through us: "We are God's workmanship *[poiēma],* created in Christ Jesus to do good works" (Eph 2:10). "God was reconciling the world to himself in Christ. . . . And he has committed to us the ministry of reconciliation" (2 Cor 5:19).

The Gospel is also the fountain of all that we mean by *the Faith.* There are several dimensions of the Faith that we derive from the Gospel. These include what we have called the Truth, the Life and the Way. By "the Truth," we refer to all the mysteries and knowledge pertaining to and deriving from the unseen God. These have been most fully disclosed in Jesus Christ. The church of Jesus, which is the "pillar and foundation of the truth" (1 Tim 3:15), is charged with the teaching of "the sound doctrine that conforms to the glorious gospel of the blessed God" (1 Tim 1:10-11). The Gospel is the plumb line by which we must measure all our teaching and all our theological commitments.

Training in "the Truth," therefore, is training in theology. Historically, the Apostles' Creed has been the church's most commonly utilized primer for such theological learning (especially in the West). But even those churches that consider themselves "noncreedal" must teach the Truth and can easily do so by appeal to any number of biblical passages and unfolding the doctrines of Scripture.

By "the Life," we refer to all the life-giving benefits and blessings that flow from the Gospel (see 2 Tim 1:10). Fundamentally, this refers to the mind-boggling reality that we have been adopted into God's family and are now his children through Christ Jesus. We were dead in our trespasses and sins, but God—because of his great love for us—has made us alive through faith in Christ (see Eph 2:1-4). We are invited to commune with God through prayer and worship, invited to call the living God *Abba*—"Dear Father." This Life is the experience of the Person and ministry of the Holy Spirit who indwells all those who belong to Christ (see Rom 8:9) and leads us onward in a life of intimacy with God (see Gal 4:4-6; 5:25). Thus training in the Life is training in communion with God—through prayer and worship. Historically, this aspect of the Faith has been taught most commonly through the Lord's Prayer and the Sacraments. Further biblical training in the Life should also include extensive use of the book of Psalms.

By "the Way," we refer to the godly manner of conduct to which the people of God are called. This pattern of living "is in accord with sound doctrine" (Tit 2:1). We are to walk in the Way of the Lord, not in the way of the world; in the Way of the righteous, not in the way of the wicked; in the Way of life, not in the way of death; in the Way of wisdom, not in the way of folly; in the Way, as opposed to *not-the-way*. The Way, in a word, is *love*. We are called to love of both God and neighbor. To love God is to obey his commands (see 1 Jn 5:3). Central to his commands is that we love our neighbors (see Lev 19:18), and especially those neighbors who are our fellow believers in the household of faith (see Gal 6:10; 1 Jn 4:7-8).

Training in the Way is training in ethics. The historic primer for this training has been, especially, the Decalogue—God's Ten Words, or the Ten Commandments. Biblical books like Proverbs, the letter of James and the Old Testament Prophets also offer much instruction in the Way of the Lord. Christ's Sermon on the Mount has been another key portion of Scripture for teaching and learning the Way.

In this chapter, we continue our exploration of these things with a view to formulating a congregational curriculum for teaching and formation. As we do so, we seek to bring together all the components that we have outlined above. These comprise the essential content at the heart of the curriculum. We are referring to our proposed content as a CORE content for congregational curriculum. We use the acronym *CORE* to communicate that the curriculum we envision is one of Comprehensive, Orthodox, Renewing Essentials. It is comprehensive in that it aims to address whole persons and to touch the entire life of the community. It is orthodox in that, as much as is possible, it is instruction in that which has been accepted "everywhere, always and by all." It is renewing in that its objective is the transformation of our lives, both individually and corporately. And its focus is on the essentials of the Faith, not on secondary doctrines. Or, to say it better, in this curriculum proposal we strive to keep primary things primary and secondary things secondary, and to help church members be clear about the distinction. Before continuing our discussion about this content, however, we must say a few words about the notion of curriculum itself.

THE CONCEPT OF CURRICULUM

Although many church members and teachers may equate the word *curriculum* with the teachers' materials and handouts for Sunday school classes, it actually has much broader implications. The English word is derived from the Latin *currere*, which means "to run." Many have thus understood curriculum as a "course to be run." For educators, this would embrace all the elements of the design for teaching, learning and formation.

We do not here attempt to offer a full introduction to the concept of curriculum. Many have written helpfully on this subject,[1] and there are numerous and competing philosophies and approaches in the world of education at large, as well as in regard to the educational practices of congregations.

For our purposes, we intend by *curriculum* both the content and processes for education and formation in congregations, and we call attention to a host of other issues regarding the people involved in those processes and the environments in which those processes occur. In other words, all of the seven questions we mentioned in the preface of this book apply to the formulation of curriculum. We have summarized these questions in the textbox on page 128 (after each question we have indicated the chapters in this book where the particular issues involved are chiefly taken up).

With these seven questions before us, it is clear that our curriculum must include far more than concern for our proclamation. It must also include significant and sustained attention to purposes, persons and practices. In part one of the book, our focus was on the purposes of our teaching. In part two, our focus has been primarily on proclamation—that is, on matters of content. In the remaining sections of the book, we deal with the persons and practices involved in ministries of teaching and formation.

EXPLICIT, IMPLICIT AND NULL CURRICULUM

The only further remark we offer about the idea of "curriculum" at this point is to draw attention to the distinction between "three types of curricula," which have been called the *explicit curriculum,* the *implicit* (or hidden) *curriculum* and the *null curriculum.*[2] Briefly put, the explicit curriculum refers to that

---

[1]For example, Maria Harris, *Fashion Me a People* (Louisville, Ky.: Westminster/John Knox, 1989); Elliot Eisner, *The Educational Imagination,* 3rd ed. (New York: Macmillan, 1994); James Gress and David Purpel, eds., *Curriculum: An Introduction to the Field,* 2nd ed. (Berkeley, Calif.: McCutchan, 1988); Dwayne Huebner, *The Lure of the Transcendent: Collected Essays by Dwayne Huebner* (Mahwah, N.J.: LEA, 1999); Robert Pazmiño, *Basics of Teaching for Christians: Preparation, Instruction, and Evaluation* (Grand Rapids: Baker, 1998).
[2]See Eisner, *Educational Imagination.* The explicit curriculum entails the teaching of goals and objectives of various subjects. The implicit curriculum is a set of messages and physical struc-

Seven Questions for Curriculum Formulation

1. *Why?* Why do we teach? What are our goals—primary and secondary? How do we conceive our task? To what do we turn as sources for framing the task? (chapters 1-2)

2. *What?* What must we teach? What is the essential content of our teaching ministry if we are to be faithful and effective in our task? (chapters 3-5)

3. *Who?* Who is charged with the responsibility of teaching? How can we best organize those who are engaged in the teaching ministry of the church? What manner of persons must teachers be in order to be faithful and effective in their task? (chapters 6-7)

4. *Whom?* Whom are we teaching? What are the sociocultural realities of our learners, and how must these affect the teaching task? (chapters 5, 8-9)

5. *When?* When should we teach what? What are the developmental realities of our learners (in terms of both natural and spiritual development), and how must these affect the teaching task? How can we build on previous learning and prepare for subsequent learning? (chapters 8-9, 11, 13-14)

6. *How?* How must we teach in order to engage whole persons—eyes and ears, heads, hearts and hands—in Christian formation? How can we challenge the community toward transformation in *all facets* of its life? (chapters 9-14)

7. *Where?* Where should the teaching occur? What are the environments in which the community and individual students are best taught and formed? (chapters 12-14)

which we actually intend to teach. The implicit curriculum refers to all that

tures that "socialize children to a set of expectations that some argue are profoundly more powerful and longer lasting than what is intentionally taught or what the explicit curriculum of the school publicly provides" (p. 213). The null curriculum is basically what a teaching institution chooses not to teach at all. Eisner contends that what a teaching institution does "not teach may be as important as what they do teach. Ignorance is not simply a neutral void; it has important effects on the kinds of options one is able to consider, the alternatives that one can examine, and the perspectives from which one can view a situation or problems. The absence of a set of considerations or perspectives or the inability to use certain processes for appraising a context biases the evidence one is able to take into account. A parochial perspective or simplistic analysis is the inevitable progeny of ignorance" (p. 97).

is taught by *the ways* (and environments) in which we teach. The null curriculum makes the point that we teach a great deal by that which we do not (explicitly) teach.

To illustrate these ideas, consider an example in which a Bible-study teacher has decided to teach a class for collegians on the subject of Christian ethics. She outlines her course based on the Sermon on the Mount and the Ten Commandments. On a given week, she prepares a presentation and discussion on what most Protestants number as the eighth commandment: "You shall not steal." This directs is her explicit curriculum for that week.

While preparing, she comes across a wonderful study guide that deals with the commandment very well. She wishes that each of her students could have a copy of the guide, but this strikes her immediately as cost prohibitive. Then an idea occurs to her: she can use the church's expensive photocopy machine and make copies for each of the students. Although the guide includes very clear instructions that it may not be reproduced in such a fashion, she reasons that the end justifies the means in this case: the lesson will be enriched, and she will be a "good steward" of church finances.

The lesson proceeds just as she hoped it would—she teaches very well (it seems to her) her explicit curriculum of "You shall not steal" by utilizing illegally photocopied teaching materials! In this case, her implicit curriculum includes (but is not limited to) the suggestion that stealing is permissible under certain circumstances. In most cases like this, what we teach implicitly outweighs what we teach explicitly. Learners tend to retain what they see in our lives far more than what they hear from our lips.

To continue the illustration, we discover that the materials the teacher has prepared for the week deal primarily with very obvious instances of stealing from others. There is little or no attention given to other forms of stealing that can be large issues for collegians in our day—issues of plagiarism, illegally photocopying, downloading music or videos from the Internet, and so on. But, by not explicitly dealing with such things, a good deal is actually being taught here as well. Similarly, if this course—set, we are supposing, in a North American context—never deals with issues like racism or poverty or warfare, then students are learning, by what is *not* taught (the null curriculum), that such issues must not be of vital concern for Christian ethics.

In planning and leading the educational ministry of the church, we must be continually attentive to all these aspects of curricula: explicit, implicit and null. Very often, we may not be teaching what we think we are teaching. In 1 Corinthians 11, for example, we see that what the Corinthians were experiencing under the designation of "the Lord's Supper" resulted in very poor learning and formation indeed.

Suppose that after one of our own "worship services," in which we have heard a stirring sermon on the importance of Christian fellowship, we send members and visitors down the hallway to the "fellowship hall" for the "fellowship hour." What they experience there, it turns out, is an uncomfortable ten or fifteen minutes of seeing many gather into small cliques while scattered others eat their donuts and drink their coffee silently and alone. In such instances, what are we really teaching about Christian fellowship (we may wonder, as well, what the ubiquitous coffee and donuts teach us about fellowship)? Similarly, by regularly avoiding all those biblical texts she finds uncomfortable and difficult, what is the preacher communicating about the "whole counsel of God"? When our worship gatherings always feature the same few church members with their particular gifts, what are we teaching about the nature of the body of Christ? The fact is, everything we do in the church is teaching something, for good or for ill.

THE FAITH AND THE STORY

Returning now to a focus on matters of content, the three key terms we have identified regarding the church's proclamation are the Gospel, the Faith and the Story. How are we to think of these terms relative to each other? We could start with the concept of the Story—that great redemptive Story into which God has invited us. In these days of renewed interest in narrative, this approach may have greater appeal for many than the seemingly more propositional approach of beginning with the Faith.[3] If we begin with the Story, we could think of the Gospel as the apex of the Story or as the summary of the Story or as the means by which we enter the Story.

On the other hand, following the outline offered in the previous chapter, we could think of the Faith as our starting point and conceive of the Gospel

---

[3]Many would relate this renewed interest in narrative (and decreased interest in propositions) to the so-called postmodern turn. For an example of how this might affect our approach to evangelism, see "From Four Laws to Four Circles," an interview by Andy Crouch in *Christianity Today,* July 2008, pp. 30-33. Crouch interviews James Choung about his "Big Story" approach to the Gospel and about Choung's recent book, *True Story: A Christianity Worthy Believing In* (Downers Grove, Ill.: InterVarsity Press, 2008). Choung introduces the Great Story by means of four circles, which he labels "designed for good," "damaged by evil," "restored for better" and "sent together."

as the foundation of that Faith, or as the fountain from which all other dimensions of the Faith derive.

Although many will be tempted to choose between *either* the more propositional approach of the Faith *or* the more narrative approach of the Story, we would urge holding fast to both concepts. The Gospel is central to both approaches, and each approach offers believers important insights regarding the meaning and implications of the Gospel.

In chapter four, we argued that we never move on *from* the Gospel. Rather, we move on *in* the Gospel. This suggests a third way of conceiving the relationship between the Gospel, the Faith and the Story. In this third approach, we begin with the Gospel in its essence. Paul writes to the Corinthians that he had passed onto them the Gospel, "as of first importance" (1 Cor 15:3). Beginning here, we could then conceive of two different paths on which to pursue further understanding and formation *in* the Gospel. At times, we let the Gospel lead us into deeper understandings of the doctrines, devotion and duties of the Faith. At other times, we follow the Gospel's lead into deeper

Table 5.1. The Gospel, the Story and the Faith

The Gospel			
The Story	The Faith		
Growing in our understanding of, and engagement in, the Story	The Truth: sound doctrine	The Life: communion with God	The Way: walking in love

engagement in the great Story of God's reconciling work. In table 5.1, we illustrate the relationships we are now suggesting.

As we continue our discussion of the church's proclamation and teaching, we recognize great value in all three approaches we have discussed above. In chapter one, we presented a sketch of the Story with the help of Paul's letter to the Ephesians. In a sense, we lent primacy to the Story by beginning the book in this way. In chapter three, we demonstrated how critical the concept of the Faith is, urging renewed attention to it in the teaching ministry of the church. Valuable as both the Story and the Faith may be as starting points, we settled on a Gospel-driven approach as our primary way of outlining what we consider the essential content of the church's proclamation. Thus our discussion continued in chapter four with an extended discussion of the Gospel and three further dimensions of the

Faith—all of which, we have argued, derive from the Gospel. By teaching and learning these elements, we are better formed to take our places in the Story, which never leaves our consciousness.

PROPOSING A CORE CONTENT

We turn now to formally explore a key component in our proposed congregational curriculum. In the table 5.2, we present an overview and summary of our proposed CORE content. We follow this with an explanation of the various elements portrayed there. Both the table itself and the explanation that

Table 5.2. CORE Content for Congregational Curriculum

A. The Story, briefly unfolded for "inquirers" (procatechesis)			
1. The Gospel, *apex and summary of* **the Story** *and fountain of* **the Faith**	Hearing and believing the Gospel (1 Cor 15:1-3)	Receiving the Gospel and the gift of the Holy Spirit (Gal 3:2)	Being reconciled to both God and neighbor (Eph 2:14-18)
2. The three summaries, *primers in* **the Faith**	The Creed	The Lord's Prayer	The Decalogue
3. Deeper immersion in **the Gospel** *and its* **implications**	Studying the Gospel: rigorous study of the Scriptures (Lk 24:27, 44)	Retelling and celebrating the Gospel: the sacraments (1 Cor 11:26)	Obeying the Gospel: learning to walk in love (Eph 2:10; Tit 2:14; 2 Tim 3:17)
4. Training for engagement in **the Story** *and* **the Faith**	Ongoing training in the Truth	Ongoing training in the Life	Ongoing training in the Way
"Ecclesia" training	*Didachē*	*Leitourgia*	*Koinōnia / Diakonia*
"Diaspora" training	*Apologia*	*Kerygma*	*Diakonia / Prophēteia*
Three dimensions of **the Faith** *(Jn 14:6)*	**the Truth**	**the Life**	**the Way**
Summary of our teaching aims	Taught by the Truth and liberated by the Life, we walk in the Way		
Teaching the Truth, Life and Way vis-à-vis . . .	False isms of the age	Idols of the age	Evil practices of the age
Seeking to nurture development of . . .	**Faith**	**Hope**	**Love**
Thus, we say, with Paul . . .	**"We proclaim him, . . . so that we may present everyone perfect in Christ"** *(Col 1:28).*		

follows (here and especially in chapters thirteen and fourteen) should make it clear that by this CORE content we do not intend at all to reduce the educational and formative ministries of the church to formal instruction in classroom settings. While that may well prove a valuable setting for some aspects of this content, the vast majority of this instruction is to take place elsewhere—in the wide variety of contexts that are part of the church's life, both when we gather together and when we disperse throughout the week.

We begin our explanation of table 5.2 from the top and move downward. The first row, set apart from the rest of the table, represents our commitment to what may be called "pre-Christian discipleship" (more on this in chapter thirteen, under "Access to the Glorious Gospel"). As we discussed in the book's introduction and first chapter, God is unfolding in history the great Story of reconciling all things to himself. It was Augustine's conviction that God's redemptive Story is the proper content for instructing those who inquire about the Faith of the church.[4] In our proposed curriculum, we follow his lead. While he intended that the Story be told from the creation account of Genesis 1 to the present history of the church, we would seek to trace the Story from creation to culmination, looking ahead to glories still to come. Our aim would be to faithfully tell the Story, trusting that the Spirit of God would convict hearers of its truthfulness and quicken in their hearts the desire and the faith to join this Story and thus be numbered among the reconciled.

As we said above, the apex and the summary of the Story is the glorious Gospel. The Gospel is our basic and essential message for both unbelievers and believers. It is named in the top left-hand corner of the table, because everything else on the table derives from it. Moving from left to right, we find in the three columns to the right of the bold line interaction with the three dimensions of the Faith that derives from the Gospel: the Truth, the Life and the Way. Moving from top to bottom, we envision movement from the *milk* of the Gospel toward the *meat* of the Gospel and an intended growth toward spiritual maturity.

In spite of the many cells on table 5.2, there are actually only five components of the proposed CORE content. All the other cells are intended to help "unpack" and explain. The five content components are as follows:

First the Story, briefly unfolded for "inquirers"—here we envision an Augustinian sort of procatechesis or protocatechesis. Then, in outline form:.

---

[4]See Augustine *De Catechesis Rudibus (On the Catechizing of the Uninstructed)* <http://www .newadvent.org/fathers/1303.htm>.

1. The Gospel, as of first importance—this is foundational to all else on the table.

    a. We hear and believe the Gospel.

    b. We receive and experience the benefits of the Gospel.

    c. We obey the Gospel by being reconciled to God and neighbor.

2. The three summaries of the one Faith—these we utilize in formal catechesis, such as in preparation for baptism or confirmation.

    a. The Apostles' Creed is our primer in the Truth (and examination of biblical books such as Genesis, Isaiah, John and the letter to the Romans).

    b. The Lord's Prayer is our primer in the Life (supplemented by such texts as the book of Psalms, the Revelation).

    c. The Decalogue is our primer in the Way (supplemented by the Sermon on the Mount, the books of Proverbs and James and so on).

3. Deeper immersion in the Gospel and its implications—this is an ongoing work, involving study, celebration and active participation.

    a. We study the unfolding of the Gospel and continually study all the Scriptures.

    b. We reenact the Gospel and celebrate it through congregational worship, including observance of the sacraments.

    c. We learn to obey the Gospel by walking in love.

4. Training for engagement in the Story and the Faith—we aim at this by means of further instruction in the Truth, the Life and the Way, in both our *ekklēsia* (when we gather together) and our *diaspora* (when we disperse throughout the week).

    a. We continually engage the Truth

        i. in our gatherings, by attending to the *didachē* (teaching) of the apostles

        ii. in our dispersals, by respectful and bold *apologia* (defense) of the Faith

    b. We continually engage the Life

        i. in our gatherings, by growing in practices of prayer and worship *(leitourgia)*

        ii. in our dispersals, by sharing the Gospel *(kerygma)* with unbelieving neighbors

c. We continually engage the Way

    i. in our gatherings, by our fellowship *(koinōnia)* and acts of mutual service *(diakonia)*.

    ii. in our dispersals, by serving *(diakonia)* our neighbors and by prophetic advocacy *(prophēteia)* for justice and mercy in the world

The last section of the table explains and summarizes some of the teaching aims for this CORE content. We proclaim Christ, who is the Truth, the Life and the Way. We proclaim Christ, contra the false isms (beliefs), the idols and the evil practices of our age. Proclaiming Christ, we seek to nurture faith, hope and love in the hearts of believing individuals and in the community as a whole. Our desire is that as we are taught by the Truth and liberated by the Life, we will more faithfully walk in the Way.

SUPPLEMENTAL OR COMPLEMENTARY TEACHING

If this CORE content represents what we consider primary content for the church, what would we count as secondary? The answer to this question, of course, will look different from context to context, since it is largely because of our secondary doctrines that there is so much (beautiful) diversity and (dreadful) division in the body of Christ. But we would suggest several broad categories to help congregations determine the teachings that might best complement and supplement the above.

First, church history. Augustine appears to have included an overview of church history in the *narratio* (the Story) he proposed for catechizing inquirers. Some may well agree with him in thus assigning to church history a place in the CORE itself. We will not loudly protest such an assignation. However, we think it best to treat this as a critical but supplemental piece of instruction because, unlike everything else in the proposed CORE, church history is not derived from the Scriptures. Therefore, our participation in God's Story—with all our failures and foibles—cannot be told with the same authority with which the Story itself is unfolded for us in Scripture, from creation to consummation. Nevertheless, somewhere in our plan we ought to include significant instruction in the church's history.

Second, denominational distinctives. This is the most obvious way to conceive of or frame those concerns we may call "secondary." The essentials of the Faith are addressed via the CORE as outlined above. Secondary doctrines are distinguished from these, and the drawing of this distinction is itself a vital part of Christian education. What makes us Baptist, for example, is vitally important

to us if we are Baptists. But it is not so important that it bars us from acknowledging as our brothers and sisters those from other traditions—so long as they
and we affirm together the Faith of the Gospel. We may add to our list of concerns at this point the matter of teaching those values and emphases that are
unique to our particular congregation. We address all this further under the
heading "Commitment to the Covenant Community" in chapter fourteen.

Third, timely teaching. Church leaders must always remain attentive to the
health and progress of their congregations and to the trends and events in the
surrounding culture. Such attentiveness will affect, on the one hand, the ways
in which we teach the essentials of the Faith. Following the lead of Jesus' own
teaching, our teaching should have the quality of "You have heard that it was
said, but God's word says to us . . ." On the other hand, paying attention to
cultural trends and events will also call forth timely topics for preaching,
teaching, reflection and action. Perhaps we will be drawn to particular biblical books or theological themes. In these ways, we labor continually to help
connect God's unchanging word to the circumstances in the ever-changing
world in which we live.

CONFRONTING THE FORCES OF MALFORMATION

One of the key ways that we have articulated our aims for the ministry of
teaching is that we labor to see people conformed to the likeness of Christ.
This is God's determination for all who are his (see Rom 8:29). When the
apostle Paul wrote of his desire to see everyone "perfect in Christ" (Col 1:28),
he was envisioning individuals and communities becoming fully formed in
Christ's likeness.

We might say that the ministry of discipleship involves *meeting people where
they are and then helping them go where they must go.* In light of what we have said
above, we have an understanding of the desired end. With Paul, we are aiming at Christlikeness, for both ourselves and those we serve—as individuals
and as congregations. We "press on to take hold of that for which Christ Jesus
took hold" of us (Phil 3:12). He laid hold of us to make us holy (see Heb 2:11)
as he is holy, and to bring us to glory (see Heb 2:10) with him (see Rom 8:28-
30; Col 3:4). We might articulate this end in various ways, but conformity to
Christ makes the point very well.

But as we noted earlier, we do not begin as unformed people and move
from there toward formation. No, we begin as *de*formed people or as *mal*-
formed people. We ourselves, as well as all those we have been called to serve,

Biblical References to Our Fallen Nature

- For no one living is righteous before you. (Ps 143:2)
- The heart is deceitful above all things and beyond cure. Who can understand it? (Jer 17:9)
- No one is good—except God alone. (Mk 10:18)
- There is no one righteous, not even one; there is no one who understands, no one who seeks God. All have turned away, they have together become worthless; there is no one who does good, not even one. (Rom 3:10-12)
- Therefore, just as sin entered the world through one man, and death through sin, and in this way death came to all men, because all sinned. (Rom 5:12)
- Through the disobedience of the one man the many were made sinners. (Rom 5:19)
- As for you, you were dead in your transgressions and sins. (Eph 2:1)
- Like the rest, we were by nature objects of wrath. (Eph 2:3)

are sinful, fallen, broken, wounded, dead and dying. Thus has it ever been from Adam forward. As the old catechetical poem in the *New England Primer* put it, "In Adam's fall, we sinned all." The biblical attestations of this reality are many (see the textbox above).

Our malformation is the product of both nature and nurture. It is confirmed and deepened by our own failings. Our malformation is further deepened by the broken world in which we live our broken lives.

ISMS, IDOLS AND EVIL PRACTICES

One feature of the malformation that we must confront concerns the cultural forces that are opposed to the heart and purposes of God. Culture is never neutral, and neither can our response to culture be neutral.[5] Where and when a given culture affirms the ways of God as revealed in Scripture, we should celebrate and connect with that culture as we teach the Gospel and implications to our community.[6]

---

[5]See Gary Parrett, "Becoming a Culturally Sensitive Minister," chapter seven in Elizabeth Conde-Frazier, S. Steve Kang and Gary A. Parrett, *A Many Colored Kingdom: Multicultural Dynamics for Spiritual Formation* (Grand Rapids: Baker, 2004), pp. 121-50.
[6]Parrett, "Becoming a Culturally Sensitive Minister," pp. 134-42.

When, on the other hand, the world's culture is moving in opposition to God, it is "the world" that we are to reject. "Do not love the world," John wrote, "or anything in the world" (1 Jn 2:15). The world, in this sense, is passing away, along with all its fallen desires (see 1 Jn 2:17). The followers of Jesus commit, rather, to do the will of the Father. Again, we do not minister to unformed people, but to malformed people. Said otherwise, it is not that people are uncatechized when we begin our ministry. Indeed, they have been very thoroughly catechized—but, tragically, in the ways of the fallen world rather than in the Way of the Lord.

With this catechetical reality in mind, we note that the world offers a fallen counterpart for every biblical path and every biblical truth. It offers counterfeit gospels and counterfeit narratives. In place of the Truth as revealed in Jesus, the world offers a variety of deceitful *isms*—false beliefs, lies that deceive and enslave. For those who refuse to believe and love the Truth and so be saved, God actually permits some to be led astray by the lies of the world (see 2 Thess 2:10-12).

In place of the Life that is found only in knowledge of the living God through Jesus Christ, the world offers an innumerable assortment of idols as vacuous substitutes for the one true God. Although we know there is only one true God, "there are many 'gods' and many 'lords'" (1 Cor 8:5). But these idols, which dazzle multitudes, ultimately offer death instead of life. For, made by hands of men, they "have eyes, but they cannot see . . . ears, but cannot hear. . . . Those who make them will be like them, and so will all who trust in them" (Ps 115:5, 8).

The false isms and the worthless idols are accompanied by evil practices that are a tragic substitute to the Way of the Lord. The Way of the Lord is a lifestyle of love—for God and neighbor, as we saw in chapter four. But the evil practices of the world move in precisely the opposite direction, with the self predominant in every decision and forging every habit.

These isms, idols and evil practices are sometimes universal, sometimes particular. Doubtless, there are certain of these that are common to all unredeemed persons, regardless of the culture or the age. But many of these will be particular to the given cultures in which we are called to minister. Therefore, the astute minister will be a faithful student of the specific culture in which he serves. He continually asks himself questions like the following:

• What are the pseudo-gospels of the culture that my congregants are trusting in?

- What is the story, the narrative, of the culture that is defining my congregants' view of themselves and of all reality?

- What are the isms of this culture in which my congregants have been catechized?

- What are the idols that compete for their affection and submission?

- What are the evil practices that they have been habituated toward?

Through all the teaching and formation ministries of the church, these isms, idols and evil practices must be actively confronted. In our preaching, our teaching, our worship, our fellowship, our service and in whatever we do as the church, we take relentless aim at these things. At times, we confront them in bold, frontal attacks. Delivering the Sermon on the Mount, Jesus repeated this refrain: "You have heard that it was said, . . . but I say to you . . ." (Mt 5:21-47). He first acknowledged the teaching that dominated the day, and then he confronted it head-on. He dismissed the popular conceptions with an authoritative word. Indeed, it was the fact that he taught as one having authority that made such an impression on his hearers.

In our various ministries, we must proceed in a similar spirit. We acknowledge the isms, idols and evil practices of the age and then confront them: "You have heard that it was said, but God's Word says to us . . ." In the history of catechetical work, this has been a common feature. The truths of the catechism are highlighted by noting the contrasts with the errors that dominate the day. In fact, without drawing the contrast, the full weight of what we intend to teach may be easily dismissed as insignificant, or simply missed altogether. When we ascend the pulpit, we do so not only with a humble spirit of fear and trembling at the awesome task ahead of us. We do so also with the authority of God's Word. We take aim at the culture's lies, at its gods and at its unholy habits. To fail to do so bespeaks either inattentiveness to the text from which we preach or a capitulation to the cultural forces at work around us. Thus many pulpits fail to assault racism, materialism, consumerism and much more. In failing to confront these things, we add our tacit approval to them. May God forgive us and change us.

As we seek to teach the CORE content—through the wide variety of activities we have noted and shall note in part four of this text—we must remain keenly aware of these countercatechetical forces that perpetually challenge us as we meet people where they are and try to help them go where they must go.

QUESTIONS FOR LEADERS TO CONSIDER

We realize that not all readers will be persuaded by our outline of what constitutes the Faith. Nevertheless, we urge all who are in positions of educational leadership in their churches to wrestle seriously with the issues we have raised concerning essential content. Along these lines, we suggest that attention be given to the following questions:

- What, if anything, is deemed essential content to help the believers in our congregation continue to grow up in their salvation?

- How many of those who regularly attend our church have been introduced to this content that we deem essential?

- What are the "delivery systems"—the processes, programs and venues— that the church utilizes to ensure that such content is reaching as many in the congregation as possible?

These questions can be applied to the education of believers of all ages. For the sake of illustration, we will focus attention on the education of adults as we try to tease out these issues.

First, it is critical that church leaders consider the matter of what they would deem essential content for the Christian education of church members, regular attendees and inquirers. The question might be framed thus: "If someone were regularly attending our church for a three-year span, what content would we want to be sure was presented (in some significant way) to him or her?" In our experiences of consulting with congregations about such matters, we have found that it is the rare pastor who has even considered such a critical question, let alone attempted to answer it.

This first question really ought to be taken up by church leaders with serious, sober and prayerful attention. In seeking to answer the question, we recommend that churches look to several sources for direction. First, primacy must be given to models and mandates of the Scriptures regarding what must be taught. Second, we ought to look to the wisdom of the church over the many centuries of its life and ministry.[7] Third, we also do well to consider the efforts of contemporary churches that are obviously approaching the teaching task very seriously.[8]

---

[7]See John Van Engen, ed., *Educating People of Faith: Exploring the History of Jewish and Christian Communities* (Grand Rapids: Eerdmans, 2004); O. C. Edwards Jr. and John Westerhoff III, *A Faithful Church: Issues in the History of Catechesis* (Eugene, Ore.: Wipf and Stock, 2003).

[8]But we caution against merely copying the efforts of those churches that appear to be successful. It is easy to fall into such a trap, in part because many large churches mass-produce their

A consideration of this first question may well produce a broad list of topics or themes that are deemed essential. To help us consider the second and third of our three questions, let us assume that a church has generated a list of themes, concluding that its members really must be instructed in the following eight areas: (1) an introduction to and overview of the Bible; (2) the basics of Christian belief; (3) Christian worship and prayer; (4) Christian worldview and ethics; (5) the life and ministry of the local church; (6) the life and health of the family; (7) spiritual gifts and Christian service; (8) evangelism and world mission. Such a list would not satisfy every church, of course, and even within a church it would probably emerge only after lengthy discussions and perhaps some difficult negotiations among those charged with generating the list.

With such a list in hand, the church can then begin to address, as honestly as possible, the second question: How many of those who regularly worship with us have, at present, been introduced to these things we consider to be essential? In many churches, the answer to this question will likely be discouraging. If we are to believe the data reported by those who have surveyed the American evangelical landscape in recent years, most churches will find that few of their members have more than a modicum of understanding about such things.[9]

Our third question deals with the matter of delivery systems—the settings and venues for offering such instruction. Perhaps the church does, after all, have some sense of what it considers essential content for its members. The list may be smaller or larger than what we have outlined above. But for the sake of argument, we will stay with the seven items that were suggested there. How has the church been presenting its members and regular attendees with this content? Is it presented in a systematic manner through the sermons and other elements of the worship service?

For many churches, this is doubtful, since many evangelical sermons tend to be primarily exhortational, rather than instructional, in nature and emphasis. As for the rest of the gathered worship, it is true that the liturgical design of the church is always powerfully formative. But sometimes our worship forms us more for ill than for good, and it is too frequently the case that our worship services are designed and led in an ad hoc fashion, with little or no effort to combine concern for worship with concern for formation and instruction.[10]

---

materials and distribute them through impressive marketing campaigns.

[9]The Barna Group, "Christians Say They Do Best at Relationships, Worst in Bible Knowledge," <www.barna.org/barna-update/article/5-barna-update/177-Christians-say-they-do-best-at-relationships-worst-in-bible-knowledge>.

[10]We address these issues at length in chapter twelve.

Is the church presenting its essential teaching in adult Sunday school classes? Perhaps some do, but many churches no longer offer Sunday school classes for adults. In fact, in an apparent effort to be as convenient as possible for as many as possible, more and more churches are offering Sunday school for children simultaneously with worship services for adults. Whatever the gains of such an approach, this typically also results in two significant losses: children are not worshiping with their parents, and parents are not being as well instructed (formally, at least) as their children are.

What of those churches where adult Sunday school is still in place? In that case, we must ask a few follow-up questions. First, how many of the regular attendees actually participate in adult Sunday school? The answer to this may also prove discouraging; perhaps only a small percentage takes advantage of this learning opportunity. Then we ask a further question: of the classes that are being offered, how many are concerned with the content that we have labeled "essential"? Even in churches where a healthy adult Sunday school program is still in place, many of the class offerings are effectively "electives" rather than "requirements."

In other words, at any given time, the church may offer several classes, and those offerings may simply be the function of who was interested in offering a certain course at that particular time. Thus one class may be a study on a book of the Bible. Another may involve discussing a Christian book that has been recently published. Yet another may be concerned with managing finances well. Still another may be an introduction to basic Christian beliefs. But these are all offered without any guidance for learners regarding the relative "weightiness" of each class. All four offerings are effectively electives—church members may elect to take any of these they wish to, though most will likely elect to participate in none of them.

Some churches, finding that their Sunday school classes were no longer being well attended, have decided to move their energy toward a small-group model. In some cases, this has resulted in a new teaching venue that is effective and is reaching a significant number of congregants. In many cases, however, the small group turns out to be a good setting for fostering fellowship and accountability, but not necessarily for substantive teaching of the essentials of the Faith. In some cases, the studies that do take place in small-group settings devolve into rather uninformed and highly subjective "sharing" about the Bible: "So, what does this text mean to *you?*"

Where then is the church offering its members deep induction into what is deemed essential? In brief, our counsel would be to retain and maximize those venues that are presently working well. Those that seem no longer to be working should not be maintained simply because "we've always done it that way." The Sunday school model, for example, may work wonderfully in one setting but horribly in another. We ought not to regard the structure itself as sacrosanct, especially since the modern Sunday school movement is less than three hundred years old. For most of two millennia, the church carried out its educational formation ministries in other ways. Many congregations may simply conclude that, while the program was effective for a time, it may not be any longer and thus should be abandoned in favor of other approaches and strategies.

I know of a church that moved its primary teaching times to Friday night because this worked very well for the congregation—made up largely of collegians and young adults. I know of another church that moved from a Sunday school program to a Thursday evening program for children. In both cases, attendance and overall effectiveness increased dramatically. In my own church, leaders have discussed initiating a quarterly seminar model. On four weekends throughout the year—from Friday evening through Saturday evening—members and all who are interested would be invited (urged, in fact) to participate in teaching sessions that focus exclusively on matters deemed essential by church leaders.

Church leaders should not make moves like these too hastily, however. To begin a new program, only to have to scuttle it shortly thereafter because it was not well thought out, often proves very disheartening to members and makes them more skeptical about future endeavors.

In any event, we need a balanced approach in the matter of "delivery systems." In most cases, no single venue can carry all the cargo we would ask it to. To truly learn in that essential component we labeled above as "Christian worship and prayer," for example, multiple venues will be necessary. Members may learn biblical principles about these things in a formal setting. But the worship gatherings and prayer groups of the church will be even more fruitful venues. Again, we are reminded that biblical teaching is multiform and that those things we consider essential content are multifaceted. A robust teaching ministry should become the backbone of all that we do as a church, to help us better connect, grow and function as the body of Jesus Christ.

HYMN FOR CONTEMPLATION AND WORSHIP

The Truth, the Life, the Way

In Jesus Christ the Way is found!
His light illumines solid ground.
O Wisdom! Hallelujah!
To love our neighbor and our God,
we walk the path that Jesus trod.
O worship and adore him.
With your strength come, bow before him.
Hallelujah!

In Jesus Christ the Truth is clear!
In him the unseen things appear.
O Myst'ry! Hallelujah!
The sacred scroll is no more sealed;
God's deepest thought has been revealed.
O worship and adore him.
With your mind come, bow before him.
Hallelujah!

In Jesus Christ the Life is ours!
Death's claim on us has lost its pow'rs.
O Fountain! Hallelujah!
The Spirit-waters in us spring,
and we cry "Abba!" to the King.
O worship and adore him.
With your soul come, bow before him.
Hallelujah!

Jesus—the Truth, the Life, the Way!
In him the veil is torn away.
O Fullness! Hallelujah!
All deity in him abides
and in our spirits he resides.
O worship and adore him.
With your heart come, bow before him.
Hallelujah!

Text: Gary A. Parrett (1999)
Tune: Lasst Uns Erfreuen
Familiar use of the tune: "All Creatures of Our God and King"

QUESTIONS FOR PLANNING AND PRACTICE

1. Rehearse the three types of curriculum—explicit, implicit and null—discussed in this chapter. Have you ever had the realization that you may not be teaching what you think you are teaching (as in the example of the Bible-study teacher described in this chapter utilizing illegal photocopies in a lesson on the eighth commandment)? We invite you to discuss with a fellow Christian any instances where something similar has occurred in your own ministry.

2. Does your church's educational ministry reflect the CORE content discussed in the chapter? In which aspect of this CORE do you see the greatest need for the church to grow? How might such growth be pursued?

3. "We might speak of the ministry of discipleship as *meeting people where they are and then helping them to go where they must go.*" Does this describe your vision of discipleship? How does this relate to the Way of the Lord that we are called to walk in, as discussed in the previous chapter? What might such a vision of discipleship actually look like in practice? How do you see this being practiced in your educational formation ministry?

4. What "isms, idols and evil practices" have you encountered that challenged you in your attempts to help people grow in discipleship? Which do you consider to be the most dangerous in the world today that could potentially test the church? Which do you personally seem especially susceptible to or sense that you have been influenced by? How is God prompting you to address some of those issues in your life or in the lives of those among whom you are called to minister?

5. Consider how educational formation ministry is conceptualized and practiced in your church. Are there various groups that are divided according to age levels, or are families together, or both? What benefits and challenges do you see in your existing structures for educational formation ministry?

6. What, if anything, is deemed essential content to help the believers in your congregation continue to grow up in their salvation? How many of those who regularly attend your church have truly been introduced to this essential content? Finally, what are the "delivery systems"—the processes, programs and venues—that the church utilizes to ensure that such content is reaching as many in the congregation as possible?

RESOURCES FOR FURTHER STUDY

Edwards, O. C., Jr., and John Westerhoff III, eds. *A Faithful Church: Issues in the History of Catechesis.* Eugene, Ore.: Wipf and Stock, 2003.

Hall, Christopher. *Reading Scripture with the Church Fathers.* Downers Grove, Ill.: InterVarsity Press, 1998.

Harris, Maria. *Fashion Me A People: Curriculum in the Church.* Louisville, Ky.: Westminster/John Knox Press, 1989.

Marthaler, Berard. *The Catechism Yesterday and Today: The Evolution of a Genre.* Collegeville, Minn.: Liturgical Press, 1995.

Noll, Mark. *Turning Points: Decisive Moments in the History of Christianity.* Grand Rapids: Baker, 1997.

Pazmiño. Robert W. *Principles and Practices of Christian Education: An Evangelical Perspective.* Grand Rapids: Baker, 1992.

PART 3

PEOPLE

Of Teachers and Learners

"What we need more than anything else today is not textbooks, but text people."

ABRAHAM HESCHEL, *I ASKED FOR WONDER*

▼

THE QUOTE ABOVE IS FROM ABRAHAM JOSHUA HESCHEL, twentieth-century rabbi, philosopher and activist. It captures well a critically important truth: the best possible way for us to teach others is in and through our very lives. Henri Nouwen, another important religious leader of the twentieth century, likewise suggested that the best that Christian leaders can offer others is themselves. He wrote, "I am fully persuaded that the Christian leader of the next century should be completely irrelevant, offering nothing to the world except his own, vulnerable self."[1]

In this book's first section, we examined the great Story into which God has called us. Helping others find their places in this Story, we who are called to teach and lead need to actively and faithfully play our own parts. In the second section of this book, we considered the glorious Gospel and various aspects of the Faith. To proclaim these well calls us once again to a certain manner of living. We must ourselves believe the Gospel we proclaim, diligently study the Truth

---

[1]Henri Nouwen, *In the Name of Jesus: Reflections on Christian Leadership* (New York: Crossroad, 1993), p. 30.

we affirm, drink deeply of the Life we offer and walk in the Way to which we point others.

This third section of the book calls attention to the people of God, in several respects. First, in chapter six, we examine the biblical data regarding who ought to assume teaching roles in the Christian community. In chapter seven, we look at a variety of attributes for Christlike teachers. In chapters eight and nine, we focus on theories of learning and development so that we may better understand how we—as the people of God—can best grow as a true community of learners and Christ-followers.

The role of interpersonal relationships has always been a vital component in ministries of Christian formation. Each of us is called to grow in intimacy with Christ, the Head of the church. We must also grow in our understandings of and partnerships with one another. Then the body "builds itself up in love, as each part does it work" (Eph 4:16) and so can walk more faithfully in the good works that God has prepared for us.

6

Teachers Among Us

Not many of you should presume to be teachers, my brothers,
because you know that we who teach will be judged more strictly.

JAMES 3:1

▼

ONE EVENING MANY YEARS AGO, at a large church where I was serving among youth and collegians, a young woman in our college ministry brought her friend as a visitor to our Friday evening gatherings. They arrived early at our facilities, and so they took a walking tour around the building. They happened on the elder who was overseeing the children's Sunday school ministry, and our member—who was herself a Sunday school teacher—warmly greeted the elder and introduced her friend to him.

The elder seemed overly enthused to meet this young woman. It turns out there was a pressing need to replace a recently resigned teacher for the children. Now, he was persuaded, God had answered his prayers and provided just the person. The young woman, who was visiting our church for the very first time, was offered the position on the spot and accepted it without hesitation. Her host did not want to embarrass her friend by telling the elder that this might not be the best idea since, after all, her friend was not a Christian. Two days later, she was on the job.

In the mercies of God, the young woman was soon converted through her own interaction with the curriculum materials that she was asked to teach to the children. But none of us, I sincerely trust and earnestly pray, will want to adopt this elder's approach to teacher recruitment.

As we have seen, the teaching ministry of the church is biblically mandated and vital to the formation of the people of God. Our mission in teaching is clear: we labor to come alongside believers and believing communities in becoming more like Jesus Christ. Our message also is clear: we proclaim Christ himself—in and through the glorious Gospel, together with the doctrines, blessings and imperatives that flow from it.

In preaching and teaching the Gospel of Christ, we recognize that we have been entrusted with a priceless treasure, and "we have this treasure in jars of clay to show that this all-surpassing power is from God and not from us" (2 Cor 4:7). As the following survey of the scriptural record indicates, God has made flawed and finite humans the stewards of this transforming message. Clearly, Christian ministers dare not depend on themselves as they engage in these works of eternal consequence. Thus Paul writes, "Not that we are competent in ourselves to claim anything for ourselves, but our competence comes from God" (2 Cor 3:5).

TEACHERS IN THE OLD TESTAMENT
AND IN JEWISH PRACTICE

When God formed a people of his own during Old Testament times, he graciously gave to the people of Israel not only the Torah but also human teachers. *Torah*—if it is to be translated into English at all—is better rendered "guidance" or "instruction" than our typical choice of "law." Deriving from the same root come a key verb for teaching, *yarah,* and two related words: *moreh* and *horeh.* A *moreh* is a teacher. *Horeh* is a very particular teacher—the male parent (*horah* is the female parent).

The Hebrew Scriptures make it clear that teaching—whether construed as inscripturated or incarnated—is primarily concerned with guidance in the Way of the Lord. The Way of the Lord is discerned by contemplation of and obedience to the Torah of the Lord. Human teachers also are to help others discern this Way. Isaiah 30:20-21 illustrates the point for us:

> Although the Lord gives you the bread of adversity and the water of affliction, your teachers [*morekha*] will be hidden no more; with your own eyes you will see them. Whether you turn to the right or to the left, your ears will hear a voice behind you, saying, "This is the way; walk in it."

The idea is present also in Psalm 32:8: "I will instruct you and teach [the verb *yarah* is used here] you in the way you should go; I will counsel you and watch over you."

The principle for teaching that we derive is clear: our aim is to help people walk in the Way of the Lord. This is no surprise to us in light of our earlier comments about *teaching unto obedience* to all that Jesus commanded (see Mt 28:20). Furthermore, it is not only that teachers are to aim at this when working with learners using biblical texts. It is also that teachers' very lives must direct disciples in the Way of the Lord. Christians can easily see the wisdom of Heschel's statement that we need "text people" more than we need textbooks (quoted at the beginning of this chapter), for God himself affirmed it when his own perfect *Logos,* his only-begotten Son, became flesh for us in the incarnation of Christ (see Jn 1:1, 14, 18).

A teacher of the Faith then can be said to be a sort of living Torah. This reminds us of Paul's words to the Corinthians: "You yourselves are our letter, written on our hearts, known and read by everybody. You show that you are a letter from Christ, the result of our ministry, written not with ink but with the Spirit of the living God, not on tablets of stone but on tablets of human hearts" (2 Cor 3:2-3). Paul's words here were a sort of appeal to the believers in Corinth to live up to such a call. All of us who are called to be teachers in faith should share similar aspirations.

This is not to suggest that the passing on of knowledge in more familiar, didactic ways is unimportant. Indeed, such work is critical. But the passing on of truth, tradition, instruction, commandment, story and so on is the penultimate, not the ultimate, concern of the teacher. The ultimate concern is obedience. Said otherwise, while information is a vital component of good teaching, it is not an end itself. Information is vital, when properly ingested for the glory of God, because of the role it plays in the formation of believers—individually and corporately—in Christlikeness.

Another insight to be drawn from the Hebrew word *yarah* and related terms concerns the preeminent place of parents as teachers in the covenant community. In Jewish thought, the father is *the* teacher who is responsible for the spiritual education of his children. The Jewish home is taken to be a small sanctuary.[2] The father is the priest, and the dinner table is the altar. All other teachers—including the mother, and any other teachers who are to be part of the upbringing of the children—have a derived teaching authority. They are authorized, as it were, by the father, who assumes a "buck stops here" responsibility in this matter.[3]

The notion of parental, and especially paternal, primacy in teaching is

---

[2]See Marvin Wilson, *Our Father Abraham: Jewish Roots of the Christian Faith* (Grand Rapids: Eerdmans, 1989), pp. 214-17.
[3]Ibid., pp. 279-80.

affirmed by both Old Testament and New Testament texts. In the Old Testament, the texts concerning the parental role in teaching are common. In passages such as Deuteronomy 6 and 11, as well as Judges 2:10 and following (sadly, a negative example), and Psalm 78, we read of the importance of passing on both the commands and the narrative of God's mighty deeds to younger generations.

In the same texts, it is evident that parents are to be the key players in these tasks. Deuteronomy 6:1-9 especially makes it clear that parents are central in this regard. Speaking about the commandments, the text says, "Impress them on your children. Talk about them when you sit at home and when you walk along the road, when you lie down and when you get up. Tie them as symbols on your hands and bind them on your foreheads. Write them on the doorframes of your houses and on your gates" (Deut 6:7-9). Clearly the primary venue for such activities is the family, in its own home and in its daily affairs. Still, the whole community must come alongside the parents to nurture the next generations together in the context of a symbiotic relationship among the families *in* the community.

Churches must realize that it takes the whole community of faith to raise the children of that community *in* the Faith. But, as we will explore in chapter eleven, many American churches have moved with fierce determination to separate the generations from one another to provide more generation-specific ministry. Tragically, such an approach to ministry can easily have the effect of encouraging the segregated "generations" to be unduly absorbed with their own needs and to have little concern for others. This runs both ways—from older to younger and younger to older. But it is the younger who suffer most in such an arrangement. And it is the older who will have to give account for shirking their God-appointed duties toward the young.

In Old Testament times, God also raised up and used other teachers to help shape his people Israel. In Jeremiah 18, three categories of teachers are mentioned. We read, "For the teaching of the law by the priest will not be lost, nor will counsel from the wise, nor the word from the prophets" (Jer 18:18). Old Testament scholar Walter Brueggemann has argued that the passage points us to three types of teachers and three types of teaching. The teachers are priests, sages and prophets. The type of teaching represented by each corresponds to the three divisions of the Hebrew Scriptures—respectively, the Torah, the Writings and the Prophets (as discssed in chapter five).

Thinking of the priests as embodying Torah, the sages as embodying wisdom and the prophets as embodying zeal for the Lord,[4] we gain insight into how we, as Christian teachers, ought to embody the content we proclaim. When we proclaim the Truth of God, we present our lives as diligent students of that Truth. When we proclaim the Life of God, we model a holy thirsting after God expressed in worship and prayer. When we proclaim the Way of God, we commit ourselves to walk in that Way with increasing integrity. When we proclaim the Gospel to others, we are careful to preach it perpetually to ourselves.

To the list of priests, prophets and sages, we must also add mention of the role of scribe. From the time of the exile onward, scribes were Torah scholars who studied and taught the Scriptures. (By Jesus' day, scribes were called rabbis.) Ezra—the Hebrew scribe who played so pivotal a role among the exiles returning to Jerusalem from captivity—provides us with a wonderful example for all engaged in ministries of teaching. We read of him that he had "set his heart to the study the Law of the LORD, and to do it and to teach his statutes and rules in Israel" (Ezra 7:10 ESV). The order of Ezra's threefold commitment is challenging and instructive. He devoted himself first to the *study* of Torah. Next, he committed himself to *do* Torah. His determination to *teach* Torah was third, built on the sure foundation of the first two commitments.

God help us who feel called to teach others to heed the wisdom here. When "teachers" teach without having first been careful students themselves, they can easily fall into error and propagate error. When they presume to teach God's commands to others but do not themselves seek to obey God's commands, they are like those scribes in Jesus' day whom the Lord rebuked for their hypocrisy. They were quick to "tie up heavy loads and put them on men's shoulders, but they themselves are not willing to lift a finger to move them" (Mt 23:4). Study, do and teach. May Ezra's way be our way.

TEACHERS IN THE NEW TESTAMENT

The most important of all the New Testament teachers is, of course, Jesus himself. (In chapter ten we will consider his teaching ministry in some detail.) Jesus extended his own teaching ministry through the apostles. Our focus at this point, however, is to consider who is called to the role of teacher in the church today, based on the witness of the New Testament writings.

As we have seen, the New Testament features many points of continuity

---

[4]Another insight from Heschel, who sees the Hebrew prophets as embodying the divine *pathos.* Abraham. J. Heschel, *The Prophets,* 2 vols. (New York: Harper & Row, 1962), 2:1-103; see also E. R. Fraser, "Symbolic Acts of the Prophets," *Studia Biblica et Theologica* 4 (1974): 45-53.

with the emphases of the Old in regard to teachers. For example, it affirms the principle of parental—especially paternal—priority in the spiritual nurture of children. Paul writes to the Ephesians, "Fathers, do not exasperate your children; instead, raise them up in the training and instruction of the Lord" (Eph 6:4). The reference to fathers affirms the principle we noted in Jewish thought—that fathers are to take final responsibility as spiritual heads of their households. But elsewhere, Paul makes it clear that the formative role of mothers is also critical. Children are to obey both their parents in the Lord (see Eph 6:1; Col 3:20), and younger women in the church are exhorted to love their husbands and children with a view to the formation of a spiritually sound household (see Tit 2:4-5; see also 2 Tim 1:5).

There are also hints of discontinuity between the Testaments on the matter of the teachers among us. Most striking is that, in light of the outpouring of the Holy Spirit during the feast of Pentecost, it is apparent that teaching gifts and responsibilities have been extended to more individuals than had been the case before. As we have seen, parents continue to have primacy, so far as the nurture of children is concerned. But whereas the Old Testament featured only a few specific teaching roles—priests, prophets, sages, scribes—from Pentecost forward, many more are charged with different aspects of the teaching task.

In Acts 2, as Peter interpreted for his hearers the strange events that occurred among the Jesus-followers in Jerusalem that day, he made appeal to a prophecy from the second chapter of Joel: "'In the last days, God says, I will pour out my Spirit on all people. Your sons and daughters will prophesy, your young men will see visions, your old men will dream dreams. Even on my servants, both men and women, I will pour out my Spirit in those days, and they will prophesy'" (Acts 2:17-18; compare Joel 2:28-29). The Spirit of God had come on only a very few with prophetic power and gifting in the Old Testament, but now he was being poured out on the entire nascent church— men and women, young and old alike!

In light of this Pentecost reality, it is no surprise that we find so many charged with the teaching task in the course of the New Testament writings. The apostles, of course, were foundational teachers. From the very beginning, the church submitted itself to their teaching (see Acts 2:42). As the Gospel moved forward with power, and as local congregations were established, it is clear that Christ distributed among the churches other gifted leaders as well: prophets, evangelists, pastors and teachers (see Eph 4:11).[5] Over time, pastors

---

[5]The passage raises several questions for us. First, is this a fourfold ministry or a fivefold minis-

and teachers (or pastor-teachers) become the most enduring leaders charged with congregational nurture. It seems most likely that "pastor-teacher" becomes synonymous with other titles used elsewhere in the New Testament, including "elder" and "overseer." These, too, are plainly charged with the tasks of teaching and shepherding (see Acts 20:28; 1 Tim 3:2; Tit 1:9; 1 Pet 5:1-4; the "leaders" mentioned in Heb 13:7, 17, are most likely also elders). Some of the elders were especially gifted and called to serve in ministries of preaching and teaching (see 1 Tim 5:17).

Aside from those in specific leadership roles such as the ones noted above, there were others in the New Testament churches who evidently were given spiritual gifts of teaching and/or responsibilities for some form of teaching. The spiritual gift of teaching is mentioned in several passages, including Romans 12:7 and 1 Corinthians 12:28-29. While it may be the case that this gift was given only to those occupying specific roles such as that of "elder," this is not made expressly clear in the passages. We do know, however, that there were many prophets functioning in various churches and that women were included in their numbers (see Acts 21:9; 1 Cor 11:5). There were also itinerant preachers and teachers who traveled from church to church for the sake of edifying the believers, as is evident from the letters of John and elsewhere.

We discover also in the New Testament that mature believers were expected to teach those younger and less mature. Thus Paul told Titus that the older women should teach the younger women in matters of appropriate lifestyle (see Tit 2:4). Similarly, Paul commanded Timothy to entrust what he had learned from Paul "to reliable men who will also be qualified to teach others" (2 Tim 2:2). And the writer to the Hebrews rebuked his readers for the fact that, though they ought to have been teaching others by then, they themselves were still in need of rudimentary instruction (see Heb 5:12).

We must speak also of the part that all members in the churches were to play in teaching one another. They were to teach one another through "psalms, hymns and spiritual songs" (Eph 5:19) and were to "admonish one another with all wisdom" (Col 3:16). When they came together for worship,

try? The answer depends on whether we see "pastor and teacher" as one role or two. Grammar seems to argue for the former, but the experience of many churches suggests that something like the latter is often in place: that is, there are many faithful and effective teachers in the church who are not pastors. A second question concerns whether or not the offices here mentioned are enduring for the entire church age. Some argue that the role of apostles was a first-century-only role that God used in laying the foundations of the church. Others would include prophets here as well, and perhaps even evangelists. Many others, however, believe that all of these areas of gifted leadership are still to be functioning in God's churches today.

everyone was to bring something for the building up of the others (see 1 Cor 14:26).[6] Peter puts special emphasis on the need to care for one's own soul as well, writing, "Make every effort to add to your faith goodness; and to goodness, knowledge" (2 Pet 1:5). He expresses similar concerns when he addresses all his readers, "But grow in the grace and knowledge of our Lord and Savior Jesus Christ" (2 Pet 3:18).

Ministering in and through all of these human teachers, of course, is the Holy Spirit. He is "the Spirit of truth" (Jn 14:17; 15:26), given to believers in order to testify about Jesus (see Jn 15:26) and guide us into all truth (see Jn 16:13). All the post-Pentecost teaching endowments that we have outlined above are fulfillments of these promises about the Spirit's ministry. Every believer has "an anointing from the Holy One," enabling us to know the truth (1 Jn 2:20). We should not merely pay lip service to the Spirit's role in teaching, but should realize that apart from his ministry in our midst we can accomplish nothing of lasting value. Thus we heed Augustine's insights that, in light of the True Teacher, we who are human teachers must be learners ourselves, and we must intercede for those we are called to serve.[7]

TEACHERS IN CONTEMPORARY CHURCHES

How do the teachers in our churches today correspond to those mentioned in the New Testament? Typically, the most prominent teachers in the educational ministry of a local congregation are volunteers who work in the Sunday school program or who lead small-group Bible studies. At first glance, it may not be obvious how such teachers correspond to the New Testament list we observed above. Are these pastors or elders? Sometimes they are, but often they are not. Are they endowed with the spiritual gift of teaching? Again, sometimes the answer is yes, but it often seems to be no. Then perhaps we have missed the mark by having the bulk of our teaching done by people other than those who seem to be biblically sanctioned for such ministries.

---

[6]One major concern that the church faces today is that many adult Christians think they no longer need to learn and continue growing in the Way of the Lord. Many convince themselves that participating in the corporate worship service once a week suffices for their life as disciples of the Lord, perhaps because they think they have learned all they needed to learn about God in Sunday school in their early years. It is no wonder that many adults in the church do not participate in the plethora of mutual teaching and learning opportunities, building one another up as fellow disciples of the Lord. It is also little wonder that the children and youth in the church are not acculturated or motivated to engage in the lifestyle of serious teaching, learning and serving.
[7]See William J. Harmless, *Augustine and the Catechumenate* (Collegeville, Minn.: Liturgical Press, 1995), pp. 221-24.

Certainly this is so if and when we have placed people in teaching roles whose Christian faith, character and knowledge are suspect.

However, many of our teaching volunteers may be doing precisely what they should be doing as they serve the congregation. In many cases, they will be applying the principle of the "more mature" teaching the "less mature," a principle we saw in passages like 2 Timothy 2:2 and Titus 2:1-8. Some are indeed also gifted with spiritual gifts of teaching, and others are, in fact, elders or pastors of the church. Sadly, however, many who ought to see themselves as key players in the educational ministry of their churches simply do not. Pastors and parents are often two examples of this.

PASTORS AND THE TEACHING MINISTRY

In recent decades, many pastors seem to have all but forsaken the teaching task as a key aspect of their ministry. This is very evident at the large Christian education conferences offered throughout the United States. These conferences are generally attended by volunteers and by associate staff members of congregations. Senior pastors are most often very conspicuous by their absence. Talk to a pastor about this, and he may reply, "Oh, we send all our CE [Christian education] people to such events." Articulated or not, this mindset reveals that the pastor does not see himself as a "CE" person. One might argue that the pastor, having been trained at a seminary or Bible college, has already received adequate training in educational ministry and thus does not need to attend such conferences. This is often simply not so, however. Many seminaries have dispensed with a requirement in this area, and those that still offer any training in it generally require only one course in the field.

The real issue seems to be that many pastors simply do not regard themselves as needing to be active leaders in the educational ministries of their churches. This may be, at least in part, an unintended outcome of the modern Sunday school movement. From its very inception, Sunday school has been a lay-driven ministry. This has had the benefit of involving more people in the teaching ministry of our churches, often bringing into the task people who had the requisite gifting and character but little opportunity to serve. On the other hand, it has often meant that pastors have moved away from active involvement in this area of ministry. The bottom line is that the one person in the congregation who probably has the most biblical and theological training and who may have the most obvious gift for teaching the Faith is often effectively absent in the formal teaching ministry of his congregation.

Of course, many pastors have diligently maintained a vital teaching role. This may take the form of teaching Bible classes on a regular basis. Or it may be that they "teach the teachers," who then teach other members of the congregation. Or they may see the weekly sermon(s) as their primary teaching venue. It seems, though, that many pastors have simply abandoned the task of significant teaching altogether. They are not involved in what is officially labeled "Christian education" in their churches. The sermon is utilized primarily for evangelism or some form of exhortation.

The notion of a pastor who is *not* fundamentally concerned with teaching would be unthinkable to many generations of pastors that have gone before us. We may think of pastors in the Reformation era—Luther and Calvin, for example, or of the great Puritan pastors, such as John Owen and Richard Baxter. Baxter's classic work *The Reformed Pastor,* though often used in pastoral ministry classes because of its clarion call to pastoral integrity in life, is really an extended argument for pastoral engagement in catechizing each member of the flock. Baxter would have regarded the idea of a pastor who is not the congregation's primary teacher as unconscionable.

When and where it is the case that pastors are no longer deliberately and actively engaged in the teaching ministry of the church, we may well ask, what exactly *are* these pastors doing? Historically, the understanding has been that every church in every age and in every culture must be engaged in three tasks: worship, teaching or nurture, and evangelism.[8] We have just suggested that many pastors have delegated the task of teaching to others. This has also been increasingly true of worship. Whereas many pastors would have previously seen themselves as the "worship leader" of their church, this is less and less often the case. We see at work here an unintended consequence of the so-called worship wars—in which "the guitars beat the organs"[9]—namely that pastors have forsaken leadership of yet another of the church's three great tasks. "Worship leading" is now often the domain of a talented young guitarist or keyboard player who, in many if not most cases, has little or no theological training.

What, then? Has the pastor now shifted all of her leadership skills and passion to the third of the great tasks, that of evangelism? In some cases, this may be so. Many pastors are certainly deeply concerned with "reaching as many people as possible for Christ." But often the pastor's energies are not really

---

[8]See Robert Webber, *Journey to Jesus: Worship, Evangelism and Nurture Mission of the Church* (Nashville: Abingdon, 2001).
[9]Michael Hamilton, "The Triumph of the Praise Songs: How Guitars Beat out the Organ in the Worship Wars," *Christianity Today,* July 12, 1999, pp. 29-35.

focused on evangelism either. So what are pastors doing? Marva Dawn has argued that many pastors have moved from having an identity of shepherd to having that of CEO.[10] Likewise, Eugene Peterson has long lamented pastors forsaking what he suggests ought always to be their principal concerns: laboring in the Word, laboring in prayer and caring for souls.[11]

Not all the blame should go to pastors, of course. The fact that many churches have so thoroughly adopted a "solo pastor" model of ministry has certainly done a great deal of damage, not only to overburdened pastors but also to the congregations themselves. Many pastors today live with the pressure of wholly unrealistic and unhealthy expectations. They are asked to fill all manner of roles, from vision caster to budget manager to facilities manager to all-purpose counselor and on and on. All such roles are expected to be above and beyond the "obvious" commitment to preach a "good sermon" each Sunday and to help, at least, with the design and conduct of the public worship services of the church.

Even as such unhealthy, unbiblical and unwise expectations are in place, pastors are abandoning their calling. Peterson writes,

> American pastors are abandoning their posts, left and right, and at an alarming rate. They are not leaving their churches and getting other jobs. Congregations still pay their salaries. Their names remain on the church stationary and they continue to appear in pulpits on Sundays. But they are abandoning their posts, their *calling*. They have gone whoring after other gods. What they do with their time under the guise of pastoral ministry hasn't the remotest connections with what the church's pastors have done for most of twenty centuries.[12]

Pastors and teachers will do well to heed Peterson's advice to resist the cries to leave their God-appointed posts. He maintains that "'working the angles' is what we do when nobody is watching. It is repetitive and often boring. It is blue collar, not dog collar work." Therefore, we are to call "the attention of [our] brothers and sisters in pastoral ministry to what all our predecessors agreed was basic in the practice of our calling, to insist that pastoral work has no integrity unconnected with the angles of prayer, Scripture, and spiritual direction."[13]

---

[10]Marva Dawn, *Is It a Lost Cause? Having the Heart of God for the Church's Children* (Grand Rapids: Eerdmans, 1997), pp. 93-95.

[11]Eugene Peterson, *Working the Angles: The Shape of Pastoral Integrity* (Grand Rapids: Eerdmans, 1987).

[12]Peterson, *Working the Angles*, p. 1.

[13]Ibid., p. 12.

PARENTS AND THE TEACHING MINISTRY

Baxter's vision of pastoral ministry, as articulated in *The Reformed Pastor,* has sometimes been critiqued as actually contributing to the problem of an unhealthy and unrealistic vision of pastoral labor. By all accounts, Baxter was able to be part of the spiritual transformation of the entire town of Kidderminster, England, during his years of ministry there in the mid-seventeenth century. But, it should be noted, he was a single man when he labored so indefatigably for the conversion and catechizing of his parish. Only after his ministry at Kidderminster did Baxter marry. He argues forcibly for the necessity of unceasing hard work, writing, "What is a candle made for but to be burnt? Burnt and wasted we must be; and is it not more reasonable that it should be in lighting men to heaven, and in working for God, than in living to the flesh?"[14]

But some may see Baxter, at this point, as not only unreasonable but also lacking a certain credibility. They may well ask, is it wise, or even possible, for a pastor today, especially one who is married with children, to follow Baxter's example? Others critique Baxter as unwisely arguing for a concentration of ministry in the hand of the pastor when it ought to be shared by the whole congregation. Baxter may have been committed to a ministry of personal catechizing, but his commitment to equipping the saints for ministry seems to have been much weaker.

These concerns about Baxter's vision of ministry are significant. But they may be a bit unfair or overstated. In the first place, it must be kept in mind that his book was addressed to fellow pastors. It is altogether reasonable then that he should focus on the duties of his pastor in his remarks, rather than on the duties of others in the flock. Even with his focus on pastors, Baxter does not envision that they should take upon themselves all the work of evangelism and instruction. He does suggest that help for the task should be sought. On the one hand, help should be sought in the form of pastoral assistants. These should be hired as needed, even if it means the pastor must share his salary with them.[15]

The primary helpers that Baxter has in view, however, are parents. He argues that parents bear primary responsibility for catechizing their chil-

---

[14]Richard Baxter, *The Reformed Pastor: A Discourse on the Pastoral Office* (London: Paternoster-Row, 1808), pp. 144-45.

[15]Baxter, *The Reformed Pastor,* pp. 34-35, in the electronic format from Christian Classical Ethereal Library at <http://www.ccel.org/ccel/baxter/pastor.pdf>. (Accessed June 30, 2008.)

dren. In this critical area, pastors take a secondary and supplementary role.[16] Baxter writes,

> We must have a special eye upon families, to see that they are well ordered, and the duties of each relation performed. The life of religion, and the welfare and glory of both the church and the State, depend much on family government and duty. If we suffer the neglect of this, we shall undo all. What are we like to do ourselves to the reforming of a congregation, if all the work be cast on us alone; and masters of families neglect that necessary duty of their own, by which they are bound to help us? If any good be begun by the ministry in any soul, a careless, prayerless, worldly family is like to stifle it, or very much hinder it; whereas, if you could but get the rulers of families to do their duty, to take up the work where you left it, and help it on, what abundance of good might be done! I beseech you, therefore, if you desire the reformation and welfare of your people, do all you can to promote family religion.[17]

In our day, many parents take the task of raising their children in the Faith very seriously. This is surely part of the impetus behind the homeschooling movement, which has been very strong in some evangelical communities, as well as the Christian schooling movement. Just as significantly, many Christian parents who have chosen to educate their children in broader environments—in public schools or nonsectarian private schools—are deeply committed to the spiritual well-being of their children. Some make this choice very intentionally, out of a desire to help their children learn to live godly lives in such contexts. Others may make this decision for other reasons, such as economic necessity.

Parents with children in schools that are not explicitly Christian must, of course, be vigilant to provide Christian education and nurture for their children in settings beyond the school. But those with children in Christian school or homeschool settings must be just as vigilant. Indeed, it may be easier for these parents to be lax about their mandate. They may unwisely assume that their children will be "fine" spiritually since the Bible is part of their daily or weekly school curriculum.

---

[16]Indeed, the family is the most natural context for teaching and learning to take place. Parents are to gently and creatively create a space for teaching and learning for their children, instead of teaching or lecturing *at* their children about what they need to believe. In other words, teaching, catechesis and so on should not be construed as a "top-down" or "banking" form of education, as if children are in desperate need of enlightenment that parents alone possess. Whenever possible, holistic and contextual teaching-learning should be the goal of parenting.

[17]Baxter, *The Reformed Pastor,* pp. 39-40, in the electronic format from Christian Classical Ethereal Library at <http://www.ccel.org/ccel/baxter/pastor.pdf>. (Accessed June 30, 2008.)

Many parents choose the church that they attend with their children's spiritual needs in view. If they are consistent in this concern, they invest themselves—as a family—deeply in the life of the congregation. Sadly, there are those parents who seem to have adopted a passive vision when it comes to the nurture of their children. "The church" should take care of their children's spiritual needs, they reason. What they mean by "the church," apparently, is somebody other than themselves, especially children's pastors, youth pastors and Sunday school teachers.

Years ago, when I was serving as a youth pastor in a large congregation, it became clear that many parents of the youth understood the spiritual nurture of their children to be primarily my job, not theirs. An elder of the church told me that his wife had been worried about the spiritual health of their teenage son. He said, "I told her, 'Don't worry about him. We have Pastor Gary in our church,'" as if to compliment me. The fact is, the mother *did* have cause for concern and so did her husband. Even if their son had been faithful in attending *all* the programs we offered through the church's youth ministry, we would have engaged that child directly no more than a few hours per week. As it was, we typically saw this boy little more than one hour per week, and often not at all. The hours at school and those at home far outweighed those spent in church-sponsored ministries.

There is also the great challenge in our day of many parents trying to provide Christian nurture for their children without the partnership of a spouse. This is the case in single-parent homes as well as when one of the parents is not a Christian believer. In such instances, particularly, we are reminded of the critical role that the church community is to play as the "household of faith." Indeed, some have argued that such circumstances can serve to remind us that it is the family of faith, not the "nuclear family," that ought to be viewed as the *primary* family of all our children.[18]

The following commitments represent the minimum that church leaders should offer by way of helping parents toward assuming their proper teaching roles in the home.

Show them—by means of example. If we are serious about helping our parents more faithfully fulfill their biblical roles in teaching and forming their children, we can offer them no better assistance than providing them with good role models. This is a call to church leaders—pastors, elders, deacons and their families—to show the way. It is not enough to wag a finger at parents

---

[18]See, for example, Mark DeVries, *Family-Based Youth Ministry,* rev. ed. (Downers Grove, Ill.: InterVarsity Press, 2004).

from behind a pulpit or lectern, chiding them for not doing their jobs well. Pastors and other church leaders who are parents themselves must provide role models for other parents in the congregation. Modeling was a chief teaching strategy of Jesus and of Paul. We will be wise to make it ours as well. However, pastors sometimes communicate, either explicitly or implicitly, that parishioners should "do as I say, not as I do." This is not only a form of hypocrisy, it is also educationally naive. People simply do not learn that way. Rather, we learn far more from how our teachers and leaders actually live their lives than we ever do from what they tell us about how *we* should live. Paul spoke of the importance of both pastor-elders and deacons managing their own families well (see 1 Tim 3:4-5, 8; Tit 1:6), and part of the reason for this concerned the power of example for members of the flock.

Paul's instruction about the families of Christian leaders, though, does not mean that pastors, elders or deacons should train their spouses and children to live a dual existence—a private life and a public one—or that they should be so demanding of having the "model" family that serious troubles are invited into it. This will not only harm the leader's family, it will seriously harm the congregation, providing precisely the wrong sort of example. Yes, church leaders should try to provide a model of loving care and nurture in their homes and of spiritual leadership for family members. But they must also model grace, mercy, forgiveness, patience, understanding and other qualities essential for healthy family life.

Often the most potent examples pastors can offer congregants are in things that appear to be simple and mundane. The pastor of my church often has left a deep impression on me in ways that he probably does not even realize. After he has finished preaching his sermon, he usually takes a seat next to his wife where, invariably, one of his young children winds up on his lap for the remainder of the service. We often receive e-mail requests, sent out to the congregation, for emergency baby-sitting help so that the pastor and his wife can enjoy their regular "date night." The pastor does not hesitate to ask for unscheduled time off if and when it is required to meet a special need that has arisen in his family. He will occasionally (and appropriately) mention his wife and children in his sermons in ways that reveal that theirs is a very "normal" family with typical struggles and that they are serious about trying to be a family that lives out its faith with integrity.

Exhort them—through the pulpit and elsewhere. Alongside the commitment to offer healthy examples for the flock regarding parenting, there is indeed a need to urge through public exhortation and instruction that parents take their roles seriously. This could come in the form of a sermon or sermon series, Sunday school classes or small groups with this particular focus. As we have seen, there are many texts that make it clear that parents are the God-ordained primary teachers and nurturers in the lives of their children. These texts can provide the basis for much preaching and teaching.

But it could also be helpful simply to note parental responsibilities within sermons or teachings that are *not* specifically concerned with parenting. After all, there are a great many biblical themes and texts that ought to be applied in the context of home and family life. In some ways, such an approach—in which concerns of the family are mentioned frequently and naturally—may prove more helpful than having a "special" focus on families. Such focused attention can lead some hearers to simply "tune out" if they believe that what is about to be said is something they have already heard or if they do not yet have a family of their own.[19]

Nurture them—in accordance with their own faith development. One of the greatest ways to help parents be better parents is simply to help them grow in their own faith and walk. In other words, encouraging them to grow as children of God will be of great help to them as they seek to encourage their children. Two examples may help illustrate this principle.

Years ago, I joined a congregation as their new pastor of Christian education. I was excited to learn that the church held a "family retreat" each year, as we had not experienced this in my previous church—much to our detriment, I believed. It was with great anticipation that I awaited preparations for that first retreat. But when I began to learn about the retreat plans, I was quite disappointed. As the new pastor on the team, I did not feel it was my place to lodge a significant protest about what I was hearing. I let things go and hoped for the best.

But the actual retreat was even more disappointing than I had feared it might be. What had been labeled a "family retreat" was, it seemed to me, anything but that. Families drove together to the retreat, but almost as soon as they arrived there, they separated from each other and thereafter did almost nothing together. The children went one direction, the youth another and the

---

[19]Whenever such incidental teaching on parenting and/or family takes place in the context of the corporate worship, it is also crucial to remind the congregation about the nature and the responsibility of the church in raising children in the household of God. It is good also to remind the congregation of the vows that they have taken during the course of the liturgy of baptism, dedication and confirmation of its children and adults to be responsible for one another's nurture.

adults yet another. They did sleep in the same cabins together, and they drove home together, but that was about the extent of family together time at this "family retreat." I was more than disappointed; I was angry.

Over the next couple of weeks, I (unwisely and immaturely) voiced my displeasure to anyone who would listen. To *almost* anyone, that is; I steadfastly avoided raising the topic to the senior pastor. Churches being what they are, however, it was not long until word of my mini-tirades reached his ears. Was it true, he finally asked me, that I was telling people that we had actually had an "anti-family retreat"? Yes, I confessed, it was true. Thus the conversation opened, awkward though it was. I voiced my complaints about what had (or, rather, had not) happened at the retreat, and he heard me out. Then he explained to me his philosophy for such retreats. He believed, very sincerely, that the best way to strengthen families was to provide a spiritually rich experience for each member of the family. That meant age-appropriate, culturally sensitive services, speakers and activities for children, youth and adults.

I found the senior pastor's arguments as unpersuasive as he found mine to be. We both left the meeting unmoved from our entrenched positions. Over the next couple of years and subsequent family retreats, I tried to be a good team player and kept most of my opinions about matters to myself. We did succeed, I recall, in finally orchestrating a few activities that brought all the groups together—a joint worship service and some recreational activities—to be a small part of the retreats.

Years later, I came to understand what he had tried to say to me. I now believe that there must have been some middle way between our two philosophies. We needed to have more time for families to interact with one another across the age spans (for more on this, please see chapter eleven). But I also came to believe there was something significant to the point the senior pastor was so passionately trying to make. If we want parents to be better parents, we do well to try to nurture their own spiritual vitality, to make their own walks with the Lord deeper.

A few years later, I found myself in another church, functioning as the lead pastor of a young congregation. About a year into the congregation's history, a young family joined us and began to get involved. They attended our services somewhat regularly and sent their children to the Sunday school program. But the husband and wife did not join the Bible-study classes available for them.

After a couple of months with us, the husband asked if he could speak with me. When we met, he revealed that he and his wife were having some marital difficulties, which he considered to be serious. After listening to him, I suggested a twofold approach that we could follow together. I would be happy to meet with them for some exploratory marital counseling. In addition, I asked him to bring his wife to the weekly Bible study, where we were studying the essentials of the Faith.

He was very enthusiastic about the former suggestion, and very unenthused about the latter. "We don't need a Bible study," he told me with exasperation in his voice. "We need serious intervention!" I replied that we would try to offer serious intervention but that I also believed that he and his wife needed to be better trained in Christian faith and life. It was clear to me that they had little church background and a fairly undeveloped faith, and that they desperately needed a new approach to life in general, an approach in which Jesus was central to their way of living. Grudgingly, he agreed to the two-pronged approach.

Without question, if we want to see parents become more faithful and effective spiritual leaders in their families, we need to provide more than parental training. We need to provide equipping for living as followers of Jesus in every area of life. In other words, we need to help them become more obedient disciples of Jesus Christ. We need to help them become immersed in the glorious Gospel and to proclaim to them the reality of Jesus Christ, who is the Truth, the Life and the Way of God incarnate.

Equip them—through seminars, resources, study groups and more. Having established the need to provide basic discipleship training for parents, we next acknowledge that there *is* a need for specific equipping for their parental roles. As we have said, it is not enough to exhort them to take their responsibilities seriously. Exhortation without necessary equipping may lead to frustration and feelings of guilt, rather than to greater faithfulness and effectiveness. As we have said, sermon series and Sunday school classes can be helpful here, as can periodic reference to parental roles and responsibilities in sermons on other topics and texts. Another venue that many churches have found to be useful in equipping parents is a weekend seminar or retreat on marriage and parenting.

Churches can provide such opportunities themselves, or they can take advantage of the numerous parachurch organizations that have risen up to address these aspects of Christian life. There are also many quality print, audio and video resources that address family ministry needs, and churches can make these available in a church resource center. Many of these resources are also available online. An e-mail newsletter or a page on the church's website can keep parents alerted to the best resources.

Support them—by recognizing the weightiness of their calling and not over-burdening them. Sometimes it seems as though church leaders have hoisted lofty expectations on the shoulders of parents but have been unwilling to help parents bear that burden. Said otherwise, church leaders may truly want the best for and from their parents but may not have adequately considered the "big picture" of the church's implicit and unreasonable expectations of what godly Christian adults ought to be contributing to the church in terms of time and energy.

For example, have we asked a young father or a young mother to take on key, time-consuming roles in the life of the congregation that will make it very difficult for him or her to fulfill ministries at home? Of course, some parents might use their family obligations as an excuse for avoiding healthy and appropriate involvement in the life of the church. Yet church leaders can be guilty of asking parents to assume unhealthy and inappropriate burdens. In the Torah, we read that newlywed men were not to join the other men in warfare during the first year of marriage, so that they could attend to their duties at home during this delicate stage of marriage (see Deut 24:5). Similarly, Paul urged that young married women focus their ministry attention on their husbands and young children (see Tit 2:4-5). Once they are married, Paul taught elsewhere, men and women both must devote themselves to ministry to one another's needs (see 1 Cor 7:32-35). There is wisdom in such passages that church leaders have often missed, with injurious results to the health of many families.

As a pastor, I confess that I was slow to learn these lessons. Like many pastoral leaders, I was always on the lookout for those in my congregation who were both competent and willing to serve in various ways. As often is the case, this meant that a handful of people were engaged in (too) many aspects of service. Over time, I came to see that this put an inordinate burden on some of my families, and I tried to adjust the shape of our ministry accordingly. In response, we tried to cease overscheduling "church events" that would take families out of the home. Too many meetings, too many ministries, too many *good* things can eventually undermine the capacity of families, as well as the extended household of God, to faithfully and effectively accomplish *better* things.

We need to change our mindset to recognize that the church is not only the church when we all gather together for large events. We are the church also when we are dispersed throughout the week. Some ministries of the church will be done far more effectively in the living rooms of our homes than in the sanctuaries of our church buildings.

We have much to learn here from the faith practices of other communities, such as those of observant Jewish families. In Jewish understanding, as we noted earlier, the home is to function as a "small sanctuary," in which the dinner table is the altar and the father is the priest.[20] In our Christian history, the same thought has been exemplified at various times. Puritan pastors, for example, regularly admonished parents to treat the home like a "little church."

> The Puritans crusaded for a high view of the family, proclaiming it both the basic unit of society and a little church in itself, with the husband as its pastor and his wife as his assistant—subordinate indeed in the chain of command, but a key figure in the ongoing pastoral process nonetheless.[21]

Worship and family devotions were to be regular features in the home. Catechizing, too, was to be a regular practice there. Families established their own days for thanksgiving and fasting.[22]

TEACHERS AND THE STRICTER JUDGMENT

Although the Spirit has released teaching gifts among believers, no one is to take a teaching role lightly or presumptuously. To the contrary, James tells us that anyone who becomes a teacher will incur a stricter judgment (see Jas 3:1). But is James referring to all those forms of teaching that we have outlined above? It seems most likely that his particular concern is not with the informal teaching that takes place in the church, in some sense, virtually all the time. Rather, James's warning is aimed at those who would assume a formal teaching office that involves presuming to speak to the congregation on behalf of the Lord, such as that of an apostle, a prophet, a teaching elder or pastor. James's point of caution at this point is far from novel. He is faithfully echoing many centuries of biblical teaching about such things.

Daring to speak on behalf of God is a fearful proposition indeed. Apart from an unshakable sense of call, a true burden from the Lord, one really ought not to proceed on such a course. The Scriptures make this clear.

---

[20]Again, see Wilson, *Our Father Abraham,* pp. 214-17.

[21]J. I. Packer, *A Quest for Godliness: The Puritan Vision of the Godly Life* (Wheaton: Crossway Books, 1990), p. 270.

[22]Leland Ryken, "The Puritan Model of Spiritual Formation," in *The Christian Educator's Handbook on Spiritual Formation,* ed. Kenneth O. Gangel and James C. Wilhoit (Grand Rapids: Baker, 1994), pp. 49-59.

Through the prophet Jeremiah, God gives a severe word of judgment against those who claim, falsely, to speak for God. Here is just a portion of what the prophet records:

> "Therefore," declares the LORD, "I am against the prophets who steal from one another words supposedly from me. Yes," declares the LORD, "I am against the prophets who wag their own tongues and yet declare, 'The LORD declares.' Indeed, I am against those who prophesy false dreams," declares the LORD. (Jer 23:30-32)

The entire twenty-third chapter of Jeremiah's prophecy, from which these verses come, should provoke the fear of God in any preacher and teacher.

Jesus similarly warned against such sins of presumption. His rebuke of many of the religious leaders during the days of his earthly ministry was severe. "Woe to you, teachers of the law and Pharisees, you hypocrites! You shut the kingdom of heaven in men's faces. You yourselves do not enter, nor will you let those enter who are trying to" (Mt 23:13). He derides those who "love to be greeted in the marketplaces and to have men call them 'Rabbi.'" Further, he commanded his disciples that "you are not to be called 'Rabbi,' for you have only one Master and you are all brothers. And do not call anyone on earth 'father,' for you have one Father, and he is in heaven. Nor are you to be called 'teacher,' for you have one Teacher, the Christ" (Mt 23:7-10).

Indeed, Jesus declared that all of us must take great care with *all* of our speech. He said, "I tell you that men will have to give account on the day of judgment for every careless word they have spoken. For by your words you will be acquitted, and by your words you will be condemned" (Mt 12:36-37). Those who, by word or deed, have caused children to turn away from Jesus receive an especially fearsome admonition: "If anyone causes one of these little ones who believe in me to sin, it would be better for him to have a large millstone hung around his neck and to be drowned in the depths of the sea" (Mt 18:6).

Surely, we ought to think of such things before we make that all-too-familiar announcement on Sunday morning, declaring that "there is a desperate need for third-grade teachers in the Sunday school. If anyone is willing to help, please see . . ." Even churches that jealously seek to guard the pulpit—wanting to ensure that the preachers are gifted and well qualified—often allow almost any willing, warm-bodied volunteer to teach the Bible lessons for the children. May God have mercy on us!

When James warned against presuming to be teachers, he went on to speak of that untamable trouble that is our tongues: "The tongue . . . is a fire, a world of evil among the parts of the body. It corrupts the whole person, sets the whole course of his life on fire, and is itself set on fire by hell. . . . No man can tame the tongue. It is a restless evil, full of deadly poison" (Jas 3:6, 8).

One wonders how anyone could ever dare to teach in our churches in light of all these biblical warnings (and we have offered only a small sampling here). But as we have seen, there are important mitigating factors that make it not only possible but necessary that some actually do become teachers. There is the Great Commission, in which Jesus actually commands that teaching be an essential part of the church's discipling of all its people. Furthermore, the Spirit has called, appointed, anointed and gifted some for teaching ministries. Still, Scripture plainly means what it says in its many warnings, and we should neither enter teaching ministries nor continue to engage in such labors without a due measure of fear and trembling. Those charged with key teaching tasks in the congregation should regularly be reminded of these things and thereby driven always to their knees.

COORDINATING THE EFFORTS OF THOSE WHO TEACH

As we have seen, many in the church are charged with teaching roles, including parents, pastors, elders, mature believers and gifted teachers. How can the efforts of so many be coordinated for faithful and effective ministry? Entire books have been written on the matters of organizing and administering Christian education programs, and we offer some suggestions for further reading at the close of this chapter. We do not propose a complete model here, but simply offer the following principles, together with some thoughts about their implications for practice.

First, in churches that have a solo pastor or a senior pastor, that person ought to play an active and intentional role in helping to shape and lead the teaching ministry of the church. This is in keeping with biblical mandates about the roles of pastors and elders, with the wisest practices of church history and with very practical considerations as well. This need not always mean that the solo or senior pastor must lead the effort in all respects, for there may be others who have greater gifting in this area.

As we noted above, churches in every age and in every culture are to be engaged in the ministries of worship, teaching and evangelism. Pastors have an obligation to play some appropriate role in each of these tasks. Concerning the task of worship, the pastor may share certain aspects of leadership with others—with gifted musicians, for example. But it is an irresponsible pastor who therefore simply withdraws his input from helping shape and lead congregational worship. So, too, pastors must not simply "hand off" the teaching task of the church to others.

Second, wise leaders in the teaching ministry of the church will see themselves as integrative partners rather than as isolated specialists. The move of some churches toward hyper-specialization is lacking in both biblical wisdom and common sense. Those charged with educational leadership for one segment of the congregation—with children or with youth, for example—should view themselves as actively partnering with other leaders in the church. For instance, those leading educational efforts with high-school students should work actively with those who minister primarily to collegians and adults, and so on. This also means that those who provide leadership to the church in the area of evangelism will not dismiss education and nurture as outside the sphere of their responsibility. In fact, we are all together in the task of making disciples.

A congregation's "leadership team" might thus look something like that in figure 6.1. The actual shape of this team could vary widely. It may be that the pastor has particular gifts in one of the other areas—worship, teaching or outreach—and thus wears two hats at once. Or it could be that any one of these leaders is also especially gifted in administration, thus eliminating the need for an additional member of the team.

We use the term *leader* in a general way in figure 6.1. Depending on ecclesial convictions and practical matters, the leader may be a paid staff member

Ministry Leadership Team

Pastor ("Lead Pastor")	Worship Ministries Team Leader	Educational Ministries Team Leader	Outreach Ministries Team Leader	Administrative Leader or Assistant

Figure 6.1. The ministry leadership team

or a "lay" leader in each case. These roles may be filled by elders or by deacons. It could be that more than one person is appointed to represent each of the three tasks. It could also be that the church wants to add more tasks to the leadership team, depending on the vision and values of the congregation.

The leadership team should meet regularly for prayer and planning and dreaming together. *All* of the three tasks are the concern of *all* the team members. At one meeting, perhaps focus turns to the task of worship. For that meeting, all team members put on their "worship hat." No one is exempted by claiming that this is not their area of specialization—certainly not the lead pastor. Worship is everyone's concern. The worship services of the church, for example, have profound impact on the ministries of formation and evangelism (much more on this in chapters twelve and thirteen). At the following meeting, each member may be asked to wear the "evangelism hat" and at the next, the "educational hat." The "prophets and teachers" at Antioch met *together,* not in two separate groups, to worship and seek the Lord (see Acts 13:1-3). It is imperative for the church to find ways to let the left hand know what the right hand is doing in leading and serving our congregations.

Third, those charged with key decision making in various aspects of educational ministry should be those who are actively engaged in those ministries. This is a not-so-subtle plea to dismantle (or radically reconfigure) the "Christian education committee" as it currently is structured in many churches. Having consulted with numerous churches about their teaching ministries, we see clearly that many of these committees are, at best, an unnecessary extra layer of bureaucracy that makes the educational ministry of the church more cumbersome than necessary. At worst, such committees actually hinder faithful and effective ministry.

Part of the problem is that these committees are often unwisely configured to include people who probably should not be there. It may be that one member is a former Sunday school teacher, another is a retired public school teacher, another is a church elder, another is a deacon and still another is an interested parent. All these people would be fine committee members, provided they were each currently and actively engaged in the educational ministry of the church. Very often, however, this is not the case. Instead, many members of such committees are simply good people with strong opinions about what ought to be done. Their opinions are then hoisted onto the shoulders of those who are actually engaged in the church's teaching ministry and who may or may not themselves be part of the committee as structured. A better structure would be to empower those who have actually been called, gifted and equipped for these ministries to make the critical decisions regarding them, in consultation with those in the first level of ministry leadership.

In light of the above, we would suggest that ministry teams be configured for each of the ministry areas that are represented in the leadership team, including worship, teaching and outreach. The person charged with leadership of each particular team will be the one who meets regularly with the church's leadership team. From the leadership team's regular meetings, this leader brings vision and guidance to the particular ministry team. The ministry team meets regularly as well, perhaps on alternating weeks with the leadership team, to further flesh out and provide guidance to that specific ministry task in the church.

The ministry team for education and nurture is made up of those who are actually engaged in hands-on leadership in that area, including those who minister with a focus on various age groups—children, youth, collegians, adults and so on. They, too, are encouraged to think together in integrated fashion about their particular ministry concerns and to avoid falling into the "isolated specialist" traps. The sort of persons that had comprised earlier iterations of a Christian education committee may continue to serve in advisory capacities, if that seems wise and beneficial to the congregation. But this newly configured educational ministry team is a working committee, partnering with one another and with the church's leadership team for faithful and effective ministry in teaching and nurture. An educational ministry team, then, might look something like that presented in figure 6.2.

Once again, the actual size and shape and titles of such a ministry team could vary widely, depending on the particular needs and commitments of the congregation. The titles here are merely suggestions. Some of these roles may be filled by paid staff, others by lay leaders, depending on the size and philosophy of the church. Responding to the unhappy fruit of fragmentation in the congregation and in the broader culture, many churches have deliberately moved to restore more integrative approaches to staffing. Thus some congregations no longer have a "youth pastor" or a "children's director" in

Educational Ministry Team

Educational Ministries Team Leader	Children's Ministries Leader	Youth Ministries Leader	College and Young Adult Ministries Leader
Adult Educational Efforts Leader	Marriage and Family Ministries Leader	Small-Group Ministries Leader	Personal Discipleship Ministries Leader

Figure 6.2. The educational ministry team

place. Instead, they have a "pastor to youth and families" or a "pastor to families and children."

Key concerns for such an educational ministry team would include coordinating efforts for a comprehensive curriculum in the congregation, the recruiting and training of teachers and helpers, and so on. In terms of training and supporting teachers, there are certain attributes and attitudes that must be championed and nurtured among those who teach. These characteristics are vital for all those engaged in the church's teaching ministry—parents, pastors, elders, small-group leaders, children's ministry leaders and so on. In the next chapter, we consider a number of such characteristics for Christlike teachers.

HYMN FOR CONTEMPLATION AND WORSHIP

We Love Your Kingdom, Lord
(Ezra 7:10; Mt 28:18-20; Eph 4:12-16)

We love your kingdom, Lord,
in all its vast array,
and pray its blessings may extend
still farther ev'ry day.

Soon ev'ry knee shall bow,
and ev'ry tongue confess.
In ev'ry tribe and land they rise,
Your awesome Name to bless.

As long as Day shall last,
may we your will obey:
to make disciples from all lands
to walk within the Way.

Our parts in this great task
God help us to fulfill:
to *be,* and *bear,* good news to all
and teach your perfect will.

May we, with humble hearts,
first hear and heed your word,
then teach the church in all the earth
till ev'ry saint has heard.

That church, equipped, shall rise,
full of good works and grace.
and by your Spirit may she stir
all flesh to seek your face.

Text: Gary A. Parrett (2003)
Tune: St. Thomas
Familiar use of the tune: "I Love Thy Kingdom, Lord"

QUESTIONS FOR PLANNING AND PRACTICE

1. Muse on the following statement: "Perhaps we have missed the mark by having the bulk of our teaching done by people other than those who seem to be biblically sanctioned for such ministries." Who are the primary people teaching in your church? In what ways is your church leadership helping to provide opportunities for the ongoing growth of teachers?

2. In this chapter, three primary areas for pastoral leadership are discussed: worship, teaching and evangelism. Many pastors today seem to have "hired out" these things to others. How do you assess this trend? What might you suggest that would allow the pastor more freedom to function in his or her individual gifting?

3. This chapter argues that parents need to take a more active role in the spiritual lives of their children, instead of leaving it up to "the church." How can the entire congregation be active in the raising of children in Christian community? What are some challenges presented to parents in the twenty-first century that perhaps generations before did not encounter? How can the church community come together amid such struggles? We invite you to create opportunities to discuss such issues with the parents in your church and to reflect with an educational minister about your findings.

4. Prayerfully reflect on James 3:1: "Not many of you should presume to be teachers, my brothers, because you know that we who teach will be judged more strictly." Have you come to a realization of the stricter judgment you come under as a leader of educational ministry? We invite you to prayerfully write a journal entry between you and the Lord to help you stay humble in this role on a daily basis.

5. How does figure 6.2, the educational ministry team outline, compare to the situation of leadership in your own church? What might be some possible advantages for configuring leadership in this way?

RESOURCES FOR FURTHER STUDY

Baxter, Richard. *The Reformed Pastor: A Discourse on the Pastoral Office.* London: Paternoster-Row, 1808.

Nouwen, Henri. *In the Name of Jesus: Reflections on Christian Leadership.* New York: Crossroad, 1993.

Osmer, Richard. *The Teaching Ministry of Congregations.* Louisville, Ky.: Westminster/John Knox Press, 2007.

Packer, J. I. *A Quest for Godliness: The Puritan Vision of the Christian Life.* Wheaton: Crossway, 1994.

Pazmiño, Robert. *Foundational Issues in Christian Education: An Introduction in Evangelical Perspective.* 3rd edition. Grand Rapids: Baker, 2008.

———. *So What Makes Our Teaching Christian? Teaching in the Name, Spirit, and Power of Jesus.* Eugene, Ore.: Wipf and Stock, 2008.

Peterson, Eugene. *Working the Angles: The Shape of Pastoral Integrity.* Grand Rapids: Eerdmans, 1987.

———. *Christ Plays in Ten Thousand Places: A Conversation in Spiritual Theology.* Grand Rapids: Eerdmans, 2005.

Tye, Karen. *Your Calling as a Teacher.* St. Louis: Chalice, 2008.

7

Attitudes and Attributes
of Christlike Teachers

The Sovereign LORD *has given me an instructed tongue,*

to know the word that sustains the weary. He wakens me morning by morning.

ISAIAH 50:4

▼

Having considered in the previous chapter the matter of who is to assume teaching roles in the church that Jesus is building, we now turn to consider some of the many characteristics befitting a Christian teacher. These attributes were evident in the Master Teacher, Jesus Christ. In many instances, we also reference how these attributes were apparent in the life and ministry of the apostle Paul or other biblical teachers. Only a brief introduction to each of these characteristics is offered here. We set this list before the reader with encouragement to contemplate these things further and to pray for God's provision of such graces, and many more, in the lives of those of us who have been called to teach.

Our list—not intended to be exhaustive—features twelve characteristics. These may be thought of loosely in terms of six pairs of attributes that are somewhat related or complementary to one another. The first pair is *belief* and *calling*. The second is *zeal* and *knowledge*. The third is *truthfulness* and *gentleness*. The fourth is *humility* and *partnership*. The fifth is *vulnerability* and *suffering*. The sixth pair, which we probe at greatest length, is *authority* and *listening*. Placing all these attributes together, we may summarize the whole by saying that those of us who are called to be teachers of the Gospel seek to live and minister in ways that are in line with the truth of the Gospel.

BELIEF

Teachers must believe. Of course, sincere belief in the Faith—as discussed in part two of this book—is critical for any who teach in our churches. As Paul commanded Timothy, leaders in the churches "must keep hold of the deep truths of the faith with a clear conscience" (1 Tim 3:9). Our concern at this point, however, is with a different application of belief. We speak now of belief in God himself and in his capacity to transform both our lives and the lives of those to whom we are called to minister. Without such belief, it will prove very difficult to sustain a ministry of teaching. With such belief, we are able actually to heed Paul's counsel to "be steadfast, immovable, always abounding in the work of the Lord, knowing that in the Lord your labor is not in vain" (1 Cor 15:58 rsv).

Jesus demonstrated belief in the Spirit's capacity to transform lives in the very selection of his apostles and in numerous encounters with others as well. We can think of the way Jesus responded to others whom the culture at large had long discounted and rejected: the woman taken in adultery, the Samaritan woman, the chief tax collector Zacchaeus and all manner of other people who had been labeled "sinners." Jesus seemed to see in such people something that others could not see. This was evidently the case with those he called to be his apostles. He saw in Thomas, Nathanael and the others not only who they were *at present* but also who they would become by the transformative power of the Holy Spirit. His first encounter with the brother of Andrew is a notable example of this. Upon seeing him, Jesus declared, "You are Simon son of John. You will be called Cephas" (Jn 1:42). Jesus saw both the present and the future in those he loved and served.

Likewise, Paul came to the point where he no longer viewed anyone "from a worldly point of view." He had once viewed Christ in such a way, but had been proved utterly wrong about him. Now he knew that if "anyone is in Christ, he is a new creation" (2 Cor 5:16-17).[1] May God give us also the grace

---

[1] We as teachers will want to commit ourselves to imagine patiently what God could do in all of us. "Let us not become weary in doing good, for at the proper time we will reap a harvest if we do not give up" (Gal 6:9). It is imperative that we take enough time to get to know those whom God has brought into our lives to teach and thus to find ways and opportunities to point them to the glorious Gospel. Perhaps, for some, it is just a word of encouragement at an appropriate time. For others, it might be more involved as we try to figure out how they learn best. For some, it might be helping students come to peace with a past that has hindered them from moving forward in freedom in Jesus Christ. Growing in our capacity to have trust in those God has entrusted to us requires taking time to invest genuinely in the various aspects of their lives as their friend, teacher and fellow traveler in the journey toward Jesus Christ.

to believe in his transforming power at work both among those we are called to serve and in our own hearts.

CALLING

This sort of belief is related to the matter of calling. Teachers not only respond to the call of God that is on their own lives, they also help others respond to God's call. Thus Paul, in the space of only a few lines, could refer to several aspects both of his own calling and of that on the believers to whom he was writing. In Romans 1:1-7, we read that Paul himself was "a servant of Christ Jesus, called to be an apostle and set apart for the gospel of God" (Rom 1:1). A few verses later, we find that his calling included the grace "to call people from among all the Gentiles to the obedience that comes from faith" (Rom 1:5). "And you also," he goes on to say, "are among those who are called to belong to Jesus Christ . . . loved by God and called to be saints" (Rom 1:6-7). As we saw in the first chapter of this book, Paul highlights in his letter to the Ephesians the lofty calling that is on all of us who are members of Christ's body.

Likewise, Jesus was both faithful to the call on his life and devoted himself to calling others. At his baptism, the Father said, "You are my Son, whom I love; with you I am well pleased" (Mk 1:11; Lk 3:22). Immediately thereafter, the Spirit led him into the wilderness, where he was to be tempted by the devil. Each temptation, in its own way, concerned and challenged Jesus' call. The temptations immediately brought the Father's declaration about Jesus into question: "*If* you are the Son of God . . ." (emphasis added). Jesus was also confronted with doubts and questions from those around him, including John the Baptist, who wondered aloud if Jesus was indeed "the one who was to come, or should we expect someone else?" (Lk 7:20). In Gethsemane, Jesus wrestled even within himself about the call to drink the cup that had been placed before him (see Mk 14:32-36). But, through all these temptations and more, Jesus remained faithful to his calling to the very end. He was obedient, even unto death (see Phil 2:8) and was proven to be "faithful as a son over God's house" (Heb 3:6).

Returning to these verses in Romans 1 and reflecting on other texts as well, we see that there are multiple aspects to the Christian's call. We are "among those who are called to belong to Jesus Christ" (Rom 1:6), the most fundamental aspect of our calling. We are called also to become like Jesus, "called to be saints" (Rom 1:7)—a reference to both our position in Christ and our pursuit of Christ. This call to sanctification (see 1 Thess 4:3) bids us love both God and neighbor. Thus we are called and chosen also to "bear fruit" through Jesus—much fruit, lasting fruit—all to the glory of God (see Jn 15:8, 16). The call to fruitfulness means that we are also called to be "pruned" with Jesus (see Jn 15:2). Through the Father's loving presence and discipline in times of trouble and tribulation, we thus become even more fruitful. As Paul writes to the Philippians, "It has been granted to you on behalf of Christ not only to believe on him, but also to suffer for him" (Phil 1:29).

Like Paul, we too may come to discover a specific call in Christ. He was called, gifted, anointed and appointed to be an apostle. We should seek to discern what God has uniquely designed us to be. Sadly, many begin and end their pursuit of God's call with a fixation on the particularity of their calling. Indeed, some expend inordinate amounts of energy trying to discover the relatively small portion of God's call that remains hidden to us—specific matters regarding career choices, marital choices and so on. Yet, at the same time, they spend little energy in obeying the vast majority of God's calling that has plainly been revealed in the pages of Scripture, such as the call to love God and neighbor, to do justice and love mercy, and to be holy. When we do pursue God's specific calling on our lives, we must never compromise his already revealed will. And we should proceed with deep humility toward our neighbors in the world, recognizing that most people in most cultures and most eras have not enjoyed the privilege that so many of us now enjoy—that of being "free" to figure out what our unique gifts are, what will most "fulfill" us, what we were "born to do."

Faithful teachers are responsive to God's call on their lives and long to see those they serve be likewise responsive and eager to see how their lives fit into God's kingdom vision. They follow the example of Jesus, also modeled for us by Paul, in obeying God's call on their own lives and pleading with others to participate fully in the further enfolding of God's redemptive drama.

ZEAL

Another feature of Jesus the teacher was that he was filled with a zeal for God, for God's honor and for the tasks that had been given him. This is perhaps most obvious in the accounts of his overturning the tables that the money lenders had set up within the temple area. Reflecting on what they had seen, "his disciples remembered that it is written: 'Zeal for your house will consume me'" (Jn 2:17). But Jesus' zeal was evident throughout the course of his life and ministry. Zeal is both a deep emotion that burns in one's heart and the actions that are thereby evoked. In and of itself, zeal is not praiseworthy (Gal 4:18). Zeal can easily be misplaced or misdirected; we can be zealous about all the wrong things. But zeal directed toward the Lord is pleasing to God. Biblical characters like Phinehas and Caleb are praised for their displays of zeal (see Num 25:1-18; 13:30; 14:6, 24).

Zeal is one of those characteristics that provokes intriguing questions. Can we really nurture such a quality in ourselves? Or is zeal something that must be inborn? Indeed, to speak of zeal may produce the image of a certain type of personality in our minds. We can imagine a particularly "passionate" individual and assume that since we are not like her, the attribute of zeal must be beyond our reach. But zeal need not always be expressed in overtly emotional ways. Even those with more quiet, contemplative and introverted temperaments can—indeed must—cultivate zeal in their hearts. "Never be lacking in zeal, but keep your spiritual fervor, serving the Lord," Paul writes (Rom 12:11). Perhaps that last phrase provides a clue about nurturing zeal. We do so by serving the Lord, and we do that, most often, by serving others.[2] Zeal is perhaps not so much a separate attribute or action as it is a commitment to do all that we do "with all our strength." As Paul writes, "Whatever you do, work at it with all your heart, as working for the Lord, not for men" (Col 3:23).

Related to being zealous for the Lord is the idea of being jealous for the Lord. Jealousy is an often-neglected characteristic of God. It may seem to us that such an attribute is not befitting the God who is love. Yet the Lord is indeed a jealous God (see, for example, Ex 20:5; 34:14; Deut 4:24; Josh 24:19; Nahum 1:2). Unlike much human jealousy, which is often rooted in pettiness, selfishness and insecurity, God's jealousy is rooted in covenant love. The Decalogue begins with God's claim to be Israel's God and Redeemer. As such, he has every right to be jealous over those with whom he has made covenant. Believers, too, must understand that God is justly jealous over us. After all, he has created us, redeemed us, adopted us and covenanted with us. More than this, God's jealousy really is an aspect of his great love for us. For God knows

---

[2]It is interesting to observe that tucked in the greatest commandments is the notion that we are to love others "as yourself." This self-love, whether proper or not, is presupposed, which suggests that it is critical that we not only love God completely and love others compassionately, but that we are also called to love ourselves accurately. This means that we are constantly to assess ourselves as God sees us—for all the wonderful gifts *and* zeal that he has given to us— evaluating, cultivating and practicing our gifts and zeal to love and serve God and others all for his glory.

that if we chase after idols and break covenant with him, we do so to our own destruction. This is not unlike a proper and holy jealousy between a husband and wife—a jealousy that is likewise based on covenant love.

Those engaged in ministries of teaching and discipling should also be jealous over those they serve. Paul manifested this often, and he mentioned it explicitly to the Corinthians: "I am jealous for you with a godly jealousy. I promised you to one husband, to Christ, so that I might present you as a pure virgin to him" (2 Cor 11:2). But let us be cautious that our jealousy is truly a godly jealousy and that its focus is on the disciple's attachment to Christ, not to ourselves. It is easy for Christian teachers to have an ungodly and improper jealousy—for example, of other teachers and ministers who seem to have more "successful" ministries than our own. Like John the Baptist, we must shun all such thinking, realizing that "a man can receive only what is given him from heaven. . . . [Jesus] must become greater; I must become less" (Jn 3:27, 30).

On the other hand, if we see those we have sought to serve for Jesus' sake being lured away from Christ toward another "Jesus" or another "gospel," our hearts should be filled with jealousy. This is a proper expression of the zeal of the Lord that should consume us as teachers. May God preserve us from passive shrugs of the shoulder where departures from the Way are concerned. Instead, like the Beloved Apostle, let us say, "I have no greater joy than to hear that my children are walking in the truth" (3 Jn 4). Christian teachers should seek to serve God's saints with all our heart, soul, mind and strength. We should be ruthless toward displays of half-heartedness, hard-heartedness or idolatrous wanderings, whether they rise up in our own hearts or in the lives of those among whom we minister.

KNOWLEDGE

As intimated above, zeal should not be a stand-alone quality for our pursuit. Rather, it is a feature of how we pursue all the attributes essential for Christlike teaching. It is especially crucial that our zeal be partnered with proper knowledge. Absent this, it is actually possible that our zeal will do more harm than good. With what must have been autobiographical insight at work as he wrote, Paul said of his fellow Jews that "they are zealous for God, but their zeal is not based on knowledge" (Rom 10:2). That is, Paul's Jewish brothers who had rejected Jesus thought themselves the zealous servants of their God. But their zeal was misguided and misshapen because it was not coupled with a growing knowledge of the God they purported to serve and persistent attentiveness to what he had revealed to them.

Paul writes elsewhere about his own misguided zeal before he had come to know the Savior. Addressing a crowd of hostile Jewish citizens in Jerusalem, he explains, "Under Gamaliel I was thoroughly trained in the law of our fathers and was just as zealous for God as any of you are today. I persecuted the followers of this Way to their death" (Acts 22:3-4). He writes of himself elsewhere, "as for zeal, persecuting the church" (Phil 3:6).

Knowledge without zeal may well be a kind of *dead* faith. But zeal without knowledge can be absolutely *deadly*—to both us and others. Thus we must consistently pursue an ever-expanding knowledge of the God we desire to serve. Paul was determined to do exactly that. He writes to the Philippians about his ongoing desire "to know Christ" (Phil 3:10). Jesus also models this commitment for us. Even as a child, he interacted with teachers at the temple, and we read that he grew in wisdom (see Lk 2:46, 52). As an observant Jew, he joined others in his community in Nazareth by worshiping, praying and studying in the synagogue each Sabbath. This "was his custom" (Lk 4:16). He was also clearly committed to study of, memorization of and meditation on the sacred Torah, as evident from the "It is written . . ." responses when the devil tempted him in the wilderness and to the various questioners who tried to trap him with theological questions throughout his ministry.

May we who teach others always seek to cultivate within ourselves a true and growing knowledge of God himself, his Word and his Way. Then, God willing, we shall be able to say to those we serve, "Follow my example, as I follow the example of Christ" (1 Cor 11:1).

TRUTHFULNESS

As we saw above in the words of the apostle John, we ought to have a passionate concern for walking in the Truth. This follows naturally from the pairing of zeal and knowledge that we considered, standing alongside our commitment to grow in our personal and experiential knowledge of God. A teacher who is not passionate about the Truth cannot be a faithful Christian teacher. In our day, when the notion of absolute truth is not only questioned but often denied, this is a critical commitment that we dare not renege on. In humility, we claim no absolute access or insight into that absolute truth. But we unashamedly confess the Truth to be perfectly incarnated in Jesus Christ (Jn 14:6; 8:31-32; 18:37) and unerringly witnessed to in the Holy Scriptures.

Another expression of this need for a teacher's truth-*full*-ness is that we must seek to speak truth to those we serve. This is not only a matter of teaching them the Truth. It also involves telling them the truth about what we see at work in their lives. Thus, if our godly jealousy is aroused within us because we see our congregants in danger of being led astray from the Way of the Lord, we must tell it like it is.

This is not an easy task. Many who are called to pastoral ministries are, by nature, people-pleasers, and we struggle mightily with speaking the truth to others when we know that their comfort levels and ours may be adversely affected by the encounter. Personally, I have struggled with confrontation all my life. This tendency is mine by both nature and nurture, and it has marked too much of my ministry as a pastor and as a professor. I used to delude myself into thinking that I avoided confrontations because I loved people and therefore did not want to hurt them. The truth, of course—if I am bold enough to confess it to myself—is usually just the opposite. It is because I have *not* loved them that I have not spoken the truth to them. I loved myself more. Or at least I loved the appearance of "peaceful and harmonious" relationships more than I loved the individuals or groups involved. My refusals to tell the truth are quite clearly sins against both God and neighbor.

GENTLENESS

Paul reminds us that we must indeed speak the truth to one another. But he qualifies this by saying that we must speak "the truth in love" (Eph 4:15). Our truth-*full*-ness must be expressed in a genuine love for others. Love that is not concerned with truth is not God-honoring; neither is truth, if and when it is severed from love. Realizing that we are to speak the truth in love, it is essential that our truthfulness be accompanied by gentleness.

Those of us who find it easy to be gentle in our ministries probably struggle with truthfulness. Those of us who do not struggle with being truthful may often find it difficult to be gentle. God, in his wisdom, has apparently not invested any of us with the perfect balance of truthfulness and gentleness. In Jesus, however, we find both attributes on full display.[3] He did not always clearly display both qualities at the same time or in the same instance. Knowing all hearts as he did, he knew when gentleness was the right medicine, and

---

[3]In the Old Testament, a very familiar pairing of divine attributes is that of *hesed* (lovingkindness, love, mercy, grace) and *emeth* (truth, truthfulness, faithfulness). These are mentioned together often (e.g., Ex 34:6; Ps 86:15; 115:1). John, in the prologue to his Gospel, says that in Jesus grace and truth were paired perfectly (compare Ps 85:9-13 with Jn 1:14-18).

he knew when nothing less than a stern rebuke was in order. But there are episodes in which both are obviously in view, such as in his dealings with the rich young man (see Mk 10:17-21) and with the woman taken in adultery (see Jn 8:1-11). By God's grace, may we strive to bring the qualities of truthfulness and gentleness together in our ministries.

Gentleness is called for in our dealings with unbelievers and believers alike. Peter reminds us that we must always be ready to give an answer to those who question us about the hope that is in us, but that we must do so "with gentleness and respect" (1 Pet 3:15). Paul reminds the Thessalonians of the gentleness of his ministry while in their midst (see 1 Thess 2:7). He writes to Timothy that the Lord's servant

> must not quarrel; instead, he must be kind to everyone, able to teach, not resentful. Those who oppose him he must gently instruct, in the hope that God will grant them repentance leading them to a knowledge of the truth, and that they will come to their senses and escape from the trap of the devil, who has taken them captive to do his will. (2 Tim 2:24-26)

The call to gentleness is thus linked to the fact that, apart from the ministry of God's Spirit, we will never succeed in persuading anyone of anything. We have no power in ourselves to convert a hardened or deceived heart. Thus we are reminded of our own limitations in ministry and are thereby prompted to humility before God and to partnership both with the Spirit and with other ministers and teachers.

HUMILITY

However praiseworthy our zeal and knowledge or our truth and gentleness may prove to be, we must guard our hearts against sinful pride. Humility, like zeal, is one of those qualities that may seem difficult to develop in our lives. After all, how does one actively acquire humility? But we ought not to think of humility as a static quality. Instead, we heed biblical mandates and models by choosing to *humble ourselves* in service of others.

Again, Jesus is the greatest model of this. Paul wrote, "Your attitude should be the same as that of Jesus Christ: Who, being in very nature God, did not consider equality with God something to be grasped, but made himself nothing, taking the very nature of a servant, being made in human likeness" (Phil 2:5-7). Paul uses this example to urge an active humility among the Philippian believers. They were to "consider others better than yourselves," to "look not only to your own interests, but also to the interests of others" (Phil 2:3-4).

Jesus did not simply "possess" humility as an abstract quality of his life; he chose humility by word and deed. In John 13, we read of his incredible display of humility among his rather proud disciples. It was he who rose from the table, took off his outer garment, took on the servant's towel and posture, and began to wash the feet of his disciples. Indeed, such humility marked his entire life, as the passage in Philippians makes clear. From his birth—through a humble young maiden and in the most humble of settings—to his death in the fashion of the lowest criminal, the path Jesus walked was one of profound humility. In 1 Peter 5:5, the apostle Peter urges his fellow elders to follow Christ's example; we who shepherd God's flock are to clothe ourselves with humility. Peter himself had been a slow and reluctant learner of these things, but finally, as Jesus had promised (see Jn 13:7), he had come to understand.

How can we, as Christian teachers, cultivate humility? Surely it is not for us, but for others to recognize the relative presence of such a virtue in our lives. It would certainly not do to pay too much attention to our own presumed humility! But we can follow Jesus in the active commitment of humbling ourselves to serve others. Indeed, Jesus commanded that we *must* do so.

> You call me "Teacher" and "Lord," and rightly so, for that is what I am. Now that I, your Lord and Teacher, have washed your feet, you also should wash one another's feet. I have set you an example that you should do as I have done for you. I tell you the truth, no servant is greater than his master, nor is a messenger greater than the one who sent him. Now that you know these things, you will be blessed if you do them. (Jn 13:13-17)

Humility, then, is something we *do*. Only in the doing are we blessed. Only in the doing are we following the example of our humble Lord. As we give ourselves to God and neighbor in these ways, God cultivates within us the virtue of true humility.

PARTNERSHIP

One way to practice humility in our teaching is by partnering with others in the work. Jesus consistently shared the works of the kingdom with his disciples. And it was not only with the Twelve that Jesus shared his ministry. There were a number of women who traveled with the Twelve in support of the work (see Lk 8:2-3). There also were occasions when Jesus employed others in kingdom labors—as when he sent out the seventy-two (see Lk 10:1-16).

The apostle Paul is sometimes thought to have been a maverick who did things his own way in ministry, a sort of "lone ranger" among the apostles. But nothing could be further from the truth. So far as we can see from the biblical data, Paul never did anything in ministry without partners. From his own testimony, we can name his ministry partners by the dozens. He partnered with those apostles who had preceded him in that calling and spoke of himself as really unworthy to be numbered among them (see 1 Cor 15:9). He partnered with many men and women whom he affectionately called his "fellow ministers" in the Gospel (1 Cor 3:9; 2 Cor 6:1). He even spoke of his relationship with God's Spirit as a partnership. It was "as though God were making his appeal through us," he wrote to the Corinthians. "We implore you on Christ's behalf: Be reconciled to God" (2 Cor 5:20; see also 2 Cor 6:1).

Paul also saw himself as partnering with those who both preceded and followed him in ministry. He had planted the seeds in Corinth, for example, and Apollos had watered them. Peter, too, had played a formative role in the development of at least some of the believers there. Paul was a coworker with both of them, and thus it was wrongheaded of the Corinthians to think they must choose among the three to attach themselves to one leader. He wrote, "So then, no more boasting about men! All things are yours, whether Paul or Apollos or Cephas or the world or life or death or the present or the future— all are yours" (1 Cor 3:21-22). "What, after all, is Apollos? And what is Paul? Only servants, through whom you came to believe—as the Lord has assigned to each his task." Neither Paul nor Apollos, then, "is anything, but only God, who makes things grow" (1 Cor 3:5-7).

Teachers in our churches should recognize both the loftiness of their calling and the serious limitations inherent as they work out that calling. We all "know in part" and therefore "prophesy in part" (1 Cor 13:9). Each of us is designed by God to play a vital but small part in the greater body of Christ, and so we must cooperate with others in the body, earnestly and consistently.

Youth pastors and teachers will recognize their need to partner with parents for the sake of building up youth in the church. After all, the ministry is primarily the responsibility of those parents, and they are best positioned to nurture true and lasting formation in their own children. In turn, parents will be very grateful to receive the help of youth ministers and teachers in so great a task. A third-grade Sunday school teacher may call on a fellow teacher or on a mature teenager for help with a musical element that she knows calls for gifts she simply does not have. A pastor scheduled to leave a congregation works hard to prepare the ground for the pastor who is soon to follow. Educators work with worship leaders and missions coordinators and those in other ministries of the church. Younger and energetic leaders seek out older members of the church for their wisdom and experience. A pastor reaches out to other pastors—who have ministries, gifts or experiences that are different in some significant ways from her own—to explore ways of mutually benefiting one another's congregations. Pastors and teachers can learn from the example of Paul and see ourselves also in partnership with both those who have preceded us in ministry and those who will one day succeed us. And on and on it goes. We are, after all, truly members of one another.

VULNERABILITY

Another attitude that flows logically from our commitment to humility is that of vulnerability. Teachers, preachers, pastors and other ministers often struggle with the issue of just how vulnerable they ought to be before those they are serving. In the class I teach on pastoral ministry, this is a much-debated topic among students. Many believe—often because this is what has been modeled for them—that pastors ought not to have close friends in their own congregation and must avoid disclosing too much of themselves in their preaching or relationships. When I was in seminary, my homiletics professor actually warned us never to use personal illustrations in our preaching. But taking such a hard line—though one can make a pragmatic argument for it—seems difficult to sustain if we take the ministry of Jesus seriously.

Jesus' earthly ministry was thoroughly an exercise in vulnerability from its very inception. The second person of the triune God became *incarnate,* authentically human. In that wondrous act, God made himself visible, tangible.[4] He is the *exegesis* and *icon* of the unseen God (see Jn 1:18; Col 1:15). It is no wonder, then, that we hear Jesus, at the earliest stages of his ministry, inviting two would-be disciples to "come and see" (Jn 1:39) where he was staying, inviting them to spend time with him. When he called the Twelve as apostles, we are told that it was preeminently a call to "be with him" (Mk 3:14). They were with him as he ate, slept, laughed, cried, worked and rested. We have mentioned as well the group of women who were also welcomed to be with Jesus and the Twelve as they traveled from village to village.

---

[4]Jesus also subjected himself fully to the frailty of human predicament, even to human temptations. He put himself in need of others and experienced deep human sufferings. In this extreme human vulnerability, Jesus Christ not only became the perfect atoning sacrifice for us but also points his followers toward how we can testify to the grace of God-with-us in this world.

At the end of his earthly ministry, Jesus' vulnerability was more striking than ever. In the garden of Gethsemane, he asked for the help of Peter, James and John, confessing to them, "My soul is overwhelmed with sorrow to the point of death" (Mk 14:34). With this single confession, Jesus showed himself more vulnerable than innumerable pastors and Christian teachers who serve in our churches today. In the end, so vulnerable was he that a friend's kiss betrayed him and his closest friends deserted him. The religious leaders and the political powers of the age then joined forces to see him tried, convicted, mocked, scourged and crucified naked before the watching world.

As vulnerable as Jesus was, however, his vulnerability was not without limits. His was a discerning vulnerability. We read that "many people saw the miraculous signs he was doing and believed in his name. But Jesus would not entrust himself to them, for he knew all men" (Jn 2:23-24). From among the multitudes that followed him, there were hundreds who were identified as his disciples at various times. From the hundreds, Jesus prayerfully appointed the Twelve to "be with him."

From the Twelve, Jesus selected three—James, John and Peter—to be with him on selected occasions. It was to these three, and only to them, that Jesus made the bold confession about his anguished soul in Gethsemane. The Twelve typically called Jesus "Teacher" and "Lord." It is not at all likely that they called him by his first name. It is on the eve of his death that Jesus said to them, "I no longer call you servants, because a servant does not know his master's business. Instead, I have called you friends" (Jn 15:15).

As Christian teachers and ministers, we do well to contemplate both the principle of vulnerability and the discernment that Jesus practiced. The "default" of our ministries ought to be an incarnational posture, a "come and see" approach to ministry. But we ought not to entrust ourselves too fully or too quickly to too many. May God raise up people in our lives and ministries to whom we can confess the state of our souls as honestly as Jesus did to his three closest friends. And may we become the kind of persons who invite such openness of heart from others.[5]

SUFFERING

To be vulnerable is to open ourselves to suffering. That suffering is an ines-

---

[5]As noted earlier, Henri Nouwen argued that such vulnerability trumps all urges to be "relevant." He wrote, as quoted earlier, "I am fully convinced that the Christian leader of the next century is to be completely irrelevant, offering nothing except his own, vulnerable self." *In the Name of Jesus: Reflections on Christian Leadership* (New York: Crossroad, 1993), p. 30.

capable part of our call to ministry has often been overlooked in an evangelical culture that tilts toward triumphalism. Thankfully, however, there have always been faithful witnesses of a countercultural message in this regard, and that continues to be the case today. Jesus' ministry could not have been fulfilled without suffering, as the author to the Hebrews makes so abundantly clear. Said otherwise, Jesus' ministry *was* suffering. We have been called not only to believe on him but to suffer for him (see Phil 1:29), called to a "fellowship of sharing in his sufferings" (Phil 3:10), to actually fill up in our own flesh "what is lacking in regard to Christ's afflictions" (Col 1:24).

We are called, to say it bluntly, to die with Jesus. Bonhoeffer offered the famous remark about the call on all disciples' lives: "When Christ calls a man, he bids him 'Come and die.'"[6] In a special sense, this is true for those who are called to teach, lead and serve in ministry roles. Such ministries are a way of laying down our lives in acts of sacrificial love for others. Paul saw his ministry as death to himself for the sake of giving life to others (see 1 Cor 4:7-12).

As Ajith Fernando beautifully pointed out in his book *The Call to Joy and Pain: Embracing Suffering in Your Ministry,* suffering is a vital aspect of the call on every minister of the Gospel.[7] My dear friend Adrian DeVisser, who leads a powerful church-planting ministry in Sri Lanka, introduced me to Ajith, his mentor, on my first visit to their homeland. Over the course of many visits to that country, I have come to realize that for these brothers, and for all who minister in such contexts, suffering is neither a surprise nor an option. As Adrian explained to me during my first visit to that beautiful but broken island, it would be unthinkable for someone ministering in the midst of such brokenness and suffering not to join themselves to that suffering with their people.

As I have also learned from Adrian and Ajith, we in the West are by no means immune to brokenness. Our particular poverty may be of a different sort than what I have witnessed in Sri Lanka, but it is no less pronounced and profound. Indeed, our poverty and pain in the West may be harder to face, because it is more easily hidden or ignored. My wife and teenage daughter joined me in a visit to Sri Lanka just a few months after the tsunami of 2004. After a few days among a people who had experienced such devastating loss— on top of decades of poverty and civil war—my daughter remarked, "They've

---

[6]Dietrich Bonhoeffer, *The Cost of Discipleship* (New York: Simon & Schuster, 1959), p. 35.
[7]Ajith Fernando, *The Call to Joy and Pain: Embracing Suffering in Your Ministry* (Wheaton: Crossway, 2007).

gone through so much, but they seem a lot happier than people back home."

In whatever contexts we may be called to minister, we must suffer for Christ and thus suffer with him for his people. The pastor of my home church, Dave Swaim, recently told our congregation about the question that was put to him when he was beginning his first ministerial service:

> When I first entered professional ministry as a twenty-two-year-old fresh out of college, I was eager and excited, and more than a little arrogant about all my gifts and the excellent ministry I planned to do with them. I began working at a church in Virginia, and a much older pastor who'd founded that church invited me to meet with him. Once an active pastor and athlete, he had been confined to a wheelchair for decades after a bizarre medical misdiagnosis resulted in the slow degeneration of all his muscles and nerves. But rather than give up ministry, he continued to serve, and his ministry became ever more influential and effective.
>
> After some initial small talk, he asked me to read from 2 Corinthians 1:3-5: "Praise be to the God and Father of our Lord Jesus Christ, the Father of compassion and the God of all comfort, who comforts us in all our troubles, so that we can comfort those in any trouble with the comfort we ourselves have received from God. For just as the sufferings of Christ flow over into our lives, so also through Christ our comfort overflows."
>
> After I read that he asked me to explain to him what it meant, to which I replied something like "we comfort others by sharing the way that God comforted us when we suffered in similar ways."
>
> "Right," he replied. "But if you want to be a pastor, then you need to be able to comfort people in every kind of suffering. Do you know what that means?"
>
> "That I have to suffer everything?"
>
> "Right."
>
> And this great, godly man who'd been in a wheelchair for decades, leaned forward and looked me straight in the eyes as he asked, "David, are you sure you want to be a pastor?"
>
> "Sure" I replied glibly. And I went on my merry way to do all of my very important ministry with all of my very excellent gifts.[8]

Dave went on to tell us of some of the ways that God has been teaching him the wisdom of the older pastor's words through the hard experiences of his own life over the years. He has suffered, and God has used it for the benefit of others. Afterward he related to me the further detail that the older pastor

---

[8]Pastor Dave Swaim of Highrock Covenant Church in Arlington, Massachusetts, related this story to the congregation in the spring of 2008.

had himself been asked the same question by his own pastor—the late Harry Ironside. All prospective pastors in our church are now asked to read the same Scripture and contemplate the same issues and the same question: "Are you sure you want to be a pastor?"

All who would follow Christ, serving him and his people, must wrestle with these things. Serving means suffering. Are we sure we want to walk this path?

AUTHORITY

Jesus taught as one who had authority, we are told. This deeply impressed the crowds who heard him, and they were struck by the contrast between Jesus and their religious authorities (see Mt 7:28-29). What was it about Jesus' teaching that marked it as authoritative, and what implications might this have for teachers in the church today?

In passages like the Sermon on the Mount, in which we have an extended account of Jesus' teaching, we find that the Lord did not base his pronouncements on the authority of rabbinic teachers who had gone before him. This stood in stark contrast with other teachers of the day, who were wont to cite those reckoned as the spiritual "fathers" of the people. At other times, it seems that Jesus' teaching struck his hearers as having an obvious divine stamp of authority because it was confirmed by miraculous signs. He demonstrated authority—visibly and dramatically—over fig trees and windstorms, over illness and death, over sins and demons. He also exercised authority in the religious realm. He forgave sins, cleansed the temple of moneychangers and claimed lordship over the Sabbath (see Mk 2:28).

When Jesus opened his mouth to speak, the words themselves rang with the air of unique authority: "You have heard that it was said . . . , *but I tell you* . . ." (as in Mt 5, emphasis added). Can Christian teachers today presume such authority in their ministries? The author to the Hebrews tells of how the message of salvation "was first announced by the Lord" and "was confirmed to us by those who heard him. God also testified to it by signs, wonders and various miracles" (Heb 2:3-4). Is this typically our experience?

There are, of course, those persistent reports from near and far—especially in cases where the Gospel is breaking new ground—that God continues to establish this "new teaching" (Mk 1:27; Acts 17:19) by means of signs and wonders. Some who preach and teach in Jesus' name experience such moments of divine authority in their ministries, and we thank God for it. But even where that does occur, it may be more exceptional than typical.

Woe to the human teacher who, having been thus favored by God on some occasion, begins to act before others as though that power is of his own making and is a permanent possession. Paul did not heal all those he ministered among (see 2 Tim 4:20). Even Jesus' healing ministry had limits. On some occasions he healed all the sick and demon possessed who were brought to him (see Mt 8:16; Lk 6:19), but on other occasions he apparently did not (see Jn 5:3-13). Even his working of wonders could be limited by circumstances (see Mk 6:4-6) and was dependent on the manifestation of the Spirit's power (see Lk 5:17).

If our teaching is not regularly accompanied by miracles, does it lack proper authority? Are we wise to begin our own pronouncements with "You have heard . . . but I tell you . . ."? We suggest, in both cases, that the answer is no. Yet we do believe that our teaching can be marked by genuine divine authority.[9]

We do well to think about Jesus' teaching authority from more than one angle. Yes, he taught as one who had authority. But we should also mark the fact that Jesus taught as one who *was under authority*. He plainly and consistently regarded Scripture as authoritative and submitted himself to it (see, for example, Mt 4:4, 7, 10; 5:17-19; 22:29-32, 37-40, 43-44; Jn 10:35). Furthermore, he lived as one utterly submitted to the authority of his Father. He did only what he saw his Father doing (see Jn 5:19) and said only what his Father gave him to say (see Jn 7:16; 14:10, 24). He labored only by the authority and in the power of his Father (see Jn 5:21-27; 14:10; 17:4). The Roman centurion had asked Jesus to heal his servant but to do so by just speaking the word rather than by coming in person to his home. He explained, "For I myself am a man under authority" (Mt 8:9). We could rightly say of Jesus that he also was one under authority. And so must we see ourselves.

The fact is, had Jesus moved out from under the authority of his Father and out from under the authority of Scripture, his own authority would have been instantly invalidated. He may still have been able to do the miraculous, but it would have been in service of another, not of God. The devil actually offered Jesus a new sort of authority and a different source of power if only he would submit to his fiendish rule instead of continuing in submission to God (see Mt 4:8-9). Jesus later made it clear that miraculous deeds in one's ministry—even

---

[9]Robert Pazmiño has written helpfully about the matter of authority in our teaching in *By What Authority Do We Teach? Sources for Empowering Christian Educators* (Eugene, Ore.: Wipf and Stock, 2002).

if exercised *in his name*—are not, in themselves, evidence of divine approval (see Mt 7:21-23).

All this ought to strike those of us who teach and preach as both sobering and encouraging. It is sobering in that it reminds us that we dare not speak on our own authority. We recall all the warnings aimed at teachers that we considered in the previous chapter and are sobered by them. But there is also encouragement for us as we find the key for teaching with proper authority: our authority is a derivative, not an inherent authority. That is, there is nothing *in us* that could mark our teaching as authoritative. Nevertheless, we have been authorized by Jesus, just as he was authorized by the Father. Thus, as long as we remain steadfastly under *that* authority, we can be assured that we teach and serve with true authority.

During his earthly ministry, Jesus often *gave authority* to others (see Mt 10:1; Lk 10:1, 17-24). The accounts of him commissioning his followers for ministry after his ascension indicate that he has given authority to the church (see Mt 28:18-20; Jn 20:21-23; Acts 1:7-8). By what authority then do we teach and preach the Gospel? We do so by the authority of Jesus himself. But we must not—we dare not—abuse this authority or in any way misuse the name of Christ. God will not hold guiltless anyone who misuses his Name (see Ex 20:7). John writes with deep respect for those servants of the church who labor "for the sake of the Name" (3 Jn 7). But he also warns against "anyone who runs ahead and does not continue in the teaching of Christ" (2 Jn 9).

Can a Christian teacher or preacher ever say, "The culture says to you . . . but I tell you . . ."? Yes, there may well be times for this. But if we speak with such language, we had better be sure that the words we speak are not our own but are fully authorized by Christ. The apostle Paul was careful to distinguish between his own advice and the Lord's command (see 1 Cor 7:6-12). Jude warns against spiritual presumption by citing the arrogance of false teachers (see Jude 8-10). We must guard against the temptation to divert toward ourselves honor that ought to belong only to the Lord (see Num 20:8-13).

We desire to be Spirit-filled, Gospel-driven and Scripture-soaked servants. We should honestly acknowledge when we are offering one among several interpretations of a long-disputed passage of Scripture and admit that we might be wrong. Some will argue that this undermines our authority. Not so—to the contrary, it reveals that real authority is found in submission to and humility before God and his Word. We ought to be boldest on those points where God's word is clearest. When we do not know the answer to a question raised by a fellow learner, we humbly confess it, rather than speak presumptuously simply to maintain an "air of authority." To say something like "That's a good question, and though I can't claim to know the answer now, I'll look into that further and will get back to you on this" is far safer than to risk confusing our hearers and incurring God's anger by making something up on the spot.

Even if we utilize every safeguard we can think of as we minister, we will err sooner or later: "We all stumble in many ways. If anyone is never at fault in what he says, he is a perfect man" (Jas 3:2). So it is that we must trust, finally, in the mercies of God. The same Gospel that we preach to others we must preach every day to ourselves. Each Lord's day, as he ascended the pulpit of London's Metropolitan Tabernacle, Charles Spurgeon is reported to have said to himself with each step he took, "I believe in the Holy Spirit. . . . I believe in the Holy Spirit." For unlike our Lord Jesus, none of us embodies either perfect deity or perfect humanity. Whatever authority we exercise in our teaching will always be limited, derivative and Spirit-dependent.

Yet our authority is real. The One to whom all authority in heaven and on earth has been given has authorized us to serve in his name. God has anointed us with the Spirit of truth (see 1 Jn 2:20, 27). The church—in which and from which we serve—is "the pillar and foundation of the truth" (1 Tim 3:15). All the holy Scriptures that we read and exposit are God-breathed and "useful for teaching, rebuking, correcting and training in righteousness" (2 Tim 3:16). The Gospel we declare is, forever and for all, the very power of God to save those who believe (see Rom 1:16). To the degree that we preach that Gospel, teach those Scriptures, identify with that church, depend on that Spirit and serve in that Name—to that degree we teach with authority. In other words, we teach *with* authority when we teach as those who are *under* authority, and only then.

Before leaving this matter of authority, we should note the distinction between an evangelical Protestant approach to this matter and that of Orthodox or Catholic believers.[10] Such an excursus is actually of vital concern to the question of the teacher's own authority. The subject is a vast one, and we refer readers to the resources listed at the close of this chapter for fuller exploration. For now, we offer these few remarks.

---

[10]For a helpful overview of some of the issues we raise here related to the "teaching office" of the church, see Richard Osmer, *A Teachable Spirit: Recovering the Teaching Office in the Church* (Louisville, Ky.: Westminster/John Knox Press, 1990).

AUTHORITY OF SCRIPTURE, AUTHORITY
OF THE CHURCH

Catholics and Orthodox Christians regard Scripture as divinely inspired, just as evangelical Protestants do. They assign to Scripture a high place of authority when it comes to teaching on matters of faith and life for believers. Yet they also assign great authority to the church and to sacred tradition. Sometimes this authority manifests itself in the form of "the proper interpretation" of Scripture. At other points, the church claims authoritative teaching that is not explicitly found in Scripture. The teaching of "the Church" or of "the Fathers" is never viewed as contradicting Scripture. Rather, it is seen as clarifying or complementing the teaching of the Bible.

From the vantage point of many evangelical Protestants, such an approach is problematic for several reasons. In the first place, it often seems that there is a gulf between theory and practice. Our Orthodox and Catholic friends may say that they assign the highest place to Scripture, but we, through our evangelical eyes, think we see numerous places where the clear teaching of Scripture has been overruled or simply ignored by the supposed clarifying or complementary teaching offered by the church. Teachings about the role of Mary in the life of the church or about the nature of the Eucharist are two commonly cited examples in this respect. Evangelicals fear—with some justification, it seems to us—that our fellow Christians run the risk at such points of nullifying "the word of God for the sake of . . . tradition" (Mt 15:6), as Jesus said religious leaders in his own day had done.

Evangelicals believe that the Word of God alone is inspired and authoritative. The tradition of the church is valuable, but it must always be tested against the plain teaching of the Bible. Writing as evangelicals, we certainly affirm this perspective. But we also acknowledge that such a view presents serious challenges. First, who is to say what constitutes "the plain teaching of the Bible"? The ever-expanding plethora of Protestant denominations today testifies against us. It is no wonder, then, that to many Catholics and Orthodox, we Protestants evoke memories of the description in the book of Judges: "In those days Israel had no king; everyone did as he saw fit" (Judg 21:25). It is not surprising that having the guidance of the Magisterium or of the Tradition is, for Catholics and Orthodox Christians, seen as preferable to such a state of affairs.

Then, too, we must acknowledge that we evangelicals have our own trouble bridging the gap between theory and practice. We profess that it is by appeal to Scripture alone that we determine our doctrines. But is that not overstating the case? We are, in fact, attentive to the tradition of the church, we exercise our reason, and we consider our experience as we interact with Scriptures. (The Wesleyan Quadrilateral—a term coined by Albert Outler to describe Wesley's approach to forming theology—is a familiar articulation of this fourfold relationship.[11])

Furthermore, for all our claims to be "Bible people," we often fail to recognize or admit that our reading of Scripture is deeply influenced by the cultures in which we live. How is it, for example, that many white American evangelicals and many black American evangelicals—while appealing to the same Bible and praying to the same Lord—can reach such different (often diametrically opposed) understandings about what is righteous and moral when it comes time to cast their votes for political leaders? In our day, such diffusion of beliefs and ethical practices among those calling themselves "Bible-believing Christians" seems only to be on the increase.

As we argued in chapter four, evangelicals are most unwise to belittle the value of the tradition of the church. When we do so, we display both ignorance and arrogance. The fact is, we depend on the diligent labors of those who have preceded us. We cited earlier the work of D. H. Williams in this regard, and many other evangelicals have also offered helpful insights in this area, especially in recent years.[12] As Catholics and Orthodox believers love to remind evangelical Protestants, every time we open our Bibles we are acknowledging our indebtedness to the church fathers who were used by God in discerning the canon of Scripture. Furthermore, all the central tenets of Orthodox Christianity have come down to us as mediated through the toils, tears and even blood of those church leaders in the first centuries. Protestants also appeal to the work of the great Reformers, and believers of various stripes appeal to the leaders in their particular church movements.

We must acknowledge all of the above. Though we evangelicals claim to be under the authority of the Scripture and of the Lord of the Scripture, it is hard work to try to live out this submission to biblical authority in particular

---

[11]For a helpful discussion on the Wesleyan Quadrilateral as it relates to biblical interpretation, see Roger Olson, *The Mosaic of Christian Belief: Twenty Centuries of Unity and Diversity* (Downers Grove, Ill.: InterVarsity Press, 2002), pp. 56-57, 63-69.

[12]D. H. Williams, *Evangelicals and Tradition: The Formative Influence of the Early Church* (Grand Rapids: Baker, 2005), and *Retrieving the Tradition and Renewing Evangelicalism: A Primer for Suspicious Protestants* (Grand Rapids: Eerdmans, 1999); Robert Wilken, *Remembering the Christian Past* (Grand Rapids: Eerdmans, 1995); Robert Webber, *Ancient-Future Faith: Rethinking Evangelicalism for a Postmodern World* (Grand Rapids: Baker, 1999).

situations of theology, ethics or worship. But hard as the work is, we feel compelled to walk such a path. It would doubtless be easier simply to follow "the teaching of the Church" or of "the Fathers" on all essential points and on most points not so essential as well. But when such teaching seems to be in conflict with the plain teaching of Scripture—a determination that must be built on diligent study of the Bible and exercised humbly as members of the one, holy, catholic and apostolic church—we cannot simply follow the lead of church authorities.

Jesus plainly opposed the religious authorities and their adherence to the "tradition of the fathers" when they themselves had come out from under the authority of Scripture. There are times for us to do the same. Like Luther at the Diet of Worms,[13] there are times when conscience binds us to take our stand. In all circumstances, we are to live as teachers who exhibit humility and a conciliatory spirit, with the posture of learners. Yet we live with proper confidence in God and in peace with fellow brothers and sisters in Christ.

An interesting angle on this dispute about final authority for life and teaching in the church is a sort of "chicken and egg" question. Did the church give us the Scriptures or did the Scriptures give us the church? The Reformers often spoke of the church as having been birthed by the Gospel, and they argued that it has no authority when it moves out from under the Gospel.

On the other hand, there really is a sense in which the church has given us the Bible. But what does that mean for the church's posture toward the Scriptures? It is well to consider some precedents for such a question. The prophets declared, "Thus saith the LORD." But though the word was spoken through them, they were the first to humble themselves and tremble before it (see Is 66:2; Jer 23:9). To Israel belonged the oracles of God—but that made God's people servants of the word, not its masters. John's ministry preceded that of Jesus, but he pointed away from himself, willfully decreasing even as Jesus' influence increased (see Jn 3:30). Mary gave birth to Christ, but she did not become Lord over the One she had birthed. Instead, her confession was, "Do whatever he tells you" (Jn 2:5). In like manner, the church that was used by

---

[13]When Luther was pushed to respond candidly as to whether he would repudiate his words and the "errors," he said, "Since then Your Majesty and your lordships desire a simple reply, I will answer without horns and without teeth. Unless I am convicted by Scriptures and plain reason—I do not accept the authority of popes and councils, for they have contradicted each other—my conscience is captive to the Word of God. I cannot and I will not recant anything, for to go against conscience is neither right nor safe. God help me. Amen." Roland Bainton, *Here I Stand: A Life of Martin Luther* (Nashville: Abingdon, 1950, 1977), p. 144.

God to give birth to the Scriptures must always submit itself to those very Scriptures. As evangelicals, we acknowledge no infallible church. Rather, we affirm the Bible as "the only infallible guide for faith and practice."[14]

LISTENING

Given the seriousness of the teacher's role and responsibilities, it is incumbent on God-honoring teachers to develop the capacity of listening. It may seem that teachers ought to be, above all, good communicators. But no. Above all, teachers must be good *listeners*. Calvin argued that a teachable spirit was the foundation of true Christian piety.[15] Surely those who would teach others must be the most teachable of all. The day we cease to be willing to learn is the day we should abandon any claim to a teaching ministry in the lives of others.

From the Bible's very beginning, we are struck with the centrality of listening in God's economy. Creation begins with the speech of God. God forms, fills, names and assigns value to all that he creates—and does all this by his word. God speaks to, and listens to, himself: "Let us make man in our image, in our likeness" (Gen 1:26). When God creates humans and places them in the garden, he speaks to them—blessings, commands and warnings. When the man and the woman rebel, God speaks again—questions, judgment, promise.

As the great work of reconciling all things to himself begins, the speech of God is once again preeminent. He raises up individuals and nations. He calls into being a people to be his very own and to serve as a witness to all the nations. To these people God sends prophets. Through the prophets, God gives Torah and other speech. The most basic of God's Torah words is the *shema* of Deuteronomy 6:4, which begins with the words "Hear, O Israel." Over the centuries, when Israel wandered from the Way, God called through the prophets, urging them to return with all their hearts. "Hear the word of the LORD" they are told again and again (for example, Is 1:10; 28:14).

The New Testament also begins with speech. John comes as another prophet of repentance, baptizing and preaching. He comes also as a forerunner, a voice of one calling in the desert, "Prepare the way for the Lord." Fulfilling John's prophecies, Jesus appears. He is himself the perfect and eternal word of God made flesh for us and for our salvation (see Jn 1:1, 14). God's

---

[14]F. F. Bruce, "The Lausanne Covenant—2: The Authority and Power of the Bible," *The Harvester* 55 (November 1976): 320.

[15]See in Osmer, *Teachable Spirit*, p. 57. See also Calvin's *Institutes* 2.1.

speech takes human form, the flawless *exegesis* of the never-been-seen-by-anyone God (see Jn 1:18). God had spoken in the past through prophets. But "in these last days" God has spoken in his Son—the "exact representation" of the invisible God (Heb 1:1-3).

The Word that became flesh devoted himself to a life of loving deeds and true speech—all of it directed by his Father. He was a prophet and teacher. Through sermon and parable, by answering and asking questions, in personal conversations and public disputations, both by gentle words and with stern rebukes, Jesus spoke, and called people to listen: Let him who has an ear, hear. His closest companions witnessed him glorified before their very eyes, and suddenly their teacher was in the company of Israel's great prophets—Moses and Elijah. But then a cloud enveloped them, and they heard a voice from heaven saying, "This is my Son, whom I love. Listen to him!" (Mk 9:1-7).

Jesus promised that after his departure, the Holy Spirit—the Spirit of truth—would come to the church, would guide them into all truth, would remind them of all that Jesus had taught them. The book of Acts is a wonderful record of that Spirit ministry, as well as a wonderful testimony of the power of listening. Nearly every page of Luke's account reveals how critical listening was in the progress of the church. We note here only a few of the highlights.

In Acts 1, the apostles listen to the Lord's instructions to wait for the Spirit's outpouring. They ask the Lord to guide them as they select a replacement for the one who had deserted them and betrayed the Lord. Acts 2 records the outpouring of the Spirit, and we read of the pilgrims to Jerusalem hearing the glories of God miraculously expounded in their own languages. They listen attentively as Peter explains what has occurred and proclaims Christ crucified and risen. In Acts 6, church leaders listen and respond graciously to grievances raised by the Hellenists who were part of the community.

Acts 7 is the most striking of several incidences of nonlistening recorded in the book of Acts. Stephen recounts God's dealings with Israel and the revelation of the Messiah Jesus. But as he rebukes his hearers for their part in the death of Jesus, they can abide no more of his words. They protect themselves from having to listen to this preacher. They cover their ears as they charge toward him (see Acts 7:57), shouting over his voice as they move. Finally, they stone him to death to finish the job of silencing him (see Acts 7:58).

Acts 8 records the account of the Gospel going to the Samaritans through the ministry of Philip. Philip is a marvelous listener. His ear is finely tuned to the leading of the Spirit, a fact made clear by all his movements in the chapter.

He was quick to listen, even when called on to move out beyond culturally acceptable boundaries. The Gospel is received by an Ethiopian official and by a group of Samaritans. The apostles, responding to Philip's ministry, listen carefully to what God is doing, and they are happily startled at God's fulfilling Jesus' words in Acts 1:8 about the spread of the Gospel. We can learn from Philip's example how important it is to keep our ears open to God's leading each day.[16]

In Acts 9, Saul of Tarsus—intent on continuing his assault of the church—hears a voice and sees a blinding light. Jesus asks Saul for an accounting of his persecuting ways. But Saul makes no defense; he simply listens as the Lord reveals to him how much he must suffer for the sake of the Name. Ananias, a faithful believer, listens with shock at his new assignment: helping this very Saul find both his sight and his place in the body of Christ.

Acts 10 tells the remarkable story of Peter learning to listen. It is not an easy affair, for Peter is being told stunning things. Through vision and visitation, he learns that God's good news is for the Gentiles too. Cornelius and other Gentiles who have gathered in his home listen as Peter proclaims Jesus once again. In Acts 11, it is now the church leaders' turn to listen as Peter explains his actions and, more importantly, God's actions among the Gentiles.

One of the most beautiful accounts of listening in the book is found in Acts 13. There we read of five servant-leaders in the church at Antioch. No one of them is marked as *the* leader. Rather, they mutually submit to one another and to the Lord. As they worship the Lord, the Holy Spirit speaks to them. Because they listened well[17] to what they were hearing, the far-flung mission to the Gentiles begins. Saul and Barnabas are marked out by the Spirit for mission—a mission that was to require many twists and turns as these ministers discerned the leading of God in the advance of the kingdom.

As God brings the Gentiles into the covenant family in such dramatic and powerful fashion, it falls to church leaders once again to listen to the accounts and try to make sense of it all. A council is convened in Jerusalem. James apparently chairs the proceedings. Paul and Barnabas offer their account of the Spirit's movements. Members of the "circumcision party" present their case for

---

[16]Two books on such listening that we would commend to our readers' attention are Klaus Bockmuehl, *Listening to the God Who Speaks: Reflections on God's Guidance from Scripture and the Lives of God's People* (Colorado Springs: Helmers & Howard, 1990); David E. Ross, *A Table Before Me: The Meditating Christian* (Longwood, Fla.: Xulon Press, 2007).

[17]They listened without prejudice or preconceived plans, as if expecting God to listen to *them* and grant *them* what *they* wished.

circumcising these Gentile believers and making them submit to the law of Moses. After much discussion, Peter speaks (Acts 15:7), recalling the episode with Cornelius and what God was clearly teaching him and all of them through such things. Finally, James speaks, and the matter is settled. In a letter sent to encourage the Gentiles who were coming to faith, James qualifies the conclusions of the group with these words: "It seemed good to the Holy Spirit and to us" (Acts 15:28). Because of the careful listening that took place on that occasion,[18] Gentiles through the ages who would follow Jesus as Savior and Lord have not been compelled to become Jewish first.

The accounts go on and on. There is the listening of Paul and his companions to the "Macedonian call," which leads to the Gospel reaching Europe for the first time. There is the contrast between the Thessalonians, who were rather poor listeners, and the noble Bereans who, after hearing Paul out fully, searched the Scriptures to see whether or not what he was saying was true. In our day, a pseudo-Berean spirit is often more evident. We tend to listen with the expectation of error. But the Bereans extended grace to this newcomer and his teaching, a grace guided and guarded by the Scriptures.

We consider just one further story from the book of Acts. In Acts 18, we read of the encounter between Apollos and two of Paul's close companions, Priscilla and Aquila. This tent-making couple is residing in Corinth, and they have occasion to hear the new preacher in town. Apollos was a trained rhetorician, was mighty in the Scriptures and had been catechized in the Way of the Lord, though he knew only the baptism of John. Priscilla and Aquila listened with appreciation but recognized that something was missing in Apollos's teaching. What did they do about it? Note what they did *not* do: they did not leave the meeting shaking their heads; they did not warn others about Apollos's shortcomings; they did not publish a tract on the errors of Apollos. Instead, they invited him to their home and shared with him what they had learned through the ministry of Paul. Their great example as listeners was matched by Apollos. He—the learned and trained teacher—accepted instruction from a pair of tent-makers. His catechesis was deepened and the result was powerful: he was sent on his way as a source of great blessing to the church (see Acts 18:18-28).

---

[18]Desiring to obey God's leading, they set aside what was comfortable and normative to their religious tradition. Listening in this instance is to the Holy Spirit who resides not only in us, the teachers, but also among those we are called to teach. The teacher's primary role is to be able to listen and to facilitate what the Holy Spirit desires to do as we—both the teachers and learners—avail ourselves to his power and will to transform us.

The theme of listening is just as clear throughout the New Testament letters. Countless examples might be cited, but the most striking is that of James, who wrote, "Everyone should be quick to listen, slow to speak and slow to become angry" (Jas 1:19). James goes on to remind us to humbly receive God's word—the word that saves us (see Jas 1:21). Furthermore, we are to "be doers of the word, and not hearers only," lest we deceive ourselves into thinking we know what we really do not know (Jas 1:22 RSV). We are to look deeply into the law that liberates. We must guard our tongues, that inferno in our faces that can cause so much trouble and grief (see Jas 3:1-12).

In the last book in the New Testament, the book of Revelation, we read of seven letters sent from our Lord to seven churches. Though the particular contents of each letter are unique, we hear this refrain in each one: "He who has an ear, let him hear what the Spirit says to the churches." The entire book is filled with God's pronouncements and praises, and listening is a persistent theme. At last, the prophecy closes even as it began, with promises and warnings relative to hearing, heeding and honoring these words from God (see Rev 1:3; 22:18-19).

Perhaps, then, the most basic duty of a believer is to listen. This is certainly so for those who would teach. We devote ourselves to the perpetual hearing of God's Word and to listening deeply to the cries of those we are called to serve. Jesus, again, is both the Word we must hear and our role model for listening. This is very clear when we meditate on the Servant Songs in the book of Isaiah (Is 42; 49; 50; 52—53). These four passages refer to a mysterious "Servant of the LORD." Christians have long believed the Servant to be personified ultimately in the Lord Jesus. A striking feature common to all four passages is that the Servant is not quick to speak.

We read of the Servant that "he will not shout or cry out, or raise his voice in the streets" (Is 42:2). Instead, he labors in mercy, faithfulness and justice. In Isaiah 49:2, the Servant says of himself that the Lord "made my mouth like a sharpened sword." The sword is frequently an image for God's Word. When this Servant *does* speak, we can be assured it will be God's word on his lips. In the most famous of the Servant Songs, Isaiah 52:13—53:12, we read that the Servant suffers silently for the salvation of his people. "He was oppressed and afflicted, yet he did not open his mouth; he was led like a lamb to the slaughter, and as a sheep before her shearers is silent, so he did not open his mouth" (Is 53:7).

Finally, we consider the testimony of Isaiah 50:4-5: "The Sovereign LORD has given me an instructed tongue, to know the word that sustains the weary.

He wakens me morning by morning, wakens my ear to listen like one being taught. The Sovereign Lord has opened my ears, and I have not been rebellious; I have not drawn back." The Servant, we are told, has been given an instructed tongue, literally, "the tongue of disciples."

A modern rendering of this text substitutes "the tongue of a teacher" for "the tongue of disciples." The translators apparently believed that the Hebrew text reflected a scribal error. "The tongue of a teacher" made sense to them, but "the tongue of disciples" did not, and so they "corrected" the text.[19] But it is not the text that needs correction. It is *we* who need correction. Would we teach others? Then we must be taught ourselves. James had written about the peril of the untamable tongue for those who teach. But the Servant offers us hope; though we may never fully tame our tongues, we can permit God to disciple them.

The key to a disciplined tongue is found in the rest of the passage. God discipled the Servant's tongue by opening his ear and by waking him morning by morning to listen like those who are taught. Literally, the Lord had "dug ears" in the head of the Servant (Is 50:5). And the Servant was not rebellious to this significant act of God. We who teach today must not rebel against the ears that God has dug in *our* heads. Instead, we must rise daily with ears and minds and hearts wide open to God and his Word. Jesus has well modeled this spiritual discipline for us (see, for example, Lk 5:16; Mk 1:35-39). Through such a practice, we will be able to discern "the word that sustains the weary one" (Is 50:4). This phrase implies that God's servants must listen in two directions—both to the Word of God and to the cries of the poor and broken whom we are called to serve.

By such a committed posture of listening, we are in position to have hearts that more faithfully reflect the living God. The idols of the nations have "eyes, but they cannot see; they have ears, but cannot hear. . . . Those who make them will become like them, and so will all who trust in them" (Ps 115:5-6, 8). If this sobering word of warning is true, so must its opposite be: we who worship the living God will become like *him*! By worshiping the God who sees all, we will come to see more clearly. By worshiping the God who hears our every cry, our hearing will be sharpened. By contemplating the glory of the risen Lord, we who are engaged in ministries of teaching will be transformed into his likeness, with ever-increasing glory, by the power of the Spirit who is at work within us (see 2 Cor 3:17-18). Here is the proper and

---

[19]The New Revised Standard Version marks the phrase in question with the notation *cn,* indicating that the text has been corrected.

worthy goal for Christian teachers: that we would be like Jesus. We often think of this in terms of personal piety alone. But let us think of it also in terms of our ministry to others as teachers in the body of Christ.

CONCLUSION

May all of the attributes we have considered in this chapter—belief and calling, zeal and knowledge, truthfulness and gentleness, humility and partnership, vulnerability and suffering, authority and listening—call us humbly onward toward greater Christlikeness as we serve the church through ministries of teaching.

We have looked thus far at the church's mission, its message and—in this just-concluded section—its ministers. In the next two chapters, we continue our consideration of its members—the people of God—by focusing attention on learners and learning. Then in the fourth and final section of the book we turn our attention to means and models for faithful and effective ministries of education and formation.

HYMN FOR CONTEMPLATION AND WORSHIP

To Hear as Those Well Taught

(Is 50:4-5)

The Sovereign Lord has given me
a well-instructed tongue
that I might understand the word
that helps the weary one.
Each morning he awakens me
unto the word of God.
My ear he wakens, day by day,
to hear as those well taught.

The Sovereign Lord has given me
an open, list'ning ear.
And I did not defy his will,
nor dare refuse to hear.
Each morning he awakens me
unto the word of God.
My ear he wakens, day by day,
to hear as those well taught.

God help us, who would dare to teach,
be swift ourselves to learn.

May your word, like an untamed fire,
within our spirits burn.
Each morning, Lord, awaken us
unto the word of God.
Our ears awaken, day by day,
to hear as those well taught.

O, may I sing the Servant's song
in humble, holy fear.
Lord, grant to me a well-trained tongue
and open wide my ear.
Each morning, Lord, awaken me
unto the Word of God.
My ear awaken, day by day,
to hear as those well taught.

Setting: Gary A. Parrett, (2005)
Tune: Kingsfold
Familiar use of the tune: "O Sing a Song of Bethlehem"

QUESTIONS FOR PLANNING AND PRACTICE

1. We invite you to evaluate your own character in light of the characteristics of teachers outlined in this chapter. What are the characteristics you see at work in your life and want to thank God for? What are the others that you desire to improve?

2. Zeal and knowledge go hand in hand; one without the other is useless. In your life, how do you seek to cultivate within yourself a true and growing knowledge of God and zeal for living out his Word as you are called to teach? As previously discussed, teachers are held to a higher standard. We invite you to prayerfully reflect on this weighty calling, that the Lord would guide your steps both within and outside of the context of formal educational ministry.

3. Reflect on a situation in your life or ministry where you found it particularly difficult to speak the truth in love (see Eph 4:15). How were you able to overcome the situation, or how could you have handled it better? What are the practices that you might introduce to your life so that you have a better balance of truthfulness and gentleness?

4. As Christians, we are called to humble ourselves before God and others. Humility is active, not passive. Reflect on Jesus' words in John 13:13-17

after he washed the feet of his disciples. What have you learned in the process of being humble before those whom you teach? How would you continue to cultivate a life and ministry of humility?

5. "We are called, to say it bluntly, to die with Jesus." This is especially true for those who are called to teach, lead and serve in educational ministry roles. In what ways is your own ministry an act of laying down your life in sacrifice for others? How do you seek to reflect this core of Christ's ministry on earth?

6. Jesus taught as one who had authority, both in the natural realm (over nature and created things) and spiritually (as the Son of God). How did Jesus exercise this authority while still remaining obedient to the will of the Father? Why is this such an important model for church workers to consider emulating today?

7. Listening is the most important discipline of every Christian. In the Scriptures, God speaks through and to his creation, and Jesus himself hears the cries of those he came to save. It is the obligation of Christians to listen both to God and to those among whom we minister. How can you become even more committed to the posture of listening? Like a humble servant, how can you discipline yourself to be slow to speak but quick to listen?

RESOURCES FOR FURTHER STUDY

Arnold, J. Heinrich. *Discipleship: Living for Christ in the Daily Grind.* Robertsbridge, U.K.. Plough, 1994.

Bonhoeffer, Dietrich. *The Cost of Discipleship.* New York: Simon and Schuster, 1959.

Braaten, Carl. "The Problem of Authority in the Church," pp. 53-66. In *The Catholicity of the Reformation,* edited by Carl Braaten and Robert Jenson. Grand Rapids: Eerdmans, 1996.

Chambers, Oswald. *My Utmost for His Highest.* Special updated edition. Translated by James Reimann. Grand Rapids: Discovery House, 1995.

Conde-Frazer, Elizabeth, S. Steve Kang and Gary Parrett. *A Many Colored Kingdom.* Grand Rapids: Baker, 2004.

Dean, Kenda Creasy, and Ron Foster. *The Godbearing Life: The Art of Soul Tending for Youth Ministry.* Nashville: Upper Room, 1998.

Fernando, Ajith. *The Call to Joy and Pain: Embracing Suffering in Your Ministry.* Wheaton: Crossway, 2007.

Mannion, Gerard, and Lewis Mudge, eds. *The Routledge Companion to the Christian Church.* New York: Routledge, 2008. See especially chapter 27, "Authority," by Mark Chapman, pp. 497-510.

Nouwen, Henri. *The Return of the Prodigal Son: A Story of Homecoming.* New York: Doubleday, 1994.

Osmer, Richard. *A Teachable Spirit: Recovering the Teaching Office in the Church.* Louisville, Ky.: Westminster/John Knox Press, 1990.

Palmer, Parker. *The Courage to Teach: Exploring the Inner Landscape of a Teacher's Life.* Special edition. San Francisco: Jossey-Bass, 2007.

———. *Let Your Life Speak: Listening for the Voice of Vocation.* San Francisco: Jossey-Bass, 1999.

Willard, Dallas. *Renovation of the Heart: Putting on the Character of Christ.* Colorado Springs: NavPress, 2002.

8

Listening to the Theorists

Let the wise listen and add to their learning, and let the discerning get guidance.

PROVERBS 1:5

▼

Throughout this book, and especially in the two previous chapters, we have been championing the ministry of teaching in the church. It is critical, however, that teachers approach their task with learning in mind. Why is this so? We do so, first of all, to ensure that we will teach as effectively as possible. Learning about learning holds great potential to increase the quality of our teaching.

There is another important reason, however, why we are wise to teach with learning in mind: it is because we teach the way we are taught.[1] Not only that, but when we teach, we often disregard "the way we were educated to teach."[2] For instance, despite much research on the clear advantage of active learning,[3] "70 to 90 percent" of those who teach at the college level and beyond continue to utilize the "traditional lecture as their primary instructional strategy."[4] Moreover, while we readily recognize the importance of the content that we are to

---

[1]Joan Stark, Malcolm Lowther, Michael Ryan and Michele Genthon, "Faculty Reflects on Course Planning," *Research in Higher Education* 29, no. 3 (1988): 219-40; Alan Gumm, *Music Teaching Style: Moving Beyond Tradition* (Galesville, Md.: Meredith Music Publication, 2003), p. 131.

[2]Gumm, *Music Teaching Style,* p. 131.

[3]For instance, see John Braxton, Willis Jones, Amy Hirschy and Harold Hartley, "The Role of Active Learning in College Student Persistence," *New Directions for Teaching and Learning* 115 (2008): 71-83; Liam Kane, "Educators, Learners and Active Learning Methodologies," *International Journal of Lifelong Education* 23, no. 3 (2004): 275-86.

[4]Lion Gardiner, "Why We Must Change: Research Evidence," *Thought & Action: The NEA Higher Educational Journal* 14 (1988): 71-88, 76.

teach our students, we often assume that our students already know how they are to study and learn. However, one study reports that merely "14 percent of 745 research university students indicated that they have received formal instruction as to how to study, in high school or in college."[5]

Howard Hendricks, widely known in evangelical circles as a teacher of teachers, asserts that if "you stop learning today, you stop living [as a teacher] tomorrow."[6] Those of us who are called to teach the Faith and form the faithful are exhorted to live as learners who are constantly in the presence of the triune God, always preoccupied with meditating on and obeying his Word so that we can aptly teach others to obey all that Jesus Christ has commanded them (see Mt 28:20).

Teaching—often insufficiently assumed to be synonymous with content transfer—is only part of what teachers are called to do. We are called to *be* teachers, not merely to be engaged in the business or profession of teaching. I remember several of my teachers in the past directing me to do what they *say*.[7] When, in my innocence, I would ask them why they were not doing what they told us to do, they would say, "Do as I *say*, not as I *do*." Perhaps I should not have expected them to be able to do all that they taught us, but I was not particularly motivated to do what they were telling me to do, especially when it came to obeying God's will.

Here I am reminded of Abraham Heschel's words, "What we need more than anything else is not textbooks but text-people. It is the personality of the teacher which is the text that the pupils read; the text they will never forget."[8] What Heschel presupposes in that statement is that teachers as "text-people" are to be readily accessible, so that their students may *experience* or *witness* the "text" fully animated by the teachers in real-life situations. When we teachers offer ourselves as fellow disciples-of-Jesus-Christ-*in-progress* among others, we begin to create a community of fellow teachers-learners who are committed to sharing life together—serving one another, exhorting one another and forming one another as the people of God.

---

[5]Lion Gardiner, "Redesigning Higher Education: Producing Dramatic Gains in Student Learning," *ASHE-ERIC Higher Education Report* 23, no. 7 (Washington, D.C.: George Washington University, Graduate School of Education and Human Development, 1996).

[6]Howard Hendricks, *Teaching to Change Lives: Seven Proven Ways to Make Teaching Come Alive* (Sisters, Ore.: Multnomah, 2003), p. 45.

[7]In this chapter, all references to "I" are Steve's.

[8]Abraham Heschel, "The Spirit of Jewish Education," *Jewish Education* 24, no. 2 (Fall 1953): 19, as quoted in Marvin Wilson, *Our Father Abraham: Jewish Roots of the Christian Faith* (Grand Rapids: Eerdmans, 1989), p. 280.

For this to happen, we who strive to be good teachers will be constantly learning about people in the context of their ordinary walks of life in the real world. Particularly, as we seek to find ways to motivate people to be lifelong learners who obey God and all that he has for us, we will want to be teachers who are committed to learning about how they develop as learners, how they experience the world and how they function as a learning community.

When the author of Proverbs admonishes the godly, "Let the wise listen and add to their learning, and let the discerning get guidance" (Prov 1:5), he is portraying the wise in a constant posture of receiving whatever God has for them to experientially acquire, namely, "the moral sense of skill in living within the moral order of Yahweh's world."[9] And "the discerning"—here another designation for "the wise"[10]—seek to grow through guidance, "the art of piloting oneself through the confusion of life." They desire to cultivate the ways of obedience unto the Lord, which "resemble buoys set out on the sea by which one can find one's position."[11]

It is clear from the proverb that wise and discerning teachers are to be habitually acquiring the art of living the life of obedience unto the Lord in the real world themselves, even as they point others to the ways of the Lord. In this sense, learning about how people develop as learners and how they experience the world as God's people becomes a crucial, yet joyous, *habitus* for teachers. What a privilege for teachers to witness God's sovereign and ongoing transformative work in the lives of his people in the world, even as we seek to testify to God's sovereign and ongoing transformative work in our own lives!

When I first started out in teaching ministry as a full-time professor, I took my responsibility seriously, as any teacher should. Yet I thought that my students' learning depended solely on my teaching. Soon I was getting so overwhelmed by the responsibility of teaching that I felt I was losing my mind. In my distress, I stopped by a colleague's office and plopped down to blurt out my fear and anxiety about my overwhelming responsibility as a teacher. After graciously listening to my rant for some time, she quietly walked over and reached for a copy of a quote on teaching and learning that she had used in her curriculum design course for some time, and she gave it to me as an encouragement. It has remained with me over all these years. It reads:

---

[9]Daniel Estes. *Hear, My Son: Teaching and Learning in Proverbs 1-9* (Downers Grove, Ill.: Inter-Varsity Press, 1997), p. 43.
[10]A typical parallel structure in Hebrew wisdom literature.
[11]Gerhard von Rad, *Old Testament Theology* (Edinburgh: Oliver and Boyd, 1962), 1:421.

In a very real sense no man can teach another; he can only aid him to teach himself. Facts can be transferred from one mind to another as a copy is made from the tape on a sound recorder. History, science, even theology, may be taught in that way, but it results in a highly artificial kind of learning and seldom has any good effect on the deep life of the student. What the learner contributes to the learning process is fully as important as anything contributed by the teacher. If nothing is contributed by the learner, the results are useless; at best there will be but the artificial creation of another teacher who can repeat the dreary work on someone else, ad infinitum.[12]

In the next two chapters, we will consider two aspects regarding a community of learners. First, in this chapter, we will ponder together how people develop as learners. As we do so, we will engage the thoughts of numerous theorists from a variety of academic disciplines who have researched and theorized about these matters. Such engagements will require us to change our "language," somewhat from that which has predominated in the book to this point. For the most part, we have been appealing to language from Scripture and from Christian theologians and educators. Without losing sight of our biblical and theological moorings, in these next two chapters we will turn our ears to hear from others—many of whom have lived and studied and written from *outside* the context of the Christian church. Engaging their thinking is an act of humility on our part that calls for a "harder" sort of listening, since some of the language we are about to encounter will be unfamiliar to us. We closed the previous chapter with a discussion of the importance of listening. We encourage the reader to read on in such a spirit.

Often when we think of how people learn, we think of how each person intentionally interacts with others in her environment. We will first consider here, however, the plethora of research on the primacy of the *ontogenesis*[13] of a human being's capacity to learn. In doing so, we will focus our attention on salient issues concerning human learning that, we believe, are germane to teaching and learning the Faith as God's people.

Second, in chapter nine, we will examine the various sociocultural realities

---

[12]A. W. Tozer, "Some Thoughts on Books and Reading," in *Man: The Dwelling Place of God* (Camp Hill, Penn.: Christian Publications, 1966), as appears on page 113 at <http://feedbooks .com/userbook/2774>. I am thankful to Dr. Scottie May, a former colleague in the Christian Formation and Ministry Department at Wheaton College, Wheaton, Illinois, for sharing this quote with me.

[13]How the individual develops as an organism through the sequence of predictable events or stages. See James Wertsch, *Voices of the Mind: A Sociocultural Approach to Mediated Action* (Cambridge, Mass.: Harvard University Press, 1991), pp. 19-25.

in which God's people experience the world as learners. Rather than copiously listing the contemporary issues or trends that Christians face in the world, we will seek to use some of those issues and trends as examples to highlight how teachers can position themselves as lifelong learners, being attentive to the times and knowing what God's people should do in this ever-protean world.[14]

More often than not, when we think about education we think of the familiar schooling model that we were brought up in. The word "education" comes from the Latin word *educare,* meaning "to draw out." It presupposes that the student has potential to learn and is capable of processing the material at hand. Some go so far as to say that the student readily processes much of the knowledge about the world and that the task of a teacher is simply to guide the students to draw knowledge out from themselves.[15] Others suggest that, contrary to the meaning of the root word, the student is a blank slate[16] that needs to be vigorously shaped and filled with knowledge.[17] Thus, depending on the view of the student and how he grows and learns, the approach to his education could vary significantly.

CONCEPTUALIZING THE LEARNER AND HER ENVIRONMENT

In the modern era, one of the first psychological treatises on the concept of human beings as learners can be traced back to William James. James drew a distinction between the self-as-knower (or the self as subject or learner) and the self-as-known (or the self as object or learned). In doing so, he paved the way for subsequent generations of researchers to advance the understanding of human beings as coherent and ordered selves.

Such human beings seek not only to circumvent diffusion and chaos in their lives but also to make sense of the self in relation to the environment they find themselves in. This is the view of human beings espoused by many since René Descartes and the Enlightenment thinkers, who tirelessly advo-

---

[14]We should be as people of Issachar in 1 Chronicles 12:32, "who understood the times and knew what Israel should do."

[15]This is the romantic approach to education. See James Wilhoit, *Christian Education and the Search for Meaning,* 2nd ed. (Grand Rapids: Baker, 1991), pp. 74-82.

[16]The seventeenth-century philosopher John Locke has popularized the notion of human beings as a blank slate, or *tabula rasa.* Yet instead of prescribing a sort of transmissive education, he advocated the autonomy and agency of human beings in the way they author their lives using sense experiences.

[17]This is what Paulo Freire calls the "banking" concept of education, which he vigorously argues against in *Pedagogy of the Oppressed* (New York: Continuum, 1970).

cated the agency and autonomy of the rational self.[18] According to James, while the self-as-knower (I) observes and experiences "myself," the self-as-known (Me) involves all that the person considers to be her own. He further conceptualized that the self-as-known (Me) consists of three aspects: the material Me (the person's body, possessions and family members), the social Me (the person's understandings of recognition she gets from other people) and the spiritual Me (the entire collection of the person's understandings of herself as the person who thinks, feels, acts and experiences life).[19]

In this scheme, we observe human beings as learners who deliberately pursue acquiring what they deem important to learn about the world, using various learning capacities. In this sense, they are not passive learners who cannot differentiate their agentic[20] selves from the reservoir of themselves that has been shaped by their own intentional interactions with their objects of learning. Instead, they are able to recognize that they are "improved," or more mature, versions of their former selves, because of deliberate actions taken to engage in learning what they deemed to be important for their growth.

James did not explicitly make connections between the impact of the social world with the development of the material and spiritual components of the Me. The subsequent generation of researchers, however, were profoundly influenced by James and thus advanced the study of the self as a learner, including emphasis on how the whole Me is formulated in the context of social relationships.[21]

For instance, James Baldwin asserts that the Me develops as a function of the interaction of the child and the social world. The process involves mutual imitation of self and other. The child's self grows by imitating her mother. As a result, the child's understanding of her mother grows, paralleling the development of the self.[22] Thus the child's imitations of her mother and numerous

---

[18]William James, *Psychology* (Greenwich, Conn.: Fawcett, 1892, 1963), pp. 166-97.

[19]For James, this distinction between I and Me does not further dichotomize the person as in the mind-body dualism advocated by the Cartesian Cogito. Instead, it embraces the intrinsic relatedness of I and (material) Me. The distinction also espouses the relatedness of I and (social) Me, while it debunks the notion of self-other dualism. For a helpful critique of the Cartesian Cogito, see Hubert J. Hermans and Harry Kempen, *The Dialogical Self: Meaning as Movement* (San Diego: Academic Press, 1993), pp. 1-10.

[20]*Agentic* refers to the capacity a person possesses to act and make choices in the world.

[21]Robert Hogan, *Personality Theory: The Personological Tradition* (Englewood Cliffs, N.J.: Prentice-Hall, 1976).

[22]James Baldwin, *Mental Development in the Child and Race* (New York: Macmillan, 1897); Jean Valsiner, *Human Development and Culture* (Lexington, Mass.: D.C. Heath, 1989).

others throughout her life—while providing fertile grounds for her growth as she navigates through her life, searching for significant others to emulate in various ways—afford her with opportunities to understand the lives of her exemplars and her relationships with them and the world.

Going a step further, Charles Cooley likened *the other* to a social mirror in which the Me is reflected, thus devising the term "looking-glass self." The self is formed as the person comes to imagine how other people observe and understand him.[23] What started out as his attempts to imitate and learn about and from others develops into an interest in learning about what each of his acquaintances thinks of him. Then the person learns to think about himself in light of what he perceives each of his acquaintances deems him to be. It is as if he is acquiring a greater number of mirrors to reflect himself from various angles as he acquaints himself with more people.

Elaborating on the themes articulated by Baldwin and Cooley, George Herbert Mead maintains that the development of the Me involves the ability to take the role of the other.[24] He argues that as a child matures, through experience in games and other complex social interactions, she formulates the concept of a "generalized other"—a personal conception of the general "audience" or "observer" of one's behavior. Thus the human learner imagines how others in general see her Me.[25] She is then able to consolidate what she thinks others perceive her to be and learns to self-modulate others' views of her, hopefully in a healthy manner, as her own view of herself. This process gives rise to what Robert Selman calls "perspective-taking" or "social understanding," in which the person grows in her ability to view other peoples' perspectives on life and learning with increasing sophistication.[26]

INSIGHTS FROM DONALD MEICHENBAUM

It has been over a century since William James and others have proposed the theories conceptualizing the reality behind how human beings as learners relate to their environment. Since then, many theorists have proposed pathways through which learners actually make the relationship a *habitus*[27] in their

---

[23]Valsiner, *Human Development*.

[24]George Herbert Mead, *Mind, Self, and Society* (Chicago: University of Chicago Press, 1934).

[25]Ibid., p. 140.

[26]Robert Selman, Mira Schorin, Carolyn Stone and Erin Phelps, "A Naturalistic Study of Children's Social Understanding," *Developmental Psychology* 19, no. 1 (1983): 82-102.

[27]By *habitus*, we refer to a person's constitutional characteristics and predispositions that are formed by the repeated behaviors as he interacts with his acquaintances in his environment.

lives. For instance, Donald Meichenbaum, a cognitive-behavior modification theorist, proposes that the human learner internalizes the authoritative figure that he interacts with.[28]

The adult begins with *cognitive modeling* by the adult's behavior, accompanied by verbal instructions, and the child is then invited to perform the desired behavior under the guidance of the adult. As the child attempts to perform the desired behavior, the adult repeats the same verbal instructions. This *overt, external guidance* step is then followed by an *overt self-guidance* step where the child is asked to repeat the behavior, but this time he repeats the same instructions out loud as he performs the task. The child is then encouraged to take the next step, *faded, overt self-guidance,* where he performs the desired behavior while whispering the instructions to himself. Through these steps, the child internalizes the desired behavior, coupled with the task instructions, so that he is able to perform the desired behavior as he thinks silently about the instructions. Finally, in *covert self-instruction,* the child will have internalized a sustainable habit of performing the desired behavior, due not to an extrinsic or "outside-in" motivation, but his to own intrinsic motivation.[29]

Meichenbaum's model might be useful in instilling or correcting certain behaviors for specific kinds of learners by having them follow each step of the various pathways. The conceptual framework—a trajectory of the integration of an intermental instruction and behavior—based on his work has been well documented elsewhere by many human learning researchers.[30]

We can observe several concepts through which human beings learn and internalize certain behaviors within a sociocultural texture: expectation, meaning, value and utility, among others. These are attached to a learner's behavior as he interacts with his life settings.[31]

First, as learners we all imitate the behaviors of those around us, which become an integral part of us as a habit. We are then further reinforced by the intricate fabric of the community we belong to, being shaped and even constrained to take on certain ways of life that range from a simple behavior to a

---

[28]Donald Meichenbaum, *Cognitive-Behavior Modification: An Integrative Approach* (New York: Plenum Press, 1977).

[29]Jeanne Ormrod, *Human Learning,* 5th ed. (Upper Saddle River, N.J.: Pearson, 2008), pp. 141-44.

[30]See Lev Vygotsky, *Mind in Society: Development of Higher Psychological Processes,* ed. Michael Cole, Vera John-Steiner, Silvia Scribner and E. Souberman (Cambridge, Mass.: Harvard University Press, 1978); Wertsch, *Voices of the Mind.*

[31]See Ormrod, *Human Learning,* pp. 118-44.

whole worldview resulting in a total transformation. Such generalized imitation could result in the kind of transformation that Ruth, a Moabite woman, went through as she decided to follow the Jewish way of life of her mother-in-law, culminating in her profound commitment to Naomi,[32] and resulting, finally, in her inclusion in the genealogy of our Lord Jesus Christ (see Ruth 4:18-22; Mt 1:5-6).

Second, learners imitate acceptable sociocultural behavior and learn from observing modeling that results in specific consequences. In such vicarious reinforcement, it is often not enough simply to observe the consequences in order to prompt learners to emulate what they observe. For instance, Genesis 29–30 depicts the classic cycle of a vicarious reinforcement as Rachel and Leah reinforce each other in the race to earn the love of Jacob.[33]

Third, human learners eventually form certain kinds of expectations when they experience the resulting consequences. Although it does not always translate into a desired course of action, human learners will likely maximize the desired consequences. In cyclical fashion, such consequences become further incentive to carry out a course of action, and in the process they become part of the *habitus* of their lives. Here neither the consequences nor the incentives necessarily need to be modeled. Sometimes they can be quite effective when merely envisioned through the mind's eyes, as with Jacob waiting and serving for seven years for Rachel, which "seemed like only a few days to him because of his love for her" (Gen 29:20). His expectation and incentive were further heightened, perhaps, because working for his wife was a custom of the time as a vicarious reinforcement.[34]

Fourth, human learners also develop "efficacy expectations" or self-efficacy, which means "beliefs about whether they themselves can execute particular behaviors successfully."[35] It is different from one's self-concept (*Who* am I?) or self-esteem (*How good* am I as a person?). Instead, they ask, "*How well* can I do such-and-such?"[36] Perhaps one of the most tragic events

---

[32]Ruth 1:16-17 (RSV): "For where you go I will go, and where you lodge I will lodge; your people shall be my people, and your God my God; where you die I will die, and there will I be buried."

[33]Rachel on Leah (Reuben, Simeon, Levi, Judah); Leah on Rachel through her servant Bilhah (Dan and Naphtali); Rachel on Leah through Zilpah (Gad and Asher); and Rachel on Leah (Issachar and Zebulum). And "God" on Rachel (Joseph and Benjamin).

[34]Gordon Wenham and Bruce Kaye, eds., *Law, Morality and the Bible* (Downers Grove, Ill.: InterVarsity Press, 1978), p. 35.

[35]Ormrod, *Human Learning*, p. 124.

[36]Ibid., p. 136.

in Scripture can serve as an example here. Samson, after disclosing to Delilah the secret between him and God,[37] had his hair cut off while sleeping, yet tried to quash the Philistines once again. Samson confidently tried to exercise his self-efficacy as before; he assumed he would go out as at other times and shake himself free. The grave mistake or self-deception on his part was that he traded his self-concept (that is, "I am the Lord's servant") for his self-efficacy (that is, "I can defeat them with my own strength"). What he did not know, however, was that "the LORD had left him" (Judg 16:20). Indeed, here was a colossal confusion between self-efficacy and self-concept. Yet in his grace, God provides (the readers) a glimmer of hope: Samson is still his servant, and he will live a bit longer to die while fulfilling his calling. Thus we read in Judges 16:22, "But the hair on his head began to grow again after it had been shaved."

INSIGHTS FROM JEAN PIAGET

While the above theories generated much conversation about the possible pathways through which human beings develop as learners in the context of social relationships, these theorists did not sense the urgency to empirically demonstrate their theories of the formation of the self as a learner. When Jean Piaget, a trained biologist, began studying the thought processes of children, however, he made a clean break from his predecessors by engaging in empirical research, which brought about a revolution in developmental psychology.[38]

From his research of children, Piaget theorized that human learning—especially in the cognitive domain—follows genetically predetermined, identifiable (invariant and sequential) stages that are universal to all human beings. He was concerned about deciphering a small set of cognitive processes that are foundational to a wide range of thinking episodes across the life span. Thus

---

[37]It is not so much the source of power but the special relationship between God and him Sampson received in his calling, as the context dictates, saying, "The LORD had left him" (Judg 16:20).

[38]"At last I had found my field of research. First of all it became clear to me that the theory of the relations between the whole and the part can be studied experimentally through analysis of the psychological processes underlying logical operations. . . . I was certain that the problem of the relation between the organism and environment extended also into the realm of knowledge, appearing here as the problem of the relation between the acting or thinking subject and the objects of his experience. Now I had the chance of studying this problem in terms of psychogenetic development." Jean Piaget, "Jean Piaget," in *A History of Psychology in Autobiography*, vol. 4, ed. Edwin Boring (Worcester, Mass.: Clark University Press, 1952), pp. 237-56, 245.

Piaget's Stages of Cognitive Development

First stage: birth to two years *(sensorimotor)*

- learns through various senses, movements, trial and error
- increasing level of intentionality
- the use of simple mental symbols
- increasing level of ability to differentiate the self from the environment[a]

Second stage: two to seven years *(preconventional)*

- more elaborate symbols (words, gestures, objects and mental images)
- rudimentary self-reflexivity (perceiving and interpreting the world in relation to the self)
- fixed thoughts (lacking reversibility and transferability of an object or person in the state or quality he first learned into other possible states or qualities through which the object or person can exist) to eventually deciphering the essence of an object (ability to understand the permanence of an object even as it changes its appearance)
- semi-logical reasoning and eventually limited social or external understanding[b]

Third stage: seven to eleven years *(concrete operational)*

- learns through operation ("an internalized mental action"— through which she can not only conserve but also reverse thought patterns), classification, seeking relations inferentially among objects and simple thoughts[c]

Fourth stage: eleven to fifteen years *(formal operational)*

- learns through hypothetical thinking, scientific thinking (observation, interpretation and application), problem solving, deductive thinking, the use of different perspectives
- ability to think about thinking[d]

---

[a]Patricia Miller, *Theories of Developmental Psychology,* 4th ed. (New York: Freeman and Company, 2002), pp. 38-46.
[b]Ibid., pp. 46-52.
[c]Ibid., pp. 52-56.
[d]Ibid., pp. 56-59.

his focus was the *noumena*[39] behind *phenomena:*[40] the cognitive structures or generalizable "schemas"[41] through which human beings learn to interact with the environment. The crux of his theory of cognitive development is that human beings at certain predictable periods upgrade themselves into a qualitatively different or "advanced" ways of thinking to "accommodate"[42] concepts and events that were previously "unassimilatable."[43] Again, the basic premise here is similar to that of James in assuming that human beings constantly seek to maintain coherence and order, which Piaget calls "equilibration."[44]

Based on these assumptions, Piaget observed several stages of cognitive development (see the textbox on page 219).

As the child grows through adolescence and young adulthood into an adult, she continues to develop her ability to learn through formal operations as they are applied to learning about a variety of content areas and episodes across the life span. What is noteworthy is that although the person continues to develop throughout her lifetime in terms of "content and stability," Piaget maintains that she does "not [develop] in the structure of thought."[45]

INSIGHTS FROM LAWRENCE KOHLBERG

Piaget's contribution toward understanding how human beings develop as learners, especially the development of the structure and dynamics of cognition and intelligence, has had a profound impact in various derivative theories describing how human beings develop, including in the areas of morality and faith.[46] Lawrence Kohlberg, for instance, engaged in cross-sectional and lon-

---

[39]Objects as they are in themselves independent of the mind, as Immanuel Kant has postulated.

[40]Appearances or events that can be perceived through human senses.

[41]Organized patterns of cognitive behaviors.

[42]*Accommodation* is defined as an interaction with a new object, event and/or concept either through modifying an existing scheme to account for the new object, event and/or concept or by forming an entirely new scheme to deal with it.

[43]*Assimilation* entails an interaction with an object, event and/or concept in a way that is consistent with an existing scheme.

[44]*Equilibration* describes the movement from equilibrium (the state where persons can comfortably interpret and respond to new events using existing schemes) to disequilibrium (the state where persons struggle with "discomfort" that spurs them to try to make sense of what they are experiencing—through replacing, reorganizing or better integrating their schemes) and back to equilibrium again.

[45]Ibid., p. 59.

[46]James Loder, *The Logic of the Spirit: Human Development in Theological Perspective* (San Francisco: Jossey-Bass, 1998), p. 23.

gitudinal studies documenting how human beings learn to negotiate the issues and spheres of morality and justice in their construal of a set of hypothetical moral dilemmas. He theorized that there exist universal stages of moral development as a person attempts to articulate a rationale for his[47] moral decisions across the life span, as outline in the textbox below.

Consonant with Piaget's emphasis, Kohlberg focused on deciphering how human beings make moral judgments (the structure and process) regardless of the various sources of morality, independent of how the nature of sources of morality shape the moral decision making of human beings. Here we observe

---

Kohlberg's Stages of Moral Development

Level 1—Preconventional Morality

Stage 1: Heteronomous morality (moral reasoning based on punishment and obedience)

Stage 2: Individualism and exchange (based on instrumental exchange)

Level 2—Conventional Morality

Stage 3: Interpersonal conformity (based on attempts to maintain favorable interpersonal relationships)

Stage 4: Law and order (based on attempts to maintain the social order)

Level 3—Postconventional Morality

Stage 5: Social contract and individual rights (based on applying uiversal, abstract and moral principles in a given situation or context)

Stage 6: Universal ethical principles (based on human rights—the equality and worth of all people).[a]

---

[a]See Brenda Munsey, ed., *Moral Development, Moral Education, and Kohlberg* (Birmingham, Ala.: Religious Education Press, 1980); Lisa Kuhmerker, *The Kohlberg Legacy for the Helping Professions* (Birmingham, Ala.: Religious Education Press, 1991); and Perry Downs, "Moral Development," in *Teaching for Spiritual Growth: An Introduction to Christian Education* (Grand Rapids: Zondervan, 1994), pp. 95-109.

---

[47]See Carol Gilligan's (one of Kohlberg's former research associates) astute critique of Kohlberg's theory-generating solely based on male research subjects in *In a Different Voice: Psychological Theory and Women's Development* (Cambridge, Mass.: Harvard University Press, 1982).

that as human learners develop as moral beings, their self-understanding as "free agents" also becomes more nuanced and complex. They learn that in order for them to live out their lives more fully in the world, they need to conform to a certain way of life—in terms of moral reasoning, moral behavior, moral expectations and so on—in which they are situated.

It is not unlike what Rollo May, a leading existential psychologist, said: "A person moves toward freedom and responsibility in his living as he becomes more conscious of the deterministic experiences in his life. . . . Freedom is thus not the opposite to determinism."[48] Human learners can understand that freedom is not always doing whatever we wish to do in our own terms. Freedom, which is always mediated and defined within the bounds of society or other circumstances, is situated and can be cultivated according to the expectations of the community of which we are a part.

In this light, human learners who belong to a Christian community can begin to understand the nature of freedom in Jesus Christ. Moreover, they can begin to grapple with the fact that human freedom and God's sovereignty over all creation and all other spheres of human lives are not mutually exclusive. If human freedom is all situated, Christians should be able to grasp the fact that the freedom we enjoy in Jesus Christ is indeed the freedom in the economy of God's kingdom, which is advancing even in our lives as kingdom citizens here and now.

INSIGHTS FROM MARY BELENKY AND COLLEAGUES

Responding to Kohlberg's moral development theory, Mary Belenky and her colleagues argue that women have traditionally had more constraints than men to negotiate in exercising freedom, thus altering the trajectory of development as human learners in such spheres as morality, self-worth and cognitive processes.[49] Their work is an extension of the work of Carol Gilligan, who judiciously demonstrated this diverging trajectory of moral development as well as identity formation in women.[50]

They contend that literature on knowledge construction has traditionally focused on men's development as human beings. In those instances when women were included, the research was generally interested in finding out

---

[48]Rollo May, *Psychology and the Human Dilemma* (New York: Norton, 1967), p. 175.
[49]Mary Belenky, Blythe Clinchy, Nancy Goldberger and Jill Tarule, *Women's Ways of Knowing: The Development of Self, Voice, and Mind* (New York: Basic Books, 1986).
[50]Gilligan, *In a Different Voice;* Carol Gilligan and Lyn Brown, *Meeting at the Crossroads* (New York: Ballantine, 1993).

Stages of Women's Development as Learners

1. The first way of knowing is referred to as "received knowledge." These women acquire their knowledge from listening to the voices of others.

2. The second is "subjective knowledge." It is the inner voice that becomes the authority where truth still remains dualistic.

3. The third, "subjective knowledge," is characterized by the quest for self. These women often have to walk away from the past to find self. In the process, new connections are made between past and future, with new and old knowledge and acquaintances, and so on.

4. The fourth way is procedural knowledge: the voice of reason. The women here are the most homogeneous group of women—most of them bright, white, young and privileged. They are most relativistic in thinking and value firsthand experience as the only reliable source of authoritative knowledge.

5. The fifth is procedural knowledge: separate and connected knowing. Women here work toward relationship with knowledge at a personal level. They seek for understanding through care.

6. The last is referred to as constructed knowledge: integrating the voices. Women here weave together the strands of seemingly dichotomistic thinking. They allow internal contradiction and ambiguity. They work to develop a narrative sense of the self and wholeness. They are called passionate knowers who value commitment and action.

7. The anomaly: "silence." The women in this state are in a denial of self and depend on external authority for direction.[a]

---

[a]Summarized from Belenky et al., *Women's Ways of Knowing.*

whether women subjects converged or diverged from male subjects in terms of the trajectories of their findings. They argue that research in this area has inordinately focused on the development of autonomy and independence, which have been values in the male-dominated American society. They also assert that the research has tended to focus on abstract critical thought as well as on the morality of rights and justice in a vacuum—in other words, in hypothetical situations.

In their observations, Belenky and her colleagues have sought to understand how women as learners develop as they negotiate their identity in the world. Their research findings demonstrate that women develop as learners as they develop in interdependence, in intimacy, in contextual thought, and in the ethics of care and responsibility, all of which remarkably coincides with Gilligan's work. Important for our discussion here is their contribution to how women develop as learners. In this regard, they delineate six ways of knowing and one anomaly (see textbox on page 223).

Belenky and her colleagues are quick to point out that these ways of knowing are not fixed, universal categories or stages, partly in their reaction against the universalistic theories such as those of Piaget and Kohlberg. They willingly admit the inherent weakness in their scheme, for its abstract or "pure"categories cannot adequately describe the complexities and uniqueness of the individual's knowing. According to them, many of these categories can be found in men's thinking as well and could be organized differently by other researchers.

However, they are convinced that human learners grow in sophistication by understanding human knowledge as socioculturally constructed and mediated. They are also convinced that women's self-concepts and ways of knowing are intertwined, engendering personal identity and commitment to evolve throughout the course of life.

INSIGHTS FROM JAMES FOWLER

In the realm of faith development, following the empirical traditions of Piaget and Kohlberg, and in consultation with Erik Erikson's psychosocial development theory (discussed in the next section), James Fowler has sought to understand how human beings engage in learning about faith across the life span. For Fowler, however, growing in faith has little to do with learning a particular content or set of cognitive beliefs. Instead, growing in faith entails development in the "pattern of our relatedness to self, others and our world in light of our relatedness to ultimacy we call faith. Faith, then, is a dynamic, evolving pattern of the ways our souls find and make meanings for our lives."[51] In other words, according to Fowler, faith is a "universal quality of human meaning making"[52] that all human beings—regardless of their

---

[51]James Fowler, *Faithful Change: The Personal and Public Challenges of Postmodern Life* (Nashville: Abingdon, 1996), p. 21.
[52]James Fowler, "The Vocation of Faith Development Theory," in *Stages of Faith and Religious Development,* ed. James Fowler, Karl Ernst Nipkow and Friedrich Schweitzer (New York: Crossroads, 1991), p. 22.

Fowler's Stages of Faith Development

Stage 1—Intuitive-projective faith. Faith is characterized by fantasy and imitation via the child's intuition, imitation and some level of imagination through what he observes in those around him.[a]

Stage 2—Mythic-literal faith. The person understands faith in its literalness based on the ability to distinguish between make-believe and real, and a principle of reciprocity between human *doer* and a divine judge. This kind of reciprocal and undifferentiated faith is a precursor to works-oriented faith (reward and punishment based on his work).

Stage 3—Synthetic-conventional faith. Faith in this stage is characterized by coherence, wholeness and generalized meanings by and interpersonal relationships with the group in which the person belongs. Thus his faith is dependent on the faith of those with whom he is in relationship and rests as his own without his needing to reexamine it.[b]

Stage 4—Individuative-reflective faith. The person in this stage becomes more critical and independent of the conventional faith that he was once content with. He asserts himself as his own authority, adjudicating the plausibility, meaning and utility of his faith. He may walk away from his faith as he notices hypocritical elements of the faith community he once belonged to, also construing his once cherished relationships as being codependent.[c]

Stage 5—Conjunctive faith. The faith in this stage is characterized by the person's recognition of the multidimensionality of faith, desire to dialogue with others about their faith, and depth in evaluating and describing his faith. The person is still committed to engage his faith critically, but it is moderated by his acceptance of ambiguities in life.[d]

Stage 6—Universalizing faith. According to Fowler, not many reach this stage, but for the person who does, his faith can be characterized by his love and justice, radical altruism and a sense of all-encompassing integrated self, so much so that his understanding and practice of faith resemble a decentralization of himself, not unlike losing himself to nothingness or transmigration of the soul.[e]

---

[a]James Fowler, *Stages of Faith: The Psychology of Human Development and the Quest for Meaning* (San Francisco: Harper & Row, 1981), p. 133

[b]Ibid., p. 173.

[c]Ibid., p. 181.

[d]Ibid., p. 183.

[e]Ibid., p. 200. For Fowler's own description of the stages, see James Fowler, "Fowler on Fowler," in *Christian Perspectives on Faith Development,* ed. Jeff Astley and Leslie Francis (Leominster, U.K.: Gracewing Fowler Wright Books, 1992), pp. 1-57; and Fowler, *Stages of Faith.*

religions and including the self-proclaimed nonreligious—are engaged in across their life spans.

Again, as did Piaget and Kohlberg, Fowler focuses on deciphering the stage-like *deep structures* of human faith, the capacity of the self to construct meaning and, according to James Loder, a preeminent authority in Christian faith development, "not stages of faith in any biblical or theological sense."[53] In the textbox on page 225 we present Fowler's stages of faith development in outline.

From our discussion of Piaget's theory of cognitive development and its derivative theories—Kohlberg's moral development and Fowler's faith development—it would seem that human learning is triggered by genetic mechanisms, moving up through each prescribed stage, a "structured whole in a state of equilibrium." Each stage is characterized by a sense of "a coming-into-being and a being," punctuated by "an initial period of preparation and a final period of achievement."[54] Each stage then functions as the foundation for the subsequent stage, providing an impetus for the higher "level" as well as greater depth of human learning.

Thus these theories of human learning rely on the sequentiality and invariance of the proposed stages of learning. Moreover, these theories maintain that behind local variations in the surface phenomena there exist constant laws of abstract structure in the way human learning happens. What this suggests is that diverse sets of learning—through myths, works of art and other practices of human flourishing—possess predictable patterns and stages that are universal across time and space for all.[55]

---

[53]Loder, *The Logic of the Spirit*, p. 255. See also James Loder and James Fowler, "Conversations on Fowler's *Stages of Faith* and Loder's *The Transforming Moment*," *Religious Education* 77, no. 2 (March/April 1982): 133-48.

[54]Miller, *Theories of Developmental Psychology*, pp. 34-35.

[55]This school of thought—structuralism—owes its origin to the work of Ferdinand de Saussure in linguistics. Saussure espoused that all sign systems are linguistic in nature and share a common belief. This resembles Noam Chomsky's view of child language acquisition, where he contends that language acquisition is not a result of sociocultural interaction, but is based on an innate disposition of the mind, an unlearned and universal grammar, supplying the kinds of rule that the child will employ in speech with which he is confronted. Moreover, Claude Lévi-Strauss of the structuralist tradition within anthropology has sought to show how a wide variety of kinship and institutional arrangements can find their origins in the basic structures of communication of fundamental patterns of the working of the mind, and from which the surface variety is generated. See François Dosse, *History of Structuralism: The Rising Sign, 1945-1966*, vol. 1, trans. Deborah Glassman (Minneapolis: University of Minnesota, 1998).

INSIGHTS FROM ERIK ERIKSON

If the stage theories of Piaget, Kohlberg and Fowler can be construed as theories describing the processes of human learning from an inside-out perspective, the "Selfing I" is more or less the locus of the conscious mind and cognitive development in interactions with the environment. Erik Erikson, a neo-Freudian psychologist,[56] sought to understand human learning through interactions among the human psyche, sociality and sexuality.[57] The starting point for Erikson's theory is the epigenetic principle, in which the person is born with a genetic ground plan that prescribes direction and a general pattern to psychosocial development of the human being. Instead of advocating some sort of genetic determinism, Erikson states that there are points of ascendancy for each of the stages of human growth for all human beings, creating "a succession of potentialities for significant interaction with a growing number of individuals and with the mores that govern them."[58] Ascendancy here suggests that there exists a generalizable period in the life cycle when the inner psychological and physical sources of human development give rise to a particular way of learning about and responding to a particular psychosocial crisis.

Yet these ways of learning do not suddenly emerge nor disappear. Instead, they are present throughout the life cycle of any human being to ascend and descend according to the social mores of a particular culture. Thus Erikson asserts that it is critical that

> all cultures must guarantee some essential "proper rate" and "proper sequence," their propriety corresponding to . . . "average expectable"; that is what is necessary and manageable for all humans, no matter how they differ in personality and cultural pattern.[59]

His major concern here is that human learners as psychosocial beings need to be properly nurtured in an environment where they learn and have a clear sense of what their community, culture and society expect them to be at various stages across their life span. In other words, human flourishing as learners requires an unambiguous set of rules or a "grammar" in the various learning communities they belong to, including the home, school, church and other sociocultural institutions.

---

[56]See his own account of the Freudian influence in his work in Erikson, *The Life Cycle Completed: A Review* (New York: Norton, 1982), pp. 15-24.
[57]Ibid., p. 15.
[58]Ibid., p. 28.
[59]Ibid.

Table 8.1. Erik Erikson's Eight Stages of Life and Life's Existential Questions[a]

Age	Psychosocial Issue	Existential Question	Associated Virtue
1. Infancy	Trust vs. mistrust	How can I be secure?	Hope
2. Early Childhood	Autonomy vs. shame and doubt	How can I be independent?	Will
3. Childhood (play age)	Initiative vs. guilt	How can I be powerful?	Purpose
4. Childhood (school age)	Industry vs. inferiority	How can I be good?	Competence
5. Adolescence and Young Adulthood	Identity vs. role confusion	Who am I? How do I fit into the adult world?	Fidelity
6. Young Adulthood	Intimacy vs. isolation	How can I love?	Love
7. Mature Adulthood	Generativity vs. stagnation (or self-absorption)	How can I fashion a "gift"?	Care
8. Old Age	Ego integrity vs. despair	How can I receive a "gift of life"?	Wisdom

[a]Adapted from Erikson, *The Life Cycle Completed,* pp. 32-33; and McAdams, *The Person,* p. 351

Based on his research primarily with people in the West,[60] Erikson conceptualized that eight stages exist in which human learners grapple with particular psychosocial tasks as they ascend at certain periods in life. The first five stages roughly correspond with Freud's five psychosexual stages.[61] As a learner, the person is faced with a "polarity in which a positive feature of the stage is pitted against a negative feature. The polarity sets up a psychosocial conflict."[62]

An example is Erikson's understanding of how a person develops a sense of identity during adolescence. According to Erikson, the person has two developmental trajectories in terms of developing a sense of identity, one positive

---

[60]Although Erikson had worked with Sioux and Yurok Indians and other ethnic-cultural groups, he stops short of entertaining a variety of differences in the construction of the self. Instead, he interpreted the findings from his crosscultural work through his psychosocial theory of human development, thus further supporting the stage scheme of his theory while acknowledging merely the variety of the content in the stage scheme. See Erik Erikson, *Childhood and Society* (New York: Norton, 1963).

[61]Dan McAdams, *The Person: An Introduction to the Science of Personality Psychology,* 5th ed. (Hoboken, N.J.: Wiley, 2009), p. 350. Freud's stages are (1) oral, (2) anal, (3) phallic, (4) latency and (5) genital.

[62]Ibid., p. 350.

and the other negative. In the positive scenario, a person's self-identity is formed through the healthy integration of all prior identifications that had provided her environs, constructing a new self-structure as a coherent whole— the desired unity of oneself. This coherence of identity provides an opportunity to learn and grow as who she is in continuity and self-sameness. In the negative scenario, the person experiences identity confusion or diffusion—a dangerous condition in which she is unable to take hold and settle into life. She is not able to forge an organizing center to her existence because her focus in life is diffused, which likely results in both intrapsychic and interpersonal difficulties. A well-synthesized identity, on the other hand, constitutes both personal and social well-being.

The general trajectory of the human learner then is to achieve a coherent self by moving *forward* through the stages of life as prescribed by society through the dialectical interaction among the body, the sense of self and the sociocultural context in which the human being is situated at a particular historical moment.[63] According to Dan McAdams, one of the most significant interpreters of Erikson, as the human learner faces the conflict between the polarity in each stage he is basically concerned about certain aspects of his existence. His experiences prompt a unique question at each stage,

> which is typically "asked" and eventually "answered" through the individual's behavior. Though this question may not be consciously posed by the individual, the overall pattern of the individual's behavior within a given stage is structured as if the individual were asking a particular question.[64]

Seen in this light, the human learner is constantly engaged in asking for and looking for responses through various ways of knowing/learning,[65] as opposed to looking only for certain "answers" that would satisfy the cognitive dimension of her self. In table 8.2, we outline Erikson's stages.

This is especially the case for the learner who is going through the first four stages in her life as a child. By the time of late adolescence and young adulthood, the human learner seeks to look for ways to respond to perhaps the most significant existential question, "Who am I?" While emerging adulthood is not the end of the person's life chronologically, it often serves as a

---

[63]As aptly demonstrated in his psycho-historical biographies on Mahatma Gandhi and Martin Luther. See Erik Erikson, *Gandhi's Truth* (New York: Norton, 1969), and *Young Man Luther* (New York: Norton, 1958).

[64]McAdams, *The Person,* p. 351.

[65]Namely, senses, reason and intuition. These will be discussed shortly.

period, as the last stage in the life span reserved to reflect on the person's whole life. Here ample opportunity is needed for her to reflect on the previous four stages of life. Such an exercise is not merely for her memory's sake, but to assess and explore her future life's trajectories by extrapolating the first half of her life's trajectory. Again, McAdams contends,

> The four stages of childhood leave the person with a unique pool of resources and handicaps, strengths, and weaknesses that will be called upon in the making of an identity. In this sense, the past (the early stages) partly determines the future (the later stages). But to a certain extent, the reverse is also true. The adolescent or young adult looks back upon childhood now and comes to *decide what childhood meant.* In that this decision is made after childhood actually happened, in some sense, the late (that which follows childhood) partly determines the early (childhood itself). We cannot literally change what has happened already, but we can change its meaning. . . . In addressing the issue of identity, we look back to the past in order to arrive at a plausible explanation that tells us how we came to be and where we may be going in the future.[66]

As human learners reach mature adulthood, they ask another important question about their lives—"How can I fashion a 'gift'?"—as they reflectively negotiate between the polarity of generativity versus stagnation (or self-absorption). A Korean proverb says, "When animals die, they leave their skins. When human beings die, they leave their names." Erikson similarly observed that the human being has "the concern in establishing and guiding the next generation."[67] And the concern turns into "a desire to invest one's substance in forms of life and work that will outlive the self."[68] This is where human learners seek out people and other resources to plan their next stage in life. For many, the concern and desire for the next generation then translate into action of at least four different types:

1. Biological generativity: only applicable to women
   a. begetting, bearing and nursing offspring

2. Parental: geared toward the child
   a. meeting basic needs
   b. loving and disciplining

---

[66]McAdams, *The Person,* p. 355.
[67]Erikson, *Childhood and Society,* p. 267.
[68]John Kotre, *Outliving the Self: Generativity and the Interpretation of Lives* (Baltimore: Johns Hopkins University Press, 1984), p. 10.

c. initiating the child into family traditions

3. Technical generativity: geared toward the apprentice and skill

a. transfer of skills

b. not generative in itself; technical transfer or teaching of skills "become generative only when it is imbued with the sense of extending oneself into the apprentice or attaching oneself to a lasting art"[69]

4. Cultural generativity

a. passing on values or the "mind" of a culture

One can observe that the distance between the giver and the recipient of generativity becomes greater as one moves from biological to cultural generativity. In all of these instances, culture becomes the vehicle through which one can learn to fashion a gift to the next generation, thus outliving oneself. However, it is entirely conceivable that even children may engage in instances of generativity-in-action. Based on the epigenetic nature of Erikson's psychosocial development, these acts are demonstrations of maturational crises to come in the future.[70]

Within this complex and richly detailed account, the main thrust of Erikson's discussion on identity formation clearly indicates the *telos* of the human learner: it is to sustain himself in a generally stable and orderly state in independency, rather than a diffused, chaotic state in dependency.[71] Erikson's notion of the coherent self shares much affinity with most of the theories of the self in the West. For instance, cultural anthropologist Clifford Geertz resonates with the concept of the coherent self when he describes the centralized, coherent self as a product of Western culture, which is "a bounded, unique, more or less integrated motivational and cognitive universe, a dynamic center of awareness, emotion, judgment, and action organized into a distinctive whole and set contrastively against other such wholes and against a social and natural background."[72] Seen in this light, Western culture—particularly mainstream American society in which Geertz is observing the phenomenon—values control, uniqueness and the ability to in-

---

[69]Ibid., p. 13.

[70]Ibid.

[71]Edward Sampson, "The Decentralization of Identity," *American Psychologist* 40, no. 11 (1985): 1203-11.

[72]Clifford Geertz, "From the Native's Point of View: On the Nature of Anthropological Understanding," in *Interpretive Social Science,* ed. Paul Rainow and William Sullivan (Berkeley: University of California Press, 1979), pp. 225-41, 229.

fluence reality as the preferred and expected attributes human learners ought to acquire.

From another vantage point, society as a broad network of learning communities inculcates independence, separateness and distinctiveness from other people and the rest of nature. It then signals that the construction of the coherent self as a learner might be at risk of becoming a private enterprise in which one finds herself alone to navigate her environment as a still agentic yet precarious being.[73] Thus it is crucial for teachers to understand the kinds of existential questions human learners "ask" about life and how they actively learn about the question at hand and collect resources—people, seminars, books, experiences and so on—to confidently respond to the psychosocial "crisis."

CONCLUSION

We have argued that our ministries of teaching and formation are vital but that we who teach must also be learners. Among the things we commit to learn about is the nature of learning itself. In this chapter, we briefly introduced the insights of a number of developmental theorists. In the next chapter, we interact further with these insights—and with those of several other thinkers—focusing our attention on implications and applications of these things for teaching and formation in the church.

HYMN FOR CONTEMPLATION AND WORSHIP
Psalm 139
O Lord, You have searched and known me.
You know when I sit and rise.
From afar, all thoughts discerning,
you know where my journey lies.
Long before I've found my own words,
you've already heard my speech.
All around me, you astound me!
Oh, such knowledge who can reach?

Where could I go from your Spirit?

---

[73]This phenomenon has been acutely documented in recent years. See Robert Bellah et al., *Habits of the Heart: Individualism and Commitment in American Life,* 3rd ed. (Berkeley: University of California Press, 2007); Anthony Giddens, *Modernity and Self-Identity: Self and Society in the Late Modern Age* (Stanford: Stanford University Press, 1991); Robert Putnam, *Bowling Alone: The Collapse and Revival of American Community* (New York: Simon & Schuster, 2001).

Can I from your presence flee?
I would find you in the heavens;
in the depths, you'd surely be.
If I flew to Earth's far corners,
your right hand would hold me tight.
If in darkness, I lay hidden,
you would make the darkness light.

In my mother's womb you formed me,
fashioned me with greatest care.
For such wonders I will praise you
who beheld me even there.
In your book, my days were written,
before one had come to be.
Thoughts so precious, who can fathom?
When I wake, you're still with me.

Oh, that you would slay the wicked
who defy your majesty.
How I hate all those who hate you,
count each one my enemy.
Search my own heart, Lord, and test me.
Know my anxious thoughts today.
From all evil, Lord, preserve me.
Lead me in the ancient Way.

Setting: Gary A. Parrett (2004)
Tune: Beach Spring[74]
Familiar Use of the Tune: "Come Ye Sinners, Poor and Needy"

QUESTIONS FOR PLANNING AND PRAXIS

1. According to the chapter, why is it important to teach with learning in mind? As educational ministers, how can we alter our perspectives on teaching to wholly incorporate learning?

2. William James argues that the self-as-known (Me) involves all that a person considers to be his own. The three aspects of Me (material, social and spiritual) then each affect the way a person thinks, feels and experiences

---

[74]Some would suggest leaving the first half of the last stanza out of this hymn for congregational singing, but these words—based on verses 19 and following—are divinely inspired (as 2 Tim 3:16 affirms) and I (Gary) have found such language very useful for purposes of spiritual warfare in the sense of Ephesians 6:12.

life. How does such an anthropological view affect the way we reach and understand others? More specifically, how does it affect the way we teach?

3. In relation to Erik Erikson's developmental theory, what is the ultimate goal of the human learner? How does this goal change depending on the age of the learner and thus his or her "psychosocial issue"? How would you theologically assess Erikson's proposed ultimate goal?

4. Adolescents and young adults are asking themselves the existential questions "Who am I? How do I fit into the adult world?" As an educational minister of people in this age group, how can you create teaching-learning experiences that foster environments conducive to answering such deep questions?

5. "The human learner is constantly engaged in asking and looking for responses through various ways of knowing/learning, as opposed to looking only for certain 'answers' that would satisfy their cognitive dimension of her self." Based on this quotation, how are educational ministers to view their task of educating others about Scripture and the Christian faith? In what ways does it make even more real the reality that teachers are to face a stricter judgment?

6. This chapter details how human beings develop into learners. No matter the focus area (cognitive, moral or faith), the trajectory remains predictably the same. In your experience as an educator, have you seen similar patterns in acquisition among various disciplines? How does it affect educational ministry in particular?

RESOURCES FOR FURTHER STUDY

Belenky, Mary, Blythe Clinchy, Nancy Goldberger and Jill Tarule. *Women's Ways of Knowing: The Development of Self, Voice, and Mind.* New York: Basic Books, 1986.

Erikson, Erik. *The Life Cycle Completed: A Review.* New York: Norton, 1982.

Estes, Daniel. *Hear, My Son: Teaching and Learning in Proverbs 1-9.* Downers Grove, Ill.: InterVarsity Press, 1997.

Fowler, James. *Faithful Change: The Personal and Public Challenges of Postmodern Life.* Nashville: Abingdon, 1996.

Giddens, Anthony. *Modernity and Self-Identity: Self and Society in the Late Modern Age.* Stanford: Stanford University Press, 1991.

Gilligan, Carol. *In a Different Voice: Psychological Theory and Women's Development*. Cambridge, Mass.: Harvard University Press, 1982.

Hendricks, Howard. *Teaching to Change Lives: Seven Proven Ways to Make Teaching Come Alive*. Sisters, Ore.: Multnomah, 2003.

Loder, James. *The Logic of the Spirit: Human Development in Theological Perspective*. San Francisco: Jossey-Bass, 1998.

McAdams, Dan. *The Person: An Introduction to the Science of Personality Psychology*. 5th ed. Hoboken, N.J.: Wiley, 2009.

Miller, Patricia. *Theories of Developmental Psychology*. 4th ed. New York: Freeman and Company, 2002.

Ormrod, Jeanne. *Human Learning*. 5th ed. Upper Saddle River, N.J.: Pearson, 2008.

9

Toward a Community of Learners

Speaking the truth in love, we will in all things grow up into him who is the Head,
that is, Christ. From him the whole body, joined and held together by every support-
ing ligament, grows and builds itself up in love, as each part does its work.

EPHESIANS 4:15-16

▼

OVER THE YEARS, MODERN HUMAN DEVELOPMENT theories, four of which we considered in the previous chapter, have generated numerous theories about government policies, development programs and the acquisition of knowledge. However, perhaps the people most influenced by these theories have been twentieth-century educators, including religious educators. Such influence, of course, has both pluses and minuses.

DESCRIPTIONS TURNED INTO PRESCRIPTIONS

It should be remembered that the focus of these theorists was to document human learning and development in a *descriptive* manner. Their intent was primarily to describe how various dimensions of human learners interact with their environment. Therefore, these theories in the hands of government agencies, educational administrators, parents, teachers and others were intended for dialogical interaction with a variety of other factors. Together with consideration of people's traditions, sociocultural factors and other forms of pertinent research (sociology, anthropology, branches of psychology other than developmental psychology and so on), these theories could be utilized toward implementing various policies, including educational ones.

However, it seems that we have pragmatism running in our veins as late-

and postmodern people in the West. These theories were intended to serve as a part of the complex ways of understanding human beings in a multifaceted world. But we have treated them as though they provided the entire answer to one of the most complex aspects of human existence: the task of education.

Again, these theories were not meant to provide all the *prescriptions* needed in modern education. Many educational leaders, however, have sought to implement their own educational commitments utilizing these theories as exclusive and universalistic educational principles and practices for large numbers of people. Thus, based on what these theorists had to say about cognitive (or moral or faith or . . .) development of learners, educators (including Christian educators) have made critical decisions regarding content and materials used for teaching. Consequently, many teachers have determined to teach only to a certain level and no further, without taking into consideration the specific needs, gifts and experiences of the individual learners, not to mention the work of the Holy Spirit "who is able to do immeasurably more than all we ask or imagine, according to his power that is at work within us" (Eph 3:20). In other words, by following these *theories* of human development as a set of prescriptions for teaching, we might be inadvertently precluding much of what God wants to do in teaching and transforming his people.

SHOULD CONTENT AFFECT THE WAY WE THINK AND OBEY?

Religious educators have not been immune to such educational approaches as we have been describing, for many of us have "baptized" these developmental theories as "sacred" prescriptions on which to base our educational practice in religious communities. Perhaps these theories may help us understand certain dimensions of how Christians learn, grow and experience certain aspects of a faith. Yet they are all fundamentally limited in that these theories cannot begin to describe the spiritual dimension of learners. Moreover, these theories all contend that the content of faith and cognition are independent of the structure of development. For the theorists, in other words, it is the structure that really matters; content is secondary. According to these theorists, the belief system—be it Christianity, Buddhism or whatever—is irrelevant to how humans develop, because development is universal. However, if learners keep feeding from a particular religious tradition, they will grow in that religious tradition and be nurtured in the cognitive structure that the tradition and the adherents of that tradition impose on them.

When those of us who are called to teach adapt a model that similarly dissects content and structure, we fail to realize that the practices of thinking profoundly shape the content, and vice versa. To teach in this way is to fundamentally forfeit the profound and mysterious encounter between the triune God and his chosen people. The mystery, awesomeness and spiritual reality all get left out in favor of written resources that are dictated by the scientific understanding of developmental theories and psychology. Teachers then rely heavily on the scientific background or cognition alone, while ignoring the mystical, inspiring aspects of God, as well as the actual teaching-learning process.

The psalmist writes, "Great is the LORD and most worthy of praise; his greatness no one can fathom" (Ps 145:3). Indeed, as human learners we are limited in our understanding of God's greatness, his character and his ways. But the unsearchable or unfathomable riches of God extend to his redemptive work among us in human history. Thus the writer of Ecclesiastes declares, "He has made everything beautiful in its time. He has also set eternity in the hearts of men; yet they cannot fathom what God has done from beginning to end" (Eccles 3:11). Even with his wonderful provisions in our hearts to know him, we cannot begin to capture all that he has done and continues to do on our behalf.

Furthermore, even "if I have the gift of prophecy and can fathom all mysteries and all knowledge, and if I have a faith than can move mountains, but have not love, I am nothing" (1 Cor 13:2). What kind of knowledge, morality, faith and life is this—that without love, we are nothing? How can we, then, claim to have figured out how all human beings learn and should be taught the Way, the Truth and the Life by using humanly generated theories based on human observations?

As moderns who have been socialized to lose "childish" ways of knowing, the modern church, especially Protestants, has privileged the use of a particular brand of reason[1] that demythologizes the Christian faith into a set of propositional truths that stem from a lifeless biblical text. In addition to our reason and in order to sanctify our reason,[2] our senses, intuition and imagination—that is, the other (and more neglected) instruments of knowledge in human

---

[1]Acontextual and ahistorical reasoning that bifurcates thought from being, reason from faith and objective from subjective faculties. See S. Steve Kang, "The Church, Spiritual Formation, and the Kingdom of God: A Case for Canonical-Communion Reading of the Bible," *Ex Auditu* 18 (2003): 137-51.

[2]See John Paul II, *"Fides et Ratio,"* Origins, October 22, 1998, pp. 315-47.

beings—must be recovered and reintegrated with our reason.[3] Let us briefly consider these.

First, all knowledge has its inception in our five senses—what we see, hear, touch, smell and taste. John testifies to the fact that the proclamation of the Gospel is firmly rooted in the holistic encounter with Jesus Christ by the disciples who have been (trans)formed by their existential encounters with him (1 Jn 1:1-4).[4] Second, intuition refers to a major capacity for knowledge with which we come into the world as children. It also refers to our fundamental capacity to receive life, strength, love and security from another. Here, to receive is not to be an empty receptacle (that is, a *tabula rasa*), but to be ready to receive patterns of life—love, security and so on—to be trained by, and in the manner consonant with, social institutions such as family, culture or society.

However, I argue that as a community of learners, the church must be the fundamental community that forms the patterns of the kingdom life through its people as the children of God. Jesus said, "I tell you the truth, anyone who will not receive the kingdom of God like a little child will never enter it" (Mk 10:15). Hans Urs von Balthasar writes,

> A child that knows God can find him at every moment because every moment opens up for him and shows him the very ground of time: as if it reposed on eternity itself. And this eternity, without undergoing change, walks hand in hand for the child with transitory time.[5]

Intuition also refers to relational knowledge (thus it is related to the repository of our emotional memories) that comes as we receive the essential nature of another into ourselves, especially in our relationship with God.

---

[3]I am deeply grateful to Dr. Carla Waterman, a former colleague in the Christian Formation and Ministry Department at Wheaton College, Wheaton, Illinois, who first introduced me to the instruments of knowledge.

[4]"That which *was* from the beginning, which we have *heard,* which we have *seen* with our eyes, which we have *looked at* and our hands have *touched*—this we *proclaim* concerning *the Word of life.* The life *appeared;* we have *seen* it and *testify* to it, and we *proclaim* to you the eternal life, which *was with* the Father and has *appeared* to us. We *proclaim* to you what we have *seen* and *heard,* so that you also may have fellowship with us. And our fellowship *is* with the Father and with his Son, Jesus Christ. We write this to make our joy complete" (emphasis added). The Word of life whose words and action coincided precisely is the Word-Action; without him there is no life or reality. What and how the apostles experienced the Word of life they experienced with their senses. They were also able to intuit as well as reason that the Word of life is, in fact, God himself and with God, and imagine life in him here and now, and forever.

[5]Hans Urs von Balthasar, *Unless You Become Like This Child* (San Francisco: Ignatius Press, 1991), p. 55.

Along these lines, we read of the Holy Spirit "whom you have *received* from God"; thus "you are not your own; you were bought at a price. Therefore honor God with your body" (1 Cor 6:19-20, emphasis added).

Third, imagination is not the capacity to see the *unreal* but the capacity to see the *unseen*. It involves an ability to remember the past, envision the future and respond to beauty with an aesthetic capacity. Using our reason alone, we cannot possibly comprehend Christ as the "image of the invisible God, the firstborn over all creation" (Col 1:15) or "the King eternal, immortal, invisible, the only God" (1 Tim 1:17). As a community of learners that has begun to live in God's eternal kingdom, the church is called to recover all the instruments of knowledge in order for us to enter into and linger in that relational realm of the triune God.

HUMAN LEARNING AS NEGOTIATING AND EXERCISING AUTHORITY

In the previous chapter we briefly examined how human beings develop as learners. To understand the relationship between the learner and her environment, we observed the advance in the theories of human knowing initially put forth by William James and others. The simple distinction between the agentic I and the reservoir-like Me provided a paradigm through which the differentiation and subsequent integration of the person in relation to others were conceptualized. We also observed that there exists a set of patterns of human learning that is often sequential and invariant based on epigenetic principles. Whether it is cognitive, moral or faith development in the lives of human learners, each of these dimensions seems to have a certain, predictable trajectory where the locus of authority for learning shifts from the outer to the inner self throughout the course of one's life.

As the contributions of William Perry[6] and of Mary Belenky and her colleagues[7] have suggested, the movement of human learning—that is, cognition, morality or faith—seems to be from authority-bound (tacit) to unqualified relativism to commitment in relativism (explicit) and to convictional commitment (paradoxical). Here we are not talking about the tenets of the Christian faith as authoritative or relative, but of how human learners make sense of, for example, the structural claim that these tenets have in the lives of

---

[6]William Perry, *Forms of Intellectual and Ethical Development in the College Years* (New York: Holt, Rinehart and Winston, 1970).

[7]Mary Belenky, Blythe Clinchy, Nancy Goldberger and Jill Tarule, *Women's Ways of Knowing: The Development of Self, Voice, and Mind* (New York: Basic Books, 1986).

believers. At another level, the philosophical commitments of human learners' progress seem to move from simple dualism to complex dualism to relativism to commitment in relativism. This is similar to how a learner who is
gradually exposed to various religious truth claims, after having been initially
acculturated into a monotheistic religious community, moves from "experienced faith" to "affiliative faith" to "searching faith" to "owned faith."[8]

Teaching and learning in any context is an exercise of authority. It is typically the people who are in charge and invested with power who develop the
content of what people "need" to be taught. Such individuals are the guardians of teaching and thus also of learning. Due to this, teachers feel constant
pressure to come across as experts in their given field, because they are dis-
pensers of what their students—the learners—"need" to know. They come to
believe that they are the only source of information for these particular learners in this particular subject area.

As a result, a strange game emerges between teachers and students: teachers
have the knowledge and students don't, thus teachers have to show constantly
that they have what it takes to "succeed" in the Christian life (which rings
strikingly familiar to the issues in modern societal education). A mysterious
divide is then formed between teachers and learners, as teachers try to keep
the authority where it "ought" to belong. This guarding of authority keeps an
ever-growing distance between teachers and learners. Teachers don't want to
give away their "cheat sheets" or "teachers' manuals," which show all the
content they are supposed to be passing along to their students, because then
students might realize that the teachers are not who they are pretending to be:
perfect imitators of Jesus Christ in all manners of life and, especially, experts
in content.

This distance between teachers and learners is often encouraged in the
church, masked in advice that teachers separate themselves from their students
in terms of their lifestyles. Being open with struggles and problems are seen as
signs of weakness that reflect poorly on their authority as educators. Keeping
"proper distance" also keeps power and authority where it "ought to be," and
results in a "do as I say, not as I do" authoritative structure. All of this, of
course, is completely the opposite of what Jesus modeled for his disciples during his earthly ministry. When such an approach to teaching occurs in theological studies, the students of these teachers will inevitably replicate the same

---

[8]John Westerhoff III, *Will Our Children Have Faith?* rev. ed. (Toronto: Morehouse, 2000), pp.
87-103.

structures—with all the related problems—when they become teachers (again, akin to what occurs in society at large). Educational ministers are essentially teaching their students not to become part of the local body of God's community for fear that their weaknesses be "found out."[9]

Since the teaching-learning process is indeed an exercise of authority, how should we teach? What is the biblical conception of this authority? If we teach students only the content we want them to acquire, what will our learners become? This philosophy of educational "ministry" turns learners into consumers and the content of teaching into commodities. If learners don't like what they're hearing (the content they're "being fed"), they can easily go to another church that better suits their desires and needs. This, in turn, forces pastors and teachers to focus primarily on the teaching event, whether it is preaching, Sunday school or any other means of information-giving in the church.[10] When pastors and teachers succumb to this model, people begin to show up in time only to hear what the pastors or teachers have to say. If they like what they hear, they keep coming back and even give their "offerings."[11]

In this extremely transactional church model, learners become passive, desiring to be entertained. They are not active participants in living out the Gospel or functioning as a healthy community. The Gospel becomes simply another recorded event, a commodity that people could just as easily download off the Internet and listen to in the comfort of their own homes without experiencing the communal, transforming aspects of the church. When the Gospel is thus turned into a content-driven commodity, people no longer feel the need to congregate together and genuinely *invest* in and among the people of God to together *obey* all that Jesus has commanded us.

WHAT DO LEARNERS BRING TO THE TEACHING-LEARNING OPPORTUNITY?

As discussed earlier, many teachers approach teaching as if their students are empty vessels or blank slates waiting to be filled with knowledge. Although they would never consciously articulate things in this way, in practice much

---

[9]Some denominations require that ordained pastors or teaching elders be the member of the denomination and not of the local assembly.
[10]In some churches, of course, the opposite can occur. That is, to keep "customers" satisfied, the pastor may downplay the importance of teaching, preaching and so on, and instead put the focus on music, drama or whatever else he perceives the people most desire.
[11]To whom? To the Lord or . . . ?

of our transmissive education sends a clear message that our students are second-class citizens who need enlightenment from us.

To remedy such an unreflective practice on the part of many teachers, the late Malcolm Knowles articulated, some forty years ago, an educational manifesto called "andragogy." Knowles's work has had a profound impact among those who have been exposed to it. His basic premise is that adults approach learning not as empty vessels but as reservoirs filled with many life experiences that have a significant influence on the way they engage in learning. Andragogy, as distinct from pedagogy (literally "child leading" in Greek), means "man leading" or "human leading." It is not interested in exploring different teaching-learning methods, but instead explicates several characteristics of adult learners as generative principles for adult teaching-learning.

Principles of Andragogy

- As a person matures, his self-concept moves from that of a dependent personality toward one of a self-directing human being.

- An adult accumulates a growing reservoir of experience, which is a rich resource for learning.

- The readiness of an adult to learn is closely related to the developmental tasks of her social role.

- There is a change in time perspective as people mature— from future application of knowledge to immediacy of application. Thus an adult is more problem-centered than subject-centered in learning.

- The most potent motivations are internal rather than external.

- Adults need to know why they need to learn something.[a]

[a]Sharan Merriam and Rosemary Caffarella, *Learning in Adulthood: A Comprehensive Guide,* 3rd ed. (San Francisco: Jossey-Bass, 2006), pp. 85-90; Malcolm Knowles, *The Modern Practice of Adult Education: From Pedagogy to Andragogy,* 2nd ed. (Englewood Cliffs, N.J.: Cambridge Press, 1980); Malcolm Knowles, Elwood Holton and Richard Swanson, *The Adult Learner: The Definitive Classic in Adult Education and Human Resource Development,* 6th ed. (Boston: Butterworth-Heinemann, 2005).

Many of these principles presuppose that there exists sociocultural capital ("social networks, mutual trust, communities of practice and relational forms of capital"[12]) in the community where adults participate in learning. This capital functions not only as a fertile atmosphere for the adult learner to engage in learning but also provides motivation, standards, expectation, encouragement and rewards for learning. Thus these principles are generative, allowing possibilities for enhancing any kind of adult teaching on any subject area.

We would argue that these generative principles apply not only to adults but to people of all ages, including children, depending on the situation. Like adults, children bring experiences to teaching-learning situations. They want to be given opportunities to share what's going on in their lives and their observations about the world. However, when we teachers focus only on what we have to give, rather than on what there is to be shared, we miss out on the beauty of viewing the world from a child's perspective. If we don't give children the opportunity to share their lives, we treat their experiences as unimportant in comparison to what their teachers have to say. Essentially, this tells the child, "God works through me only when I teach from the Bible," rather than saying that the Holy Spirit allows them to have experiences in their lives. There are things children are actively learning on a daily basis that they are bursting to share with those they love. These things often testify to God's grace in everyday life. Teachers should strive to allow students to be active participants—not passive "vessels"—no matter their ages.

The pedagogy-andragogy continuum can be construed as the continuum from teaching-focused to teaching-learning focused to learning-focused education, as table 9.1 outlines.

As a supporter of the teaching-learning educational approach, Thomas Groome, a Roman Catholic religious educator, has steadfastly advocated the kind of teaching-learning experience where what the learners bring is not only valued but also utilized as an integral part of the teaching-learning experience. He calls this approach "shared Christian praxis."[13] The five movements of this teaching-learning model provide an opportunity to forge critical self-reflection in and through communal reflection in the lives of the participants, with a threefold purpose: education for the reign of God, for

---

[12]Merriam and Caffarella, *Learning in Adulthood,* p. 87.

[13]Thomas Groome, *Christian Religious Education: Sharing Our Story and Vision* (San Francisco: Harper and Row, 1980), and *Sharing Faith: A Comprehensive Approach to Religious Education and Pastoral Ministry: The Way of Shared Praxis* (San Francisco: HarperCollins, 1991).

Table 9.1. Teaching and Learning in Focus

	Teaching Focused	**Teaching-Learning Focused**	**Learning Focused**
Content is defined and planned by	Teacher	Both teacher and learners	Learners with teacher serving as a consultant
Motivation (assumed)	Extrinsic	Intrinsic and communal	Intrinsic
Locus of education	Classroom	Community	Independent
Relationship between student and learners	Dependence	Interdependence and dependence	Self-directing and interdependence
Form of education	Formal, highly structured	Nonformal, semi-structured	Informal, dearth of structure
Resources	A set, written resources	Availability of rich and diverging resources	Independent research
Educational process	Transmission, mastery learning	Various interactive teaching-learning activities dictated by the nature of content (decided by both the teacher and learners)	Research and open learning activities

Christian faith and for human freedom.[14] His praxis model is not merely a teaching method but a meta-approach that is an overarching perspective and mode for proceeding that can be readily adapted to a great variety of teaching and learning occasions and ministerial tasks.[15]

At the outset, participants are invited to explore the ways in which a "generative theme"[16] (a lively focus that will engage all participants, chosen as a theme for a session of shared learning) is important in their lives; Groome calls this movement "Naming/Expressing Present Action." This movement includes the expression of the aspirations, feelings, needs, hopes and beliefs of those present. The important goal here is to elicit a personal statement on present action rather than a statement of *theoria* based on what "they" say. This is ensured by having participants reflect on their *own* feelings and actions,

---

[14]For a complete discussion, see Groome, *Sharing Faith,* pp. 175-293.

[15]Ibid., p. 2.

[16]"Generative theme" refers to themes that are relevant or of critical concern to the participants and that would potentially motivate them to develop ownership in their teaching-learning experience as well as in their lives.

rather than on what they are supposed to think or on the store of knowledge from their tradition.

The second movement, "Critical Reflection on Present Action," is the beginning of critical reflection proper. It concerns directly the questions "Why do we do as we do?" and "What do we hope to get out of it?" It involves a shared reflection of the theme introduced in movement one on all the underlying factors, particularly the internal factors, that involve the deep-seated attitudes, interests and beliefs of the participants themselves. The focus is particularly on the participants' own social conditioning (answering "Why do we do what we do?") and visions of the future (answering "What do we hope to get out of this?").

The third movement, "Making Accessible the Christian Story and Vision,"[17] brings Scripture and religious tradition to bear on the generative theme. Groome calls this "the Christian Story/Vision." Participants are invited to search what is critical to the theme, drawing on Scripture, tradition and liturgy to present the variety of options that Christianity has offered, rightly or wrongly, on the theme. The Story/Vision must be presented in a way that continues the praxis mentality in order to ensure that the participants reflect on, grapple with, question and personally encounter that which is presented.

In movement four, "Dialectical Hermeneutic to Appropriate Story/Vision to Participants' Stories and Visions," participants consider what they have seen of the theme within themselves and in society. Both are interpreted in light of what they now understand as the Christian Story/Vision. The Story is appropriated in dialectic with their own (personal) stories. They are challenged to ask if their practices are affirmed or challenged by the Christian Story/Vision. They are also encouraged to search for honest ways to fuse their own life stories/visions with the Christian Story/Vision so that both are more faithful to the reign of God. This is the beginning of the decision-making phase.

In the last movement, "Decision/Response for Lived Christian Faith," participants are given the opportunity to decide how to live the truths they have arrived at in the preceding movement, a dialectic between Vision and vision. This is the point at which praxis develops, the practical action that will

---

[17] *Story* (uppercase) refers to the whole faith tradition of Christians that is expressed or embodied; and *Vision* refers to the response of Christians to, and God's promise in, the Story, whereas *story* and *vision* refer to participants' own stories and vision through which they reflect and lead their lives.

restore the imbalance and inconsistencies noted and draw closer together the practice and the theory (that is, the way it is and the way it should be begin to merge). As with all critical education, the assumption is that religious education is not complete until the students possess both the will and a mechanism for change.

LEARNERS POSSESS MORE THAN TEACHERS REALIZE

When we congregate together as a community of learners, we bring together all that God has endowed us with in terms of our gifts, passion, character, life experiences, interests and more. Whenever we meet in the name of the Lord, we have all we need to be transformed by God—not because we have all the necessary ingredients to conjure up transformation ourselves, but because when we bring ourselves and all we have as our offerings to the Lord, the Holy Spirit who resides in each of us and among us mysteriously animates us to bring about transformation that he is so desirous to bring to us.

Because of this, we the teachers will want to be committed to create a teaching-learning atmosphere where the learners can intentionally and fully engage in learning as whole persons. Practically, rather than merely focusing on what we want to "cover" in terms of content, we will want to guide the learners to discover what God might have us learn together. Unfortunately, most teachers I have worked with over the years consider teaching preparation as content mastery or review of the old content that they have taught previously. One way to conceptualize teaching with learners in mind is to recognize that God has endowed us with various ways through which we can learn and grow in him.

Over the years, our society—and the church not being an exception to this—has privileged logical and verbal ways of knowing. For instance, studies have repeatedly shown that there is a positive correlation between the Scholastic Aptitude Test (SAT) scores (verbal, math and analytic) and the average income level in the United States. Those with rhetorical gifts and a wider range of vocabulary are likely to be more successful in society. Those who are gifted in the arts, for instance, are encouraged to get a degree in something else because the "less marketable" and thus less important degree is not a reliable investment.

Many other ways of knowing continue to be seen as second-rate abilities, and therefore our churches do not call forth those intelligences in the learners.

Table 9.2. Multiple Intelligences and Teaching-Learning Opportunities and Possibilities[c]

	Commonly found in	Example of famous person	Likely traits	To strengthen for learning
Linguistic	Novelists, poets, orators, journalists, preachers	C. S. Lewis, Martin Luther King Jr., John Donne	• sensitive to patterns • orderly • systematic • able to reason • likes to listen, read and write • likes word games • has good memory for trivia • may be a good public speaker and/or writer	• tell stories • play memory games with names, places • read stories • write stories, jokes • use journal writing • interviewing • integrate writing and reading with other subject areas • produce, edit and supervise magazine • discussions
Logical-Mathematical	Mathematicians, scientists, engineers, lawyers, theologians, accountants	Isaac Newton, John Calvin, Charles Colson	• likes abstract thinking • likes being precise • enjoys counting • likes being organized • uses logical structure • enjoys problem solving • enjoys experimenting in logical way	• stimulate problem solving • analyze and interpret data • use reasoning • encourage practical experiments • use prediction • allow things to be done step by step • use deductive thinking • use computers for spreadsheets, calculations
Visual-Spatial	Architects, painters, sculptors, navigators, naturalists	Rembrandt, Michelangelo, Neil Armstrong	• thinks in pictures • creates mental images • uses metaphor • has sense of gestalt • likes art—drawing, painting and sculpting • easily reads maps, charts and diagrams • remembers with pictures • has good color sense • uses all senses for imaging	• use pictures, diagrams and maps to learn • create doodles, symbols • integrate art with other subjects • use mind-mapping and clustering • do visualization activities • change places in the room to gain a different perspective • use organizers or goal-setting charts • highlight with color • use computer graphics

[c]Adapted from Gordon Dryden and Jeannette Vos, *The Learning Revolution: To Change the Way the World Learns* (Torrance, Calif.: The Learning Web, 1999), pp. 341-54. See also Howard Gardner, *Frames of Mind: The Theory of Multiple Intelligences* (New York: Basic Books, 1983); *Multiple Intelligences: New Horizons in Theory and Practice* (New York: Basic Books, 2006); *Creating Minds: An Anatomy of Creativity as Seen Through the Lives of Freud, Einstein, Picasso, Stravinsky, Eliot, Graham, and Gandhi* (New York: Basic Books, 1994)

Table 9.2. continued

	Commonly found in	Example of famous person	Likely traits	To strengthen for learning
Musical	Performers, composers, musical audiences, cultures without traditional written language	Mozart, Bach, Handel	• sensitive to pitch, rhythm, timbre • sensitive to emotional power of music • sensitive to complex organization of music • may be deeply spiritual	• play a musical instrument • learn through songs • study with baroque music • work out with music • write music • use music to relax and change mood • learn through raps such as timetable, whole-language poems, choral reading
Bodily-Kinesthetic	Dancers, actors, athletes, inventors, mechanics	Mother Teresa, Ignatius of Loyola, Eric Liddell, Catherine Booth	• exceptional control of one's body • good timing and trained responses • learns best by moving and acting out • likes to engage in physical sports • skilled at handcrafts • learns through participation • responsive to physical environment	• engage in active role-play • use movement, manipulatives and dancing to learn • act out the learning • take lots of "state changes" and breaks • use models, machines, handicrafts • use field trips, learning games and simulations • use drama, role-plays
Interpersonal or "Social"	Teachers, pastors, counselors, managers, "people people"	St. Benedict of Nursa, Desmond Tutu, Paul Tournier	• negotiates well, relates well, mixes well • able to read others' intentions • enjoys being with people and has many friends • communicates well, sometimes manipulates • enjoys group activities • likes to mediate disputes and cooperate • "reads" social situations well	• do learning activities cooperatively • use "pair and share" learning activities • use relationships and communication skills • work in teams • learn through service • tutor others • use cause and effect

Table 9.2. continued

	Commonly found in	Example of famous person	Likely traits	To strengthen for learning
Intrapersonal or Intuitive	Counselors, wise elders, spiritual directors, philosophers	Plato, Martin Buber, Henri Nouwen, Brother Lawrence	• self-knowledge and knowledge of one's own values • deeply aware of one's own feelings • sensitivity to one's purpose in life • intuitive ability and self-motivated • very private person and desires to be different from mainstream	• use personal-growth activities to break learning blocks • debrief activities • think about your thinking • take time for inner reflection and reflective writing • do independent study • teach questioning
Naturalistic	Environmentalists, outdoor enthusiasts, biologists	Wendell Berry, St. Francis of Assisi	• uses all senses for learning • learns best through bodily experiences • panentheistic in understanding God's immanence • respectful of nature • observant	• do reading outside • do outdoor projects • go on a nature walk • build a garden • study nature • reflect while going for walk

By privileging the verbal and logical ways of knowing, we inadvertently treat the Word of God as if it were merely a set of words that we are to *do study on,* thus *mastering them* logically for our verbal teaching. May it not be! If the Gospel of Jesus Christ is to continue transforming our whole being, we want to seriously consider how best to design teaching-learning experiences where the learners participate, utilizing all the ways of learning with which they are endowed by God.

Howard Gardner has systematically articulated the theory of multiple intelligences, which describes eight ways of learning and their possible implications (see table 9.2).[18]

How are we to lead the teaching-learning experience in which, while everything needful for transformation by God is present within the community of the learners, every learner brings his own set of preferences in learning, passion, interests, gifts and needs? Moreover, how can we as teachers possibly extend ourselves beyond our preferred teaching styles and strategies to become master teachers—like Jesus? The answer is simple: we can't! And that's all right. What our Lord wants from us who teach is to be humble, teachable and dependent on him.

When some of us as teachers think of "being teachable," we often think of those students who come to our classes on time, without absences, sit in front, take notes and agree with all we have to say. But is there more to being teachable, especially for us as teachers? We need to admit that we who are called to teach God's authoritative Word subconsciously come to believe that what we have prepared in our study to teach becomes authoritative.

At this point, some readers might be up in arms, saying, "Of course what I teach is authoritative!" But let's think about this for a moment. Yes, God's Word *is* authoritative. But when we approach God's Word with our limited perspectives, ways of knowing, knowledge base and assumptions, we have to admit that it is only by God's grace that we can even begin to acknowledge that the Bible is indeed the Word of God. Moreover, it is only through the work of the Holy Spirit that we can begin to understand what God has for us to study and learn, not so that we can stand up before our students and teach, but so that we let God's Word dwell in us richly and get ahold of us as we obey.

Yet as teachers we often engage in what I call a "Saturday Night Spe-

---

[18]Gardner, *Frames of Mind; Multiple Intelligences;* and *Creating Minds.*

cial" or a "Sunday Express"—just barely getting the content down enough
so that we can impress our students. Are we teachable yet? Rather than
bemoaning the illiteracy and lack of obedience and growth on the part of
our students, perhaps we should admit that we have not lived as teachers
who truly submit ourselves to the Lord and are captivated by his Word for
the ongoing transformation that is desperately needed—in us, first of all.
Only if we do so will we begin to teach from the overflow of hearts that
are saturated with his Word and enabled to live in accord with the Word
that we have studied and experienced. When we practice like this, we will
have nothing to prove and won't feel the need to fill the classroom with our
eloquent words. Perhaps then we will feel enabled to envision how we can
teach with the students' learning in mind, getting our students to actively
participate together as a community of learners that includes us, the teachers as learners.

We will also want to pay special attention to learning how our students
experience the teaching-learning experience themselves. Some might see this
as an evaluation of how well the teacher has performed, yet there is more here.
The focus of such assessment is to observe how the learning community has
experienced God corporately and individually. Questions such as the following can frame ways for the teacher to facilitate self-assessment as a learning
community in light of God's work among them.

- Who is God?
- Who is God *to us?*
- Who are we *in God?*
- Who are we in relation to *one another?*
- How are we to live *in God?* What is God claiming in us?
- How are we to live *in the world?* How are we to relate to *the other?*

This set of questions can be useful both for designing one lesson and for planning the entire educational ministry of the church.

Another aspect of assessing teaching-learning times that often gets overlooked is a corporate prayer time. Prayer, as communication with God, especially as *listening to God,* is essential in creating strong and healthy Christian
communities. Too many times, however, corporate prayer is simply a short
blessing before a class—and a forgotten moment at the end. What valid reasons could a teacher have for "not having enough time" and thus missing the

opportunity to bring their students and the teaching-learning encounter before the Lord in prayer as a community?

HUMAN LEARNING IS ALWAYS *IN SITU*

We discussed earlier how human learners are not concerned merely about interacting with the world in a cognitive manner but also about interacting in an existential manner. In other words, human beings as learners do not merely choose to interact with our environment as an object or the *other*. Instead, they are situated beings who cannot escape the world in which they find themselves. Emphasizing the sociocultural shaping of human learning and the central function it plays in human action, Jerome Bruner argues that as human beings participate *in* culture, their mental functioning and powers are realized *through* culture.

> Human beings do not terminate at their own skins; they are expressions of a culture. To treat the world as an indifferent flow of information to be processed by individuals each on his or her own terms is to lose sight of how individuals are *formed* and how they *function*. . . . There is no such thing as human nature independent of culture.[19]

Bruner basically asserts that it is culture that shapes human life, human knowing, the human mind and the biology that constrains us. Culture, not biology, situates human beings' underlying intentional states in an interpretive system by imposing patterns inherent in the culture's symbolic systems: "its language and discourse modes, the forms of logical and narrative explication, and the patterns of mutually dependent communal life."[20] As socioculturally situated, however, human learners are not merely passive beings who are constructed unilaterally by culture, but they are preoccupied with meaning-making and meaning-using processes that connect them with fellow human beings and to culture, mediated by symbolic systems of culture. These processes take place in the form of narrative, Bruner asserts, which comprises the notions of sequentiality, real and imagined links between exceptional and ordinary, and dramatic quality.[21]

We as teachers can sometimes be quick to judge certain learners by inadvertently constructing a false narrative about them based on our limited

---

[19]Jerome Bruner, *Acts of Meaning: Four Lectures on Mind and Culture* (Cambridge, Mass.: Harvard University Press, 1990), p. 11.
[20]Ibid., p. 34.
[21]Ibid., pp. 43-52.

knowledge and our assumptions. For instance, I may deem a particular person who listens well as one who is motivated to learn. On the other hand, I may deem one who comes to class consistently late as either having a character issue or as disrespectful of me, the teacher. But later, perhaps, I learn that he has to drop off his son at a nursery at exactly the same time as the start of my class. And it turns out that his wife has to be at work an hour before class begins. I could easily have asked him about his lateness after two sessions. Yes, he could have told me beforehand why he would have to be late by five minutes to the class, but perhaps I come across to him as a teacher who is hard to approach with such a "petty" personal problem.

In other words, we teachers often judge our students by their actions in ways that we do not judge ourselves. We reason that if the student does something wrong, she's an immature person, but if we do the same wrong, we have simply made a mistake. As teachers, we should be extremely careful not to characterize learners by their observed behavior. Instead, may we learn to cultivate great patience. More often than not, we don't know what kind of lives our students have to live before coming to participate in the teaching-learning experience we have prepared.

Uri Bronfenbrenner, whose life has been devoted to documenting how human beings' environments shape their development and learning, asserts that the learner's life context has a profound impact on the manner in which he approaches learning and, in turn, how teaching-learning designed with his context in mind could potentially transform his learning as well as his life.[22] Bronfenbrenner's ecology of human development theory construes that human beings live and have their being in a set of complex interlocking systems. In such systems, humans grow through processes and interactions that occur both within systems and across systems, which Bronfenbrenner illustrated through a set of concentric circles.

Examples of this are easily seen. A poor person may not have had breakfast that day and is therefore not actively engaged in class. A mom and dad could have had a fight in the car on the way to the church, causing the child to be upset and not to have a good learning experience and to wonder about God the Father's unconditional love. A father struggles to keep his job even after a hefty pay cut during hard economic times and then brings his emotions home, causing his children to have a difficult time concentrating on their school

---

[22]Urie Bronfenbrenner, *The Ecology of Human Development: Experiments by Nature and Design* (Cambridge, Mass.: Harvard University Press, 1979).

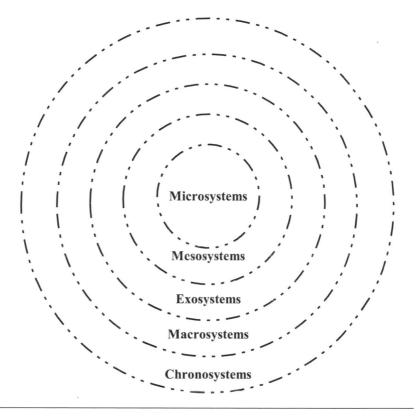

Figure 9.1. The ecology of human development

work and their youth group commitments; perhaps they feel guilty that they are not working to contribute financially to the family. When a society is in an economic depression, it affects the smaller structures, too, such as the local church. In such situations, pastors are typically impatient and quick to give the "annual giving" sermon, requesting more funds and emphasizing faithfulness to God through finances. But they may fail to recognize the pains and concerns of those sitting in the pews.

Here, in brief, are descriptions of Bronfenbrenner's categories:

1. *Microsystems* denote a set of patterns of activities, social roles and interpersonal relations experienced by the learner within the immediate environment. These proximal processes are the ways through which the learner grows as a person, but her power to do so depends on the content and structure of the microsystem, such as family, church, school, peer group and workplace.

2. *Mesosystems* comprise the linkages and processes taking place between two or more settings containing the person. In other words, a mesosystem is a system of microsystems. Some examples include the relations between home and school, and school and workplace. According to James Epstein, elementary school pupils from classrooms in which joint involvement (that is, two-way communication and participation in decision making by parents and teachers) was high not only exhibited greater initiative but also received higher grades.[23] The effects of family and school processes were greater than those attributable to socioeconomic status or race.

3. *Exosystems* consist of the linkage and processes taking place between two or more settings, at least one of which does not contain the developing person. Here, events occur that indirectly influence processes within the immediate setting in which the developing person lives. For instance, a child can be influenced by how his home life is affected by what goes on at his parents' workplace. A mother's parenting style could be influenced by how she discerns the parenting styles that are promoted by her church and that are routinely exhibited by her neighborhood mothers with children. The parents' workplace, family social networks and neighborhood-community contexts, and spheres of adult Christians are especially likely to affect the development of children and youth as learners indirectly through their influence on the family, the school and the peer group.

4. *Macrosystems* house the overarching pattern (that is, a societal blueprint) of micro-, meso- and exosystems, characterizing a given culture's milieu. They include belief systems, bodies of knowledge, material resources, customs, lifestyles, opportunity structures, hazards and life course options that are embedded in each of these broader systems. For example, capitalism, consumerism, individualism, liberal democracy, racial and class segregations, and suburban-urban differences are some of the macrosystemic patterns in the United States. Macrosystems also include specific social and psychological features that affect the particular conditions and processes occurring in the microsystem.

5. *Chronosystems* extend the environment into a third dimension. They encompass change or consistency over time, not only in the characteristics of the person but also of the environment in which she lives. Some examples

---

[23]James Epstein, "School/Family/Community Partnerships: Caring for the Children We Share," *Phi Delta Kappan* 76, no. 9 (1995): 701-12.

might be generational shifts; modern, late-modern and postmodern shifts; pre- and post-9/11; and changes over the life course—in family structure, socioeconomic status, employment, place of residence or the degree of busyness and ability in everyday life. Glen Elder's classic study[24] demonstrated that youngsters who were teenagers during the Depression years and whose parents' income fell by 35 percent or more displayed a greater desire to achieve and a firmer sense of career goals, and attained greater satisfaction in life—both by their own and societal standards—than those teenagers whose parents' income level either stayed the same or fell less than 35 percent and youngsters who became teenagers eight years after the Depression and did not experience the direct effects of the Depression.[25]

Recently, I had a chance to attend a men's Bible study at a nearby church. At the leader's initiative, the men were invited to share their prayer concerns. With the exception of one man, who spoke of an impending divorce proceeding, all the other men shared some kind of financial worry in this major economic downturn. Some had lost their long-held employment. Some retirees were concerned that their retirement money would run out much quicker than anticipated. Some were worried about their children's college education. Yet, even in a context with such serious needs, the teacher "had to" move on to what he came prepared to teach for that Sunday.

Afterward, in the corporate worship service, the pastor preached a polished sermon from the series he had been preaching on for some time, apparently oblivious to the plight of many in the pews. I wondered how the men at the Bible study were able to worship God with their heavy hearts. Pastors, teachers and leaders often seem so preoccupied with the operations of their church— budgets, programs and other matters—that they are unaware of the issues their people are bringing into the church. "Church" then gradually becomes only a segment of people's lives, rather than the vital community of God's people that provides the hope, vision and service God has called us to.

However, this does not mean that pastors and teachers are to be all things to all people, abandoning their own lives and families. We who are teachers need to have good advisers, as well as fellow disciples with whom we can mutually share our lives and concerns. We can also selectively invest in visiting and learning about our learners' typical spheres of life—their work, fami-

---

[24]Originally published in 1974. See Glen Elder, *Children of the Great Depression,* updated ed. (Boulder, Colo.: Westview Press, 1998).
[25]Adapted from Bronfenbrenner, *Ecology of Human Development.*

lies and places where they spend much time. It behooves us to embrace a lifestyle of "ethnographic research,"[26] in which we are constantly learning about the people God has entrusted to us.

Our focus should be on the various aspects of their lives and the sociocultural contexts in which they live—"thick" description, rather than simple explanations of their behaviors or contexts.[27] It is crucial to remind ourselves that our goal is to *learn from* them rather than to *study* them. This involves a "disciplined study of what the world is like for people who have learned to see, hear, speak, think, and act in ways that are different"[28]—the sociocultural prescriptions of their everyday behaviors, beliefs, attitudes, values and ideals.[29] In doing so we as teachers serve those God has entrusted to us to *co-construct* the reality of God's kingdom in their lives, being more reflective of God's presence and critiquing the incessant influence of their environs.

The vast majority of intercessory prayer requests I have heard over the years in churches and places of Christian learning have been prayers for physical healing. Does that mean that the people are all fine in other spheres of life? Some lose employment, suffer mental illnesses, are estranged from their loved ones, struggle with various addictions and face many other challenges frowned on not only by society but also in the church. We are graciously invited by the triune God to "engage in *regular practices of truth telling, forgiveness, and reconciliation.* These communities must have the skills of engaging one another in humility and listening until the point they can all come together and recognize the Spirit in one another's lives."[30]

As the people of God, we are called to cultivate and practice *hospitality* in the name of the Lord. Even a cursory look at the root of that term reminds us of at least two other familiar terms: *hospital* and *hospice.* We are to minister to the lost, care for the sick and help the dying to die well. Here we are not just talking about what we are called to do *for others,* which is both an enormous responsibility and a wonderful privilege that we have as God's children. It is

---

[26]J. L. Peacock, *The Anthropological Lens: Harsh Lights, Soft Focus* (Cambridge: Cambridge University Press, 1986).

[27]Earl Babbie, *The Practice of Social Research* (Belmont, Calif.: Wadsworth, 2001).

[28]James P. Spradley, *Participant Observation* (New York: Holt, Rinehart and Winston, 1980), p. 3.

[29]In other words, we ought to grow in our understanding of the *emic* perspective of a culture in order to realize *their* vision of *their* world. Bronislaw Malinowski, *Argonauts of the Western Pacific* (London: Routledge, 1922), p. 25.

[30]David Fitch, *The Great Giveaway: Reclaiming the Mission of the Church from Big Business, Parachurch Organizations, Psychotherapy, Consumer Capitalism, and Other Modern Maladies* (Grand Rapids: Baker, 2005), p. 137.

also *for us*. We are called to be hospitable with one another so that we can share our lives together and grow together to be more like Christ as the body of Christ. We are also called to be like a hospital, where only those who admit and exhibit their illnesses are admitted. We are to be vulnerable by being open and honest about our struggles and challenges, so that we can confess and be forgiven, and be on the path of God's redeeming work.

Moreover, we are called to be a hospice where we help one another die well. Though the term *discipleship* has morphed over the centuries since the inception of the church, it in fact refers to "a process of learning—not merely the acquisition of knowledge, but the surrender of one's person to Christ in faith and service."[31] In this sense, as the people of God we are to learn to die well, for it is only when we know how to die to ourselves daily and are unafraid of physical death that we can truly begin to live well in the Lord. Rather than being content to retain a professional, sterile, schoollike learning environment, we who teach can begin to reenvision a teaching-learning environment where the community of learners—ourselves included—are invited to engage in teaching-learning experiences with our whole beings.

LEARNING TO BE CHILDREN AGAIN

We who are called to be teachers want to be careful when consulting the theories of human learning that we have been discussing. The goals of the various theorists are not the same as the end goal of the teaching ministry of the church. In using these theories without a critical (yet charitable) theological assessment, Christian teachers can easily end up offering students a form of teaching-learning that is devoid of God.

For instance, independence becomes one of the major goals in our teaching as biblical characters are made out to be heroes (consider Samson, David and many others), as we conveniently gloss over the fallen nature of these characters and rarely provide an opportunity for our students to learn the complete story. In doing so, we often neglect the themes of the dark side of human beings and how God's mercy shows through it over and over again. Teaching

---

[31]Robert Hoerber, "Mathetes," *Concordia Journal* 6, no. 5 (Spring 1980): 181-82. "A *mathetes* is much more than a follower; he is one who hears the call of Jesus and joins Him. When crowds of people—including the curious—merely follow Jesus, the New Testament frequently employs the verb *akoloutheo* (Mt 4:25; 8:1; 21:9). *Mathetes,* however, is cognate to *manthano* (aorist stem: *math*), which involves a process of learning—not merely the acquisition of knowledge, but the surrender of one's person to Christ in faith and service. . . . The New Testament evangelists . . . employ *mathetes* to indicate total attachment to someone in discipleship."

the Bible as a collection of heroes strung together inevitably makes a mockery of God's Word and character. The triune God himself is the *only* "hero" of the Bible; human beings are in constant need of his grace, mercy and justice.

In terms of the cognitive dimension, we usually think about the "age appropriateness" of certain biblical material. In reality, children have a much bigger capacity to intuit and see through the eyes of faith and spiritual realities than adults do in many instances. God has given human beings several ways of knowing and learning: senses, intuition, imagination and reasoning,[32] yet we tend to think that reason alone is the proper way to understand the God of the Bible. For example, we might assume that sensitivity and intuition belong to children and women,[33] and are thus considered inferior. Children are allowed to imagine for the time being, but we really want them to grow up to be rational beings (like ourselves!). With this predisposition, we short-circuit the wonderful confluence of all the ways of knowing and learning that God has endowed us with—not just our children, but people of all ages.

When Jesus tells his followers to be more childlike, perhaps he is speaking of recovering all the ways of knowing and learning, and integrating them in our submission to him. Jesus proclaims, "Anyone who will not receive the kingdom of God like a little child will never enter it" (Lk 18:17). Commenting on the way Jesus uses the image of a child as the only proper recipient of God's kingdom, Walter Liefeld writes, "It is not age *per se* that is in view but childlike qualities such as trust, openness, and the absence of holier-than-thou-attitudes."[34] Yet we want to be quick to recognize that being children in the first century was not at all glamorous. There was a high mortality rate among young children, and they were often construed as "not adults," meaning that

> they might be valued for their present or future contribution to the family business, especially in an agricultural context, but otherwise they possessed little if any intrinsic value as human beings. Luke's phrase "even infants" draws attention to the particular vulnerability of the smallest of children, perhaps accounting for the widespread practice of infanticide and child abandonment. . . . "Little children" . . . translates a term used for household slaves and children, those maintained in a relationship of subordination in a Greco-Roman household.[35]

---

[32]See pages 238-40.
[33]Often referred to as "women's intuition."
[34]Walter Liefeld, "Luke," *The Expositor's Bible Commentary,* vol. 8, ed. Frank Gabelein (Grand Rapids: Zondervan, 1984), p. 1002.
[35]Joel Green, *The Gospel of Luke* (Grand Rapids: Eerdmans, 1997), p. 651.

Here lies an important point: Jesus was saying that

> "receiving little children" is tantamount to granting them hospitality, perform-
> ing for them actions normally reserved for those of equal or higher status. That
> is, Jesus is asking his followers to embrace a topsy-turvy system of values and to
> extend respectful service to that social group most often overlooked.[36]

In this sense, "'receiving the Kingdom' is intimately tied to 'receiving little children.'"[37] The child is at the mercy of the adults. The disciples are to extend hospitality, and it is like receiving the kingdom. This is what it means to be childlike. There definitely exists a circularity here in the passage: We are called to become like a child who is at God's mercy. We are also to be hospitable to our fellow children of God and to receive and extend to one another God's mercy, the message of the cross, which is "foolishness," yet "the power of God" (1 Cor 1:18).

This posture of receiving the power of God by becoming a fool for God emerges from "a transformed sense of the way the world works, one based on the power of the Kingdom of God to deconstruct those worldly systems and values that stand in opposition to God's project."[38] This requires learning to learn together, yielding ourselves to the Holy Spirit to bring us closer as a community so we can *see* the kingdom of God corporately.[39] In the process, what began as a quest for the independence of the agentic I learns what it means to have our true identity in receptive We, the people of God who together daily surrender our *it's-all-about-Me* and daily learn to be the *teachable Us* for the glory of God.

CONCLUSION

The church exists in time and space to glorify God through good works of reconciliation. To fulfill this task more faithfully, the church builds itself up in love, in part, through ministries of teaching and learning. The content of our teaching, at the most basic level, is the Gospel and its implications for faith and living. God graciously raises up, within the church, gifted servant-leaders to champion the formative ministry of teaching the body.

Those who are called to teach need to understand the purposes toward which they teach. They also need to be deeply acquainted with the message

---

[36]Ibid.
[37]Ibid.
[38]Green, *Gospel of Luke,* p. 651.
[39]Matthew 5:8: "Blessed are the pure in heart, for they will see God."

they are to obey themselves and to proclaim to others. But it is also vital that teachers study the people among whom they minister. Thus, in the last two chapters, we have considered some of the dynamics of how the people of God learn and develop. With all the above concerns ringing in our minds and hearts, we now turn our attention to an exploration of strategies and practices for teaching and forming the faithful.

HYMN FOR CONTEMPLATION AND WORSHIP

Sanctuary

In a dry and barren land
you've called us to be
a people who stand apart
a sanctuary.

You draw us into your sight
and bring shame to light.
Through mercy found in your scars
we come as we are.

Make us a sanctuary
where grace would overflow.
Make us a sanctuary
for lost and weary souls.
Grant us true community where we'll find
a house of safety where there's nothing to hide.
Make us a sanctuary
where we can be made whole.

Words and Music by Eugene Kim[40]

QUESTIONS FOR PLANNING AND PRACTICE

1. What issues arise when educators take the human development theories from the twentieth century and make them prescriptions instead of descriptions of the educational process? What effects do these have on formational ministry?

2. This chapter discusses how the developmental theories by Piaget, Kohlberg, Erikson and others have given us great insight into the learning pro-

---

[40]"Sanctuary," by Eugene P. Kim, 2003, from *Songs at 3*. Used by permission. You can listen to some of Eugene's beautiful songs at <http://profile.myspace.com/index.cfm?fuseaction=user.viewprofile&friendID=30634964>.

cess and also how they do not go far enough in terms of formational ministry. How do you perceive these things to be true, based on the exposition in the beginning of this chapter?

3. In what ways is teaching-learning an exercise of biblical authority? This chapter discusses how the teacher-learner relationship often gets skewed because of a misuse of such authority. What steps can be taken to ensure that this authority is exercised biblically?

4. Malcolm Knowles's "andragogy" states that adults approach learning not as empty vessels but as reservoirs filled with life experiences that influence the way they engage as learners. We invite you to reflect on your experiences as an adult learner: How did you view yourself—as a blank slate or as a filled reservoir? How did that affect the process and outcome of your learning experience?

5. We invite you to reflect on the concept of children as filled reservoirs, entering teaching-learning environments with experiences and stories to tell. Reflect with another educational minister on methods by which you can effectively engage young learners as people with something to contribute, yet still with much content to learn. Essentially, how do you engage children as both learners and teachers in their own right?

6. What does it mean to be teachable as educational ministers? What kind of teacher does Jesus call his disciples to be?

7. "The focus . . . is to observe how the learning community has experienced God corporately and individually." Educational ministers often need the reminder that our teaching is to be completely about God and that our focus needs to be on how our students can be transformed to be more like Christ. With this in mind, as an educational minister, how do you respond to the above statement both in planning and executing teaching-learning times?

RESOURCES FOR FURTHER STUDY

Balthasar, Hans Urs von. *Unless You Become Like This Child*. San Francisco: Ignatius Press, 1991.

Bronfenbrenner, Urie. *The Ecology of Human Development: Experiments by Nature and Design*. Cambridge, Mass.: Harvard University Press, 1979.

Gardner, Howard. *Multiple Intelligences: New Horizons in Theory and Practice*. New York: Basic Books, 2006.

————. *Creating Minds: An Anatomy of Creativity as Seen Through the Lives of Freud, Einstein, Picasso, Stravinsky, Eliot, Graham, and Gandhi*. New York: Basic Books, 1994.

Groome, Thomas. *Christian Religious Education: Sharing Our Story and Vision*. San Francisco: Harper and Row, 1980.

Knowles, Malcolm. *The Modern Practice of Adult Education: From Pedagogy to Andragogy*. 2nd ed. Englewood Cliffs, N.J.: Cambridge Press, 1980.

Knowles, Malcolm, Elwood Holton and Richard Swanson. *The Adult Learner: The Definitive Classic in Adult Education and Human Resource Development*. 6th ed. Boston: Butterworth-Heinemann, 2005.

Spradley, James P. *Participant Observation*. New York: Holt, Rinehart and Winston, 1980.

Westerhoff, John, III. *Will Our Children Have Faith?* Rev. ed. Toronto: Morehouse, 2000.

PART 4

PRACTICES

Strategies for Teaching and Forming

"Meet them where they are; help them go where they need to go."

▼

I (GARY) HAVE OFTEN USED THE WORDS ABOVE TO articulate some of the basic concerns involved in the making of disciples. We must meet people where they are. Jesus has modeled this in many ways, most dramatically by his incarnation. In a similar spirit, the apostle Paul was dedicated to becoming "all things to all men so that by all possible means I might save some" (1 Cor 9:22).

We do not meet people where they are as though this were the goal in and of itself. The goal is to help them go where they must go. As teachers, we are also fellow learners who are ready to journey with them toward the goal. We discussed what that goal is at length in chapter two: we are aiming at becoming like Christ. This was the motivation for the incarnation. Jesus became like us that he might make us like himself.

The starting place in the saying above, then, is not really "meet them where they are." We start instead with a vision of the end, of the *telos*. It is with this fixed in our minds and hearts that we then seek to meet people where they are. Long before the Word became flesh, meeting us where we were (see Jn 1:14), he had eternally been in that presence of the Father (see Jn 1:1, 18). Too often, our ministries of discipleship, of teaching and formation, begin with a concern for relevance. But this misses the mark. We begin with a concern for faithfulness to God's purposes, such as those we outlined in chapters one and two. Otherwise, our efforts at "relevance" will be completely irrelevant.

In this, the final major section of the book, we aim to fill out our proposed curriculum for congregational teaching and formation. We have already attended to questions of aims (part one), content (part two) and participants (part three). We now consider processes and practices. As we do so, we seek to keep in mind all that we have considered thus far. In our proposal, we pay special attention to the spiritual development of learners as we try to meet them where they are and help them go where they must go.

As we have repeatedly said, we know in part. What we offer here is a work still very much in progress. Yet we pray that the readers of this text will find in our proposal ideas that can stimulate their thinking and can somehow serve to spur them on toward love and good deeds in their lives and ministries.

Part four begins with chapter ten, on the nature and aims of Christian teaching. Chapter eleven is primarily a call to intergenerational love and faithfulness. In chapter twelve we consider the formative power of congregational worship. Finally, in chapters thirteen and fourteen, we propose a model of seven commitments for congregational formation.

10

Visions of Christian Teaching

". . . and teaching them to obey everything I have commanded you."

MATTHEW 28:20

▼

I<small>N THE PREVIOUS SECTION OF THE BOOK,</small> WE examined issues related to the person of the teacher and the nature of the learner. We now turn to consider the teaching task itself.

How should we envision teaching? After all, innumerable definitions have been offered through the centuries. Contexts in which good teaching occurs vary so widely that any definition will likely seem ill fit for use in some settings. In this chapter we seek to rehabilitate the full meaning of teaching from a Christian perspective, keeping in mind some of the concerns raised about teaching in recent years. Toward this end, we will interact with a now familiar (to some) definition of teaching and will also propose and unpack a definition of our own.

It seems that some evangelicals look on commitment to intentional teaching with suspicion today. Many would argue that the emphasis ought to be on learning, not on teaching. Others would take this one step further by replacing the word *educational* with *formative*. Still others emphasize *faithful practices* rather than *teaching* or *teaching ministry* as the preferred term for our task. But, in fact, we do not diminish proper emphasis on learning, education, formation or faithful practices when we take teaching seriously. On the contrary, to neglect a serious and biblically informed commitment to teaching is to imperil sound learning, education and formation. It is also to be guilty of neglecting one of the most biblically sanctioned of all faithful practices.

In both Old and New Testaments we find numerous models and mandates for teaching. In table 10.1, we offer a partial list of the many Hebrew and Greek words that speak to different aspects of teaching. The list itself makes it evident that a biblical vision of teaching embraces all the concerns we have outlined above—concerns for learning and forming, for sound education and for faithful practices—and much more. The list also makes it obvious that no single definition of teaching can suffice to say all that could and should be said. However, through the following discussion, we aim to provide a framework through which a holistic understanding of teaching may be conceptualized and practiced.

TEACHING AS "CREATING SPACE" FOR OBEDIENCE

One of the descriptions of teaching we have found very helpful was put forth by Parker Palmer in *To Know as We Are Known*.[1] Palmer's book took the educational world by storm when it was first published in 1983. He had intended to write for Christian educators and was surprised to see how much the little book seemed to resonate with educators in a wide variety of settings. Palmer argued for an approach to education that is rooted in love. Rejecting the kind of educational practices that are hypercompetitive and concerned with helping people gain control over knowledge, Palmer advocated an approach marked by humility, mutuality and an open-hearted attitude toward truth and toward fellow learners. At the heart of Palmer's book is his definition of teaching: "To teach is to create a space in which obedience to truth is practiced."[2]

The definition is abstract and evocative, and it invites a wide range of possible applications. To help his readers understand the spirit of the definition, Palmer illustrates by appealing to the desert fathers. He relates the following account of Abba Felix:

Some brothers . . . went to see Abba Felix and they begged him to say a word

---

[1]This early work of Palmer (New York: Harper & Row, 1983) was one of the most explicitly Christian of his works. In later works, he has ventured into more general musings on teaching, mentoring and spiritual direction.

[2]Ibid., p. 69. In response to readers who were suspicious of the word *obedience,* Palmer later changed the definition thus: "To teach is to create a space in which the community of truth is practiced." *The Courage to Teach: Exploring the Inner Landscape of a Teacher's Life* (San Francisco: Jossey-Bass, 1997), p. 90. While we understand the concerns and the change, we deal with the original definition here, believing that (1) *obedience* is a word worthy of being both retained and, as necessary, "redeemed" from any abuse it has either suffered and caused, and (2) that taking seriously such obedience will lead to the faithful practice of true community.

Table 10.1. Key Bible Verbs Related to Teaching[a]

Hebrew word	emphasis	root meaning(s)	examples of usage
lamadh—usual OT word for teaching	discipline	to beat, to goad, to teach	2 Chron 17:7; Ps 71:17; Prov 5:13
yarah—from the same root as *Torah*	law, guidance, direction	to cast (as an arrow or lots), to flow	Ex 35:34-35; 2 Chron 6:27; Ps 32:8
byn	discernment	to separate, to distinguish	Dan 8:16; Neh 8:7-9; Ps 119:34
shanan	impress upon	to point, to pierce, to whet	Deut 6:7
sakhal	wisdom	to be wise, to look at, behold	Prov 16:23; 21:11
yada	knowledge	to see, to perceive, to know	Ex 18:16, 20; Prov 9:9; 22:19
yasar	discipline	to chasten, instruct discipline	Prov 29:17
zahar	illumination	to shine, to admonish	Ex 18:20; 2 Chron 19:8-10
hanak	dedication	to dedicate, train, inaugurate	Prov 22:6
ra'ah	nourishment	to feed a flock, to shepherd	2 Sam 5:2; Prov 10:21
Greek word	**emphasis**	**root meaning(s)**	**examples of usage**
didaskō—usual NT word for teaching	instruction	to teach	Mt 4:23; 28:20; Jn 6:59
paratithēmi—used regarding parables of Jesus	presentation	to place beside	Mt 13:24; Mk 8:6; Acts 16:34
symbibazō	persuasion	to put together, cause to coalesce	Acts 9:22
diermēneuō	elucidation	to interpret, to explain thoroughly	Lk 24:27; 2 Cor 12:30
ektithēmi	exposition	to set or place out	Acts 11:4; 18:26; 28:23
paideuō	training	to train a child, to chastise, discipline	Eph 6:4
noutheteō	admonition	to warn, admonish, exhort	Col 1:28
prophēteuō	authority	to prophesy, to speak for	Mt 11:13; 15:7; 1 Cor 13:9
katēcheō	verbal instruction	to echo, sound from above, resound	Lk 1:4; Acts 18:25; Gal 6:6
katangellō	proclamation	to announce, make known, declare	Acts 17:3
paradidōmi	tradition	to pass on, to hand over	1 Cor 11:2, 23; 15:3

[a]This table is based on a variety of sources, including especially Byron H. DeMent's entry on "teach" in International Standard Bible Encyclopaedia, Electronic Database Copyright © 1996, 2003, 2006 by Biblesoft. All rights reserved.

to them. But the old man kept silence. After they had asked for a long time he said to them, "You wish to hear a word?" They said, "Yes, abba." Then the old man said to them, "There are no more words nowadays. When the brothers used to consult the old men and when they did what was said to them, God showed them how to speak. But now, since they ask without doing that which they hear, God has withdrawn the grace of the word from the old men and they do not find anything to say, since there are no longer any who carry their words out." Hearing this, the brothers groaned, saying, "Pray for us, abba."[3]

Much of Palmer's book reads like a commentary on this story. Abba Felix becomes the exemplar for would-be teachers. We see that he "creates space" in the hearts and minds of his hearers, in part by using silence and story. We see also that his hearers, in the end, take a first step toward obeying Truth. They groan and ask for Abba's prayers. They have come to recognize their own disobedience and have taken the first steps on the road to recovery from their error.

There is much that we find commendable in Palmer's definition of teaching. In the first place, he affirms the existence of truth and believes it is to be taken very seriously. The Truth, as we explored in chapter five and as Palmer affirms in his book, has been incarnated in the person of Jesus Christ. Jesus is *the Truth* in its fullest possible expression. This is not to deny that truth is not evident elsewhere or has no other witnesses in other religious or philosophical teachings. It is simply to assert that there is no expression or articulation of the Truth that is so full, so perfect and so ultimate as that in Jesus. In saying this, we affirm the clear teaching of many biblical texts.[4]

A second appealing aspect of Palmer's definition is his insistence on obedience or, if we use language from the later version of his definition, on practice. We have already argued that this is a nonnegotiable for Christian teaching. Knowledge is never the goal in and of itself, not even knowledge of the Truth. Obedience to that Truth is required. If we stayed closer to the Hebrew conceptions of our terms, this would hardly surprise us. The key Hebrew word for knowledge, *yada*—as we saw in chapter two—actually implies a

---

[3]Palmer, *To Know as We Are Known*, p. 41.
[4]For example, John 1:1, 14, 18; Hebrews 1:1-3; Colossians 1:15; 2:9; John 14:6. Though Palmer clearly affirms that truth has been incarnated in the person of Jesus Christ, many evangelicals will find his overall approach to truth in this book to be somewhat elusive. Palmer's subsequent writings are less explicitly Christian in tone.

deep, personal encounter with the Truth and will not permit claims of disinterested, objectified detachment. In the Hebrew concept of *yada,* "to know is to do," Marv Wilson argues.[5] Biblical knowing is "an act involving concern, inner engagement, dedication, or attachment to a person. It also means to have sympathy, pity, or affection for someone." Wilson continues: "A grasp of so much information was not enough; it also implied a response in the practical domain of life, in behavior and morals."[6]

Palmer demonstrates this personal commitment to truth by pointing out that even the English term makes such a demand. *Truth,* he reminds us, is etymologically related to *troth.* Commenting on this fact, he writes,

> To know something or someone in truth is to enter troth with the known, to rejoin with new knowing what our minds have put asunder. To know in truth is to become betrothed, to engage the known with one's whole self, an engagement one enters with attentiveness, care, and good will. To know in truth is to allow one's self to be known as well, to be vulnerable to the challenges and changes any true relationship brings. To know in truth is to enter into the life of that which we know and to allow it to enter into ours. Truthful knowing weds the knower and the known; even in separation, the two become part of each other's life and fate.[7]

In Palmer's definition of teaching, then, we have attention to *content*—that is, to truth. We also have attention to *purpose*—obedience to that truth. Furthermore, by speaking of the need to "create space" for obedience to truth, Palmer's definition also embraces the matter of *process.* Good teaching requires thoughtful work on the part of the teacher. She must plan with intentionality and be sensitive to how learners are able to engage the teaching-learning process in order to move with fellow learners toward the desired end. Obedience to truth does not happen simply by presenting that truth to others. We are not naturally inclined toward seeking truth, and we are surely not inclined to submit to it if and when we do discover it. Something in the mind, heart and will of humans must be "opened" if good is to emerge.

THREE EXAMPLES FROM THE TEACHING OF JESUS

Palmer's vision of teaching reminds us of aspects of the teaching of Jesus. As

[5]Marvin Wilson, *Our Father Abraham: Jewish Roots of the Christian Faith* (Grand Rapids: Eerdmans, 1989), pp. 287-89.
[6]Ibid., p. 288.
[7]Palmer, *To Know as We Are Known,* p. 31.

we have already noted, Jesus was concerned with obedience to the Truth, not merely with affirmation of it. In teaching toward such an end, Jesus employed various elements that could help to "create space" in the hearts and minds of his hearers.

To illustrate this approach to teaching in the ministry of Jesus, we consider briefly three examples of Jesus' teaching as recorded in the Gospels. The first involves his parable of the two sons, as recorded in Matthew 21:28-31:

> What do you think? There was a man who had two sons. He went to the first and said, "Son, go and work today in the vineyard."
>
> "I will not," he answered, but later he changed his mind and went.
>
> Then the father went to the other son and said the same thing. He answered, "I will, sir," but he did not go.
>
> Which of the two did what the father wanted?

The religious leaders to whom Jesus addressed this parable could answer his question only by saying, "The first," for it was obviously so.

In this episode, the Lord sets forth the will of God. The Truth to which he points his hearers is that God requires obedience to his will, not mere lip service to it. To "create space" toward this obedience, Jesus tells a parable, as he so often did. He asks a question at the story's end—again, something he often did. All of this is to provoke, to open space for them to grapple existentially with the matter of obedience. His hearers immediately put forth the proper answer to the question, but it is not at all clear that they have become more obedient to the Truth.

Soon after they had answered his question, Jesus tells them that "tax collectors and prostitutes" are entering the kingdom of heaven ahead of them. It is a severe rebuke. But in the larger scheme of things, even this rebuke can be seen as a loving effort to "create space" in his hearers. Only God knows if this teaching ultimately bore fruit in one or more of those who heard him that day.

Our second example of Jesus' teaching is his encounter with the rich young man, as recorded in Mark 10:17-28. The young man is desperately seeking peace with God. He runs to Jesus and falls on his knees. "Good teacher," he asks, "what must I do to inherit eternal life?" Jesus answers, "Why do you call me good?" and continues, "No one is good—except God alone."

To evangelical readers of this story, Jesus' reply may be troubling and confusing. "But Jesus," we may wonder, "you *are* God. Why would you then protest such an address?" Compounding our confusion is the fact that Jesus turns to the commands of the Torah. "You know the commandments," he says, and then lists several. This, too, might confuse us: perhaps we think that Jesus should have pointed to himself, not to the law, if he truly wanted to help this young man find eternal life.

The young man dismisses Jesus' words about the commandments. Without hesitating, he says, "Teacher . . . all these I have kept since I was a boy." At this, Mark records, "Jesus looked at him and loved him. 'One thing you lack,' he said. 'Go, sell everything you have and give to the poor, and you will have treasure in heaven. Then come, follow me.'" We are then told, "At this, the man's face fell. He went away sad, because he had great wealth." Again, we see no evidence that the teaching actually helped the young man to open his heart and mind to obedience. But what exactly was the Truth that Jesus wanted the young man to obey?

In the first place, it seems that Jesus was aiming to help this young man realize that there is no one good but God. This means that he—the young man—was not as good as he thought himself to be and had not obeyed the commandments as he supposed he had. Thus, if he would truly find eternal life, he must let go of his idolatrous grip on his wealth and join himself to Jesus and to the true life that only Jesus can offer. The point of Jesus' words, "No one is good—except God" was not a denial of Jesus' own goodness or of his deity. It was a word *for the young man,* who apparently thought of himself as good.

Quite sincerely, he had tried to obey the commands of God but had failed to grasp that God's law calls for obedience of the heart, as well as for external obedience. This he had not fulfilled. The reference to the divine commands, had it been seriously and soberly considered, would have helped the young man to realize it. Had he truly "kept all of these" since his childhood? Plainly, he had not obeyed even the first of the Ten Commandments: "You shall have no other god before me." The young man was struggling with idolatry, worshiping his wealth, and was desperately in need of salvation from this sin. Yet he had convinced himself that he was a law-abiding Jew with good standing before God. Jesus used questions, the commandments and the admonition to sell all and give to the poor in an effort to "create space" in the heart of this inquirer. Again, we cannot know this for certain. Sometimes, it must be remembered, even the best teaching does not achieve its desired ends.

There is another layer to this story, as there so often is in the Gospel accounts. After the young man leaves, Jesus turns to the Twelve and says to them, "Children, how hard it is to enter the kingdom of God! It is easier for a camel to go through the eye of a needle than for a rich man to enter the kingdom of God." This astounds the disciples, who wonder, "Who then can be saved?" Jesus explains that "with man this is impossible, but not with God; all things are possible with God" (Mk 10:24-27).

The whole matter of salvation, it is clear, depends on the gracious intervention of God, not on human power, wealth, goodness or ingenuity. Jesus, the Master Teacher, cannot let this encounter with the young man be lost on the Twelve. He uses the encounter, together with his own follow-up statements and evocative illustration, to create space in *their* hearts for genuine obedience—in this case, for greater dependence on the living God.

A third example of this sort of teaching in Jesus' ministry is recorded in Luke 10:25-37. Luke writes of another occasion of someone putting the very same question to Jesus. The questioner is a scribe—a Torah scholar. "Teacher," he asks, "what must I do to inherit eternal life?" Here, however, the motivation seems very different. The rich young man had seemed sincerely desperate for his own soul. In this case, the scribe is motivated by a desire "to test" Jesus. "What is written in the Law?" Jesus asks the inquirer. "How do you read it?" Jesus often "answered" questions by posing a question of his own. The tables have turned quickly in this story: who, now, is testing whom?

Without thinking reflectively about his own life, the scribe has no problem offering the correct answer. Citing Deuteronomy 6:5 and Leviticus 19:18, he places together what had come to be widely regarded as the two greatest commands: love of God and love of neighbor. Jesus replies, "You have answered correctly. . . . Do this and you will live." The Torah had promised, after all, that whoever obeys the commands of God shall live by them (see Lev 18:5). But the same Torah also warned that whoever fails to continue in obedience to all that is written in it is under a curse (see Deut 27:26).[8]

What this scribe had intended as a conversation to put Jesus on the spot was over before it had hardly begun. He sought to test Jesus, but Jesus had actually tested him—and in doing so was graciously inviting him to consider the chasm between his life's profession and his actual practice. The scribe had uttered "the right answer." He and Jesus apparently agreed on their reading of Torah. "But he wanted to justify himself," Luke tells us of the scribe. Does this mean that the scribe wanted to justify his manner of life, or was it simply that he wanted to save face before Jesus and the listeners, rather than be dis-

---

[8]Note Paul's use of these references in Romans 10:5-13 and Galatians 3:10-14.

missed as someone who had asked an easy and obvious question? In either case, he asks a follow-up question, one he must have thought would lead to full-blown debate: "And who is my neighbor?" But Jesus has no interest in joining this scribe in debate. His interest is that this scribe (as well as the others who were looking on and listening) would become more obedient to God's Truth and God's commands. So he tells a story.

The story he tells we have come to know as the parable of "the good Samaritan." In it, a priest and a Levite fail to offer aid to a man who had fallen prey to robbers and thugs. But along comes a Samaritan—one whom Jesus' hearers would have thought most unlikely of all to offer assistance to the fallen Jew. Yet it is this Samaritan who helps the victim, at great cost and personal risk to himself. Jesus follows the story with a question: "Which of these three do you think was a neighbor to the man who fell into the hands of robbers?" To this question, the expert in the Law replied, correctly, "The one who had mercy on him." Then Jesus concluded the conversation with the invariable call to obedience, "Go and do likewise" (Lk 10:36-38).

In this instance, what is the truth to which Jesus was demanding obedience? It is the command to "love your neighbor as yourself." Jesus would show this scribe the condition of his own heart and the hopelessness of his own law-observance apart from surrendering his self-righteous, defective heart to God in trust and surrender. Therefore, he, the Master Teacher, labors to "create space" for obedience in this man's heart. He does so with a combination of a question, a command, a provocative story, another question and another command. Once again, we have no evidence recorded here about the "success" or "failure" of the teaching. But the teaching itself was masterful, and provides a wonderful example for our own endeavors.

In the Gospel account of John, we read of several more encounters that illustrate Jesus creating space in the hearts of his hearers. We could think of Jesus' encounter with Nicodemus (see Jn 3), of Jesus' washing of the disciples' feet (see Jn 13), of his meeting with the woman of Samaria (see Jn 4), of the episode regarding the woman caught in adultery (see Jn 8) and more. Each powerfully illustrates the Master Teacher at work. The latter two events illustrate, further, that Jesus often taught more than one person or one group at the same time.

In John 4, for example, Jesus works to transform not only the woman's life but also the lives of her fellow townspeople and of his own disciples. In John 8, his concern for the hearts and lives of both the woman and her accusers is apparent in what he does, what he says and what he does *not* say. In this episode, as elsewhere,[9] silence is a critical device[10] that Jesus utilizes to "create space" for obedience to the Truth.

When Jesus was confronted with questions, especially questions that arose from improper motives stemming from a misplaced priority and values, it was typical for him to reply with searching questions of his own, with compelling stories, with provocative or utterly shocking speech, with deafening silence or with other such "space creating" devices. What he almost never did was answer such questions in a direct manner; he seldom, if ever, gave disingenuous questioners what they wanted. His concerns were always of far greater import.[11]

Jesus taught in order to call others toward greater obedience to the Truth, and he himself was utterly committed to obedience. He took his directions from his Father, not from any of his inquirers. He did what he saw his Father doing (see Jn 5:19) and said only what his Father gave him to say (see Jn 14:10, 24). In all these things, Jesus has given us an example that we who would dare teach others should follow in his footsteps (see Jn 13:15-17). Here is wisdom for parents with their children, for preachers with their congregations, for elders with the members of their flocks, for Sunday school teachers with their students, for anyone engaged in helping others become more faithful disciples of Jesus.

We offer one further thought evoked by Palmer's definition and by the examples we have discussed above. Since Christian teaching is concerned with the Truth, it must always be fundamentally a witness to Jesus Christ. As we noted earlier, the Truth has been expressed fully and perfectly in the Person and work of Christ. He had come, as he told Pilate, to testify to the truth (see Jn 18:37). But more than this, Jesus *is* the Truth (see Jn 14:6). In his own teaching, he was concerned with drawing men and women to himself. He urged them to follow *him,* to obey *him,* not some abstract conception of truth. Parents, pastors and all Christian teachers dare not lose sight of this. Directing ourselves and others to Christ himself is ever our central concern. We teach to create space for obedience *to Jesus.*

---

[9]In Isaiah 53, we read that the Servant of the Lord remained silent as a lamb before its shearers. We recall also Jesus' silence before the Sanhedrin, the high priests and Herod.

[10]It seems that "creating space" here and in our teaching is for the purpose of allowing God to stir our heart and thus to expand our heart's capacity to obey him.

[11]Jesus' genuine concern for them often led him to provide a space where they were forced to assess their own soul and make a decision either to repent and follow him or to reject him and his Way.

TEACHING AS "TAKING AIM"

We turn now to our own proposed definition of teaching for Christians.[12] It is much wordier than Palmer's. A longer definition invites opportunity to consider more dimensions of the matter, though it is far less easy to commit to memory and involves the risk of stifling the imagination of the teacher with too much detail. Here is the definition, followed by commentary on each of its key elements:

> To teach is to come alongside another,
> in the power of the Spirit and in the company of the faithful,
>   to seek an encounter together with the Truth:
>   taking aim to perceive it more clearly,
>   consider it more critically, embrace it more passionately,
> obey it more faithfully, and embody it with greater integrity.[13]

TO TEACH IS TO COME ALONGSIDE ANOTHER

We begin our unpacking of the definition with the phrase "to come alongside another." Several things are intended here. First, we understand teaching to be a *paraklētos* role. This Greek word, which could be rendered "one who comes alongside to help," is applied in Scripture to both Jesus (see 1 Jn 2:2) and the Holy Spirit (see Jn 14:16). English versions of the New Testament struggle to find the best translation of the term. Among the renderings that have been offered by major Bible translations are *comforter, counselor, advocate, helper* and *one who speaks to the Father on our behalf.* It is clear that the word is pregnant with meaning and implications. Our use of it here suggests that a Christian teacher will assume in humble and awesome partnership with God (1 Cor 3:9) similar roles at times. We provide comfort and counsel as needed. We are advocates and helpers as necessary. We intercede with the Father on behalf of those we serve. We are, in sum, called truly to come alongside those we teach. We are companions on the journey toward Truth and obedience to all that Jesus has commanded.

The word *another* is an intentional choice for the singular, as opposed to

---

[12]The phrases "in the power of the Spirit," and "in the company of the faithful" in the following make it clear that this is a definition of teaching for Christians. Were these two phrases removed, the definition might prove useful for teaching in general, although the expression "the Truth" would likely be objectionable for some.

[13]This definition first appeared in print in the introduction of *A Many Colored Kingdom,* although it was not explicated there as we have done in these pages. The definition has been expanded here to include the phrase "and in the company of the faithful."

saying, "come alongside *others*." Christian formation occurs in the context of community, but a Christian teacher retains a pastoral heart toward each individual member of that community, seeking to know and care for each one as a unique person with a unique story and unique needs. As a shepherd must know his sheep by name (see Jn 10:3) and be willing to leave the ninety-nine for the sake of the one (see Lk 15:4), so we resist every temptation to reduce those we serve to the status of merely faces in the crowd. We also resist an even darker sort of temptation: to treat individuals whom we are called to love and nurture as objects that can somehow be useful to us in advancing "our" ministries. When we perceive people merely as objects of our ministry, we depart from the Way of Jesus.

Jesus is "that great Shepherd of the sheep" (Heb 13:20), "the Chief Shepherd" (1 Pet 5:4) and "the good shepherd" who lays down his life for the sheep (Jn 10:11), who knows and is known by his sheep (see Jn 10:14). He knows each one by name and leads them (see Jn 10:3). His sheep follow him, because they know his voice (see Jn 10:4). They listen to his voice; he knows them, and they follow him (see Jn 10:27). By contrast, the "hired hand" flees when trouble comes, abandoning the flock because he cares nothing for the sheep (see Jn 10:12-13). Jesus incarnates the heart of God, who has always had a heart to shepherd his people (see Ps 23; 80 as examples), who is severe with those who prove to be false or otherwise unworthy shepherds (see Ezek 34) and to whom all human shepherds must give account (see 1 Pet 5:4). We are to imitate that Shepherd's heart among those we serve (see Acts 20:28-31; 1 Pet 5:1-3).

The Hebrew verb for shepherding, *ra'ah,* is one of many words for teaching in the Old Testament. Teachers act as shepherds by coming alongside students as leader-companions in the journey, supporting them when they need encouragement, guiding them when they feel lost and serving them when they are down and out. Teachers can also serve as a sort of base from which learners can explore and step out of their comfort zones to grow in obedience to Christ. To be such shepherds, teachers are to be vigilant in learning and closely monitoring the health and well-being of their students in various aspects of their life.

IN THE POWER OF THE SPIRIT

A Christian teacher comes alongside another "in the power of the Spirit." Otherwise, no lasting good can possibly result. The Holy Spirit is "the Spirit of truth" (Jn 14:17; 15:26), who anoints all believers unto knowledge of the Truth (see 1 Jn 2:20, 27) and guides us to all truth (see Jn 16:13). Augustine spoke of the Holy Spirit as "the true Teacher," and argued that human teachers must bear this in mind and take this very seriously. If the Spirit alone is the true Teacher, then the human teacher must be both a petitioner and a hearer before she is anything else.[14] The human teacher is a "petitioner" on behalf of those she serves, interceding in prayer for them, because she knows that only the Spirit can finally guide believers into truth (see Jn 16:13). She is also a "hearer" before ever presuming to teach others. Jesus modeled both of these attitudes for us in his earthly ministry. He continually prayed for those who were with him as disciples (see Lk 5:16; 22:32; Jn 17), and he offered to them only those words that he himself had heard from his Father (see Jn 7:16; 14:24).

AND IN THE COMPANY OF THE FAITHFUL

Our definition continues with "and in the company of the faithful." With this phrase, we acknowledge that although we must exhibit pastoral care toward each individual sheep, we teach with a consciousness that we are fellow learners in a great community. That community includes, most obviously, members of our own congregation. But its reach goes much further, including all those across the earth and through the ages who belong to Jesus Christ. The wise teacher practices his ministry in serious and humble partnerships with all of these groups of believers.

Toward the saints who have gone before us, we humble ourselves in recognition that we are not the *first* to ask questions about how believers ought to be taught or formed. We glean wisdom concerning both the content of our teaching and the faithful and effective practices for teaching and formation. Toward our fellow saints who fill the earth today, we humble ourselves in recognition that we are not the *only* ones asking such questions today. This means, for example, that as the Spirit of God moves so powerfully in the global South and East in our times, we in the West have a great deal we can learn from our brothers and sisters in the rest of the world.

Within our local communities, as well, we humble ourselves, recognizing that we dare not attempt to teach or form others without the context and re-

---

[14]For example, see Augustine *On Christian Doctrine* bk. 4: "Containing a General View of the Subjects Treated in Holy Scripture," chap. 16, at <http://www.ccel.org/ccel/augustine/doctrine.html>.

sources of the entire congregation. Whether we are concerned with the formation of young children or the ongoing education of adults, it takes a whole community to grow and sustain a faithful believer.[15] It is critical then that every disciple-in-the-making and every "disciple maker" be actively engaged in the full life of the church in its wide variety of expressions. There will certainly and necessarily be a place for significant one-on-one ministry between teacher and learner, but it is never finally one-on-one. We are part of something much larger than that, always. The question is, are we cognizant of and properly responsive to that larger relationship?

TO SEEK AN ENCOUNTER TOGETHER WITH THE TRUTH

Next in our definition of teaching for Christians come the words "to seek an encounter together with the Truth." We say "encounter *together*" because teachers need always to see themselves as fellow learners. After all, what percentage of the Truth has any of us mastered? (Or, better, what percentage of the Truth has presently *mastered us?*) Together with Paul, Christian teachers confess, "We know in part and we prophesy in part" (1 Cor 13:9). This should be not merely a verbal confession but a consciousness that pervades all the teacher does or aspires to do. A teacher may well be further along than some other learners in this pursuit of the Truth, but she is still a fellow seeker, still desperately in need of continuing the chase.

But what do we mean by *the Truth?* This is obviously a vital question within this definition. In discussing teaching that creates space for obedience to Truth, Palmer arrues that truth is neither an object "out there" nor a proposition about such objects. Instead, truth is personal, and all truth is known in personal relationships. Jesus is a paradigm, a model of this personal truth. In him, truth, once understood as abstract, principled, propositional, suddenly takes on a human face and a human frame. In Jesus, the disembodied "word" takes flesh and walks among us. His call to truth is a call to community—with him, with each other, with creation and its Creator.[16]

For our part, we would make the definition sharper, adding the definite article to indicate that it is *the* Truth we pursue, an objective reality[17] that is

---

[15]A variation, of course, on the African proverb "It takes a village to raise a child."

[16]Palmer, *To Know as We Are Known,* pp. 48-49.

[17]We maintain that there exists reality *out there,* independent of human knowing, and not in a sense that humans can scientifically decipher the reality as in a one-to-one correspondence. See Kevin Vanhoozer, "Pilgrim's Digress: Christian Thinking on and About the Post/Modern Way," in *Christianity and the Postmodern Turn,* ed. Myron Penner (Grand Rapids: Brazos, 2005), pp. 71-103.

perfectly embodied in Christ and faithfully recorded for us in the pages of Scripture. The Truth speaks powerfully to us also in other ways—in the glories of creation, for example (see, for example, Ps 8; 19; Rom 1:18-20), for God has graced us not only with *special* revelation but also with *general* revelation. Through general revelation, we begin to perceive, by faith, glimpses of the special revelation of Jesus Christ who is the Lord of that general revelation. We wholeheartedly affirm, then, that absolute Truth *is*. But we make no claim to have absolute access to or perception of that Truth.[18] Again, we know in part and we prophesy in part. It cannot be otherwise this side of glory, because we are all finite, sinful and situated[19] humans.

TAKING AIM . . .

"Taking aim" is the next expression in the definition. These words attempt to capture the sense of another key Hebrew verb for teaching, *yarah*. As we discussed earlier, this word means, literally, "to shoot" or "to cast." One of its ancient uses was in reference to an archer taking aim with bow and arrow. It becomes an important word for teaching in the Old Testament and indicates that a teacher's role involves pointing learners toward the right path. A teacher is a guide in the Way of the Lord.

From the same Hebrew root come words for both parent and teacher. Also from the same root comes the weighty word *Torah*. The teacher is, as we have said, always a fellow learner in encounters with the Truth. But it is the teacher's burden to help give intention and focus to the encounter. It is the teacher's responsibility to help all involved keep their aim focused on the Truth.

At this point in the definition, we begin to consider what sorts of interaction with the Truth we are actually aiming at. As we do so, we are reminded of a familiar triad of educational domains: cognitive, affective and behavioral.[20] Put more simply, many Christian educators have written of the need for

---

[18]Yet we are graced, as the body of Christ, to grow in knowledge and love to understand the depth and breadth of the infinite riches of the Truth, in relationship with God and through obedience to him who is the Way, the Truth and the Life. See the discussion "Reformed Christian Critical Realism" in Kevin Vanhoozer, "But That's Your Interpretation: Realism, Reading, and Reformation," in *Modern Reformation,* July/August 1999, pp. 21-27.

[19]That is, we are situated in specific contexts of time, space, socioeconomic class, gender, nationality and so on.

[20]The cognitive (the recall or recognition of knowledge and the development of intellectual abilities), the affective (interests, attitudes, appreciations, values and emotional sets) and the psychomotor (the manipulative or motor-skill area). See Benjamin Bloom, ed., *Cognitive Domain,* bk. 1 of *Taxonomy of Educational Objectives* (New York: Longman, 1956/1984); David

our teaching to engage learners' heads, hearts and hands.[21] Being attentive to these three is not to suggest that learners can be neatly divided into these three domains. Nor do we suggest that a teacher can seek to engage a learner's mind without also engaging the heart, or vice versa. Rather, the point of this three-fold attention is that if we are not serious about engaging the whole person, it is very possible that something will be overlooked. It is only when we con-sider these domains independently that we can develop precise goals. The aim is not to address these as three disparate domains, but to bring these together to forge a set of holistic goals appropriate for creating a teaching-learning space in which the truth is practiced and obeyed as sustained habits of the learners are cultivated.

TO PERCEIVE IT MORE CLEARLY

We will soon address the familiar triad we have just noted. Before doing so, however, we have added one aspect of learning that is often overlooked. To cognition, affection and behavior, we add the notion of perception. In other words, to head, heart and hands we add the need to engage the eyes and ears of learners. Thus our definition includes the words "taking aim to perceive[22] it more clearly." Our first concern in our mutual encounter with the Truth is to help both ourselves and our fellow learners move toward a more accurate perception of the Truth. We long to see things that are easily missed and to see things that we *think we already see* even more clearly.

Part of the concern with enhancing our perception is to help learners be more attentive and engaged with the world. Sometimes teachers expect more from their learners than those learners can presently muster. We want them to think critically, to feel deeply and to act faithfully about important issues. But it may be that the learners do not regard the issues as particularly important. Indeed, they may not "see" that there is any issue at all. For example, a teacher working with a youth group in suburban America may wish to engage his

---

Krathwohl, Benjamin Bloom and Bertram Masia, *Affective Domain,* bk. 2 of *Taxonomy of Edu-cational Objective* (New York: Longman, 1964).

[21]Johann Heinrich Pestalozzi, *Leonard and Gertrude* (1801; reprint, Whitefish, Mont.: Kessinger, 2004). Rick Yount, *Created to Learn: A Christian Teacher's Introduction to Educational Psychology* (Nashville: Broadman & Holman, 1996).

[22]*Perceive* has a sense of active passivity. It refers to becoming aware of or being able to identify, or decipher, by using the senses, intuition, reason and/or imagination. It also refers to receiv-ing, collecting and deducing a set of data with care and reflection, as opposed to making a rash judgment or unreflective assimilation. It is more like grasping with the mind's heart—from the Latin *per,* "thoroughly," and *capere,* "to grasp."

students on the subjects of poverty, hunger and other global issues, but perhaps the students cannot see how such things concern them. As Christians, we may wish to challenge our fellow believers regarding racialization[23] or racism, only to discover that many or most in the congregation believe that this is no longer a pressing matter in American life. A teacher will need to raise levels of attentiveness and find ways to motivate students to perceive critical issues that are close to God's heart if there is to be a meaningful and fruitful encounter with God's Truth.

Some pastors regularly labor to raise awareness in their preaching by means of carefully prepared sermon introductions and illustrations. Our colleague Haddon Robinson has argued that a preacher has only seconds to "win or lose" the attention of the congregation.[24] The use of a provocative question or statement, or the telling of a compelling story, can help members of the congregation realize that what the preacher is about to say is of vital importance. John Stott has also articulated that it is the preacher's task to help hearers connect the timeless word of God with the ever-shifting world in which they live.[25] When congregants are inattentive or apathetic to what is being proclaimed from the pulpit, we do well to consider what the underlying problem really is. In some cases, it may be that the preacher is assuming a level of engagement that is not congruent with the realities in the pew. While the preacher is expecting critical engagement, heartfelt repentance and decisive action, members of the congregation may actually be quite disengaged from the texts and topics of the sermon.

Sunday school teachers are likely to be familiar with the concept we are considering here. For decades now, American Sunday school curricula have used—in one form or another—the organizing formula of "Hook, Book, Look, Took." Popularized by Christian educator Larry Richards,[26] this commonly used outline begins with the "Hook"—an attention-grabbing opening to the lesson (which corresponds to the preacher's provocative sermon intro-

---

[23]"A racialized society is a society wherein race matters profoundly for differences in life experiences, life opportunities, and social relationships." Michael Emerson and Christian Smith, *Divided by Faith: Evangelical Religion and the Problem of Race in America* (New York: Oxford University Press, 2000), p. 7.

[24]In his classes on preaching, Robinson uses this point to emphasize the importance of a stimulating and provocative introduction to the sermon.

[25]John Stott, *Between Two Worlds: The Challenge of Preaching Today* (Grand Rapids: Eerdmans, 1994).

[26]Lawrence Richards and Gary Bredfeldt, *Creative Bible Teaching*, rev. ed. (Chicago: Moody Press, 1998).

duction). Another approach to this has also made inroads in evangelical Christian education: the "split-rail fence" illustration,[27] which is associated with Lois LeBar,[28] Ted Ward, Jim Plueddemann and others. In this illustration, the teacher begins where the learners actually live, symbolized by the lower rail in the fence. The teacher and the teaching process itself are like the posts that link the lower rail to the upper rail, which represents the timeless Word of God. Jesus used parables to help his hearers look through the present and familiar to things mysterious and eternal. Again, good teachers meet learners where they are and help them go where they truly need to go.

Many helpful insights on the matter of increased or improved perception are found in the writings of Annie Dillard. Her Pulitzer Prize–winning book, *Pilgrim at Tinker Creek,* is a testament to the wonders of attentiveness. In chapter after chapter, Dillard both models and exhorts her readers simply to pay attention. In one passage, after detailing the rapid vertical descent and graceful landing of a mockingbird—an event that she simply chanced to see—she writes, "The fact of his free fall was like the old philosophical conundrum about the tree that falls in the forest. The answer must be, I think, that beauty and grace are performed whether or not we will or sense them. The least we can do is try to be there."[29]

But growing in the art of perception is not easy. In a chapter titled "Seeing," Dillard interacts with a book that recounts the experiences of people who have had their sight restored through surgery. For the newly sighted, according to those accounts, life can be beautiful or harrowing, or both. After describing some of the ways in which the newly sighted learn to use their new perceptive skills, Dillard writes of how wrenchingly difficult it is for some to make the transition. "A disheartening number of them refuse to use their new vision, continuing to go over objects with their tongues, and lapsing into apathy and despair."[30]

To help our fellow learners be more attentive and perceptive, we who teach

---

[27]Ted Ward discussed the illustration in 1969: "The Split-Rail Fence: An Analogy for the Education of Professionals" Learning Systems Institute report (East Lansing: Learning Systems Institute and Human Learning Research Institute of Michigan State University, 1969), p. 64. Later Jim Plueddemann, then a Ph.D. student of Ward at Michigan State, popularized it.

[28]Lois LeBar introduced a simple formula, the boy-book-boy model (later known as the way-truth-life model). Plueddemann asserts that this has made a significant contribution to evangelical curriculum, in Lois LeBar and James Plueddemann, *Education That Is Christian,* rev. ed. (Wheaton: Victor Press, 1995), p. 101.

[29]Annie Dillard, *Pilgrim at Tinker Creek* (New York: Bantam, 1975), p. 10.

[30]Ibid., p. 30.

ought to be diligent to open our own eyes and ears more often and more faithfully. As we have already noted, our most potent form of teaching is modeling for others the Truth we desire to teach. This applies to cultivating our own perceptive capacities. Do we see well? Do we listen well? What might we do to help ourselves become better listeners?

One discipline that may help us in this regard is to seek relationships with people who speak, in some significant way, very differently than the way we speak. For many of us, this could mean getting to know a person whose native language is not English. As a seminary professor and pastor, I have often been stunned to see how impatient and rude students or parishioners can be in such relationships. I have also caught myself being both ungracious and unwise. But I have been trying to learn.

Years ago, I was teaching a class about teaching. The class was designed with the expectation that there would be about a dozen students, but more than double that number enrolled. One of the assignments was a fifteen- to twenty-minute classroom presentation by each student that was to be based on one of the alternative texts that had been assigned for the class. Midway through the term, it finally occurred to me that we had too many students to pull this assignment off as designed, and so I offered students an alternative. Instead of the full presentation, they could choose to write a paper about the additional text and present a five-minute summary to the class. Only two took me up on this offer, however. I was not surprised that these two were international students for whom English was a second language. To that point in class, neither had spoken unless I had specifically called on them, which I had not often done.

When the time came for the public presentations, we at last had the chance to actually hear from those two students. Both of them chose simply to read the papers they had written. The first did a fine job with his paper. It was a clear, cogent and effective summary. The second student did not do a fine job—to say that he did would be to grossly understate the case. As he read his paper, which turned out to be based on his interaction with Palmer's *To Know as We Are Known,* I could actually see jaws dropping throughout the class. Frankly, we were all astonished by what we heard, and for two reasons. First, the student's interaction was both deeply personal and truly profound. Second, we were surprised that all this was coming from *him.* He had been so quiet—virtually silent—for a full semester. What happened on this day was that I, as the teacher of the class, had finally given his voice a viable opportunity to speak. All of us were far richer for it.

I have been thinking ever since about how I, as a classroom teacher, need to find ways to apply Matthew 25:35. In that verse Jesus tells us, "I was a stranger and you invited me in." How can I better welcome into the learning community, into our common pursuit of the Truth, those who are in some significant way *xenoi* to the majority in the room?

More recently, I had another experience with an international student. Her English seemed even more limited than that of the student in the story above. She seemed to follow lectures well, but when I tried to invite her voice to speak to us in class, she struggled mightily. One of my faculty colleagues said to me bluntly that this student "shouldn't be here." But I sensed from her presence in class and from her written assignments that she was actually one of the hardest working and most attentive students I have been privileged to teach.

In one class she was seated next to a student who spoke both her native language and very fine English. In one of our sessions, the two of them were paired together as the class wrestled with a question in small groups. When it was time to report what each group had discussed, the young man spoke on behalf of this pair. He began to summarize their discussion. "Well, actually, this is really all from what *she* said," he continued. What followed were the most helpful and perceptive comments that were said in the entire three-hour session on that day.[31]

It seems to me that multiple benefits resulted from these two experiences. First, substantive and significant content was added to the classroom discussion by giving voice to two students who had not previously been able to contribute very much to the class. Second, many of us in the classroom learned the immense value of hearing from those we do not often hear from. We learned that the hard work of listening can reap great rewards.

Furthermore, on these occasions two students found themselves newly empowered. I have since heard from each, more than once, how these episodes

---

[31]I considered using pseudonyms in these two illustrations to help personalize the stories. I have opted not to do so, in part because of the fact that in both cases the students were essentially nameless to most of their classmates. Their names were difficult to pronounce for our mostly American-born students, and few made the effort to listen and to learn their names well enough to repeat them in class. Leaving them nameless, then, actually *does* help personalize these students' experiences. In recent years, I have asked students to write their names out for each other's sakes on the first day of the class. Then we take time to practice pronouncing the names together. This is, in itself, an exercise in improving our listening skills, our overall attentiveness and perception.

were transformative for them. These two students had previously felt consistently marginalized in class (not only in mine but in most of their other classes as well). They, too, saw and heard things more clearly because of these episodes. In particular, they saw and heard themselves in new ways. My guess is that they also saw their classmates—and perhaps their professor—in new ways.

I often encourage students to build relationships with those who have come from other nations or from American cultural backgrounds other than their own. I encourage them to get to know students from different denominational backgrounds and theological perspectives as well. I have tried to do the same myself through the years. It seems to me not only to be a good discipline for increasing perception in general but also a great help in learning to listen to God. For God has said, "My thoughts are not your thoughts, neither are your ways my ways" (Is 55:8-9). When I listen to those who are in some way *xenoi* to me, I am training myself to interact with the One who is (from our vantage point) the greatest *xenos* of all—the living God.[32]

In a congregational setting, there are numerous strategies that may help church members see and hear more clearly. We can invite guests into the pulpit from other national, ethnic, socioeconomic and denominational backgrounds. This can flow out of relationships pastors build with pastors of other congregations and a commitment to a regularly scheduled "pulpit exchange" that can prove mutually beneficial. Guests can also be invited to share their testimonies in the church assemblies or in small-group settings. One church near us has a missions conference each year that seems to bear great fruit in the congregation. A full week is devoted to hearing their "own" missionaries bring reports from near and far, and a guest speaker is purposely chosen to provoke and stimulate the flock to see the world, and their place in that world, in new ways.

Perhaps even more helpful than bringing people into the church commu-

---

[32]Our friend and colleague Paul Lim has noted that it is with God that we must first face our xenophobia. His point is not unlike Karl Barth's observation that there is absolutely no *analogia entis,* no natural correspondence, between the infinite God—the Creator or the uncreated—and the created. If revelation is to occur, "then this occurrence will necessarily be one in which God takes objects, events, words, ideas and other this-worldly entities and bestows upon them a capacity which in and of themselves they do not possess." Trevor Hart, "Revelation," in *The Cambridge Companion to Karl Barth,* ed. John Webster (Cambridge: Cambridge University Press, 2000), p. 46. Lim ascertains the notion of xenophobia from our perspective, one of estrangement as human beings with our total otherness, creatureliness and sinfulness. Barth was contemplating the utter radicalness of the incarnation of God the Son, Jesus Christ, on our behalf.

nity is taking the church to the community. This is, of course, a strategy that Jesus employed in the training of the Twelve. Churches can send teams abroad for short-term learning opportunities.[33] Just as pastors can engage in a pulpit exchange with other pastors, whole congregations can form "sister" relationships with other churches that involve periodic gatherings for fellowship, worship and service together with people from some significantly different backgrounds.[34] Study groups can read books together or watch films that are chosen intentionally because of their potential to open eyes and ears. Activities that seem "nonreligious" can also prove very helpful in this regard. Visits to nearby museums can, with proper guidance and debriefing, help believers learn to see more clearly. Attendance at concerts and other performances can stimulate better hearing. Outings to enjoy the wonders of creation can be utterly transformative in increasing our ability to appreciate.

The possibilities are really limitless. Prayerful creativity on the part of church leaders and teachers can go a long way toward increasing levels of attentiveness.[35] We can help ourselves and our fellow learners to "look at the birds of the air" and "see . . . the lilies of the field" (Mt 6:26, 28), to "go to the ant . . . consider its ways and be wise" (Prov 6:6). We can help adults watch and learn from young children and help church members be more attentive to current events and their lessons for us (see Mt 18:1-4).[36] By encouraging our

---

[33]Pastor Oscar Muriu of Nairobi Chapel, Nairobi, Kenya, introduced this term to me, explaining that his church uses it when they send out short-term teams, rather than their earlier and more familiar term "short-term missions." It is not that the teams do not go out to serve. But, he explained, the primary outcome of such ventures is the opening of the eyes and forming of the hearts of his church members.

[34]When such groups serve together, they not only serve their neighbors, they also learn how to relate to one another and learn varying perspectives from each other. Furthermore, those who are on the receiving end witness how Jesus Christ can indeed bring people of different races, ethnicities and socioeconomic classes to love one another and testify to the unity they have in Jesus Christ. All the while, participants strengthen together the spheres of ministry and help transform the local communities of both churches. Thus global church partnership is not merely an intriguing option. It is a way for our churches not only to survive but also to thrive.

[35]We often look for outside experts to introduce some new program to help revitalize our churches. Typically, however, these "experts" have no clue about how God has brought together the unique blend of gifts, ages, races and life experiences that characterize a congregation. Or on the other extreme, some local churches or denominations become so closed off from others that they stagnate. Erring in either direction reveals a grossly inadequate understanding of ecclesiology.

[36]The socioculturally constructed uniqueness of the generational cohorts—builders, boomers, busters, millennials and so on—must be acknowledged, and mistrust along the generational lines in the church must be confessed and ruthlessly purged. Intentional and mutual submission ought to characterize the household of God, rather than constantly breaking apart (self-

fellow learners to perceive things more clearly, we will be in a far better position to help them also consider the Truth more critically, embrace it more passionately, obey it more faithfully and embody it with greater integrity.

TO CONSIDER IT MORE CRITICALLY

Next, we turn to the matter of more fully engaging our minds with the Truth. Our definition of teaching continues with the phrase "consider it more critically." Cognitive engagement with the Truth is frequently at the center of disputes about good education. There is often something of a pendulum swing between two extremes. On the one hand, some educators—in both public and church arenas—have championed the teaching of solid content as the most important ingredient in education. On the other side of the spectrum are those who insist that meaningful and engaging processes are the hallmark of good education.

Although it should be obvious that both of these concerns are essential for effective education, it is easy to slip into polarizing attitudes and rhetoric. Thus, on the one side, people clamor for drumming into learners' minds the essentials of what is thought to constitute "core knowledge." From the other side come the cries for "critical thinking." Each side feels compelled to belittle those who advocate the other perspective. "Critical thinking about *what,* exactly?" complain the content folks. "Mere transmission of content is not education," retort the process people.

When we speak here of considering the Truth more critically, however, we refuse to take sides in the content-process debates. Rather, we aim at faithfulness in regard to both concerns. We cannot be satisfied with "mere transmission of content." But we know how easily this line of reasoning can lead to replacing *mere* transmission of content with *no* real transmission of content. This will not do. Surely we must seek to cultivate critical-thinking skills in Christian disciples. But it is vital that there be a sufficient and growing deposit of content about which, and from which, learners can truly engage in such critical thinking.

One approach to pursuing faithfulness in engaging minds with the Truth is to pay attention to both natural and spiritual developmental concerns. For example, we may introduce to a young child the Ten Commandments. Many children will be able to easily memorize the Ten Words that God uttered at Sinai, and teachers can offer a rudimentary introduction to their meaning. A

---

destructing or dismembering) God's household.

deposit of riches is thus made in the child's mind and heart.

As the years go on, and the child grows in both natural and spiritual abilities, we return to the treasure store and revisit the commands in perpetual and progressive contemplation. We challenge the high-school student to consider implications and applications in their daily lives of the word they memorized so long ago: "you shall not bear false witness against your neighbor." It is much harder to engage adolescent learners critically about content they have never heard or considered before. Pedagogical wisdom calls for a path of depositing good content early and revisiting it again and again through the seasons of life. As someone has put it, when our children are young we should try to fill their cupboards with all manner of good things so that, when they grow older, they will be able to open those cupboards and benefit from those goods.[37]

The same approach can be applied when we are addressing issues of spiritual maturity. An adult convert to the Faith may be very capable of critical thinking. But in the early experience of her Christian life, through serious and intentional catechesis, we must introduce her to the new world she has been called to inhabit, a world with a new language, a new ethic, a new theology and a new spirituality. It is folly to leap straight to critical thinking without laying the firm foundation of a knowledge base that can sustain genuine critical engagement.

In neither instance—whether we mean spiritual or natural development—do we draw hard lines between content and process. There is a great deal of overlap here, and each dimension affects the other. But being inattentive to the distinctive concerns of each, and of their interrelationship, will greatly hinder the potential for spiritual growth in our learners.

Why is there such a profound biblical illiteracy today when the church is replete with an unprecedented richness of print and Internet resources for Christian learning? Why such an inverse proportionality? Perhaps one of the causes is the saturation of available resources. Multiple textbooks in the form of material accumulation has brought on a critical shortage of critical thinking in the form of serious grappling with the content of the Faith. How then can the church begin to recover the critical thinking and engagement necessary for the church to grow as the people of God who can genuinely live as his text-people?

---

[37]I first heard this idea from theologian and educator Robbie Castleman during a presentation to a Doctor of Ministry class at Gordon-Conwell Theological Seminary, May 2007. For more of her thinking on ministry to children, see Robbie Castleman, *Parenting in the Pew: Guiding Your Children into the Joy of Worship* (Downers Grove, Ill.: InterVarsity Press, 2002).

We suggest that such a recovery starts with interrogating or unearthing our own assumptions. We examine those things we take for granted that so affect the manner in which we think about issues and the manner in which we go about making life's decisions. It is no surprise to us that our own assumptions seem most natural and self-evident to us, for they have been deposited in us without much question or resistance. These assumptions continue to shape us in more profound ways as we grow older, because we not only base our decisions on our assumptions, but they reinforce our identity and provide us with a sense of coherence in life. In turn, we become more committed to our way of life and learn to defend or rationalize it. In this way, we further legitimize our identity, allowing those often-unexamined assumptions to have enduring influence in our lives. Some go as far to say that "in many ways, we *are* our assumptions."[38]

How then do we begin to delineate our assumptions so that we can avail ourselves of God's grace to continue the transformation that he has begun in us? Stephen Brookfield delineates three broad categories of assumptions, where paradigmatic assumptions function as an umbrella that subsumes the latter two. *Paradigmatic assumptions* provide basic structures in our lives through which we organize or approach the world around us. Under that broad category, we have *prescriptive assumptions,* through which we think of what ought to be happening in life. The other would be *causal assumptions,* through which we predict or explain how various things in everyday life take place.[39]

As followers of Jesus Christ, perhaps we will want to acknowledge that there is within us an even greater set of assumptions that has a profound influence on our paradigmatic assumptions. Brookfield calls these "hegemonic assumptions," those that we think are in our own best interests but that have actually been designed by more powerful others to work against us in the long term.[40] But as Christians we know that they are the spiritual forces of evil in the heavenly places—the rulers, the authorities and the cosmic powers over this present darkness. If such is the case, and it is, thinking critically as the people of God is essential to become increasingly aware of and to interrogate the ways in which our God-given faculties of knowing[41] have been seriously marred by sin. Further, we are also under constant assault by the spiritual

---

[38]Stephen Brookfield, *Becoming a Critically Reflective Teacher* (San Francisco: Jossey-Bass, 1995), p. 2.

[39]Ibid., pp. 2-3.

[40]Ibid., p. 15.

[41]In its fullest sense, as discussed a number of times throughout the book.

forces of evil in the heavenly places. The most tragic irony of all is that we, the people of God, have become such faithful citizens of this world that we have lost the zeal for being the text-people that God has intended us to be.

The time has come for us, who are called by his name, to humble ourselves and pray, to seek his face and turn from our wicked ways and unexamined lives (see 2 Chron 7:14). In that light, we the teachers of the Gospel are to create a space where God's people can reflect and wrestle together "against the rulers, against the authorities, against the powers of this dark world and against the spiritual forces of evil in the heavenly realms" (Eph 6:12).

Again, teaching is not merely a transfer of knowledge to our students. It is nothing less than stimulating God's people to interrogate and resist the influences of the spiritual forces of evil in the fabric of the church and in this present world that we live in. We must see how they systematically influence us to choose the paths of least resistance that are not the Way, to sell our souls to the teachings that are antithetical to the Truth and to live comfortably in a death that pulls us away from the Life.

Thus, thinking about the Truth more critically is not merely some mimicking of the latest fad in the academy to dislocate, disembody or deconstruct every truth to oblivion. Rather, by unveiling the systemic and hideous nature of all sins in and about us, we become more fully captivated and enraptured by the Truth and so more clearly and fully become like Jesus Christ as God's people. May the Lord who hears and sees from heaven restore us and heal his church once again.

TO EMBRACE IT MORE PASSIONATELY

Important as it is to direct our minds toward a more critical engagement with the Truth, we do not stop there. We take further aim at the Truth, to "embrace it more passionately." This phrase in the definition calls to mind the affective domain of learning. This domain is concerned with values, emotion and volition.[42] In other words, we may refer to this as formation of the heart. In the original languages of Scripture, it is typically not the heart but other

---

[42]Some theorists have handled the matter of volition separately, sometimes referring to this as the "conative" domain. See chapters one and three in Thomas Groome, *Sharing Faith: A Comprehensive Approach to Religious Education and Pastoral Ministry: The Way of Shared Praxis* (San Francisco: HarperSanFrancisco, 1991). According to Groome, conation is "what is realized when the whole ontic being of 'agent-subjects-in-relationship' is actively engaged to consciously know, desire and do what is most humanizing and life-giving for all." In his schema, *wisdom* comes close to being its synonym.

human organs that are used to refer to deep-seated emotions, including the kidneys, liver, spleen and bowels.[43] The heart, though, is also sometimes referred to as the seat of emotion and is the locus of the will as well. The heart is often presented as representing a person's deepest self, the very essence of a human.[44] It is reasonable, then, to speak of the need to help learners engage the Truth with their hearts as well as with their heads.[45]

This heart-realm, as we are calling it, may already be emphasized in some church settings. Some congregations, for example, are already very emotive in the ways they relate to God, though not necessarily in ways that are particularly healthy.[46] In such cases, we minister toward the end that our hearts be not just inclined but *properly* inclined.[47] That is, we labor to see our emotions and our wills subservient to the Truth as it in Christ. In many evangelical churches, however, the heart-life may be neglected. Perhaps we prize the mind in our church, or perhaps we strive to stay busy for Jesus. Either way, we may think it unnecessary or even dangerous to pay too much attention to the affective domain.

In the history of Christian teaching, however, there was not always such reticence to address this dimension of our faith. The great catechetical efforts of the church's early centuries unabashedly included attention to the affections.[48] In more recent church history, we can consider the classic work of

---

[43]Geoffrey Bromiley, *Theological Dictionary of the New Testament, Abridged in One Volume,* ed. Gerhard Kittel and Gerhard Friedrich (Grand Rapids: Eerdmans, 1985), p. 630.

[44]See chapter four in Matthew Elliott, *Faithful Feelings: Rethinking Emotion in the New Testament* (Grand Rapids: Kregel, 2006).

[45]Dallas Willard reminds us that genuine spiritual formation can take place only when all "essential aspects of the person come into line with the intent of a will brought to newness of life 'from above' by the Word and the Spirit." *Renovation of the Heart* (Colorado Springs: NavPress, 2002), p. 253.

[46]See Peter Scazzero, *Emotionally Healthy Churches: A Strategy for Discipleship That Actually Changes Lives* (Grand Rapids: Zondervan, 2003).

[47]In *Renovation of the Heart,* Willard contends that feelings can be successfully "reasoned with" and can be corrected by reality, only in those who have the habit "and are given the grace of *listening* to reason . . . [and] they will carefully keep the pathway open to the house of reason and go there regularly to listen" (pp. 124-25). However, even the capacity of reason has been affected by depravity and functions improperly because feeling has overpowered the capacity of reason. For example, Willard observes that, for many Christians, hope has been understood as "subjective psychological states such as 'being sure of' or 'having a conviction of'" (p. 129). Instead, hope is closely related to faith, as in confidence grounded in the substance and evidence or proof of reality in Jesus Christ. Yet he still maintains that effective action toward spiritual formation is possible through "order, subordination, and progression, developing from the inside of the personality" (p. 83).

[48]See, for example, John A. Berntsen, "Christian Affections and the Catechumenate," in *Theological Perspectives on Christian Formation: A Reader on Theology and Christian Education,* ed. Jeff

Jonathan Edwards in his *Treatise Concerning Religious Affections*. Edwards examines the affections at length and in great depth, and argues persuasively that right affections are the chief evidence of true and efficacious Christian faith.[49]

We recall from our exploration of Palmer's notion of "creating space" the power of silence, story and searching questions. These are all very critical for the education of the heart. Additional tools for such engagement could include the use of music, drama, the arts, testimony, relationships and much more. In preaching and teaching, we can and should take intentional aim at hearts. Did not Paul do as much when he spoke of imploring people on Christ's behalf to be reconciled to God (see 2 Cor 5:20)? Was this not Peter's aim when he appealed to his fellow elders to humbly shepherd God's flock (see 1 Pet 5:1-2)? Surely John was aiming at hearts as he addressed his readers as "Dear children" and "Dear friends" again and again (throughout the Johannine letters).

Jesus' teaching of the heart is quite potent. Episode after episode reveals his intentionality and effectiveness in this regard. As we join our fellow learners in encounters with the Truth, we work to see eyes and ears more fully opened and our intellects more critically engaged. We work also to soften the soil of our hearts. Hardened hearts are death to spiritual progress, as the Scriptures continually testify (for example, Is 6:9-10, which actually combines elements of perception, cognition and affection; Ps 119:70; Is 29:13; Jer 12:2; Mk 10:5). We should be bold and unapologetic about challenging the misalignment of our affections. As teachers, we should also guard our own hearts against becoming calloused toward God and others.

TO OBEY IT MORE FAITHFULLY

We seek an encounter together with the Truth in order to perceive it more clearly, consider it more critically, embrace it more passionately and "obey it more faithfully." As we saw in chapter two, we teach *out of* obedience and *unto* obedience. It is *out of* obedience to Jesus' mandate to disciple the nations that we teach. Since there can be no disciples without teaching, we must teach. And since there are no disciples except those who obey their Master, we teach *unto* obedience. As Jesus said, we teach others (and ourselves) "to obey everything I have commanded you" (Mt 28:20). We saw that this was the consistent

---

Astley, Leslie J. Francis and Colin Crowder (Grand Rapids: Eerdmans, 1996), pp. 229-43.
[49]Jonathan Edwards, *Treatise Concerning the Religious Affections* (Uhrichsville, Ohio: Barbour, 1999).

emphasis of Jesus and that this was reflective of the pattern of all Scripture. Only when we *do* God's Word can we claim to *know* it.

Having discussed all this at length, we need not repeat it fully here. We simply note that obedience is a proper aim in teaching, part of the larger aim of forming us into the image of Christ. It is far too easy to err by simply passing along more information to learners and then congratulate ourselves for the apparent increases in "biblical literacy" that result. But we have never been called to raise Bible trivia champions or even to raise biblical scholars. We have been called to make disciples—*learner-followers* of Jesus.

Our obedience to the Truth is not always as cut and dry as we might suppose, however. In some matters, the choice between obedience and disobedience will be very clear and easily discerned. But in many areas of our faith walk, obedience is something we progress in. Thus our definition says, "to obey it more faithfully." Even those who are *already* obedient to the Truth of Christ can become *more* obedient. Thus Paul encourages the believers in Thessolonica for how well they have been living, yet adds an exhortation to go further still: "Finally, brothers, we instructed you how to live in order to please God, as in fact you are living. Now we ask you and urge you in the Lord Jesus to do this more and more" (1 Thess 4:1). What we already know of the Truth, we must strive to live up to (see Phil 3:16). This commitment toward progress, however, also calls us onward in our knowledge. We seek ever deeper acquaintance with the Truth in terms of perception, cognition and affection, and all this calls us to even more faithful obedience.

AND EMBODY IT WITH GREATER INTEGRITY

Our ultimate aim as Christian teachers is that we and our fellow learners become like Jesus. The life of discipleship is not simply a matter of comprehending what Jesus taught. Nor is it only a matter of doing what Jesus did. It is, ultimately, a matter of *becoming what Jesus is*. The author of Hebrews informs us that it was necessary that Jesus be made like us "in every way" (Heb 2:17) to fulfill his appointed mission of making us holy and bringing us to glory (see Heb 2:10-11). Paul's language for such transformation includes words like *sanctification, renewal* and *glorification*.[50] The aim is godliness (being like God), toward which we strive and for which we train ourselves (see 1 Tim 4:7). But for all our effort, it is *God* who is at work in us, trans-

---

[50]See David Peterson, *Possessed by God: A New Testament Theology of Sanctification and Holiness* (Downers Grove, Ill.: InterVarsity Press, 2001).

forming us from glory to glory by the liberating power of the Holy Spirit (see Phil 2:13; 2 Cor 3:17-18).

Perhaps the most striking biblical language about this *becoming* like God is found in 2 Peter 1:3-4:

> His divine power has given us everything we need for life and godliness through our knowledge of him who called us by his own glory and goodness. Through these he has given us his very great and precious promises, so that through them you may participate in the divine nature and escape the corruption in the world caused by evil desires.

We are invited, as Peter puts it, to participate in the divine nature! In Orthodox traditions, this wonder is referred to as *theosis*. It is not necessary that evangelical Protestants fully embrace this notion of divination or deification as the Orthodox articulate it. But we really must bow before the great mystery that we are called into union with the triune God and wrestle with the implications of this mystery for our teaching ministries.

Luther was forthright in going beyond even his radical younger disciples by making the claim that God's elect are united with Christ in "a real communion of divine attributes." He wrote, "Every Christian fills heaven and earth in his faith."[51] This communion, though, is definitely

> not dissolution in God or even any usual sort of mysticism or idealism, for the Christ who is one with me so that I am one with God is precisely Christ in "flesh and bones." The "righteousness of God" [in Romans] . . . is the righteousness by which God is righteous, so that God and we are righteous by the same righteousness, just as by the same word God makes us and we indeed are what he is, so that we may be in him and his being may be our being.[52]

In God's inaugurated kingdom, we have begun to be part of the triune Community, having accepted the work of Jesus in time and by virtue of union with Christ. The union with Christ is through the Spirit alone, according to Calvin, for it is by the "sacred wedlock," that the elect are made "flesh of his flesh and bone of his bone, and thus one with him."[53] It is by the grace and power of the same Spirit that the elect are made his members, "to keep us

---

[51]Martin Luther, *A Commentary on Saint Paul's Epistle to the Galatians: A New Edition* (London: B. Blake, 1833), p. 187.

[52]Robert W. Jenson, *Systematic Theology: The Works of God* (New York: Oxford University Press, 1999), 2:297.

[53]John Calvin, *Institutes of the Christian Religion* (Philadelphia: Westminster, 1960), p. 541.

under himself and in turn to *possess* him."[54] As Luther put it, "For what greater fame and pride could we have . . . than to be called the children of the Highest and to *have all he is and has?*"[55]

What does it really mean to be vitally "in Christ"—a phrase that Paul uses again and again? What did Jesus mean when he prayed to the Father that all who ever believe in him "may be one, Father, just as you are in me and I am in you" (Jn 17:21)? Jesus' prayer deepens further into the unfathomable: "I have given them the glory that you gave me, that they may be one as we are one: I in them and you in me" (Jn 17:22-23). When John writes that "God's seed remains" in those who have been born of God (1 Jn 3:9), do we understand his full meaning? Have we searched out, as yet, the meaning of Paul's teaching that we are already risen with Christ and that our life "is now hidden with Christ in God" (Col 3:3)?

Returning to 2 Peter 1, we see that the apostle's response to such mysteries seems very practical, and so should ours be. In view of God's invitation into the eternal *perichōrēsis*[56] of the Trinity, Peter reminds us that there are actually things we can and must *do* to live into our calling and new identity.

> For this very reason, make every effort to add to your faith goodness; and to goodness, knowledge; and to knowledge, self-control; and to self control, perseverance; and to perseverance, godliness; and to godliness, brotherly kindness; and to brotherly kindness, love. (2 Pet 1:5-7)

Paul, too, not only invites us to marvel at the sovereign will of God in saving us, but he also implores us to respond faithfully to it all. God is at work within us, but our part in the pursuit of godliness is active, not passive. Indeed, it is precisely because we know that the living God is at work in us that we are to "work out" our "salvation with fear and trembling" (Phil 2:12-13). These things, too, we must earnestly and perseveringly teach.

In our ministries then let us be clear that our aim is to embody the Truth, even as Jesus embodied the Truth. As Jesus was the incarnation, the *eikōn,* the *exēgēsis* of the unseen Father, so the church is the body of Christ in the world, the *eikōn* and the *exēgēsis* of our risen, glorious Lord. McKnight further elucidates this privilege:

---

[54]Ibid.

[55]Jenson, *Systematic Theology,* p. 311.

[56]The active relation of the triune persons. God's eternity must be construed as love in continual action, precisely because his eternity is intensely personal, decisive in his freedom and conversational in his creativity.

To be an Eikon means, first of all, to be in union with God as Eikons; second, it means to be in communion with other Eikons; and third, it means to *participate* with God in his creating, his ruling, his speaking, his naming, his ordering, his variety and beauty, his location, his partnering, and his resting, and to oblige God in his obligating of us. Thus an Eikon is God-oriented, self-oriented, other-oriented, and cosmos-oriented. To be an Eikon is to be a missional being.[57]

Dare we apply the same sort of language to the individual believer as well? We do so, but with this important caveat: while the individual believer should strive to be the embodied reflection of the risen Lord, he cannot possibly be such without being vitally and intentionally part of the body of Christ. The whole is in the part, but the part is not alive if it is severed from the whole. We are reminded, therefore, that our spiritual growth—by whatever name we call it—cannot occur apart from the context of Christian community, the *poiēma* of God.

EYES AND EARS, HEADS AND HEARTS, HANDS AND FEET

Finally, we need to address the question of whether or not it matters where our encounter with the Truth begins. We aim at transformation of the whole person—of this there can be no question. Toward that end, all aspects of our humanity must be engaged, including our eyes and ears (perception), heads (cognition), hearts (affection), and hands and feet (behavior). Each of these areas may be viewed as an entry point into the center of our being, and each entry point has its own doorway.

Does it matter which doorway we utilize first? Is it always the case that we must begin with perception, then move on to address cognition, affection and behavior, in that order? We suggest that it does not matter which doorway we pass through first. What matters is that we touch all the critical points of our being on the journey toward transformation. In figure 10.1, we have attempted to illustrate this.

Good teaching will be responsive to the present realities of the individual or group, to the particular aspect(s) of the Truth that we are taking aim at, to the learning situation that has presented itself, and more. As we weigh all these factors, it may become clear which doorway must be utilized first in a given situation.

Jesus' training of the Twelve provides wonderful examples of variety in

---

[57]Scot McKnight, *A Community Called Atonement* (Nashville: Abingdon, 2007), p. 21.

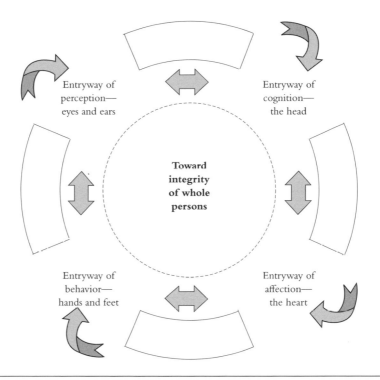

Figure 10.1. Entryways for teaching and formation

teaching with regard to these doorways. On one occasion, we find Jesus walking with the Twelve and responding to circumstances that arise along the way. "Do you see these stones?" he asks them. Or he says, "Consider the birds of the air" and "the flowers of the field." Or he calls attention to the poor widow who has just offered two small coins to the Lord. At many points, Jesus thus begins a Truth-encounter with the doorway of perception by helping his disciples to see things they have often missed, to see them more clearly for what they truly are. From this increased perception, he moves on to engage their minds, their hearts, their hands and feet.

At other times, Jesus begins by engaging the hands and feet of the Twelve. In Jonn 4, he follows the Father's direction by traveling to an out-of-the-way village in Samaria. He sends the Twelve off to buy food, and while they are away, reads a broken woman's life story to her, much to her astonishment. When the Twelve return, the woman departs to tell her townspeople about this amazing man.

When she and the villagers return to Jesus and the Twelve, they plead with him to stay longer. For two days, Jesus and his followers engage in God's works in this most unlikely of places. His very Jewish followers live among these Samaritans—eating, ministering, praying, conversing, sleeping along-side these people whom they had always regarded with ill will. This experience all proves to be very eye-opening (perception) for the Twelve, resulting in changed minds (cognition) and stirred hearts (affection).

There are other episodes when Jesus simply opens his mouth to teach them the Twelve. This is the case during the Sermon on the Mount (Mt 5—7) and elsewhere. The teaching is both content-rich and provocative. Elsewhere, he asks them questions or tells them stories or parables. Sometimes he says something bizarre, startling or downright shocking. In other words, Jesus often seems to be "messing with their heads" and by doing so he leads them to a transformative encounter with the Truth.

Then there are events, teaching-learning encounters, that seem to begin with the hearts of the Twelve. They have gathered together at the time of Passover to feast with Jesus on the eve of his crucifixion. During the meal, Jesus rises from the table, takes off his outer garment, girds himself with a servant's towel and washes the feet of his disciples. He says very little; it is a nearly wordless sermon that will be followed by a simple and sober debriefing. But he says a great deal indeed. This picture paints a thousand words and more. He shatters the pride-hardened hearts of his followers on this, the eve of his death.

Again, it should be clear that we cannot really draw lines between these various aspects of learning. Though we have suggested that the foot-washing episode was a "heart" event, it is clear that this action on the part of Jesus was also "eye opening" and "mind stretching" in the extreme. But as we stated earlier, the point is not that any one of these learning "domains" can or should be approached in isolation from the others. The point is, rather, that we must not overlook essential aspects of our teaching. Jesus could simply have instructed the Twelve verbally about their need to humbly minister to one another. He had done so on other occasions. But although this information might well have passed from his mind to their minds by such means, truly teaching what he intended to teach them called for more. And so, through this very startling and dramatic act that evening, Jesus instructed their *hearts*. Then, in the debriefing that followed, he once again made it clear that "now that you know these things, you will be blessed if you do them" (Jn 13:17), reminding them that even serving the Truth with their hearts will not be suf-

Table 10.2. A Vision of Christian Teaching

To teach is . . .	biblical words that inform the definition[a]	the teacher commits to . . .	Educational domains	Aspects of our humanity	Palmer's definition: "To teach is . . .
to come alongside	*paraklētos* (Gk—one alongside to help)	meet them; help them go where they need to go			
another	*ra'ah* (Heb—to shepherd)	care for each individual			
in the power of the Spirit	*exousia* (Gk—power, authority)	depend on God's power			
and in the company of the faithful,	*pistois* (Gk—faithful, believing ones)	humbly draw on the one, holy church			
to seek an encounter together	*sakhal* (Heb to be wise, look at, behold)	see oneself as a fellow learner in pursuit of the Truth			
with the Truth:	*alētheia* (Gk—truth)	the Truth as it is in Christ			
taking aim	*yarah* (Heb—to point, cast, guide)	guide toward Christ's Way			
to perceive it more clearly,	*eidon* (Gk—to see, perceive)	help to see things as they truly are	perception	eyes and ears	to create a space
consider it more critically,	*biyn* (Heb—to discern, distinguish)	help to think things through more deeply	cognition	heads	to create a space
embrace it more passionately,	*shanan* (Heb—to impress upon)	seek out and reflect God's heart	affection	hearts	to create a space
obey it more faithfully	*tēreō* (Gk—to keep, guard, observe)	be an example in word and deed	behavior	hands and feet	in which obedience to truth is practiced.
and embody it with greater integrity.	*yada* (Heb—to know)	love God with heart, soul, mind and strength	integrity	whole being	in which obedience to truth is practiced.

[a]Some of these terms are included on table 10.1, presented earlier in this chapter.

ficient. They must serve the Truth with their bodies as well. They must *do* the Truth. *We* must do the Truth.

Different seasons and different settings will call for increased attention to one or more of the dimensions of teaching we have been discussing. For example, congregations, like individuals, develop distinct personalities and tendencies. Some of our churches may tend to be more cognitive, others more affective and still others more activist. Effective teachers will be sensitive to this and give attention where it is most needed. A church that is always busy doing good—rather Martha-like in character, we might say—may need to be urged to slow down, to engage in more study or contemplation. A Mary-like church, on the other hand, may need admonishing in the opposite direction, toward acting on that which they have been contemplating for so long. A church that has proudly prized the life of the mind may need a season of ministry focused on heart warming or heart breaking.

CONCLUSION

Palmer's definition of teaching and our own lengthier definition offered in this chapter share several points in common. Both seek to balance concern for process and content. Both aim at obedience, but do so while acknowledging the vital role of the mind and heart in moving toward that obedience. The final aim of each definition is wholeness. This wholeness, both definitions affirm, is found only in relationship with Jesus Christ.

As each member of the body is instructed and formed through ministries of teaching and nurture such as we have envisioned here, the body as a whole is built up and enabled to walk more faithfully in the Way of the Lord, to the glory of our great God.

In table 10.2, we have attempted to bring together many of the elements that we explored in this chapter.

HYMN FOR CONTEMPLATION AND WORSHIP

As a Witness
For the Gospel of the Lord
I would yield my grateful heart.
God saves sinners, first to last.
God alone can life impart.
As a witness to your grace,
help me serve you with my heart.

For the life of holiness
I would thirst with all my soul.
May your Spirit's cleansing font
fill me till I overflow.

As a witness to your life,
help me serve you with my soul.

For the teachings of God's Word
I would humbly bow my mind.
God All-Knowing would be known.
Those who seek the Lord shall find.
As a witness to your truth,
help me serve you with my mind.

For the oneness of the church
I would work with all my might:
joining Jesus in his prayer,
loving all for whom he died.
As a witness to your love,
help me serve you with my might.

For the glory of our God,
I would ever give my all,
till, confessing, "Christ is Lord,"
on their knees all men shall bow.
Help me, as a witness, Lord,
For your glory give my all.

Text: Gary A. Parrett (2006)
Tune: DIX
Familiar use of the tune: "For the Beauty of the Earth"

QUESTIONS FOR PLANNING AND PRACTICE

1. As discussed in this chapter, Parker Palmer asserts that "to teach is to create a space in which obedience to truth is practiced." How do you evaluate your teaching ministry to date in light of his definition?

2. Reflect on Mark 10:17-22, concerning Jesus and the young rich man. Here Jesus is creating the opportunity for the young man to reflect critically on his spirituality and salvation, yet the man goes away sorrowful. Reflect on a time when, as a teacher, you tried to create space for a pupil to learn but did not get the desired result. What were your reactions and feelings?

3. When planning for teaching-learning times, how do you plan with intentionality, being sensitive to the needs of your learners? What concrete steps

might you take the next time you prepare a lesson in order to create opportunities for a more powerful learning experience?

4. Think of some learners in your community who are quiet, shy, perhaps nonnative speaking and from whom you rarely hear in your ministries and meetings? What strategies could you (and fellow leaders) employ to give them opportunities to vocalize the work of the Holy Spirit within their hearts and lives?

5. In your own teaching, which way do you tend most to engage your learners—by perception (eyes and ears), cognition (the mind), affection (the heart) or behavior (hands and feet)? Do you think it's necessary to walk through other doorways to reach the whole person?

6. Consider the following presented by the authors: "To teach is to come alongside another, in the power of the Spirit and in the company of the faithful, to seek an encounter together with the Truth: taking aim to perceive it more clearly, consider it more critically, embrace is more passionately, obey it more faithfully and embody it with greater integrity." What aspects of this definition resonate for you? Why? What aspects do not resonate for you? Why? How might you change something of your approach to educational ministry in light of this definition?

7. With another educational minister, work together on creating your own description of teaching. Be sure to consider why, how, what and whom you teach, in addition to the matter of desired outcomes of educational ministry.

RESOURCES FOR FURTHER STUDY

Brookfield, Stephen. *Becoming a Critically Reflective Teacher.* San Francisco: Jossey-Bass, 1995.

———. *The Skillful Teacher: On Technique, Trust, and Responsiveness in the Classroom.* 2nd ed. San Francisco: Jossey-Bass, 2006.

Foster, Richard. *Streams of Living Water: Celebrating the Great Traditions of Christian Faith.* San Francisco: HarperSanFrancisco, 1998.

Harris, Maria. *Women and Teaching.* New York: Paulist Press, 1988.

Hendricks, Howard. *Teaching to Change Lives.* Portland: Multnomah, 1987.

Hollinger, Dennis. *Head, Heart and Hands: Bringing Together Christian Thought, Passion and Action.* Downers Grove, Ill.: InterVarsity Press, 2005.

Joyce, Bruce, and Marsha Weil with Emily Calhoun. *Models of Teaching.* 8th ed. Boston: Allyn and Bacon, 2008.

Osmer, Richard. *Teaching for Faith.* Louisville, Ky.: Westminster/John Knox Press, 1992.

Packer, J. I. *Rediscovering Holiness: Know the Fullness of Life with God.* Ventura, Calif.: Regal, 2009.

Palmer, Parker. *To Know as We Are Known: A Spirituality of Education.* New York: Harper and Row, 1983.

Pazmiño, Robert. *Basics of Teaching for Christians: Preparation, Instruction, and Evaluation.* Grand Rapids: Baker, 1998.

Richards, Lawrence, and Gary Bredfeldt. *Creative Bible Teaching.* Chicago: Moody Press, 1998.

Vella, Jane. *Learning to Listen, Learning to Teach: The Power of Dialogue in Educating Adults.* Rev. ed. San Francisco: Jossey-Bass, 2002.

Wiggins, Grant, and Jay McTighe. *Understanding by Design.* 2nd ed. Alexandria, Va.: Association of Supervision and Curriculum Development, 2005.

11

From Generation to Generation

We will tell the next generation

the praiseworthy deeds of the LORD,

his power, and the wonders he has done.

He decreed statutes for Jacob

and established the law in Israel,

which he commanded our forefathers

to teach their children.

PSALM 78:4-5

▼

In recent decades, we have witnessed a trend toward age segmentation in many North American churches.[1] A family may drive to the church facilities together on Sunday morning, but after arriving, it is likely they will immediately disperse according to age. The children will be off to the "children's church" or to Sunday school classes, and parents will find their way into the

---

[1]Throughout its history, the church of Jesus Christ has witnessed many fragmentations. Some were necessary as they had to deal with theological controversies, such as heresy within the church, and for the sake of theological renewal. However, much of the fragmentation came about due to varying preferences, which were often couched in the name of theological differences. In recent centuries we have witnessed fragmentation of the church via proliferation of denominations and along racial and ethnic lines, as well as theological lines, among other issues. In recent decades we have seen the North American church fragmenting along generational lines and, within the church, along the lines of age segmentation. Thankfully, a number of challenges to this trend have recently arisen. See, for example, Mark DeVries, *Family-Based Youth Ministry,* rev. ed. (Downers Grove, Ill.: InterVarsity Press, 2004); Maria Harris, *Fashion Me a People* (Louisville, Ky.: Westminster/John Knox, 1989); Mariette Martineau, Joan Weber and Leif Kehrwald, *Intergenerational Faith Formation: Learning the Way We Live* (New London, Conn.: Twenty-Third Publications, 2008); C. Ellis Nelson, *Growing Up Christian: A Congregational Strategy for Nurturing Disciples* (Macon, Ga.: Smyth & Helwys, 2008); John Westerhoff III, *Will Our Children Have Faith?* rev. ed. (Toronto: Morehouse, 2000).

main sanctuary for a worship service. In some cases, teenagers may head in still another direction to experience ministries that are specially designed for them. An hour or two later, the family reconvenes for the ride back home. Something similar may occur later in the week, perhaps on a Wednesday evening, when, on their arrival at the church facilities, the family members go their separate ways again for their various activities.

The segmentation is also apparent in the hiring practices of many churches. A new staff member assumes the role of "children's pastor," while another couple ministers to the "thirtysomethings." It is increasingly rare that a growing church with an expanding staff will hire a "minister of Christian education" with educational oversight that crosses the generations or a pastor of congregational life and growth who will coordinate the formational education of the whole congregation. Far more likely, the church will hire staff for specific assignments to a specific age group in the congregation. The church may gather for an annual "family retreat" at some point in the year. But once again, that may mean little more than a long car ride together before the family members go their separate ways.

Of course there are benefits from such approaches to ministry. If one is charged to teach or preach to middle-schoolers—and nobody but middle-schoolers—it will likely prove easier to craft a message or discussion that is developmentally appropriate and culturally suited to the audience. It is certainly a harder task to prepare and present a teaching or sermon for an audience that features listeners who may range in age from four to ninety-four.

An extension of this segmentation is evident when churches move toward multiple worship services with different styles of worship for each. It is not too surprising in such churches to see that one service may be attended predominately by younger members of the church with older members mostly attending another service. Again, planning a worship service for a more particular audience is often easier than trying to be sensitive to the needs of a diverse congregation.

With a view to evangelism, it has long been argued that such particularizing of ministry to meet the needs of a very particular audience is especially helpful in terms of reaching people who are not yet believers. This is a sort of application of the so-called homogeneous unit principle that has long been associated with the modern church-growth movement.[2] Whether the matter

---

[2]This perspective was originally conceptualized by missiologists to reach the unreached people groups around the world. But soon this principle took on prominence in the United States as

is difference in age or in race, difference in socioeconomic status or in educational background, it seems easier to "reach people for Christ" if we have a specific group of people in mind. This evangelistic burden can affect nearly everything about how a congregation chooses to "do church"—from the music in worship to the approach to preaching to the structuring of discipleship ministries, and much more. Most congregations, at least at times, make decisions along these lines of thinking.

There is a legitimate question about how much all of our trends toward such practices in the church are mirroring larger cultural trends. Many have written about how, for example, the marketing world has driven the development of "generational" consciousness within American society.[3] Have churches simply learned from the marketplace that you need to know your audience and target that audience with whatever it is you are trying to sell?

Aside from the pragmatic questions involved in all this, there is also the matter of biblical fidelity. What are the mandates and the models of Scripture regarding intergenerational life and ministry in our churches? For some, the question may simply be answered by sweeping it under what are perceived to be larger concerns. Surely, some will argue, the overriding concern of the church must always be to reach as many people as possible for Christ at all cost.[4] But what does it mean to reach people for Christ? Are we to reduce this to simply a concern for evangelism. As we noted in chapter two, the goal of our teaching must embrace "teaching them to obey all I have commanded you." The goal of our ministry is making disciples of Jesus. Thus it is not enough to ask merely about how we can "reach" people. Attentiveness to this goal may well help us succeed in getting people to come. But what manner of

---

churches sought to reach certain segments of the population, often along socioeconomic class, ethnic and generational lines.

[3]According to some, generational differentiation in the United States is largely the invention of Madison Avenue, reflecting an attempt to create marketing niches and fads to boost sales. "Generations," which were typically grouped into forty-year windows in Bible times, were reintroduced several decades ago in North America, now segmented into twenty-year windows as "builders, boomers, busters and millennials." Now, due to the rapid pace of changes in society, there are often subcategories conceived within each generation. Among the millennials, for instance, are Generation Z, homelanders (born between 1990 and 1996) and Generation I, the Internet or Net generation (born between 1996 and 2006). See, for instance, Neil Howe and William Strauss, *Millennials Rising: The Next Great Generation* (New York: Vintage, 2000).

[4]Unfortunately, such a practice of ministry comes with a high cost of its own. Recently, one "seeker-driven" church, for the sake of solving the parking congestion between two services, decided to do away with Sunday school hour between the two services to make a smooth transition from one service to the next.

people will they *become* if our philosophy of ministry is dominated by catering to personal and generational preferences?[5]

Unquestionably, ministry that is intentionally aimed at particular audiences can be very fruitful. It is a wise church that seeks to make its ministries culturally congruent for the realities of its congregants. This means we must pay attention to all aspects of the cultural milieu that continue to shape both our members and those outside the church whom we are seeking to serve. Developmental realities and generational issues[6] are a large part of such attention, and we certainly must try to minister in age-appropriate ways.

Yet many churches seem to have gone overboard in this regard, structuring all, or nearly all, their ministries with this issue of "age appropriateness"[7] in mind. Whatever gains there may be in approaching ministry along this age-segmented path, however, we must recognize that there are significant corresponding losses. For one, children lose the opportunity to be with adults in worship, to learn by example what it means to pray, praise, listen, partake. As I worship in my own congregation, I am often watched very closely by babies in their parents' arms, by toddlers and other young children. They watch me as I sing to the Lord and as I listen to the preaching of the Word. What are they thinking as they watch? I have no idea. But I am glad they are watching, and I pray that such a seemingly small matter will bear kingdom fruit one day.[8]

---

[5]Without full commitment to holistic and intergenerational discipleship as a congregation, the church will likely become like a revolving door—people coming and leaving based on their satisfaction level: how their needs and preferences are addressed and met. During the period they stay at a church, they remain "consumers" merely occupying the pews as passive Christians. They feel satisfied with what they are getting, which likely means that they are affirmed by the church leaders as precisely the targeted population of that church. The problem is that they then translate such messages to mean there is no need to change or grow in Jesus Christ any further. When they are "pushed" to examine their lives and change their ways in the Lord, they can always pack up and venture into another church that would welcome them "just as they are." So the great migration cycle continues.

[6]It may be instructive to delineate the age-related groups and the generational cohorts here. By *developmental issues* we mean the enduring traits in terms of abilities and other ontogenetic issues that are generally accepted as normative throughout time and space for certain age groups, for example, certain cognitive abilities of preadolescents. By *generational issues* we mean the characteristics that are unique to a certain group of people who grew up together, sharing a set of unique experiences in a particular period and/or in a particular region of the world, for example, so-called baby boomers in America.

[7]We really should call the very term into question in certain respects. Is it not "age appropriate," after all, to have significant interaction with persons of other ages within one's family, church and community?

[8]We are called to live as a "congregation," a local gathering of the family of God and the manifestation of the kingdom life. This means that we are called to model for one another how we

Just as important, of course, the adults in the congregation need to see, hear and be with the children. We have much to learn from those younger than us. Jesus evidently thought that this was so. On one occasion, when his disciples were (once again) disputing among themselves about who would be greatest in the kingdom of God, Jesus had a young child stand in the midst of his disciples and taught them that they needed to learn from this young one and, indeed, needed to become like him (see Mk 9:33-37).

Many adult worshipers seem to think that children will be a distraction to real learning and worship—for themselves, for the preacher or teacher, or for both. The disciples thought this way, at least on one occasion. They rebuked a group of mothers who wanted to bring their babies[9] to Jesus to receive a blessing from him. When Jesus saw the disciples' actions, "he was indignant. He said to them, 'Let the little children come to me, and do not hinder them, for the kingdom of God belongs to such as these.'" Here again, he told his disciples that they had much to learn from such children (Mk 10:13-16). The attitude the disciples displayed on this occasion seems to have mirrored the broader culture. We recall the episode some time after this event when the religious authorities asked Jesus to quiet the children who were shouting their hosannas upon his entry to Jerusalem. But Jesus rebuked those who rebuked, and he warmly welcomed the children and their praise (see Mt 21:15-16).

Jesus' attitude toward children mirrored not the culture at large but the heart of his heavenly Father. A straightforward reading of the Scriptures reveals that God's heart for them is much more open than ours very often are. Children are at the center of his attentions, not at the periphery. Israel was commanded to keep the instruction and formation of their children as a chief priority. Children were welcomed into the covenant community while they

---

are to live as a kingdom family in the context of the various aspects of life together: prayer, worship, teaching, service and so on. This can happen only when we submit ourselves to one another across generations, genders, socioeconomic status, ethnic and racial "differences," and so on. These differences should be construed as openings or opportunities through which we can create space for God to transform us as a kingdom family. More often than not, when we live in the "silos" of our differences, we end up truncating the Gospel according to the perceived needs of the group and creating a set of standards the group needs to conform to in order to be part of that group. At the same time, these silos need to be recognized, celebrated and even strengthened. This is not, however, for the purpose of being comfortable with those who share similarities/familiarities that are often socioculturally constructed for them. Instead, it is for the purpose of deciphering together how they are to build one another up in the church, by listening, equipping, serving, teaching and so on, as partners in God's ongoing transformational work in the family of God and beyond.

[9]While the other Gospel accounts use the general word for "young children," Luke makes it clear that these were, in fact, babies who were brought to Jesus by their mothers (Lk 18:15).

were but infants and were to be raised and nurtured within the very heart of that community (see Deut 6:1-9; 11:1-7, 16-21). This priority was reiterated in New Testament teaching (see Eph 6:4; Col 3:21; Tit 2:4). When Paul addressed letters to the congregations, he included instruction for the children (see Eph 6:1-3; Col 3:20).

In the Old Testament, we read of several occasions when children gathered with the whole assembly for solemn and serious matters (see, for example, Deut 31:12-13; Josh 8:35; 2 Kings 23:2). When Ezra and the Israelites stood for his reading the Torah scroll, the assembly included "men and women and all who were able to understand. He read it aloud from daybreak till noon . . . in the presence of the men, women and others who could understand" (Neh 8:23). "Others" here includes the children in the community who were old enough to follow along.[10] Perhaps the high platform that had been built to make Ezra more visible to the assembly (see Neh 8:4) was built in part with them in mind.

This account of Ezra's public reading, by the way, offers a possible guideline for us to follow when we design our own gatherings and discuss who should participate. If we welcomed children old enough to understand what is said and done in our various gatherings, what difference might that make for our approach to those meetings? In some cases, perhaps this would mean fewer children would attend some of our services. I have sat in worship services where I was initially thrilled to see children and youth worshiping alongside their parents, only to have my initial enthusiasm give way to sadness when I saw that the presence of these children was not acknowledged in the least. Neither the songs nor the sermon, nor any other element seemed to consider the presence of the children. In some cases, the church actually provided kids with coloring crayons and paper to keep them busy. In other cases, parents packed their own "keep them busy" supplies or scrambled to come up with something on the spot. If we are not going to act as though the children are actually in our midst and are part of the assembly, it would be better to provide them with another venue where they would be treated as though their spiritual well-being was taken seriously.[11]

---

[10]It also included those Gentiles who came into the fold of the Israelites and, by living among them, now understand God's heart for them as well.

[11]Having children in worship reading a book that has nothing to do with a Christian theme during the service is problematic. Yet having kids color and engage in any kind of potentially worshipful and "responsive" (to God) activities might not be a bad idea. The leaders of the church, as well as the worship committee, can work with parents to provide materials (inten-

In many cases, children could join with the adults and profit from the experience. Typically, we do not give children enough credit for what they are capable of understanding. This seems to be especially true of our approach to church matters. Consider the contrast, for example, between what we ask of our high-school students when they are at school during the week and what we seem to expect of them during youth group or youth Bible studies. Our students are in classes for many hours each week, asked to read meaty academic textbooks on a wide variety of subjects, to do hours of homework, to generate sizable papers, presentations, projects and so on. When it comes to the church's youth group meetings, what do *we* offer them? Perhaps it is best to let the reader answer that question based on her experiences and observations. In too many cases, what we offer our youth and expect from them—in view of what they are actually capable of—is both insulting to them and shameful for us.[12]

Our children and youth would profit even more from our gatherings if pastors and other worship leaders planned services with them in mind. All too frequently, it seems that churches consider their worship services to be adult services, rather than services for the whole community. This may be an example of our failure to properly "[recognize] the body" (1 Cor 11:29). In some circles, the tendency to segregate the church family based on age has made the "adult services" approach almost unavoidable. We have become so hyper-specialized that we believe that only the "experts" can minister effectively to particular age groups. Senior pastors often find the prospect of having to preach in such a way that even young children are engaged either terrifying or unduly burdensome. It is rare to find a preacher today who has heeded Luther's counsel to preach in such a way that young children can understand.

---

tionally designed for the theme of the corporate worship that Sunday) that kids can interact with during the worship service. Also, parents can be trained to nurture their kids before, during and after the service to understand the meaning of various aspects of the service and to participate more intentionally and thus voluntarily take part in worship. For more on the parental role in helping children experience congregational worship, see Robbie Castleman, *Parenting in the Pew: Guiding Your Children into the Joy of Worship* (Downers Grove, Ill.: Inter-Varsity Press, 2002).

[12]Do we dare extend the same phenomenon to the adults as well? We hardly have any expectation for one another as Christian adults in the church in terms of taking our spiritual walk as seriously or more than what they are accustomed to in their employment, their parenting, their leisure activities and so on. We observe that in a typical North American evangelical church, the sermon has become the lowest common denominator of what most adults should adhere to or agree with. Unfortunately for many, that lowest common denominator has turned into the one and only avenue through which they seriously ponder God throughout the week.

When people from other nations and cultures visit services in some American evangelical churches, they are often struck by how the cult of ageism has deeply infiltrated our congregations. American worshipers often have the opposite experience when they travel abroad and worship with whole families, including many young children.

Thankfully, there are church leaders in North America who have been rebelling against the age-segmentation phenomenon. Many are becoming passionate in their advocacy of intergenerational ministry. One can find many wonderful resources for designing and leading multigenerational worship services,[13] small groups, Bible studies and more—online and in print. Some evangelical authors also have made thoughtful contributions about the spiritual formation of children and youth in recent years.[14] Perhaps we are turning the corner on these matters, moving closer to God's heart in determining to include our children into the full life of the body and to nurture them in the Faith as we have been commanded.

As the apostle Peter finally came to learn, God's heart embraces children into his family and demands that we do the same. On the very day the church was born, by that Pentecostal outpouring of God's Spirit, Peter urged the wondering crowds to repent and be baptized, "every one of you, in the name of Jesus Christ for the forgiveness of your sins. And you will receive the gift of the Holy Spirit. The promise is for you and your children and for all who are far off—for all whom the Lord our God will call" (Acts 2:38-39).

The reality is that our children may be *our* children, according to the flesh, for a brief season in this temporal life. But in the Spirit and for all eternity, they are our brothers and our sisters.[15] May we increasingly come to believe

---

[13]See, for example, the recently released Howard Vanderwell, ed., *The Church of All Ages* (Herndon, Va.: The Alban Institute. 2008).

[14]Marva Dawn, *Is It a Lost Cause? Having the Heart of God for the Church's Children* (Grand Rapids: Eerdmans, 1997); Holly Allen, *Nurturing Children's Spirituality: Christian Perspectives and Best Practices* (Eugene, Ore.: Cascade, 2008); Beth Posterski, Linda Cannell, Catherine Stonehouse and Scottie May, *Children Matter: Celebrating Their Place in the Church, Family and Community* (Grand Rapids: Eerdmans, 2005); Rick Dunn, *Shaping the Spiritual Life of Students: A Guide for Youth Workers, Pastors, Teachers and Campus Ministers* (Downers Grove, Ill.: InterVarsity Press, 2001); Kenda Creasy Dean and Ron Foster, *The Godbearing Life: The Art of Soul Tending for Youth Ministry* (Nashville: Upper Room, 1998); Kenda Creasy Dean, *Practicing Passion: Youth and the Quest for a Passionate Church* (Grand Rapids: Zondervan, 2006).

[15]Mutual and intentional discipleship thus can start early in the family. Asking children to pray for their parents, having parents be accountable to their children about certain aspects of their lives, training children to ask appropriate questions when studying the Bible, preparing them gradually to take turns with parents in leading family worship—all these would be wonderful places to begin.

these words and to act accordingly as we plan and lead our ministries to the church, the household of faith. Seeking to minister well to all our members, we will undoubtedly continue to have various ministries designed for congregants of particular ages. But we will also have many more times when we—as the family of God—are praying, playing, worshiping and working together, *all* together.

We are called to take children very seriously. Jesus taught that we are never to "look down on one of these little ones. For I tell you that their angels in heaven always see the face of my Father in heaven" (Mt 18:10). In our approach and attitude toward ministry, whose heart are we imitating? Is it the attitude of the surrounding culture or that of our Father in heaven? Do we really welcome children into the full life of our community? Do we recognize that they are not "the church of the future" but are, in fact, a vital part of the church today? To welcome children in our midst—to truly welcome them with open minds and hearts—is not only to imitate the Lord Jesus and the Father who sent him; it is also to welcome both the Son and the Father into our lives (see Mk 9:37).[16]

GOD'S MIGHTY DEEDS AND RIGHTEOUS COMMANDS

When we set our hearts fully on nurturing our children in the Faith, we must be clear about both the content and the processes of that ministry. We have dealt with issues of content at length in part two of this book. The content we consider essential for children and youth is the same content we consider essential for all members. Simply put, we must nurture our children in the Gospel. This commitment leads us also to invite them to the Story of God's redemptive works in the world and to instruct them in the three dimensions of the one Faith that we observed in chapter five: the Truth, the Life and the Way.

When we are addressing our message to children, we must take particular care that our message to them is at its heart the word of the Gospel. We can miss this mark very easily if we are not very deliberate about our message. To illustrate this, we can consider wisdom from Psalm 78. The psalmist calls God's people to make a transgenerational commitment. There are things "we have heard and known," he writes, things that "our fathers have told us." The psalmist is committed to binding himself to the generations

---

[16]We maintain that how we engage and serve the children in the congregation is an excellent indicator of its spiritual maturity. How we treat and value one of the groups that might be called "the least of these" is also a good indicator of the church's desire for outreach to the other groups of "the least of these" in the community and beyond.

that have preceded his own. And what is to be done with these treasures gleaned from the past? The psalmist continues, "We will not hide them from their children; we will tell the next generation." (Ps 78:3-4). A few verses later it becomes clear that it is not only "the next generation" that the psalmist has in mind. He is looking beyond to "even the children yet to be born" who "in turn would tell their children" (Ps 78:6).

The psalmist is determined that the future generations "would put their trust in God and would not forget his deeds but would keep his commands. They would not be like their forefathers—a stubborn and rebellious generation, whose hearts were not loyal to God, whose spirits were not faithful to him" (Ps 78:7-8). Israel had gotten it wrong before. The psalmist recalls episodes from the past when a godly generation of Israelites gave way to a rebellious generation. He longs that such history not be repeated again.

In Judges 2, we read the account of such a tragic generational shift. Joshua and his contemporaries, we are told, have passed away: "After that whole generation had been gathered to their fathers, another generation grew up, who knew neither the LORD nor what he had done for Israel. Then the Israelites did evil in the eyes of the LORD and served the Baals" (Judg 2:10-11). If the text said only of this new generation that they did not know the Lord, perhaps we could excuse the generation of their parents. After all, even if parents do everything right, there is no guarantee that their children will know the Lord. No one is ever invited to call God "Grandfather." We do not pray to him as such. No, we each must come to know God as Father. Having godly parents does not automatically make us God's children ourselves.

But the account in Judges 2 says more. Not only did this new generation not know the Lord. We read further that they did not know "what he had done for Israel" (Judg 2:10). Joshua's generation had witnessed God's mighty dealings on their behalf, and they had heard what God had done for the generation that preceded them. But it seems that they had failed to pass on to their own children the accounts of God's wondrous works. They may or may not have passed on God's commands. They undoubtedly passed on at least certain rituals of the community. But they had not told their children of God's redemptive deeds on Israel's behalf.[17]

---

[17]Each generation was charged to pass on the acts of God's gracious deeds in such a way that the subsequent generation would truly encounter God in a transforming manner. Perhaps the "passing on" is far more than the passing on of rituals and even stories. The passing on entails the genuine obedience of heart, attitude, character and integrity where all the inner-life issues coincide with the outer obedience.

Returning to Psalm 78, we can almost hear the psalmist saying about such things, "Not on our watch!" However often it might have occurred in their history, he writes, we will not neglect to pass on to our children what our fathers have told us. In particular, the psalmist commits his generation to the passing on of two things. First, he will tell the next generation "the praise-worthy deeds of the LORD, his power, and the wonders he has done" (Ps 78:4). Second, God has "decreed statutes for Jacob and established the law in Israel, which he commanded our forefathers to teach their children" (Ps 78:5). God's wondrous works and his righteous requirements—these are two features of the essential content for this transgenerational ministry. The pair is repeated in verse seven more simply as "his deeds" and "his commands."[18]

It is easy for parents in faith communities to fail in regard to this twofold message. I can easily think of my own Christian story as an example. Not raised in a devout home, I became a Christian at age sixteen. A few years later, I married a young woman of similar background—like me, a first-generation believer. When we became parents, we desired to raise our daughter differ-ently—in terms of "spiritual" matters, at least—than we ourselves had been raised. We wanted our daughter to grow up in a "Christian home." Surely this was a reflection of our desire to do what Scripture tells us we must do: raise our child up in the Faith.

Consciously or not, however, raising our daughter in a "Christian" home often meant that we would say or imply things like this: "Remember, we are Christians, and so we don't . . ." "This is a Christian home, and that means we have to . . ." "Because we're a Christian family, we . . ." Without realizing it, we often reduced our Christian faith to a list of dos and don'ts for our daugh-ter. When my wife and I first became believers it was, for each of us, a power-ful Gospel experience. God broke into our lives in wonderful and dramatic ways, transforming us. It was truly all Gospel. But what was Gospel for us was becoming law for our daughter.

Here is a temptation common to many of us who are first-generation Christians called to raise our children in the Faith. Instead of the mighty deeds of the Lord on our behalf, we offer our children a list of what we should and should not do. In the process, we might potentially sap the spirit right out of the glorious, life-transforming Gospel, extricating the amazing grace from

---

[18]Interestingly, the word rendered *teaching* in Psalm 78:1 and *law* in Psalm 78:5 is actually *Torah*. We are reminded that the Torah itself (that is, the five books of Moses) records the narrative both of God's wondrous works and of his righteous commands.

God's character. In the end, all we offer is the Gospel according to our own image and pass that on to our children.

In doing so, of course, we are setting forth a perverted vision of the Faith and may be setting both our children and ourselves on a course of lifeless legalism. Perhaps such problems have contributed to what Christian Smith and his team of researchers found when they analyzed the spirituality and theology of evangelical young people in the United States. The researchers concluded that the faith of many of these American Christian teens could best be described as a "moralistic, therapeutic deism."[19]

The wisdom of Psalm 78 reminds us that we must teach both what God requires of us and what God has done for us. If we speak only of grace and never refer to the commands of the Lord, we are unfaithful to our mandate in one direction. Such teaching may well lead to antinomianism, to a disobedient faith. But erring on the other side is not the solution. Emphasizing God's commands to the exclusion of his saving grace can surely lead to disillusionment and despair.

Psalm 85 also provides language to describe the sort of dual concern that we must pursue in our ministries. The psalmist here prays for God's forgiveness and salvation for his people. Having made his request, he writes, "I will listen to what God the LORD will say; he promises peace to his people, his saints—but let them not return to folly" (Ps 85:8). The potent poetry continues in Psalm 85:10 with these words: "Love and faithfulness meet together; righteousness and peace kiss each other."

Such language reminds us of the encounter recorded in John 8 between Jesus and the woman taken in adultery. He assures us that she is not condemned, but he also charges her to "go, and sin no more" (Jn 8:11 KJV). Jesus brings the woman peace but does not cease to call for righteousness. In the ministry of Christ, in other words, righteousness *(tsedek)* and peace *(shalom)* "kiss each other." This happened most profoundly at the cross, where God revealed himself to be both just (righteous in himself) and justifier of those who believe (saving us, bringing us to shalom).

These divine qualities met not only in the *deeds* of Jesus, however. They were also married in his very *person*. The expression "love and faithfulness meet together" brings together the Hebrew words *hesed* and *emeth*. *Hesed* is variously rendered in English Bibles as "loving kindness," "faithful love,"

---

[19]Christian Smith, *Soul Searching: The Religious and Spiritual Lives of American Teenagers* (New York: Oxford University Press, 2005).

"mercy" and so on. One viable rendering is simply "grace." *Emeth* can be rendered "faithfulness," as the NIV has it here. But it could also be rendered "truth." Thus we could translate the expression "Grace and truth have embraced." Doing so takes us into the language of John's prologue: "The Word became flesh and made his dwelling among us. We have seen his glory, the glory of the One and Only, who came from the Father, full of grace and truth. . . . Grace and truth came through Jesus Christ" (Jn 1:14, 17).

Thus we are once again reminded that Jesus himself must ever be the center of our proclamation and teaching. This is certainly so when we consider the essential content that we would teach to our children. We must stand guard, then, against the temptation to teach Sunday school Bible stories in ways that emphasize obedience over grace. When our children learn the story of Jonah, instead of highlighting God's great mercy, is the conclusion something like, "So we shouldn't be like Jonah who ran away from God's call"? When they learn about Mary, instead of underscoring the presence and power of the Holy Spirit in her life, does the lesson simply amount to "And so we should be like Mary who obeyed the Lord"? Tragically, many of our Sunday school lessons for children are reduced in this way to moralistic tales that emphasize the response of human love above the revelation of divine love. To help us avoid this tendency, we must refuse to detach particular stories of the Bible from the grand Story of God's redemptive dealings with sinful humanity.

The same sort of temptation can influence our teaching and preaching among adults as well. Do we preach and teach in such a way as to leave parishioners with the impression that God is calling us to "be good," as if that were possible apart from the redeeming and regenerating grace of God? On the other hand, do we teach or preach the grace of God in a way that calls forth no response or denies that the Gospel has transformative power? In Jesus, God reconciles all things to himself. This reconciliation includes forgiveness of our sins and transformation into a godliness that is reflected in love of God and neighbor. Christ died to redeem for himself a people of his very own who would be eager to do good (see Tit 2:14). Thus Jesus—in whom righteousness and shalom kiss, and in whom grace and truth embrace—must remain central in all our teaching and preaching.[20]

---

[20]When we teach the Scriptures, we will want to focus on two basic things: First, what does the passage or story say about God's character and plan? Second, what does it say about who we are in light of God's character and how God wishes to include us in his plan? As we enter, dwell and linger in God's presence by utilizing all the faculties that he has endowed us with to delight in who he is and what he is doing, only then can we understand our identity and

THE TORAH OF THE LORD

In Deuteronomy 6 and 11, we read of Moses' charge to those who were about to enter the land of promise. That charge called for both adherence to God's commands for themselves and the obligation to pass on to their children these commands and the account of God's mighty deeds. After delivering to the people the *shema*—the central affirmation of all observant Jews: "Hear, O Israel: The LORD our God, the LORD is one" (Deut 6:4)—and commanding further that the Israelites were to love the Lord their God with all their heart, soul and strength (see Deut 6:5), Moses instructs,

> These commandments that I give you today are to be upon your hearts. Impress them on your children. Talk about them when you sit at home and when you walk along the road, when you lie down and when you get up. Tie them as symbols on your hands and bind them on your foreheads. Write them on the doorframes of your houses and on your gates. (Deut 6:6-9)

God's purposes in commanding such practices among his people included both his glory and their good. They would fear, obey and love him. But they, in turn, would find that obeying and teaching these things would bring great blessing to them: "so that you may enjoy long life . . . so that it may go well with you and that you may increase greatly in a land flowing with milk and honey" (Deut 6:2-3). Very similar injunctions and promises are repeated in Deuteronomy 11. Added is the command to recount for their children the mighty deeds God had done before their own eyes: "It was not your children who saw what [the Lord] did for you in the desert. . . . But it was your own eyes that saw all these great things the LORD has done" (Deut 11:5, 7). That which God had revealed to one generation obligated that generation to pass on this history to subsequent generations.[21]

The twofold emphasis of reciting both redemptive history and divine

---

our vocation more fully. In the process, we realize that only the Holy Spirit who works in us and among us can enable us to respond to God in obedience to participate in his plan with gratitude. It will serve us well if we truly recognize that our obedience to his will, plan and commands is not ultimately for God's benefit, as if he needs our help(!). Instead, it is God's commitment to continue to transform us as he enables us to obey him. In his grace, it is God who called us to be his children. In his grace, it is God who stirs our hearts to respond to him with gratitude. And in his grace, it is God who even enables us to obey him with our good works. This is God's plan for the gracious transformation of his people in Jesus Christ.

[21]Again, it is not merely retelling the story as if it were the story of old, but truly dwelling in that story so that children can readily witness that the story the parents talk about is unmistakably what informs every aspect of their lives. "Passing on" thus means testifying to those around what God has done for his people, endowing them with true identity and life's project in relation to him.

commands is captured by one rich and complex Hebrew term—*Torah*. The word *Torah* has been used in multiple ways by practicing Jews through the centuries. For some today, the word is primarily understood as the title of the five books of Moses, what many Christians call the Pentateuch.[22] Others think of the term as representing all the divine commands, or the Ten Commandments in particular. Still others see in the word the Lord's instruction and guidance for an entire way of life. Again, it is taken by some to refer to the entirety of God's revelation. In Judaism, there is also a distinction between the written Torah (the Scriptures) and the oral Torah (the rabbinic teaching that has been codified in the Talmud and other Jewish legal works).

The word *Torah* is often translated into English as "law." This is the common practice in most English translations of the Bible. But this is more in line with the meaning of the Greek word *nomos*. While this word is the typical choice in the Septuagint for translating *Torah,* and while the writers of the New Testament also used this term to represent Torah, it seems that the Greek term simply cannot bear the weight of all that is intended by the Hebrew original.

While *nomos* can refer to any sort of law or to any sort of tradition, custom or usage that is enjoined on someone,[23] the word *torah* permits a greater range of nuance and application. It is not surprising that many contemporary Jewish writers either simply leave the word *torah* as is, without translation, or render it "guidance" or "instruction," rather than "law." If our modern ears experience a twinge of repulsion when we hear the word "law," we are quite obviously experiencing something far different than the psalmist experienced when he contemplated the words of *Torah,* as Psalms 1; 19 and 119 so powerfully demonstrate. We hear him sing, "Oh, how I love your law *[torah]*! I meditate on it all day long" (Ps 119:97). Rejoicing, he says elsewhere, "I run in the path of your commands, for you have set my heart free" (Ps 119:32).

Is the point of our argument in the preceding pages that the Torah, properly understood, actually includes the Gospel? There is indeed much grace in God's commands, and God has promised that all who walk in the Way of these commands will be blessed. But the commands of God are not presented as the pathway to a relationship with God. Entry into covenant relationship with God is rooted entirely in his sovereign grace and saving deeds. As we

---

[22]This term, meaning "five scrolls," is from the Septuagint. See Gordon Wenham, *Exploring the Old Testament: A Guide to the Pentateuch* (Downers Grove, Ill.: InterVarsity Press, 2003).

[23]See Geoffrey Bromiley, *Theological Dictionary of the New Testament, Abridged in One Volume,* ed. Gerhard Kittel and Gerhard Friedrich (Grand Rapids: Eerdmans, 1985), pp. 646-55.

noted earlier, the first of the Ten Words is not a command. It is rather "I am the LORD your God, who brought you out of Egypt, out the land of slavery" (Ex 20:2). No one will be justified in God's sight by obeying his commands (see Rom 3:20). We reject then any vision of a neo-nomian "gospel," as though the good news were that God will enable us to obey the law and justify us on the basis of our obedience. As we argued at length in chapter four, we are justified freely by God's grace, through faith alone in Christ alone.

On the other hand, we must reject any vision of the Christian life that does not take holiness, righteousness and obedience very seriously. That is, we reject all forms of antinomianism, as if God's people were under no obligation to observe God's commands today. We reject as well any simplistic understanding of the Reformation "law and Gospel" dialectic that suggests that the Old Testament knows nothing of Gospel and the New Testament knows nothing of law. Rather, as many Lutheran scholars more wisely suggest, we regard law and Gospel as two principles revealed throughout the Scriptures. Wise and faithful preaching continually moves back and forth between these two principles, applying the word of the law and the word of the Gospel as required,[24] and thereby "comforting the afflicted and afflicting the comfortable."

RITUAL AND REMEMBRANCE

Having addressed issues of content in the preceding pages of this chapter, we return now to issues of educational processes for ministry "from generation to generation." One of the most important and powerful of all formative tools is ritual. Ritual is a daily part of all of our lives—individually and corporately—and, as is so often the case, it can be formative for either good or ill. There are national and cultural rituals, family rituals and personal rituals. Churches and all other religious groups depend largely on the role of ritual in worship, teaching and formation.

In both Old and New Testaments, ritual plays a critical role. The people of Israel were commanded to observe a great number of rituals in their homes and in their assemblies. Often the rituals were to be practiced especially for

---

[24]Thanks to our friend and colleague Gordon Isaac for (re)introducing us to these insights. For helpful treatments of the law and Gospel dialectic, see Robert Kolb and Charles Arand, *The Genius of Luther's Theology: A Wittenberg Way of Thinking for the Contemporary Church* (Grand Rapids: Baker, 2008). For an engaging presentation of these principles in narrative fiction, see Bo Giertz, *The Hammer of God,* rev. ed. (Minneapolis: Augsburg, 2005).

the instruction and formation of the community's children.[25] The ritual of the Passover meal, for example, was to involve answering questions raised by the children:

> Obey these instructions as a lasting ordinance for you and your descendants. When you enter the land that the LORD will give you as he promised, observe this ceremony. And when your children ask you, "What does this ceremony mean to you?" then tell them, "It is the Passover sacrifice to the LORD, who passed over the houses of the Israelites in Egypt and spared our homes when he struck down the Egyptians." (Ex 12:24-27)

I have been privileged to participate in the Passover Seder (the ritual meal) on several occasions with observant Jewish families. The youngest child who is present at the meal is to recite or sing four questions during the unfolding of the Haggadah (the liturgy of the Seder). The questions concern particular elements of the meal—what is eaten, and how. Each question gives occasion for rehearsing features of the Passover story. One of the more striking things for me was that the language of the entire Haggadah is designed so participants understand that the story is not merely about what happened to our forefathers. It happened to *us!* "With a mighty hand the LORD brought us out of Egypt, out of the land of slavery" (Ex 13:14). Here is a powerful ritual of remembrance for children of the community. They are asked to remember *their* participation in events that occurred long before they were born. The community is theirs, thus the story is also theirs.

At other times, the Israelites erected memorial stones that would serve as powerful, visual, tactile testimonies to the children of future generations:[26]

> So Joshua called together the twelve men he had appointed from the Israelites, one from each tribe, and said to them, "Go over before the ark of the LORD your God into the middle of the Jordan. Each of you is to take up a stone on his shoulder, according to the number of the tribes of the Israelites, to serve as a sign among you. In the future, when your children ask you, 'What do these stones mean?' tell them that the flow of the Jordan was cut off before the ark of the covenant of the LORD.

---

[25]For children, these are identity-shaping, and for adults, identity-affirming as they point to the right way of living in light of the identity-setting narrative for the community. Thus we are called to narrate God's story even as we find ourselves in that story.

[26]The children were to be taught to remember who God is, what he has done, what he has done *for them* and who he calls them to be. It was thus to prompt them to rededicate themselves to be the people God called them to be. Sharing or teaching also shapes teachers and parents even as they try to shape their children. Rituals thus have a profound way of reinforcing their own identity and their life's project.

When it crossed the Jordan, the waters of the Jordan were cut off. These stones are
to be a memorial to the people of Israel forever." (Josh 4:4-7)

In much of today's evangelical world, however, we have not been careful
to raise our "Ebenezers"[27] for the glory of God and for the sake of our children. Indeed, it is commonplace in some evangelical circles to decry the
"empty ritualism" of more highly liturgical churches. But this rings hollow,
for several reasons. First, we are often criticizing things we have not really
experienced and do not understand.

This was true of me when I was first exposed to the Lutheran liturgy.
When I began to attend a Lutheran seminary as a young man, the school's
chapel services startled me. At the time I was attending an independent charismatic church that sang mostly choruses and had no stated liturgical design.
Reciting prayers and confessions written by others seemed wholly inauthentic
and inappropriate to me, convinced, as I was then, that only truly spontaneous prayer could be heartfelt and God-pleasing. I became very critical of these
services, usually sat (and stood and sat and stood) at the back of the chapel and
even joined in sarcastic critique with a fellow student.

One day, in the middle of a church history class, my ignorance and arrogance were challenged. My professor was a lifelong Lutheran, still teaching—
very well—while then in his mid-eighties. I do not recall why or how this
came about in class, but he began to quote from memory a lengthy passage
from the liturgy. After speaking, his eyes welled up with tears as he looked at
the class and said, "Isn't it beautiful? It's all Scripture!" Once I had removed
the spear that had just pierced my heart, I found myself seeing things with
new eyes. How could I have been so blind? He was right—the liturgy we
were reciting in chapel day by day was Scripture-saturated. And it really *was*
beautiful. Whatever I had been doing in those services, this man had been
seeking sincerely to worship the Lord in spirit and truth.

My approach to those chapel services began to change. I listened, I learned,
I prayed, I sang "a new song" to the Lord because my attitude was being renewed. But it was not only the Lutheran liturgy I saw differently. I began to
see my own church's worship differently as well. Were we really as spontaneous as I had assumed? We were not. Our services were remarkably similar

---

[27]See the account in 1 Samuel 7, and note the name that was given to the memorial stone there.
Ebenezer means "stone of help." The stone and its name were to be a reminder that "thus far has
the LORD helped us." See Gary A. Parrett, "Raising Ebenezer," *Christianity Today,* January 2006,
p. 26.

from week to week. A word of welcome and opening prayer were followed by twenty minutes or so of lively singing—often of songs we had sung many times before. The songs we sang and prayed were not spontaneous or original to me or to most of my fellow worshipers. We made them our own in the attitude of our hearts, not because we had composed them ourselves. Our liturgy continued with outbursts of prayer and praise that may well have been "fresh," though they usually occurred at about the same time in the service each week. One could almost guess, even, when it would be time for Mrs. So-and-so to stand and "prophesy" to the congregation. More singing and then a prayer of dismissal would follow a thoughtful sermon. This was our liturgy—in rough outline—and we followed it nearly every week. Unlike the Lutheran liturgy, however, ours was not so thoroughly Scripture-soaked. Nor was it vitally connected to practices of the historic church.

Yes, our harangues against the "empty ritualism" of highly liturgical churches often ring hollow. The fact is that we all have our rituals; we all *need* our rituals. Baptism itself is, of course, a ritual, no less so when practiced in "low church" settings than when performed in "high church" settings. The Lord's Supper is a ritual that we typically perform even more often. Most evangelical Protestants have no problem accepting these two rituals. Whether we call them "sacraments" or "ordinances," we acknowledge them as acts we must perform because Jesus himself commanded us to do so. The fact is, they *are* rituals, whether we call them that or not.

A BRIEF CASE STUDY ON RITUAL AND FORMATION

Some of our rituals occur weekly in our worship services, but most in attendance would not think of them as rituals. In my own church home,[28] we hear several times during the worship service this refrain: "Hi, I'm _____, and I'm one of the pastors here at _____." Indeed, this seems to be the most frequently repeated ritual phrase of our church. When I pointed this out to church leaders, they may have been a bit surprised. But upon reflection, they were not apologetic, for this ritual is an intentional reflection of a key value of the church.

The church fully expects that there will be new visitors each week (and this has been the case for quite some time). Both the pastoral staff and the members have committed themselves to do whatever they can to make those visitors feel

---

[28]Many thanks to Pastor Dave Swaim for his kind permission to include this brief case study regarding the congregation he serves, Highrock Covenant Church of Arlington, Massachusetts.

welcome. This value is also reflected in the community meal that we serve between services each Sunday. This meal is a critical ritual for us, costing countless hours of volunteer service and a sizable chunk of our annual budget.

Still another ritual behavior based on the same value is the wearing of nametags. Our welcome ministers greet all newcomers at the front doors. Members and regular attenders have printed nametags that are reused and returned when they leave the facilities. Visitors are greeted warmly and given a temporary nametag. This is replaced with a permanent tag of their own upon their request. Such a ritual might seem problematic in some settings, but it has been very helpful in ours.

Some of the many rituals in our church are more obviously "spiritual" than those noted above and are based on our understanding of Scripture and our desire to connect with historical and global practices of the church. Some of our rituals are repeated weekly. Others are repeated monthly, such as our celebration of the Lord's Supper.[29] Still others are repeated annually. Each year we rehearse the Redemptive Story by paying attention to the church calendar, observing the seasons of Advent and Lent, for example. These practices have been increasingly meaningful for our members, most of whom have come from backgrounds where little attention was paid to the church year.

Some of our rituals occur irregularly, but frequently. We have testimonies, called "life stories," in our church once or twice per month. We also have a system for providing meals for families with new babies—another important ritual that reflects key values of the congregation.

Some of the rituals in any congregation occur without intentionality or perhaps reflect a certain ambivalence on the part of church leaders. As another reflection of my congregation's desire to be visitor-friendly, it became the church's practice to have the Scripture text for the sermon available in either printed or projected form. The expectation was that the visitors would not be bringing Bibles with them on Sunday. The unexpected outcome was that believers stopped bringing their Bibles. The church finally bought pew Bibles. No longer is the sermon's text projected for worshipers. They are invited to stand as the text is read and to "follow along in your own Bible or in one of the pew Bibles." It has become a familiar ritual now to see folks stand, open a pew Bible and follow along as the text is read. A second unintended part of the

---

[29]The church has recently begun a third service—on Sunday evenings—that features the same sermon and mostly the same songs as the two morning services. However, several features are different. Among these is the fact that the Lord's Supper is observed weekly, instead of monthly.

ritual has also emerged. As they are returning to their seats, most people close the pew Bible and put it away. It is seldom opened again during the course of the sermon. After all, once the sermon is underway, all biblical texts that are referred to will be projected. We stopped projecting texts during the Scripture reading but continued projecting texts while the sermon is preached.

I have used my home church to illustrate some of the possibilities and pitfalls of the use of ritual in congregational life. On balance, I find that our rituals sometimes serve us very well and other times less so. We have strong and healthy rituals related to welcoming newcomers, singing songs of heart-felt praise and adoration, serving one another and serving in acts of justice and mercy in our congregation. We also have a strong tradition of listening deeply to the thoughtful sermons we hear each week. We are growing well in our observance of the church year and drawing life from practices associated with it.

At the time of this writing, however, I think our congregation is less healthy in terms of our rituals relative to the Scripture texts themselves and in our intentional teaching of the Faith. We do not seem to have strong ritual commitments to intentional evangelism. We are not as strong in prayer as our leaders wish we were. I also wish that we were much more intentional about connecting with the historic hymns and confessions of the church. Still I rejoice that our church leaders are committed to ongoing evaluation of our rituals and that we have rejected any naive denial that we, like all congregations, are inherently and inescapably ritualistic people.

REFRESHING OUR RITUALS

There are times when the rituals of a congregation need to be refreshed. Before our Scripture reading, for example, members of our congregation rise to pray a corporate "Prayer for Illumination." At the close of our Scripture readings, we repeat a historically practiced refrain: "This is the word of the Lord," says the Scripture reader. "Thanks be to God!" the congregation replies. Over time, rituals like these can lose some of their significance in the minds of congregants. Occasional words of instruction about why we do such things can be helpful both for our members who need reminders and for newcomers who may wonder why we do such things. A word of explanation in the weekly "worship folder" or on the church's website can also help in this regard. It may be helpful to vary our rituals from time to time to keep us from falling into a relatively "mindless" ritualism. Church leaders should compare notes regularly to see which of the many ritual practices we perform may need such refreshing.

How else might our rituals be refreshed? It may be wise to throw a curveball at our people every once in a while. Have we been reciting the Lord's Prayer? Perhaps we can sing it for several weeks before returning to recitation. Have we been confessing the Apostles' Creed each week? It is wise to alternate occasionally with other creeds, such as the Nicene Creed or perhaps another form of faith affirmation. Biblical passages can be recited or adapted as faith confessions. Many churches have found it helpful to use questions and answers from a catechism as a form of affirming the faith. For example, the first question and answer from the Heidelberg Catechism offer congregants a beautiful summary of critical components of a Gospel-centric worldview:

> Question 1: What is your only comfort, in life and in death?
> Answer: That I am not my own, but belong—body and soul, in life and in death—to my faithful Savior, Jesus Christ. He has fully paid for all my sins with his precious blood, and has set me free from the tyranny of the devil. He also watches over me in such a way that not a hair can fall from my head without the will of my Father in heaven: in fact, all things must work together for my salvation.
>
> Because I belong to him, Christ, by his Holy Spirit, assures me of eternal life and makes me wholeheartedly willing and ready from now on to live for him.

Sometimes the most effective way to refresh a ritual is to suspend its usage temporarily. In many traditions, a dramatic form of something like this is practiced annually during the Lenten season. The word *Hallelujah,* or *Alleluia,* is removed from prayers, confessions and songs throughout the six weeks of Lent. During this season, the congregation reflects on the passion of the Christ and our role in that suffering because of our sin. This sober repentance is finally broken at the great Easter Vigil. At the pivotal moment in that service, the congregation cries out, "Christ is risen. Hallelujah! Hallelujah! He is risen indeed!" The stifled "Hallelujah" finally erupts after weeks of dormancy in an experience that can be very rich with meaning. In some churches, congregants come to the gathering equipped for the celebration—bringing with them bells, chimes, tambourines and other "joyful noise" makers.

Perhaps a church's music team can temporarily suspend the singing of a certain genre of songs, "contemporary choruses," for example. C. S. Lewis argued that for every book we read by a living author we ought to read one by an author who has passed away. A church could take such an approach to its hymnody—with a possible twist. A month could be set aside during which the church sings no songs written by composers who are still living.[30] Or a church could decide to sing all its songs without instrumental accompaniment for a week or more. Or the instrumentation could be dramatically altered for a season—from guitars and keyboards to a string or wind ensemble, for example. A choir could be assembled to lead the congregation in song, instead of the traditional "praise band" that typically leads.[31]

QUESTIONING OUR RITUALS

As we have seen, all congregations have their rituals—intentional or accidental, conscious or unconscious, thoughtful or thoughtless, full of meaning or lacking meaning. The question, then, is never "Do we observe rituals in our church?" The important questions concern the nature of our rituals and of their formative power—for good or for ill—in the life of the church. In the textbox on the next page we propose a number of questions that church leaders could explore together regarding the congregation's rituals.

RITUALS AND CHILDREN

The last of our questions reminds us that if we have segmented our meetings according to age, we may well be undermining the value of our rituals. In my experience, children often love ritual, both at home and in the wider gatherings of the church. When our daughter was very young, she refused to let us take a night off from the Advent traditions we had established. Years later, she still seems to expect and appreciate our dinnertime rituals that include (often, but not always) the singing of a family-composed song before the meal and Scripture reading and prayer after the meal. Other family rituals are also highly valued, everything from eating at our favorite restaurants to certain birthday traditions to singing together as we drive from place to place. Just as we said about the rituals of the church community, we should seek to be intentional about the rituals we develop in the home. These can also easily become unhealthy and unproductive, can lose their meaning and may need periodic refreshing.

In the worship gatherings of the church, rituals are full of formative poten-

---

[30]N. T. Wright suggested during a November 2008 chapel service at Gordon-Conwell that if the worship service is to have more than one song, the songs should be from more than one century. His comment provoked loud approval from many who were present.

[31]The use of the word *traditional* is ironic, but not inappropriate.

Questions Regarding Church Rituals

- Can we articulate a biblically informed rationale for our intentional rituals?

- How do our rituals connect us meaningfully to the one, holy, catholic, apostolic church?

- Do our rituals serve to unite the diverse elements of the congregation? How so? Might some rituals actually be divisive in the church? If so, what can be done about this?

- How do our rituals confirm, or disconfirm, the stated vision and values of the congregation?

- In what ways do our rituals seem to form us for good? In what ways do they seem to form us more for ill?

- In the eyes of most congregants, are our rituals filled with meaning? Do the worshipers know what the rituals represent? Are members encouraged to employ rituals in ways that not only involve outward expression but also engage their minds and hearts?

- Which of our rituals need "refreshing"? How might we aim to accomplish this?

- Which of our rituals should we seriously consider abandoning at this time? Why?

- Which rituals have we neglected that need new, or renewed, attention?

- How are we making our rituals accessible and meaningful for our children, youth and others who may need extra help toward understanding them?

tial for our children. Many years ago our family visited a local Episcopal church for Sunday-morning worship. Unlike the worship services we had been regularly experiencing at the time, here was a highly liturgical experience based on the liturgy of the *Book of Common Prayer*. All of us struggled to keep up with the ritual speech and actions of the service—standing one minute, sitting the next; now confessing our sins, now praying a corporate prayer of adoration—moving (too) rapidly back and forth between the worship folder and the prayer book. In many ways, it was a rich experience, for the liturgy was plainly steeped in biblical language. But my wife and I both found ourselves rather worn out by it all. Our daughter was a young elementary-school student at the time, and I was fairly sure that she was even more exasperated than her mother and I were. But no sooner had we climbed into our car than she exclaimed, "That was cool!"

As we debriefed, our daughter's comments began to make perfect sense. We had been attending a church in those days that offered no "children's worship," and I was very glad to have our daughter with us for the community's worship. But the worship was not really crafted for the whole community; it was designed for adults. That meant that our poor daughter sat through a service that included very few elements she could actually participate in. The sermon—which my wife and I both found very stimulating—was typically not at all suitable for our daughter, and so she was largely disengaged Sunday after Sunday. But this day she had been more involved than ever before. There were many things for her to say and do. She was a full participant. Even the sermon—which was too brief and too simple for my wife's and my tastes— had been very accessible for our daughter.

There are many worship rituals that can engage our children very meaningfully—if we allow them to do so. This requires several commitments. First, we must choose our rituals carefully. Second, we must invite our children to experience these rituals with us. And third, we must be sure that the rituals are as meaningful for our children as possible. In a church that has a simple liturgy, like the one our family now attends, we can still maximize the possibilities to welcome the children fully into the experience. Confessions, affirmations and songs that can be easily read or memorized are a great place to start. Personal testimonies are often very powerful for children. The sermon can address children and teens, as well as adults. Visual and tactile ritual acts like baptism and the Lord's Supper can be explained and, in ways appropriate to our various traditions, can be experienced or witnessed by children. For example, I have observed the following ritual of one church that practices infant baptism. Before the actual baptism of the baby being presented, the pastor calls all the children of the congregation forward and explains to them what they are about to witness, reminding them that most of them have already experienced this same event.

One particular aspect of formative ritual concerns rites of passage for children and youth. In Jewish tradition, rites of passage have been integral to education and formation and tied to a child's growth in wisdom.[32] In Catholic tradition, as well, rites of passage have long been a critical component of one's spiritual formation. Indeed, the seven sacraments recognized in the Church of Rome are tied to key rites of passage in the life of an individual.[33]

Many evangelicals have rejected such practices as unnecessary or even unhealthy. But such an attitude simply betrays, once more, our lack of wisdom. Where we fail to provide or give shape to meaningful and intentional rites of passage for our children, the surrounding market-driven culture will rush in with alternatives to fill the void. Thus we in North America have been shaped by the powerful social rituals surrounding a young girl turning "sweet sixteen," the prom for high-schoolers, engagements to be married, the multibillion-dollar wedding industry, the multibillion-dollar baby industry, and on and on. The need for meaningful rites of passage is inherent in our humanity, and the church is wise to address it. Thankfully, many evangelical churches have shown signs of helping us correct course in this regard.[34]

CONCLUSION

Old Testament scholar Bruce Waltke argues that the opposite of remembering is not forgetting, but *dis*membering. In the broad culture of our day, as well as in much contemporary church practice, we have been effectively dismembering our children by stripping them of the memories they so desperately need.[35] May God help us to repent in these areas and to more faithfully help our children take their places alongside us in the great Story that God is unfolding. May we reject the well-intentioned but deeply erroneous idea that "our children are the church of tomorrow" and come to see that they are every bit as much a part of today's church as are the adults. May we learn to pray together and play together, to worship together and work together across the generations. May we reject ungodly ageism on either end—laboring diligently in-

---

[32]For a highly accessible work on this and many other aspects of Judaism, see Robert Schoen, *What I Wish My Christian Friends Knew About Judaism* (Chicago: Loyola University Press, 2004).

[33]See "Part 2, The Sacraments: The Faith Celebrated," in *United States Catholic Catechism for Adults* (Washington, D.C.: United States Conference of Catholic Bishops, 2007).

[34]See, for example, Chris McNair, *Young Lions: Christian Rites of Passage for African American Young Men* (Nashville: Abingdon, 2001); Walker Moore, *Rite of Passage Parenting: Four Essential Experiences to Equip Your Kids for Life* (Nashville: Nelson, 2008).

[35]Bruce Waltke, "The Way of Wisdom from the Book of Proverbs," audiocassette (Vancouver: Regent Audio, 2002).

stead to marginalize neither our youngest nor our oldest members.[36] May we choose our rituals more carefully and keep them as full of meaning as possible for as many of our members as possible.

HYMN FOR CONTEMPLATION AND WORSHIP

Let the Children Come to Me

(Mk 10:13-16)

Let the children come to me.
Let them know my heart and mind.
Come, my children, taste and see
grace so good and love so kind.
All that you have known thus far—
ev'ry tear and ev'ry scar;
from such depths, new life shall spring.
I will loose your tongues to sing.

Let the children come to me.
Do not hinder them at all.
Let my words, alive and free,
on their hearts like manna fall.
Come, my children, take and eat:
words like honey, pure and sweet;
words to fill the hungry soul;
words of life to make you whole.

Let the children come to me.
Serve them well in deed and prayer
till my Son shall set them free,
making each a royal heir.
O my people, hear me now:
you have made a solemn vow.
Raise these young ones with great care,
or my righteous anger bear.

Let the children come to me
from the corners of the earth.

---

[36]The marginalization of older members is a growing crisis in our churches today. For discussions concerning this, please see Gary McIntosh, *One Church, Four Generations: Understanding and Reaching All Ages in Your Church* (Grand Rapids: Baker, 2002); James Knapp, *The Graying of the Flock: A New Model for Ministry* (Abilene, Tex.: Leafwood Publishers, 2003); Linda Vogel, *Rituals for Resurrection: Celebrating Life and Death* (Nashville: Upper Room, 1996).

By my Spirit, they must be
offspring of a second birth.
In each nation, tribe and tongue,
let this song of hope be sung:
"Jesus loves me, this I know,
for the Bible tells me so."

Text: Gary A. Parrett (2002)
Tune: Aberystwyth; Alt: Martyn
Familiar use of the tunes: "Jesus, Lover of My Soul"

QUESTIONS FOR PLANNING AND PRAXIS

1. In what ways does your church embrace the "homogenous unit principle" as outlined on page 307? After reading this chapter, has your understanding or attitude toward this principle changed? If so, how?

2. How do you plan on nurturing children in the Faith within the larger context of the body of Christ? What intergenerational teaching-learning experiences can you create that will enhance the formation of children, give older church members the opportunity to teach and model for children, and allow older members, in turn, to be affected for good by children?

3. Psalm 78 reminds us to teach our children: "I will open my mouth in parables; I will utter hidden things, things from of old—what we have heard and known, what our fathers have told us. We will not hide them from their children; we will tell the next generation the praiseworthy deeds of the LORD, his power, and the wonders that he has done" (Ps 78:2-4). It speaks also of the statutes God has given us to teach our children. Thinking of your own faith community, discuss with a ministry partner how you might better implement the wisdom of this psalm in your context?

4. Sometimes rituals in the church serve us very well. At other times they do not. For example, churches may be strong in welcoming newcomers and singing songs of worship to God, but weaker in their rituals of intentional teaching of the Faith. How can you, as a church leader, commit to the ongoing evaluation of—and, as needed, making changes in—your church's rituals?

5. With another person in educational ministry in your church, we invite you to reflect on the intentional rituals used in your church. Do you have a biblically informed rational for such rituals? How do they connect you to

the larger body of Christ? Are they filled with meaning known by the congregants? Most importantly, are they accessible and meaningful to the children in your congregation?

6. What are your thoughts concerning children's rites of passage in the church? Are there rituals to recover that have been lost by modern evangelicalism? We invite you to prayerfully reflect on these matters and how they can potentially become an integral part of educational ministry in your church.

RESOURCES FOR FURTHER STUDY

Dawn, Marva. *Is It a Lost Cause? Having the Heart of God for the Church's Children*. Grand Rapids: Eerdmans, 1997.

Dean, Kenda Creasy. *Practicing Passion: Youth and the Quest for a Passionate Church*. Grand Rapids: Zondervan, 2006.

DeVries, Mark. *Family-Based Youth Ministry*. Rev. ed. Downers Grove, Ill.: InterVarsity Press, 2004.

Garber, Steve. *The Fabric of Faithfulness: Weaving Together Belief and Behavior*. Downers Grove, Ill.: InterVarsity Press, 2007.

Garland, Diana. *Family Ministry: A Comprehensive Guide*. Downers Grove, Ill.: InterVarsity Press, 1999.

Howe, Neil, and William Strauss. *Millennials Rising: The Next Great Generation*. New York: Vintage, 2000.

Posterski, Beth, Linda Cannell, Catherine Stonehouse and Scottie May. *Children Matter: Celebrating Their Place in the Church, Family, and Community*. Grand Rapids: Eerdmans, 2005.

Scazzero, Peter. *Emotionally Healthy Churches: A Strategy for Discipleship That Actually Changes Lives*. Grand Rapids: Zondervan, 2003.

Smith, Christian. *Soul Searching: The Religious and Spiritual Lives of American Teenagers*. New York: Oxford University Press, 2005.

Stonehouse, Catherine. *Joining Children on the Spiritual Journey: Nurturing a Life of Faith*. Grand Rapids: Baker, 1998.

Vanderwell, Howard. *The Church of All Ages: Generations Worshipping Together*. Herndon, Va.: The Alban Institute, 2008.

Westerhoff, John H., III. *Will Our Children Have Faith?* New York: Morehouse, 2000.

Wuthnow, Robert. *After the Baby Boomers: How Twenty-and Thirty-Somethings Are Shaping the Future of American Religion*. Princeton, N.J.: Princeton University Press, 2007.

12

When You Come Together

Worship and Formation

What shall we say, brothers? When you come together, everyone has a hymn,
or a word of instruction, a revelation, a tongue or an interpretation.
All of these must be done for the strengthening of the church.

1 CORINTHIANS 14:26

▼

I DO NOT REMEMBER ANYTHING FROM THAT FINAL worship service—except the last thing we did. Hundreds of us spread out and stood against the walls of the sanctuary and were asked to join hands with one another. We then lifted our voices in an emotional singing of the chorus "We Are One in the Bond of Love." When we finished our singing, hugs and tears were everywhere. The ending of the song was not only the ending of the service. The church that I (as a teenager and new believer) had come to know and love also ceased to exist that day. This Sunday had been designated as our last service together.

The church, like so many North American congregations in the 1970s, had experienced an awful split over issues related to the charismatic movement and the so-called worship wars. For the most part, older folks would stay behind and try to recapture "church" as they had once known it, and younger folks would form a new church to follow the "movement of the Spirit." Generations of families would not henceforth worship with one another again. Over time, I became very struck by the irony and (it now seems clear to me) hypocrisy of our final song. We were *not* "one in the bond of love." I was still bearing those scars when, several years later, I preached my first sermon in a local church setting. My text was John 13:34-35, "A new commandment I give you: Love one another." In one way or another, I have been preaching the same message ever since.

Without question, one of the most powerfully formative things that a church does together is to engage in worship as a community. Worship always forms its participants—for good or for ill. Historically, worship has been considered to be one of the "three great tasks of the church," together with evangelism (and other forms of outreach in the world) and teaching (nurturing, forming believers).

Understood biblically, worship is a lifestyle commitment of every believer, the offering of our full selves in obedient love and service of the living God (see Rom 12:1). It is our proper and appropriate response to God's gracious revelation of himself, of his redemptive work on our behalf and of his present will for our lives. Worship is a call to do justly, love mercy and walk humbly with our God (see Mic 6:8). We are to worship God in spirit and truth (see Jn 4:23-24), at all times and in all places. One vital expression of our perpetual worship of God is joining together with others as an assembly of worshipers. Paul sometimes speaks of such occasions by use of the phrase "when you come together" (1 Cor 11:18, 20, 33; 14:23).

Our congregational worship gatherings must be first and foremost about the worship of the living God. We dare not turn these services into primarily evangelistic events. Several authors have sounded this warning in recent years. Marva Dawn, for example, has been especially outspoken about this.[1] Some might charge, however, that Dawn herself falls into a similar problem, focusing so much on the formative power of worship that she muddies the line between worship and Christian formation. In other words, we may ask, is Dawn guilty of turning congregational worship into a primarily educational or formative experience? Dawn writes often of her concern about the kind of Christians we are producing in our worship services. Are we, in our commitments to an evangelistic "reaching out," guilty of seriously "dumbing down" the Faith and thus hindering the formation of believers? Michael Horton has made a similar lament, asserting that many of our efforts to reach out to the unchurched have actually been far more effective at "unchurching the churched."[2]

---

[1]See especially Marva Dawn, *Reaching Out Without Dumbing Down* (Grand Rapids: Eerdmans, 1995), and *A Royal "Waste" of Time: The Splendor of Worshiping God and Being the Church for the World* (Grand Rapids: Eerdmans, 1999).

[2]See especially chapters ten, eleven and twelve in Michael Horton, *A Better Way: Rediscovering*

In her book *Teaching That Transforms: Worship as the Heart of Christian Education,*[3] Debra Dean Murphy might also be charged with blurring the lines between worship and formation. Murphy focuses a good deal of her attention on the ancient practice of catechesis. Her central argument seems to be that, since the primary venue for the catechumenate of old was actually the liturgy of the church, contemporary educators would be wise to follow suit. Yet, while Murphy is correct in her identification of the liturgy as the central venue for ancient catechesis, we must also acknowledge the historic commitment to other aspects of the catechetical experiences that go beyond the liturgy, including rigorously didactic experiences, especially in preparation for baptism. Furthermore, by setting forth the liturgy as so formative an experience, Murphy may unintentionally leave the reader with the impression that its primary value is in the formation of believers rather than in the worship of God.

What are we to make of such concerns about the work of Dawn, Horton, Murphy and others? Have they overstated the formative role of congregational worship? If they have, we would argue that what they have done is not as serious a problem as that of turning congregational worship into evangelistic outreach. But such a statement requires some explanation.

THREE GREAT TASKS OF THE CHURCH

We have stated that there are three great tasks churches consistently engage in: worship, formation (or teaching) and outreach (evangelism, or work and witness in the world). But as we have seen, these tasks overlap and each directly impinges on the other. We may picture their interrelationships as in figure 12.1. The three circles—representing the three tasks—are presented as overlapping. Note that the area of overlap between worship and formation is larger than that between worship and evangelism.

While the worship of the living God must always be the first agenda for our gatherings of worship, it would not be wholly improper to suggest that there are secondary concerns that are appropriate as well. Consider, for example, Paul's extended instructions regarding the worship gatherings in Corinth, as recorded in 1 Corinthians 11—14. His concern throughout this section is, as we have already said, for those times "when you come together."

---

the *Drama of God-Centered Worship* (Grand Rapids: Baker, 2003).
[3]Debra Dean Murphy, *Teaching That Transforms: Worship as the Heart of Christian Education* (Grand Rapids: Brazos, 2004).

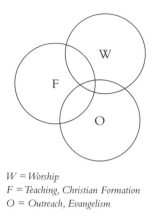

W = Worship
F = Teaching, Christian Formation
O = Outreach, Evangelism

Figure 12.1. Worship, formation and outreach

Thus he speaks at length about various worship practices that are to be exercised in the gatherings of God's people, including the celebration of the Lord's Supper, the use of the various spiritual gifts, the reading of Scriptures, the singing of hymns and so on. But although these gatherings aim primarily at giving God the worship he is due, Paul never loses sight of both the formative and the evangelistic impact of these gatherings.

In the first place, Paul mentions that everything done in these meetings is to be done for the building up of the entire body. He therefore harshly criticizes their practice of what they were calling "the Lord's Supper" (1 Cor 11:20). Rather than building up the body, the Corinthian practices were, at this point and others, doing "more harm than good" (1 Cor 11:17). Rich members of the congregation apparently were despising and shaming those members of the church "who have nothing" (1 Cor 11:21-22). They were failing to recognize that they were, together, the body of the Lord (see 1 Cor 11:29; compare 1 Cor 10:16-17). The whole process was being done "in an unworthy manner" and causing great harm in the congregation (1 Cor 11:27, 30-32).

The exercise of their spiritual gifts also was off the mark. The gift of tongues becomes the focus of Paul's critique at this point. This gift—which Paul himself utilized "more than all of you" (1 Cor 14:18)—had become quite prized among the Corinthians. But the "haves" were apparently looking down on the "have nots" (1 Cor 12:30), and the gift was being exercised in ways that might have been personally edifying but were not helpful for the body as a whole. Without interpretation, Paul argued, the gift of tongues could not prove edifying for the gathered assembly (see 1 Cor 14:6-17). Thus he asserted that he—when "in the church"—would "rather speak five intelligible words . . . than ten thousand words in a tongue" in order that he might instruct (literally, *catechize*) others (1 Cor 14:19).

Likewise Paul did not lose sight of the impact of the assemblies on unbelievers who might be present. Again, his reflections on uninterpreted tongues are the focal point for his remarks. If the church is gathered together, he writes, and all are speaking in tongues without interpretation, "and some who do not understand or some unbelievers come in, will they not say that you are out of your mind?" (1 Cor 14:23). Paying attention to the impact of our worship gatherings for both formation and evangelism, then, does not represent unfaithfulness. What matters, it seems to us, is that our agendas be properly ordered.

Thus we suggest that while worshiping God is the proper and primary agenda for Christian gatherings of worship, the formation of believers is an altogether appropriate secondary agenda for such meetings. This is evident from the history of worship as recorded in both the Old and New Testaments. Whenever we see reference to the worship gatherings of God's people, it seems clear that the gatherings functioned as a means of encounter between God and his people. In this encounter, God was to be worshiped *and* the people were to be formed. Formation is an essential, even if a secondary, purpose of the meetings.

On the other hand, evangelizing in the context of community worship is a more peripheral concern in Scripture. While there may be God-fearing "outsiders" present at the worship gatherings, the meeting was never to be "about" them,[4] although their presence was certainly to be noted (more on this later, under the heading of "Access to the Glorious Gospel" in the chapter thirteen).

WORSHIP AND CHRISTIAN FORMATION

That the formation of God's people is a legitimate concern of our worship gatherings can be demonstrated by appeal to a number of biblical passages. First of all, worship itself is presented as intrinsically formative—for good or for ill. We read in several Old Testament passages, for example, that those who

---

[4]Nor, again, is worship primarily "about" believers. The primary purpose of corporate worship is the worship of the triune God. When we "seek first his kingdom and his righteousness" in our corporate worship, "all these things will be added to" us, including his presence and all we need to worship him continually in the course of our lives (Mt 6:33).

worship idols are doomed to become like the objects of their worship.[5] In Psalm 115:4-8, we read of the idols, their makers and their worshipers:

> But their idols are silver and gold, made by the hands of men. They have mouths, but cannot speak, eyes, but they cannot see; they have ears, but cannot hear, noses, but they cannot smell; they have hands, but cannot feel, feet, but they cannot walk; nor can they utter a sound with their throats. Those who make them will be like them, and so will all who trust in them.

The same idea is expressed in Psalm 135, as well as in prophetic passages like Jeremiah 10 and Isaiah 44. In the New Testament, as well, we are alerted to the tragic possibility that our gatherings for worship can sometimes do the participants more harm than good (see 1 Cor 11:17, 30).

That which is true in such profoundly negative and destructive ways, however, is also true in the positive. In other words, those who worship the living God will become like the object of their worship. Those who abide in the presence of the Lord, reflecting or contemplating his glory, are "transformed into his likeness with ever-increasing glory, which comes from the Lord, who is the Spirit" (2 Cor 3:18). Worshiping the God who is love, who is holy and righteous and true, we shall ourselves become more loving, holy, righteous and true.

We find further biblical evidence that instructional and formational elements are not only permissible in worship, they are mandated. The Jewish celebration of Passover, as with all the holy festivals, might justly be classified as a part of that people's *cultus*—acts of worship by which they communed with the Lord their God. Ritual behavior for the observance of this event is detailed in Exodus, Leviticus, Numbers and Deuteronomy. It is an act of worship, but it is clearly to be an educational and formative experience as well. Children's questions about the meaning of the ceremony were to be answered with such ends plainly in view:

> "And when your children ask you, 'What does this ceremony mean to you?' then tell them, 'It is the Passover sacrifice to the LORD, who passed over the house of the Israelites in Egypt and spared our homes when he struck down the Egyptians.'" Then the people bowed down and worshiped. (Ex 12:26-27)

Is the Passover festival, then, an act of worship or of formation? It is quite obviously both. Similar Old Testament examples are found in pas-

---

[5]For a full exploration of this, see Greg Beale, *We Become What We Worship: A Biblical Theology of Idolatry* (Downers Grove, Ill.: InterVarsity Press, 2008).

sages such as Exodus 13:8, 14, and Joshua 4:4-7.

In the New Testament, we find a similar both/and principle at work. There is the account in Acts 20, of the believers gathering "on the first day of the week . . . to break bread" (Acts 20:7). Most scholars accept that this was precisely one of those "when you come together" episodes Paul had described in his Corinthian correspondence.[6] The believers had gathered on the Lord's Day for worship that included the celebration of the Lord's Supper. "Paul spoke to the people," we read, "and, because he intended to leave the next day, kept on talking until midnight" (Acts 20:7). It is evident that he felt instruction to be a component vital to this worship gathering.

Aside from the earlier Pauline references we noted in 1 Corinthians 11—14, we can also consider his commands to both the Ephesian and Colossian churches about their hymnody:

> Let the word of Christ dwell in you richly as you teach and admonish one another with all wisdom, and as you sing psalms, hymns and spiritual songs with gratitude in your hearts to God. (Col 3:16)

> Instead, be filled with the Spirit. Speak to one another with psalms, hymns and spiritual songs. Sing and make music in your heart to the Lord. (Eph 5:18-19)

In view of these two passages, we may well ask, to whom were the believers to direct their singing? On the one hand, their hearts were to be filled with praise "to God," "to the Lord." But, simultaneously, their hymnody was a form of speaking "to one another." By means of that "speaking," the community would experience in greater measure the fullness of both "the word of Christ" and "the Spirit."

Our hymnody, it turns out, is both worship offered to God and instruction, or exhortation, directed to one another. The fact is, even if the songs we sing are directed Godward, the words leaving our lips also fall on the ears of all those present, including our own. We are all formed—again, for good or for ill—by what we say and sing in our gatherings. This being quite evidently the case, we ought to be very thoughtful about our selections for song, as well as for all the other liturgical elements of our gathering.

Worship, then, should be both God-honoring and church-edifying. How does Christian worship actually form its participants? In many ways, as the textbox on pages 342-43 illustrates.

---

[6]John Stott, *The Message of Acts,* The Bible Speaks Today Commentary (Downers Grove, Ill.: InterVarsity Press, 1990), pp. 319-20.

Formational Effects of Christian Worship

- Our minds are renewed by truth—as God's Word is read and exposited—leading us toward conformity to Christlikeness rather than conformity to the world's pattern (see Rom 12:1-2).

- Truth is spoken by the people of God to one another in psalms, hymns and spiritual songs (see Eph 5:18-20; Col 3:16) and helps worshipers toward greater experience of the fullness of the word of Christ (see Col 3:16) and of the Holy Spirit (see Eph 5:18-20).

- The Spirit is present among God's people in liberating power, transforming us into Christlikeness, from glory to glory (see 2 Cor 3:17-18).

- The Lord is especially present when his people gather in his name (see Mt 18:20; Ps 22:3).

- Our participation in the Lord's Supper is a participation in Christ's body and blood (see 1 Cor 10:16-17; 11:26-29).

- Our vision is clarified and corrected, and we begin to see things as they truly are, not as they appear to be (see Ps 73).

- All the rituals of worship shape our understanding of reality, of the Story in which we live. This is part of the reason why observance of redemptive history by means of holy days and festivals can be so powerfully formative.

- Space for listening to the Lord to receive his direction and instruction is opened among us (see Acts 13:1-3).

- The rhythm of revelation and response gives shape to our lives (see Is 6:1-8; compare Rom 12:1). As we worship, God's person, work and will[a] are revealed among us in greater measure, and we are called toward more faithful response at each point.

---

[a]In the Isaiah 6 passage, God's unfolding revelation to Isaiah includes at least these three features: (1) something about who God is in essence ("holy, holy, holy"); (2) something about God's redeeming work on behalf of the sinner ("your sin is atoned for"); and (3) something about God's present will for Isaiah ("Whom shall we send? Who will go for us?"). We suggest including each of these three elements in worship gatherings.

- Worship teaches us how to pray and praise, how to lament, confess and much more. The words of our songs and confessions work their way into our souls via our mouths, ears and eyes. Repetition helps us to retain these words and gives us a vocabulary for life and worship for those times when we are *not* gathered with God's people but are on our own at home, at work, in our neighborhoods and so on.

- Worship teaches us not only how to think but also how to feel and what to desire. That is, it shapes both our intellects and our affections. Further, as implied above, worship shapes us physically, teaching us how to use our speech to bless both God and neighbor (and thus avoid the error identified in Jas 3:9-10), how to kneel before the King of kings, how to lift our hands to praise God and extend them to embrace our brothers and sisters, and more.

QUESTIONS FOR LEADERS OF CONGREGATIONAL WORSHIP

As we have seen, the worship gatherings of the community are powerfully formative—for good or for ill. To a great extent, of course, we must respect the sovereign work of the Spirit in making the final difference between the good or the ill we speak of. But as the Scriptures do not hesitate to offer counsel about what should happen when we gather, it is clear that those who design and lead services of worship are obligated to do so as thoughtfully and faithfully as possible. It has been said of Augustine that "he liturgized catechetically."[7] The expression reminds us that Augustine seized opportunities to let the worship of the saints be as instructional and formative as possible. The questions and suggestions below are offered in this Augustinian spirit.

To reiterate, the triune God and his glory must ever be the preeminent concern in the design of our worship. While we can justly concern ourselves

---

[7]"Augustine the liturgist and sacramental theologian was at one and the same time Augustine the catechist; and it was precisely as catechist that he did his liturgical and sacramental ruminating. He liturgized catechetically; that is, publicly, orally." William J. Harmless, *Augustine and the Catechumenate* (Collegeville, Minn.: Liturgical Press, 1995), p. 338.

with questions about formation and evangelistic significance, we do not let
such issues predominate our thinking. To do so is to veer off course. Matters
of substance as well as matters of style cannot simply be regarded as matters of
personal or group preference. Rather, we ought to be diligent students of
what God has said that he requires and desires in and through our worship.
There is much guidance in Scripture regarding these points.[8]

Having established what our priority is and must be, we should indeed ask
the questions "How is our worship forming us?" and "What can be done—
without in any way compromising our primary calling in worship—to help
ensure that our worship forms us for good, rather than for ill?" These sorts of
questions ought to be asked continually by church leaders. In light of what we
have seen above about how worship does, in fact, form its participants, we
suggest attention to the following questions.[9]

Is our worship Scripture-saturated? Worship always involves a rhythm of
revelation and response. Since Scripture is the record both of what God has
revealed to us and of what God requires of us, we must use generous portions
of Scripture in our services. It is very evident that this was the case in biblical
worship and in the ancient church. Sadly, many evangelical churches that
pride themselves on being "Bible churches" actually feature minimal amounts
of Scripture in their services. There may well be a fine expository sermon
based on a few verses of a biblical passage. But are those the only verses of
Scripture the congregation will hear on that particular Lord's Day?

From descriptions of the worship gatherings of the ancient church, we
know that there was a good deal of Scripture read in the assemblies of believers. This was driven, in part, by the fact that worshipers did not commonly
own copies of the Bible, and some would not have been able to read them in
any case. In our day, we might reason, our church members likely own multiple copies of the Bible and can utilize them in their own personal devotional
life. Even if this is true for some of those in attendance on a Sunday morning,
can we really assume that they are regularly reading large portions of Scripture? What of those for whom this is not the case? What about visitors who

---

[8]We have found the following books to be particularly helpful in summing up the biblical teaching in these regards: David Peterson, *Engaging with God: A Biblical Theology of Worship* (Downers
Grove, Ill.: InterVarsity Press, 2002); James Torrance, *Worship, Community and the Triune God of
Grace* (Downers Grove, Ill.: InterVarsity Press, 1997); and Robert Webber, *Ancient-Future Worship: Proclaiming and Enacting God's Narrative* (Grand Rapids: Baker, 2008).
[9]For another exploration of related issues, see Gary Parrett, "9.5 Theses on Worship: A disputa-
tion on the role of music," *Christianity Today,* February 2005. See <http://www.ctlibrary.com/
ct/2005/february/3.38.html>.

may never read the Bible on their own and perhaps do not even have a copy? What about those who are illiterate?

Furthermore, shall we dismiss the biblical models and mandates simply because there are more copies of the Scriptures available to us these days? This seems to us both unwise and unfaithful. Paul commanded Timothy to devote himself "to the public reading of Scripture, to preaching and to teaching" (1 Tim 4:13). In our day, with so many fine Christian books available, as well as video and audio recordings of sermons and teaching, not to mention the virtually unlimited resources now available online, some might make the case that we do not need to gather at all to hear good preaching and teaching. Would we dismiss these practices because of our new technologies? Thankfully, most churches have not yet been inclined to do so. Why then would we make such an argument about the public reading of Scripture?

Though God's Word ought to be faithfully proclaimed and explained by gifted preachers and teachers, those who can do so well should also read it publicly. Do we believe that God's Word is living and powerful in its own right? If we do, then we will read it and let it speak. Hearing God's Word read publicly may well allow it to speak into our ears, minds and hearts in ways that do not happen through our personal and silent readings or through our hearing as "assisted" by the gifts of preachers and teachers.

Ezra read the book of the Torah to God's people from sunrise until midday (both he and the people apparently standing during the entire reading). He stood on a large platform constructed for that very occasion, so that he could be seen and better heard as well. This extended public reading was followed by exposition and explanation. The people's responses to this twofold experience of God's Word indicate that this *reading plus explanation* was a potent combination (see Neh 8:1-12).

Churches can increase the amount of exposure to and participation with the Scriptures in numerous ways. An obvious and very helpful strategy is to employ one of the various lectionaries that are available.[10] These are typically designed to ensure that broad and coherent exposure to the Scriptures is experienced in congregational worship over a given period, such as one year or three years. Other churches—especially those that are less formally liturgical

---

[10]The most popular being *The Book of Common Prayer: An Administration of the Sacraments and Other Rites and Ceremonies of the Church* (New York: Church Publishing, 2001). Also, *Revised Common Lectionary Prayers: Proposed by the Consultation on Common Texts* (Minneapolis: Augsburg, 2002); and *The Revised Common Lectionary: Consultation on Common Texts: Includes Complete List of Lections for Years A, B, and C* (Nashville: Abingdon, 1992).

in their tradition of worship—can simply complement the sermon text for the day with related readings from the other Testament. If the sermon is based on a New Testament passage, a related passage from the Old Testament can be read as well. Scripture's presence in our midst can also be increased through other elements of the liturgy: responsive readings, corporate prayers and confessions, the singing of psalms and other Scripture portions, and so on.

Is our worship Christocentric? Another way we can attend to the revelation-and-response rhythm of worship is to focus our worship on the person and work of Jesus Christ. As we have seen, Christ is the perfect revelation of the unseen God. By focusing our worship on him, all three of the features of revelation that we mentioned above—who God is, what God has done for us and what God is calling us to do—become clearer. Indeed, Christian worship ought always to involve "celebrating the saving work of Christ."[11] In fact, if we remove the Gospel from the heart of our worship, our worship itself will cease to be distinctively Christian worship.

But Christ is not only the perfect revelation of God; he is also the model for our faithful response to God's revelation. During the days of his life on earth, Jesus modeled for us in every way the proper human response to God. He sought his Father always, obeyed his Father's commands, walked in the Way of the Lord and fulfilled the ministry that was given him to do. Focusing our worship on Jesus Christ then enhances our experience as worshipers in terms of both revelation and response. Thus our worship becomes more powerfully formative for good, helping us be transformed more fully into the Lord's likeness, from glory to glory, by the Spirit (see 2 Cor 3:17-18).

How can we be more Christocentric in our congregational worship? More faithful attention to the Scriptures—the point we argued for above—will surely help with this concern, for the Scriptures testify to Christ (see Lk 24:27; Jn 5:49). It is also critical that our preaching be Gospel-centered. We must resolve with Paul "to know nothing" in our preaching and teaching except Jesus Christ crucified (see 1 Cor 1:23; Gal 3:1). This does not mean that we focus on only a few texts of Scripture that seem obviously Christocentric. It means that we understand that all the Scriptures, as we saw in the references above, point us to Christ. This understanding must affect, even transform, our entire approach to preaching.[12]

---

[11]See Robert E. Webber, *Worship: Old and New,* rev. ed. (Grand Rapids: Zondervan, 1994).

[12]See Sidney Greidanus, *Preaching Christ from the Old Testament: A Contemporary Hermeneutical Method* (Grand Rapids: Eerdmans, 1999); Bryan Chapell, *Christ-Centered Preaching: Redeeming the Expository Sermon* (Grand Rapids: Baker, 1994); Christopher Wright, *Knowing Jesus Through*

Observing at least a simplified version of the church calendar can also help us to exalt Christ in our worship. The church year provides an effective means of retelling the great Story of God's reconciling and redemptive work, of which Jesus Christ is the central figure. Following the lectionary readings from Advent through Pentecost, for example, helps ensure that both our public reading of Scripture and the texts we exposit are clearly presenting this Christocentric drama over the course of several months and are doing so on an annual basis.[13]

Our hymnody also should be Christ-focused. Whether we are singing "contemporary choruses" or "traditional hymns,"[14] we should follow the pattern of the church for two millennia by singing continually of the Savior. This commitment can be seen even in the writings of the New Testament, where we perhaps find evidence of some of the earliest Christian hymns.[15] Finally, we celebrate Christ well by observing the sacraments regularly. Baptism and the Lord's Supper are both Christ-centered and Christ-exalting rituals.

Is our worship trinitarian—both explicitly and implicitly? It is a wonderful gift to the church that so much recent attention has been paid to developing or recovering a robust trinitarian theology and to considering its implications for the life and ministry of the church.[16] All of the divine work—from creation to redemption to culmination—is accomplished by the triune God revealed to us in the Bible. Our worship, therefore, must be explicitly trinitarian. James B. Torrance has offered the following definition of worship, which we find pregnant with insight: "Worship is the gift of participating through the Spirit in the incarnate Son's communion with the Father."[17]

Our worship is intentionally and explicitly trinitarian when we acknowledge that it is in Christ and through the Spirit that we have communion with the living God. We ought to regularly acknowledge the Persons of the Godhead in our worship. We address our prayers primarily to the Father, since this is how most biblical prayers are addressed. But we do not hesitate to pray to

---

the Old Testament (Downers Grove, Ill.: InterVarsity Press, 1992).

[13]See Robert Webber, *Ancient-Future Time: Forming Spirituality Through the Christian Year* (Grand Rapids: Baker, 2004).

[14]Both of these terms, though very common, are misleading.

[15]Femi Adedeji, "An Analysis of Selected New Testament Hymns," *Asian Theological Journal* 17, no. 2 (October 2003): 301-14; Ralph Martin, "Hymns in the New Testament: An Evolving Pattern of Worship Responses," *Ex Auditu*, August 1992, pp. 33-44.

[16]See Roderick Leupp, *The Renewal of Trinitarian Theology: Themes, Patterns and Explorations* (Downers Grove, Ill.: InterVarsity Press, 2008).

[17]Torrance, *Worship, Community*, p. 30.

the Son and to the Spirit as well, since we find evidence in Scripture indicating that such prayers can be valid.[18] We "name" the Trinity in our hymns as well and in our confessions, readings and other elements of our liturgical design. Furthermore, we faithfully proclaim and teach the biblical doctrine of the triune God through our preaching and teaching and in our administration of the sacraments.

Beyond such practices for explicitly trinitarian worship, we should also be attentive to implicit features of our worship and what we are communicating about God by *how* we worship. The tri-unity of God reveals to us that God is, in himself, a loving community of diversity in unity. Is this truth being illustrated, incarnated, in our worship gatherings? We ask this in regard to both the assembly itself and the way the assembly is led in worship. Regarding the assembly itself, does the congregation reflect this trinitarian notion of unity in diversity? Or is that diversity suppressed or discouraged? Is unity rejected in favor of uniformity?[19]

In regard to the leading of congregational worship, is place given for a diversity of gifts and personalities? In a congregation of several hundred, are there many whose gifts are consistently and systematically ignored, given no opportunity for expression? Of course, not all are gifted for leadership in assembled worship. Most persons in the church have primary giftings that are best expressed when the church is dispersed throughout the week. On the other hand, there are often many in our churches who could contribute in significant ways but are never given the opportunity to do so. This can be exacerbated in churches where "the guitars beat the organs in the worship wars."[20] In some congregations, one part of the fallout of this is that a forty-person choir has given way to a five-person band. A few new instruments may now be used that previously were not, but others are likely no longer heard in the services. Often people have been marginalized in the process. The points we are trying to raise here involve other of our questions, and this should become clear as we press on to address those below.

Does our worship feature whole-person participation of the whole community? The issue of "imaging" the tri-unity of God in our worship is related to this fourth question regarding congregational participation. Worship is in-

---

[18]See, for example, John 14:13-14; Acts 13:1-4 (cf. 2 Cor 3:17-18; 12:8).

[19]For fuller exploration of these questions, please see our previous work *A Many Colored Kingdom*.

[20]As discussed earlier, Michael Hamilton, "The Triumph of the Praise Songs: How Guitars Beat out the Organ in the Worship Wars," *Christianity Today,* July 12, 1999, pp. 29-35.

tended to be a participatory act of the people of God. This was plainly the case with Old Testament worship.[21] In the New Testament, as well, we read that everyone was to bring something to the gathering for the good of the whole (see 1 Cor 14:26). As we saw earlier, Paul wrote also of the importance of the congregation's ministry to one another in singing and teaching (see Col 3:16; Eph 5:19-20). There is also the exercise of the various spiritual gifts that Paul mentions in 1 Corinthians 12 and 14, and in Romans 12. In response to what is shared through these various gifts, the people are to respond to what they have heard in the services by saying "the Amen" (1 Cor 14:16; 2 Cor 1:20).

Too often, worship services in our churches reduce congregants to passive observers rather than active participants. Our aim should be that the whole assembly is actively engaged in the worship of God and that they are encouraged to bless the Lord with all that is within them (see Ps 103:1)—hearts, souls, minds and strength (see Mk 12:29-31). God is worthy of all that we have, and nothing should be held back. It is the whole person that needs to be transformed into the likeness of Christ. We offer him the raw materials of our cognition and affections. Our thinking, our willing and our emotions are all fallen and in need of being more wholly reconciled to God. It was, we remember, the *believers* in Corinth whom Paul was urging to "be reconciled to God" (2 Cor 5:20). Because we are not yet living fully for the one who died for us and rose again (see 2 Cor 5:15), we place all that is within us before the Lord and ask him to change us further into his likeness as we worship him.

Our bodies, too, are called into action. Our ears hear, our eyes watch, our lips speak and sing and shout and close shut. We lift our hands and clap our hands. We bend our knees to kneel and straighten them to stand. We greet one another with our voices, our eyes and with a handshake, hug or holy kiss. The postures of worship are important in Scripture, but we often fail to pay attention to this matter in our churches. One wonders, for example, what is happening in the hearts and minds of worshipers when they sing praises or recite confessions of the Faith while their hands are buried in their pants pockets or when, during the sermon, they sit leaning back in the pews with arms folded across their chests.

Is our preaching potent—biblically sound, taking aim at the idols, false isms

---

[21]See "The Gift of Liturgy," chap. 16 in Bruce Waltke, *An Old Testament Theology: An Exegetical, Canonical, and Thematic Approach* (Grand Rapids: Zondervan, 2007). In the chapter, while expounding a biblical theology of the book of Exodus, Waltke develops a theology of worship-liturgy in a thematic manner as well, discussing the participatory nature of worship in the Old Testament.

and evil practices of the culture? Does the preaching demonstrate a comprehen-
sive concern—at times evangelistic, at times exhortational, at times confronta-
tional and at times catechetical? It is easy to make any number of mistakes in
regard to our ministries of preaching. On the one hand, we can overvalue the
role of the sermon in such a way as to suggest that it is the only vital part of
the worship experience, everything else being treated as mere filler. On the
other hand, we can treat the sermon as an awkward and not particularly vital
element in what would otherwise be an "exciting" service of "worship." This
may happen where the word *worship* has been reduced to a synonym for singing songs of praise. Sermons may also be seen as relatively insignificant for
worshipers in churches that fix all attention on the Eucharist.

In any type of service, the sermon can and should be a powerful element
for expositing and declaring "the whole counsel of God" (Acts 20:27 ESV).
This calls us, once again, to a disciplined approach toward expositing all the
Scriptures, and not only those books and passages that the pastor may find
especially intriguing or easiest or safest to handle. Paying attention to the
broad range of biblical emphases will mean that some sermons will be largely
evangelistic, others largely exhortational. Some will be confrontational in
nature and others catechetical. On the one hand, our sermons should be
largely *con*structive as we grow and exalt a vision of the Truth, the Life and
the Way of the Lord, leading people ever deeper in the Gospel. But our
preaching must also be *de*structive—taking relentless aim at the false isms, the
idols and the evil practices of the age.

Tragically, it too often happens that such influences are not sufficiently
confronted or, worse, are actually affirmed in the name of the Lord. If the
pastor is more interested in winning approval from the congregation than
from God, such things may be inevitable. May the day come soon when such
accolades as "Nice sermon, pastor" and "I really enjoyed your message, pastor" are replaced by responses that are far more fitting for faithful proclam-
tions and expositions of the potent Word of God—the Word that burns like
fire, breaks like a hammer, cuts like a sword—and the Word that heals the
brokenhearted, sustains the weary and raises the dead.[22]

---

[22]In his magisterial work *The Drama of Doctrine: A Canonical Linguistic Approach to Christian
Theology* (Louisville, Ky.: Westminster/John Knox Press, 2005), Kevin Vanhoozer asserts that
doctrine ought to serve the church, which he calls the theater of the Gospel. By grounding
his assertion using the speech-act theory, Vanhoozer argues that every mode of the church's
proclamation and performance must be construed as "the means by which the Gospel becomes
that all-encompassing framework that allows us to think and experience truth, goodness, and

Does our worship consciously connect us to the church that is one, holy, catholic and apostolic? Truly Christian worship does, in fact, connect its participants to the one church. Whether or not it does so in a way that makes the worshipers conscious of this reality is quite another question. Too many times, worshipers come and go believing that the entire experience was intended to be simply a personal encounter with God or, even worse, simply an individual religious experience. Indeed, we often are not even called to attend to the fact that we are worshiping in community with those who are actually physically present with us at the time. Especially in the West, where we are so deeply influenced by a thoroughgoing individualism, this is a problem that should be addressed.

However, there is much that could be done to help the situation. To begin with, we could change the balance of our songs, incorporating more that remind us we are part of the people of God and are worshiping God in that community. A step as simple as singing a few more songs each month that use the first person plural pronoun *we* instead of the singular *I* will prove significant. We would be unwise to argue for dismissing all the *I* songs—perhaps two-thirds of the Psalter would qualify as such. But we should definitely call for adjusting the ratios that are common in so many evangelical circles today, especially where "contemporary choruses" predominate. Many of these choruses have helped worshipers celebrate the invitation to intimacy with God that is ours through the Gospel. Unfortunately, this gain often comes with the corresponding loss of community consciousness. To correct the growing imbalance, adding a few more songs that remind us of our place in the church is critical. If we manage to improve the I/we ratio from what often seems about 90/10 to 70/30 or even 50/50, we will have made great strides indeed.

We can also improve the situation by means of additional corporate acts of worship. Corporate readings of Scripture, corporate affirmations of faith, corporate confessions of sin and other such liturgical elements can be disequilibrating for those who have not commonly experienced them. I have found some young "worship leaders" to be rather uncomfortable with the concept of corporately confessing sin. Usually, however, a brief survey of biblical narratives and theological realities quickly helps them overcome their reticence. The experience itself often proves to be quite powerful. We are "all

---

beauty in light of the history of Jesus Christ. The ministry of the Word involves more than communicating a few truths; it involves transmitting a whole way of thinking and experiencing. Preaching and teaching should be 'evangelistic,' then, in the sense of enabling people to indwell the Gospel *(evangel)* as the primary framework for all that they say and do" (p. 74).

in this together"—what any one of us does for good or for ill truly affects the health and well-being of the whole body.

As we engage in our corporate acts of worship—singing, praying, reading, listening, confessing, greeting, partaking of the elements—we also help the situation greatly when we make it easier to see and hear one another. Some churches have discovered how important the architecture and arrangements of our worship spaces are in this regard. For example, a semicircular seating arrangement can have the benefit of helping worshipers see both the front of the sanctuary and one another. Celebrating the Lord's Supper in ways—even limited ones—that capture the intimate setting of a communal meal can be helpful. Turning down the volume on our amplifiers (or even turning them off altogether) can help congregants hear each other's voices as they sing. If the resulting sound is not as professional and polished, we may still find our hearts strangely warmed as we "speak to one another in psalms, hymns and spiritual songs" in new ways.

But it is not only the immediate community that we must call attention to. Moving from the consciousness of "I worship God" to "we worship God" is a great beginning step to take. But we also must move from "we" to "We," growing, that is, in our awareness of how vast the church of the living God is, how rich in diversity this one body of Christ is.

The Nicene Creed and other historic confessions of the Faith remind us that the church is one, holy, catholic and apostolic. Scripture elsewhere makes it clear that we worship as part of something even larger than that, for we join the hosts of heaven in awe of the living God, the Master of the universe. These are powerfully important realities. The author to the Hebrews writes, "You have come to thousands upon thousands of angels in joyful assembly, to the church of the firstborn, whose names are written in heaven" (Heb 12:22-23). John writes that he saw "a great multitude that no one could count, from every nation, tribe, people and language, standing before the throne and in front of the Lamb. . . . And they cried out in a loud voice: 'Salvation belongs to our God, who sits on the throne, and to the Lamb'" (Rev 7:9-10). Do those worshiping in our churches today have any consciousness of such amazing things?

How can we expand our vision of the We with whom we join in worship of the living God? There is much we might do, including expanding the range of our liturgical elements. We can and should employ songs and confessions and prayers from the historic church. In this way, we invite worshipers to consciously enjoy the "communion of the saints" as they worship with Ambrose,

Luther, Charles Wesley, Frances Ridley Havergal and other hymnists of the past. When we confess the Apostles' Creed or pray together the Lord's Prayer, we are joining voices, minds and hearts with millions upon millions of others across the earth and through the ages. When we learn songs of the saints or recite affirmations of faith that have arisen from ethnic communities and nations other than our own, we experience a taste of the Revelation 7:9-10 realities. Paying closer attention to the church year—with its historic colors and symbols—and utilizing a common lectionary can also make us more conscious of our place within the much larger community of God's people.

Preaching and teaching can address these realities—all the while hitting hard against the isms, idols and practices that keep us from embracing these truths about God's church, from experiencing the Life that flows from the Truth and from walking in the Way of love to which these truths call us. Every baptism performed in the congregation provides a reminder that there is "one Lord, one Faith, one baptism." Eucharistic celebrations likewise can remind us that the "one loaf, one body" mystery is far deeper than we realize.

It should be clear that more planning in all these areas can make a great difference in helping God's people more fully realize that we "are among those who are called to belong to Jesus Christ" (Rom 1:6).

Is the hymnody of the church biblically sound, helpful in regard to both revelation and response, and culturally and generationally sensitive? Our songs of worship are powerfully formative—again we must say it—for either good or for ill. Our songs should help with all the points we have already mentioned. Well chosen, our songs can help us be Scripture-soaked, Christ-centered, and explicitly and implicitly trinitarian. They can be chosen and led with a view to increasing whole-person participation of the whole community. They can play both a constructive and a destructive role in the shaping of a godly worldview and the tearing down of strongholds that have been erected against God. They can help us recognize our connection to the church that is one, holy, catholic and apostolic. They can be a means of inviting the Spirit's powerful presence to minister in our midst.

For the sake of all the above, our songs must be chosen very carefully. Let the songs be biblically sound. If there is a clear scriptural basis for a song, that fact can be noted in such a way that the worshipers are reminded that they are singing God's Word.[23] If we cannot think of a biblical basis for a song that we

---

[23]Such practice is not only encouraged in our hymn singing or when singing praise songs but also in the way the church has prayed the Scriptures, as in *lectio divina,* throughout the church

are singing, perhaps we should not be singing it. We cannot expect any single song to declare the whole truth about a given theme, but we can demand that we be singing nothing that is less than true.[24]

Do our hymns of worship help us with the revelation-and-response pattern? We can consider the contribution of each song to our understanding of what God has revealed concerning his character, concerning the redemption wrought for us in Christ or concerning God's present will for our lives. Alternatively, our worship can help us in responding to one or more of these three concerns. Again, if our songs do not help us with either revelation or response, perhaps we are singing the wrong songs.

Do our songs represent a broad range of human experience? Staying close to the Psalter will help enormously in this point as we find therein "the whole anatomy of the human soul."[25] If we are singing only songs of praise, we are missing the mark. We also need songs of confession, of instruction, of lamentation, of spiritual warfare and more. Naming our song leaders "the worship team" communicates that only our singing is worship. But a title like "the praise team" will not do either, unless we also have a "lament team," "a confession team" and so on.[26] Perhaps our best choice for naming the musicians and singers is to call them "the musicians" and "singers." (This seems to have been David's preferred choice of terms; see, for example, 1 Chron 15:16-22.)

Do our songs have staying power? Will they form believers over a lifetime? Many of us have doubtless had the experience of visiting with an aged believer who has lost most of her memory functions, yet can sing every line of a familiar hymn. It used to be commonplace for believers to have something like a canon of hymns. The repetition of these texts—many of them profoundly biblical—worked these truths deep into minds and hearts. In our day, many of our songs are obviously disposable. We sing them for a few months or a few weeks and then toss them aside in favor of something newer and fresher. One can only wonder how many of these throw-away songs will still be within

---

history.

[24]In *Is It a Lost Cause?* (Grand Rapids: Eerdmans, 1997), Dawn asserts that "worship can never give us the whole truth, but worship must never give us untruth or less than truth. . . . Every time the community gathers we have the opportunity to add to our total store of truth what this time of corporate worship contributes" (p. 80).

[25]John Calvin, *Commentary on the Book of Psalms*, trans. James Anderson (Grand Rapids: Baker, 2003), p. xxxvii.

[26]Regarding the place of lament in our hymnody, see Gary Parrett, "Singing in the Night," *Contact*, Winter 2007, pp. 26-28.

reach of our recall when our own memories have largely failed us.[27]

Finally, we ask which members in our congregation are being marginalized by our hymnody. In some cases, it may be children and youth who are asked to participate in a worship service but are never acknowledged in the selection of songs for worship. In many cases it seems that it is older members who are being marginalized. Since our "worship leaders" are often young musicians, it is not surprising that our songs also grow younger and younger. Are older members of the congregation given opportunity to sing some of the songs of worship that have been most meaningful and formative in their lives? Or are they made to feel, week after week, as though the services are being designed and led with someone else in mind (which is sadly but most probably the case). Of course, on any given Sunday, it may be unavoidable that some will feel this way. But if someone attends the services of their church over a period of many months and yet regularly feels ignored in this regard, we are again failing to "recognize the body of Christ" in a very tangible and important way.

Is our worship bathed in prayer? We have offered a number of questions and suggestions about how our gatherings of worship can be more faithfully and effectively formative. It should be obvious from the above that more thoughtful planning, design and conduct of our worship gatherings can make a great deal of difference for good. May God help us who are called to serve the church in such ways be more faithful stewards of these responsibilities. And may God deliver us from the tendency to do what we do in our worship simply because it is what other, apparently "successful" churches seem to do, or because this is "the way we've always done things." May God deliver us from pastors who would wash their hands of these matters and leave it all up to their "worship people." On the other hand, may God deliver us from "worship leaders" or liturgists who exercise a prideful possessiveness about the design and conduct of our worship services and are unwilling to partner with others in the body who have much to offer.

As critical as all our planning and thinking is, there is something even more helpful that we can and must do concerning these things: pray. If we would see God's people formed into Christ's likeness, we must recognize that this is a work only the Spirit of God can perform. Second Corinthians 3:17-18

---

[27]Another example, perhaps, of the "dismembering" of ourselves and our children that Bruce Waltke warns against in "The Way of Wisdom from the Book of Proverbs," audiocassette (Vancouver: Regent Audio, 2002).

makes this clear: "Now the Lord is the Spirit, and where the Spirit of the Lord is, there is freedom. And we, who with unveiled faces all reflect the Lord's glory, are being transformed into his likeness with ever-increasing glory, which comes from the Lord, who is the Spirit."

What shall we pray? We can do no better than to pray God's Word back to him, for we are thereby assured that what we ask is according to his will and that he hears all such prayer (see 1 Jn 5:14). It was Paul's pattern to offer prayers on behalf of the churches to which he addressed his letters. We should follow this pattern and, indeed, we should utilize Paul's very prayers. Do we long for our congregants to more fully understand their glorious inheritance in Christ? Then let us pray Ephesians 1:15-23. Would we see them come to a greater grasp of God's ungraspable love and to experience this "together with all the saints"? Then let us pray Ephesians 3:14-21. Paul's prayers in Philippians 1:9-11 and in Colossians 1:9-12 are two more wonderful prayers that we can regularly employ.

Of course, Jesus also prayed for those whom he loved and served. We have record of his prayers as well, and we are especially reminded now of his prayer as recorded in John 17. From this text we can learn to pray with Christ that God's people be sanctified by truth, that they be protected from the evil one, that they be finally and fully delivered to glory. We can pray further "that all of them may be one, just as you are in me and I am in you. May they also may be in us so that the world may believe that you have sent me" (Jn 17:21).

One of the four commitments of the first believers was to "the prayers" (Acts 2:42 rsv). This was not a generic commitment to prayer, but a commitment to prayers in, of and for the community. Therefore, prayer should be offered for our worship services, but should also be a primary ingredient *within* our worship services.

Once again, the Psalter is a great resource in this regard. Jews and Christians have historically employed the Psalter as both hymnal and prayer book. The Anglican *Book of Common Prayer* is a beautiful reminder and a helpful tool here, as most editions contain the entire Psalter arranged for community prayer. The psalms are also evident throughout that prayer book (as well as in the worship resources of many other denominations) in the various collects, litanies and other prayers assembled for various aspects of the daily services and for numerous special occasions. Aside from the Psalms, countless other passages of Scripture can be prayed "as is" or easily arranged for congregational prayer. Churches also can utilize the prayers of the church throughout the ages and from among the nations.

CONCLUSION

As we noted above, Marva Dawn has written that we cannot expect a service of worship to tell us the whole truth, but we can expect that nothing less than truth be communicated through our worship.[28] Perhaps this is a bit too idealistic. After all, we are a sinful and situated people; we are bound, therefore, to get things wrong—seriously and frequently—in spite of our best efforts. Still, Dawn makes an important point. Through prayerful design and conduct of our community gatherings of worship, we can surely move nearer to the truth. Following in the spirit of Paul, Ambrose, Augustine, Luther and Calvin, we can more faithfully and effectively liturgize catechetically. The formation that occurs in such gatherings of worship is a critical component among all our efforts to teach and form God's people more fully into the beautiful body of Christ that we are called and created to be. It is as such a body that we will have an impact for healing and hope in the broken world that we share with one another and with all our neighbors.

HYMN FOR CONTEMPLATION AND WORSHIP

Come, Lord Jesus, to Redeem Us

(for the season of Advent)

Come, Lord Jesus, to redeem us
from our foes and from our fears.
We await the hand of mercy
that will wipe away our tears.
We have labored long in darkness,
even now our hearts grow weak.
How we long for your appearing
and your great salvation seek.
(Rev 21:4; Rom 8:23; 2 Tim 4:8)

Come, Lord Jesus, true and righteous,
bring your pure and piercing light.
For we know when you appear, Lord,
ev'ry wrong shall be made right.
You will vanquish all the proud ones;

---

[28] Dawn, *Is It a Lost Cause?* p. 80.

you will fill all those who thirst.
Oh, the first shall be the last then
and the last shall be the first.
(Rev 16:5-7; Mt 19:30; 20:16)

Now prepare a path before him:
in the desert make a way.
Take the Gospel to the nations
and proclaim his coming Day.
Ev'ry mountain must be leveled;
ev'ry valley must be raised.
Then all flesh will see his glory.
God shall be forever praised!
(Is 40:3-5; Mt 24:14)

Raise the cry of "Maranatha!"
We shall soon behold our King.
To the Alpha and Omega,
this one prayer and plea we sing:
joining voices with the Spirit,
we, the bride of Christ, say, "Come!"
Come, Lord Jesus, come and free us
from this death and bring us home.
(1 Cor 16:22; Rev 22:13, 17)

Text: Gary A. Parrett (2002)
Tune: Nettleton
Familiar use of the tune: "Come, Thou Fount of Every Blessing"

QUESTIONS FOR PLANNING AND PRACTICE

1. One of the most formative things a church does together is engage in worship as a community. Worship is offered to God, and instruction (or exhortation) is directed toward one another. How does educational ministry play a role in creating communities of worshipers and instructors?

2. How is the worship in your church forming the body of Christ? What steps can you, in an act of educational ministry formation, take to encourage your church to form healthy, Spirit-filled worship habits?

3. Consider some of the characteristics of worship as outlined in this chapter: Scripture-saturated, Christocentric, explicitly and implicitly trinitarian. In what ways do you see your church engaging these characteristics in its

worship services? What about in your own personal worship? How are you engaging these characteristics in your "prayer closet"?

4. Does the worship of your church encourage participation by the whole person and the whole community? How can Christocentric, trinitarian worship that is Scripture-saturated more fully involve the whole person and community in your context?

5. Does the worship of your church make people aware of the church that is "one, holy, catholic and apostolic"? This chapter suggests moving away from the individualistic worship typical in the West toward a more communal worship service. Have you experienced such a service before? If so, how could this enhance the educational ministry of your church?

6. Many have assumed that worship is synonymous with singing. What steps might you take to educate your parishioners that God desires worship in all that we do? How do you model this biblical truth with your own life? We invite you to discuss with the other educational ministers in your church and those from other Christian traditions how to help avoid this misconception.

RESOURCES FOR FURTHER STUDY

Beale, G. K. *We Become What We Worship: A Biblical Theology of Idolatry.* Downers Grove, Ill.: IVP Academic, 2008.

The Book of Common Prayer: An Administration of the Sacraments and Other Rites and Ceremonies of the Church. New York: Church Publishing, 2001.

Dawn, Marva. *How Then Shall We Worship?* Wheaton: Tyndale, 2003.

———. *A Royal "Waste" of Time: The Splendor of Worshiping God and Being the Church for the World.* Grand Rapids: Eerdmans, 1999.

Greidanus, Sidney. *Preaching Christ from the Old Testament: A Contemporary Hermeneutical Method.* Grand Rapids: Eerdmans, 1999.

Horton, Michael. *A Better Way: Rediscovering the Drama of God-Centered Worship.* Grand Rapids: Baker, 2002.

Labberton, Mark. *The Dangerous Act of Worship: Living God's Call to Justice.* Downers Grove, Ill.: InterVarsity Press, 2007.

Murphy, Debra Dean. *Teaching That Transforms: Worship as the Heart of Christian Education.* Grand Rapids: Brazos, 2004.

Parrett, Gary, and Julie Tennent. *Psalms, Hymns and Spiritual Songs.* Chicago: MorgenBooks, 2009.

Peterson, David. *Engaging with God: A Biblical Theology of Worship.* Downers
    Grove, Ill.: InterVarsity Press, 2002.
Richardson, Rick. *Experiencing Healing Prayer: How God Turns Our Hurts into
    Wholeness.* Downers Grove, Ill.: InterVarsity Press, 2005.
Torrance, James. *Worship, Community and the Triune God of Grace.* Downers
    Grove, Ill.: InterVarsity Press, 1996.
Webber, Robert. *Ancient-Future Time: Forming Spirituality Through the Christian
    Year.* Grand Rapids: Baker, 2004.
———. *Ancient-Future Worship: Proclaiming and Enacting God's Narrative.* Grand
    Rapids: Baker, 2008.

13

Commitments for a Congregational Curriculum

(Part 1)

Then Jesus came to them and said,
"All authority in heaven and on earth has been given to me.
Therefore go and make disciples of all nations, baptizing them
in the name of the Father and of the Son and of the Holy Spirit,
and teaching them to obey everything I have commanded you.
And surely I am with you always, to the very end of the age."

MATTHEW 28:18-20

▼

IN THIS CHAPTER AND THE NEXT, we propose seven commitments for teaching and formation in the local church. The first five of these commitments might justly be called phases, for they represent something of a chronological progression or perhaps a logical progression. The last two commitments are more concerned with the overall ethos of the congregation. We envision all of the commitments as being present in the life of a congregation all the time. Our steps are outlined using an acrostic device—in this case, utilizing letters A to G. Together with the CORE content we presented in chapter five, the practices associated with the seven commitments outlined in this chapter represent the outline of our proposal for a comprehensive curriculum for congregational formation.

Before going any further with explanatory comments, we invite you to peruse table 13.1 to see the big picture of what we are suggesting. Please note

that in the left-hand column of the table we have indicated which elements of
our proposed CORE content might principally be addressed within each of
the seven commitments. The remainder of the chapter is devoted to detailed
descriptions of the commitments. These seven commitments are, we believe,
birthed out of the biblical vision for teaching and formation we have been
seeking to discern and suggest throughout the course of the book.

Table 13.1. Seven Commitments for Teaching and Formation

	Grounding	*Growing*	*Giving*	*Going*
1. Access to the glorious Gospel —*the Story unfolded* —*the Gospel, as of first importance*	An Alpha type experience for inquirers. Ideally in homes, hosted by lay members. Focus on the Story and the Gospel.			
2. Baptism Preparation, Confirmation and Recollection —*the Gospel* —*the three historic summaries*	Formal catechumenal experience in preparation for baptism, featuring instruction in the "three summaries." Open to candidates for baptism and confirmation, and to those who are already members. Taught by pastoral staff and mature lay members. Baptism and confirmation joyously celebrated by the church.			
3. Commitment to the Covenant Community —*the Gospel* —*three facets of the one Faith* —*distinctives of the denomination* —*history, vision and values of the church*	An intensive course of instruction in preparation for becoming members of the church (or additional elements of instruction prior to baptism). Taught by pastoral staff and mature lay members. Further instruction in the Gospel, in the three "great streams" of the Truth, Life and Way. Instruction in the distinctives of the church and its denomination or other affiliation. Instruction in the privileges and responsibilities of membership. Beginning steps are taken in vocational understanding and involvement.			
4. Deepening and **Developing** in the Gospel —*the Gospel* —*three facets of the Faith* —*Story immersion* —*training in Word, work and witness*	Members submit to the discipline and instruction of the church, participating regularly in the four commitments of Acts 2:42. In addition to participating in the liturgy and in formal learning experiences, growth occurs in a wide variety of informal settings. Along with continued growth in the Truth, Life and Way, emphasis is on ongoing training in the Word, sharing life in community and growing in vocational understanding. Small groups and Bible studies may be "labeled" to help understand intended sequence or priority (for example, Grounding, Growing, Giving, Going). Members are trained and involved in both ecclesia (when the church assembles) ministry and diaspora (when the church disperses) ministries.			

5. Engagement in the Ministry of Reconciliation —*the Gospel* —*active ministry involvement* —*leadership training*		Those who have become members (and others who are interested in joining them, when this is appropriate) engage in a wide variety of ministries (both ecclesia and diaspora). There is an emphasis on vocational training, via ministry opportunities, service projects, mission trips, seminars regarding Christianity in the workplace and so on. Ongoing leadership training raises up and sustains leaders (who must be members) for the various ministries of the church.
6. Follow-Up Care of the Flock —*the Gospel*	Those who have walked through the "A through E" process as outlined above have not "arrived." They are still sheep who must be lovingly tended by the shepherds of the flock—pastoral staff, elders, mature believers—who are ever watchful, prayerful and careful for the well-being of the flock.	
7. Grace Cultivation as the *Ethos* of the Church —*the Gospel*	Lest the processes outlined above fall victim to legalistic abuse, grace must be central in the preaching, teaching, hymnody, fellowship and every ministry of the church. This must be intentionally cultivated by the leaders of the body and prayerfully guarded by all members.	

Looking at the table from the top and moving downward reveals the sense of the spiritual development we are envisioning. This is based loosely on the catechetical development that was recognized by ancient church leaders, such as Cyril and Augustine: an individual moves from being an inquirer to a formal catechumen to a member of the faithful.[1]

Looking at the table from left to right, a different angle on spiritual development is intended. We have labeled the movement here as "Grounding, Growing, Giving, Going." The point here is simply to suggest that the A to G commitments focus on different sorts of development. For example, the Baptism commitment focuses on Grounding and Growing, whereas the Engagement commitment focuses on Growing, Giving and Going. Of course, the lines between these stages of development are "fuzzy," and there is plenty of overlap.

In the further unfolding of the seven commitments below, we will be referring to other materials presented earlier in the book.

ACCESS TO THE GLORIOUS GOSPEL

The first educational commitment of the church is to ensure that the Gospel

---

[1]See our comments about this progression below, especially under the headings "Access to the Glorious Gospel" and "Baptism: Preparation, Confirmation and Recollection."

is as accessible as possible to as many as possible. By "as many as possible" we
mean that the Gospel ought to be clearly proclaimed among the believers who
regularly attend the church and to unbelieving friends who are within the
"reach" of the congregation. Our primary focus at this point is on the latter
audience—those friends, family members and neighbors of the church community who do not yet know the Savior.

In recent history, a commitment to making the Gospel accessible to unbelievers has been well championed by ministries such as Alpha[2] and Christianity Explored.[3] These endeavors, designed to introduce unbelievers to the central tenets of Christianity, may seem like contemporary innovations. In fact,
they are a sort of rediscovery of a very ancient practice. Augustine might have
described such a work as *procatechesis,* a first or preliminary catechesis for "inquirers." His work on the subject, *De catechizandis rudibus,* was written in response to a question from a church deacon named Deogratius, concerning
how to instruct those who approached the church with interest in the Faith.[4]

An interesting difference between Augustine's approach and that of, say,
the Alpha program concerns the content of such instruction. Whereas Alpha
introduces Christianity in topical fashion, Augustine argues for a more narrative approach.[5] He reasons that it is the great *narratio* that inquirers must
hear—the great redemptive Story of God. This story must be told in compelling fashion, beginning with the creation of the world and continuing on
through the present history of the church. We would suggest presenting this
great Story from creation to consummation.[6]

---

[2]The Alpha course is a movement that started in 1973 in England and has been revitalized under
Nicky Gumbel's leadership since 1990. The course seeks to provide a safe and hospitable space
where people of every walk of life are invited to explore the Christian faith in a relaxed, small-
group setting over ten thought-provoking weekly sessions based on Gumbel's book *Questions
of Life* and related resources. As of July 2008, up to thirteen million people have participated in
the program worldwide. See <http://www.alphana.org/Group/Group.aspx?ID=1000016933>.
(Accessed on July 1, 2008.)

[3]Christianity Explored is another informal course for people who are open to learning about
Christianity or to "just brush up on the basics." The course basically explores who Jesus was,
what his aims were and what it means to follow him. <http://www.christianityexplored.org/>.
(Accessed on July 1, 2008.)

[4]William J. Harmless, *Augustine and the Catechumenate* (Collegeville, Minn.: Liturgical Press,
1995), p. 107.

[5]Christianity Explored takes a more narrative approach than Alpha, as the content is based
largely on Mark's Gospel.

[6]"Two Ways to Live" is a simple evangelistic message based on the crux of the biblical narrative,
developed by Matthias Media in Sydney. The ministry is based on classic evangelical principles:
Christ alone, Scripture alone, grace alone and faith alone, all to the glory of God alone. See
<http://www.matthiasmedia.com.au/usa/>.

Augustine's fifth-century wisdom could not be more timely for us today. By all accounts, the power of story is very compelling to postmodern hearers. Ironically, even as so many have dismissed the possibility of a metanarrative or a meganarrative that could possibly be "true" for all persons, interest and openness to hearing another individual's or community's story seems greater than ever in our lifetimes.[7] When I am on a flight, for example, I often find myself caught up in spiritual conversations. There was once a time when mentioning to the person seated next to me that I was a pastor seemed to stop a conversation. Now it very often seems to open a conversation or deepen a conversation. People seem genuinely interested to hear "my story."[8] This is a marvelous opportunity for the Christian community. As we tell "our story" we do so faithfully and prayerfully, pointing away from ourselves to Christ the Redeemer and asking the Spirit of God to persuade our hearers that "our story" is, in fact, connected to *the* Story—the very Story that they most desperately need to hear and engage. Many find the biblical Story attractive because it is coherent, is historically rooted and has proven life-giving for so many people.

The Access commitment of our teaching plan demonstrates that the line between evangelism and education is not as clear as we often suppose it to be. Indeed, although it is common for Christians to speak of evangelism as being

---

[7]In fact, the notion of metanarrative as coined and critiqued by Jean-François Lyotard (*The Postmodern Condition: A Report on Knowledge* [Minneapolis: University of Minneapolis, 1984]) was largely not the scope of *grand recit* but the *nature* of the claims of the humanly generated constructs such as the Hegelian system, Marx's historical materialism and the modern scientific narrative of progress. In other words, what Lyotard was critiquing was the distinctly modern, Enlightenment presuppositions behind these grand stories. James K. A. Smith astutely summarizes the kind of metanarrative Lyotard was critiquing when he writes, "For Lyotard, metanarratives are a distinctly *modern* phenomenon: They are stories which not only tell a grand story (since even premodern and tribal stories do this), but also claim to be able to *legitimate* the story and its claims *by an appeal to universal Reason*." ("A Little Story About Metanarratives: Lyotard, Religion, and Postmodernism Revisited" in *Christianity and the Postmodern Turn,* ed. Myron Penner [Grand Rapids: Brazos, 2005], pp. 124-25.) In sum, most of so-called postmodern theorists' criticism of the notion of metanarrative was not necessarily its *scope* but its *nature,* that is, its modern foundationalistic assumptions. In other words, the biblical story as a "metanarrative" was largely *not* in the purview of these theorists or the object of their contemplation. One wonders whether many Christian thinkers with a modern mindset have overreacted in assuming that the postmodern theorists' critiques of modernism are attempts to dismantle the Christian metanarrative. This reflects a lack of careful interaction with various postmodern theorists' works.

[8]People are interested in hearing or encountering the whole-story-in-context—the story that is shaped at the intersections of historical, cultural, familial, personal and other elements of life's predicaments. There seems to be much less interest in being told merely propositional, universalizing and/or totalizing statements and imperatives that are stripped of the "stuff" of real life, devoid of life's situated or textured milieu.

followed by discipleship, the structure of Matthew 28:18-20 argues for a better conceptualization, as we saw in chapter two. That is, discipleship includes *both* evangelism and ongoing instruction. Ministries such as Alpha then can justly be called a form of pre-Christian discipleship. Indeed, they are precisely this, for they represent an invitation to join a certain way of living. The concept of pre-Christian discipleship should be no surprise to those who have studied the way Jesus himself made disciples. It is clear that people followed him and spent significant time with him even before entrusting their lives to him. Or, rather, as they spent time with him, their faith in him developed. In some instances, the faith of would-be followers faltered as they saw and heard more. In other instances, their faith in Jesus deepened.

It is often the case that through prolonged exposure to the Gospel and its accompanying doctrines and implications, faith comes alive. In my home church, we have witnessed numerous instances of people coming to faith in such ways. There is, for instance, the brother from India who had come to the States for study. After completing his degree, he took a position at a local company. One of his coworkers, who is a member of our church, invited him to visit our services.

This young man, who had been raised a Hindu and knew no Christians in his home country, became a deeply committed "seeker" for the next many months. He was attracted by what he was hearing in church but, even more, by what he was seeing in the lives of the church members—their love, joy and commitment to serving others. He came faithfully to services and Bible studies. He noticed that many of those around him were serving the church in some way, and so he volunteered to do so himself. He took attendance at the services, helped with social justice projects and more. He was deeply involved in the fellowship of the congregation and finally asked if he could be part of a mission trip abroad. He had never been anything but honest about the fact that he was not yet a Christian, but he was welcomed to join the mission trip with clear boundaries about what his role would be. Upon returning from the trip, he announced to his teammates that he had yielded his heart to Jesus. Now, just a few years later, he is himself actively engaged in the ministry of reconciliation in his home country.

Stories of this sort of gradual transformation are becoming increasingly common in Christian churches today, perhaps especially among young adults who may in some sense be identified as postmodern in their orientation. Part of such an orientation is often an openness to experience the world and the story of others. People seem to be more open and honest about their spiritual journeys than Americans of an earlier generation often were. But again, none of this is as novel as it may seem. It is reminiscent of faith journeys we read about in Scripture—from the God-fearing Gentiles who attended synagogue services, to the followers of John who were invited by Jesus to "come and see" where and how he lived, to those who moved from observing the followers of the Way to becoming obedient to the Way themselves. In fact, many have argued that this is precisely the sort of evangelism desperately needed for times like ours.[9]

None of this is to suggest that the church ought to evangelize only passively, by waiting for folks to "come to us." We must also engage actively in reaching out to those who do not yet believe the Gospel. In doing so, however, we need to acknowledge that the Gospel we want them to consider bears eternal consequences for them. This means that we as Christians should be patient and persevering as we invest in those who are open to explore the Gospel of eternal consequences, rather than "pushing" for a quick decision. It would be wise for Christians to heed an ancient Jewish tradition in which rabbis turn away three times a candidate wanting to convert to Judaism, in order to test the candidate's sincerity.[10] In all this, we are called to be in step with them in their lives, invoking the Holy Spirit to bring about transformation in them.

GOD IS REALLY AMONG YOU!

Aside from specific ministry programs, like a multiweek course on the basics of Christianity, the congregation must exercise this Access commitment in other ways.[11] For example, the worship service can be examined with a view to show concern for nonbelieving visitors. Of course, there has been much debate about how to respond to "seekers." The more common approaches that churches have adopted might be plotted on a continuum, as follows.[12]

⬅————————————————————————➡

seeker hostile   *seeker indifferent*   *seeker friendly*   *seeker driven*

---

[9]For instance, George Hunter III, *The Celtic Way of Evangelism: How Christianity Can Reach the West . . . Again* (Nashville: Abingdon, 2000).

[10]See "The Conversion Process" <http://www.convert.org/conversion_process.html>.

[11]For such a course to be a potentially life-transforming encounter for the seekers, the congregation must be a place where the transformative power of God's grace is readily manifested and authenticated.

[12]This sort of continuum and related principles are expanded on in Mary Scifres, *Searching for Seekers: Ministry with a New Generation of the Unchurched* (Nashville: Abingdon, 1998).

Before briefly exploring these options, we must first explore the word *seeker* itself, in light of the fact that "there is . . . no one who seeks God" (Rom 3:11; compare Ps 53:1-3). Although Scripture does say elsewhere that those who seek the Lord shall find him (see, for example, Jer 29:13; Mt 7:7), such verses are typically spoken to those who have already been identified as God's people. For aside from God's prevenient grace working in the heart of a person, there are none who seek God on their own initiative. Should we then use the word *inquirer,* as the ancients did? This may be better, but it still begs the question of who is pursuing whom. Shall we call them *the being sought?* In light of verses like Galatians 4:9, this might be a wise choice. But so long as we understand that those we dub "seekers" are in fact seeking because God has initiated something in their hearts, we may perhaps retain the word for the sake of engaging this discussion with familiar terms. By placing it in quotation marks, we are reminded of its significant limitations.

What should a church's approach to worship be, relative to the impact of the service on those who are not yet believers? The view adopted here might well be called *"seeker" friendly.* However, what we intend by this is not what many churches today might understand by the term. Rather, it is an attempt to grasp the spirit of Paul revealed in 1 Corinthians 11—14. This section clearly concerns the gatherings of believers for worship. It is all under the heading of "your meetings" and "when you come together" and "in the church" (1 Cor 11:17-18; 14:19, 26).

Paul clearly suggests that when the church has gathered for worship, the emphasis must be on the encounter between God and his people. He certainly does not favor shifting the emphasis of such meetings primarily to accommodate unbelievers. Nothing must take the focus off the true worship of God and the meaningful instruction and edification of the body of Christ. Thus Paul cannot be described as advocating a "seeker"-*driven* worship service. Yet he would ensure that God-fearers be welcomed in the worship experience as far as possible without compromise. No doubt he would favor creating a safe and hospitable space where they could encounter the living God.

Paul's sensitivity toward unbelievers who may be present at the meetings is clear in his discussion regarding the use of the gift of tongues in 1 Corinthians 14. He writes, "So if the whole church comes together and everyone speaks in tongues, and some inquirers[13] or some unbelievers come in, will they not say that you are out of your mind?" (1 Cor 14:23). Paul is mindful

---

[13]This alternative translation is from the NIV footnote.

of the impact of all that occurs in the assemblies of the saints—not only on believers (as in 1 Cor 14:16-19) but also on unbelievers.[14] His solution, however, is not to advocate a total recasting of everything for the sake of unbelievers. His concern is that the unbeliever in the midst of the assembly would be able to hear a clear word from God and so come to acknowledge that God was truly present among this people.

In another sense, however, we may well call Paul Seeker-sensitive, even Seeker-driven. But by *Seeker,* we are now referring to the living God,[15] not to those who appear to be reaching for him. For while there is "no one who seeks God" (Rom 3:11), God is the true and great Seeker. From the cry of "Where are you?" in the garden (Gen 3:9), to the pursuit of his wandering sheep (see Ez 34:12, 16) and straying bride (as in Hosea), to the sending of Jesus who came "to seek and save the lost" (Lk 19:10; compare 1 Tim 1:15), to continually seeking worshipers who will worship him in spirit and truth (see Jn 4:23), God has long and passionately sought after us. Paul was certainly sensitive to and driven by this Seeker, for he had himself been sought and powerfully saved by him. We too have experienced the gracious and relentless pursuit of God. May God help us share his heart for all those around us.

What might it look like to have services of worship that are sensitive to the true Seeker? Such worship will have the glory and honor of God as its primary agenda. And, as we discussed in chapter eleven, it will also take very seriously the matter of forming the believers who have gathered to worship the living God. But worship that is attentive to the true Seeker will also manifest a heart for those who do not yet know the Lord. The following principles can, we trust, help churches toward more faithful practices in reflection of such a heart.

First, committing ourselves to worship God in Spirit and truth is the very best gift we can offer to unbelieving friends who may be visiting our services. We pray that they will be able to sense that "God really is among you." Therefore, we do not recast the "event" for the sake of unbelievers. If they really are "seekers," we should not disappoint them by using our time together for something other than the worship of the living God.

Second, without compromising the central focus on worship, we can and should practice genuine hospitality in our services, thereby accentuating focus on the God who seeks and saves and who has welcomed us into his family.

---

[14]As background, we might consider the "God-fearing Gentiles" who attended synagogue services. F. F. Bruce, *The Book of the Acts,* New International Commentary on the New Testament (Grand Rapids: Eerdmans, 1988), pp. 276-77.

[15]Not unlike when we call the triune God a missionary God when we speak of *missio Dei.*

This means committing ourselves to welcome all visitors warmly and to help them "find their way" in our services, both literally and figuratively. A well-trained welcome team is a great start here, but beyond this, we should create a congregational ethos of hospitality. This attitude should be clearly evident in those who are leading the service as well. Words of welcome should be included at some point in the service. A "welcome package" of some sort and/or a brief welcome gathering after the service can be very helpful. In all these things, no assumption should be made that visitors are already believers. Thus it is essential to include some introduction to the Gospel in whatever materials are made available to visitors. We should also consider including some sort of guide that introduces the elements of the worship service prepared especially with newcomers—including unbelieving visitors—in mind.

Third, to ensure that there are no unnecessary barriers to the Gospel, church leaders should have guidelines for what needs to be explained when, and how. "The natural man" cannot discern the things of God, we are told (see 1 Cor 2:14), and the Gospel itself is a scandal to unbelievers (see 1 Cor 1:23). These realities do not suggest that we are simply wasting our time if we try to explain ourselves to unbelievers. To the contrary, they suggest that we should work carefully to proclaim the Gospel and the things of God as clearly as possible, doing all we can to avoid *unnecessary* barriers. In other words, we want people to stumble over the right thing—over the Gospel itself, not over such things as our lack of hospitality, compassion, courtesy or godliness. Any help offered in this regard can also prove very helpful for the sake of children in the congregation and serve mature believers by way of reminder.

BAPTISM: PREPARATION, CONFIRMATION AND RECOLLECTION

In the section above, we focused on what we called *procatechesis,* a catechizing or instruction aimed at those who are not yet believers. We now turn our attention to formal catechesis. Historically, catechesis has been associated primarily with two things: the instruction of children and the preparation of candidates for baptism. We will discuss both of these and will offer suggestions for contemporary instructional practices in evangelical congregations.

We have already suggested that catechesis is the very biblical concern to ground believers in the essentials of the Faith. We also saw that this means far more than simply inculcating into new believers certain doctrinal beliefs. It means helping them become immersed in the glorious Gospel of God, that they may begin to discern and accept their places in the grand Story of God's reconciling all things to himself in Christ. It means, further, beginning a journey of growth in three facets of the Faith: the Truth, the Life and the Way. Learning all this is a lifelong process. In preparing adult converts for baptism and in introducing the Faith to children who are born and nurtured in our congregations, there are certain initial practices and emphases we are wise to engage.

Considering historical precedents. Over the first five centuries of the church's history, the preparation of adult converts for baptism was linked to what was called the catechumenate. Although this ancient school of the Faith took various shapes in various places and times, certain characteristics became quite common, if not entirely normative. By the time we reach the catechumenal ministry of Augustine in northern Africa at the beginning of the fifth century, these common practices had become quite standardized.[16] However, what Augustine formalized was not novel to him. His practices were largely in keeping with what had been developing for centuries and was widely practiced by the church in numerous locations.

A would-be convert to the Faith typically passed through several phases on the journey toward baptism. To begin with, *inquirers* were interviewed to determine their spiritual condition and to discern their motivation for approaching the church. The bishop, pastor or other church leader would conduct the interview. Through this it would be determined whether or not the inquirer was sincerely desirous of becoming Christian or, at the very least, sincerely wanting to know more about the Christian teaching and manner of life. The interview could also help the catechist to determine where to begin instruction. For Augustine, as we saw earlier, inquirers ought to be presented with the great Story of redemptive history. Those who found the Story compelling or at least intriguing, and who had been deemed sincere in their searching, would then become *catechumens.*

A catechumen was one under the instruction of the church. Sometimes this person, having received preliminary instruction in the *narratio,* had accepted this good news of the Gospel and had already become a believer. At

---

[16]We offer only a brief overview of these practices here. For more, please see Harmless, *Augustine and the Catechumenate;* O. C. Edwards Jr. and John Westerhoff III, *A Faithful Church: Issues in the History of Catechesis* (Eugene, Ore.: Wipf and Stock, 2003); Robert Webber, *Journey to Jesus: The Worship, Evangelism, and Nurture Mission of the Church* (Nashville: Abingdon, 2001). See also J. I. Packer and Gary A. Parrett, *Grounded in the Gospel: Building Believers the Old-Fashioned Way* (Grand Rapids: Baker, forthcoming).

other times, he did not yet fully believe but longed to learn more and was journeying toward faith. In either case, the catechumen was now a "hearer of the Word." A catechumen might thus hear the Word for a period of many months or several years before becoming a candidate for baptism.

Most of the instruction during this time took place in the gathered worship of the community. They "heard" the Word through the elements of the liturgy: Scripture readings, confessions of faith, prayers of the people, testimonies, hymns and public preaching. By this time, the worship services were typically divided into two portions: the service of the Word and the service of the Table. Catechumens were dismissed with prayers for blessing after the service of the Word. Sometimes this dismissal included a ceremonial closing of the doors, reminiscent of the closing of the door on Noah's ark. Although these men and women were beloved and were on their way toward faith in Christ, they were not yet counted among the *faithful*.

After much sustained hearing, the catechumen, with the recommendation of a sponsor—one of the faithful—could become a candidate for baptism. To become a candidate, one needed to demonstrate both an affirmation of the Truth and a determination to live according to the Way of the Lord, and the sponsor was a witness of these things. The catechumen then began a new, final and more intentional stage of catechesis. She was now numbered among the *competentes* (or *electi, illuminati, photozomenoi* or similar term).[17]

This final phase of baptism was made in time to correspond with the Lenten season. During the six weeks of Lent, the candidates for baptism underwent intense and holistic instruction. They received daily teaching in the doctrines of the church. This included instruction in the Lord's Prayer and in the creed of the church. The creed was verbally "handed over" to the candidates. They learned it line by line, with the bishop or pastor explaining each line. The creed was to be committed to memory and was not to be written down. This was a treasure that was reserved only for *competentes* and the faithful. It was not to be shared with either unbelievers or ordinary catechumens.[18]

In addition to the instruction they received, the candidates for baptism engaged in various fasts and other ascetic acts. They offered daily prayers and

---

[17]Various terms were used to describe the candidates for baptism, but all placed emphasis on the work God was doing in the candidates rather than on what the candidates were themselves "doing" for God. Thus these candidates were called "the elect" or "those being enlightened."

[18]This was an application of the principle of *disciplina arcani,* the discipline of the secret—a law imposing silence for Christians regarding rites and doctrines.

received prayer from church leaders. They were also exorcised daily. They were being transferred from the kingdom of darkness to the kingdom of God's beloved Son, and all powers of darkness had to be dealt with and overcome. The *competentes* were set apart during congregational worship over this period of weeks that all might remember to pray for them as they approached baptism. A day or a few days before the actual baptism, the candidates "gave back" the creed in public confession. This was the final step in determining their readiness to fully join the faithful.

At last the day arrived. The candidates were baptized during the Great Easter Vigil. The ceremony was ritually rich and emotionally stirring. Men and women were baptized only in the company of members of the same gender, for they were baptized naked. Before disrobing for baptism, candidates faced west as they renounced the devil and all his works. They trampled their discarded robes beneath their feet. Turning to the east (toward Jerusalem), they entered the baptismal font. Baptism was by immersion in "living waters," which symbolized the life-giving Holy Spirit. The Spirit's work was also pictured as the newly baptized were anointed with oil. Then attendants placed on them new, white linen robes to symbolize that they were now clothed with righteousness. Witnesses celebrated enthusiastically the reception of these *neophytes* who now, for the first time, were about to partake of the Lord's Supper together with the faithful.[19]

Evaluation and implications for contemporary practice. This brief description of these ancient practices is likely to evoke a wide variety of responses from evangelical Protestants today. Some may find these things mysterious yet intriguing. Some may be excited about certain aspects of what we sketched out above, but highly skeptical about others. Still others may find the whole scheme deeply disturbing and wonder why we would bother even considering it. The approach we will advocate is one of humility, discernment and creativity. After explaining what we mean by such terms, we will move on to propose several practices for implementation.

To begin with, we suggest looking at these ancient practices with humility. As we have said before, we are not the first to wrestle with the question of how to make disciples. Our ministry contexts are certainly very different from those of the first few centuries of the church. But the question before us is this: Is there something that God would have us learn by humbly consider-

---

[19]Again, an application of the *disciplina arcani*. The Eucharist was received only by the baptized, and only those who had been duly instructed received baptism.

ing the meaning behind these ancient practices? Are all these practices praiseworthy in the light of biblical testimony? We suggest that they are not. But
then how might our forebears evaluate *our* practices? Is all that we do in typical American evangelical churches today praiseworthy and scripturally sound?
That is certainly not the case. We humble ourselves further by taking on the
attitude that these practices are not those of "somebody else." They are *our
own* practices, in the sense that they were carried out by the saints who have
gone before us, our predecessors in the one, holy, catholic and apostolic church
of Jesus Christ. They belong to us, and we to them. The approach outlined
above dominated Christian practice for centuries. At least we can seek to
learn our own history and ponder it, and let it sink into us.

Our listening, of course, calls not only for humility but also for discernment. These practices are ancient and belong to members of our own faith
family, but that does not mean that they are all wise practices that ought to be
emulated. Before turning to consideration of the things we find most helpful
in the ancient pattern, we will admit that there are certain features of it that
seem at least questionable, if not outright objectionable.[20]

Is it wise, first of all, to withhold baptism for so long a season to those who
have truly believed the Gospel? There is biblical warrant for being sure that
one has attained some understanding of the Gospel before baptism, but who
could argue—in the light of biblical examples—that several years is a reasonable norm? The book of Acts offers only a few examples of people beng baptized. In each case, the baptism followed soon on the heels of believing the
good news (though there was always *some* instruction prior to baptism). Does
not such a drawn-out process run the risk of diverting attention from the
grace of God displayed in the waters of baptism and putting too much emphasis on the "worth" of the candidate?

Second, we may well wonder if dismissing the unbaptized from worship
services prior to the service of the Table was a good idea. Did not the secrecy
of these early Christians in fact invite all kinds of accusation and slander from
outsiders? And then there is the whole notion of the *disciplina arcani*. Not only
were the sacraments of the Lord's Supper and even baptism reserved as closely
guarded secrets, even the teaching of the creed was a privilege reserved only
for those in the final phases of catechesis. Luther, Calvin, their fellow reform-

---

[20]What we are called to do is to listen to them and their practices on their own terms, rather
than jumping into evaluating their practices using our own ways of thinking—perspectives,
paradigms, sensibilities and so on.

ers and later Catholics did not hesitate to have the creed printed and distributed widely as a central part of the catechisms they prepared. Paul preached and taught openly, as did all the apostles, as did their Lord before them. Why then did the ancients take such care that an "ordinary catechumen" would not overhear one working on his memorization of the creed?

All these questions—as well as others—deserve to be asked. All the elaborate ritual that surrounded the services of baptism will also trouble some. Ritual turnings, disrobings, anointings, robings and so on are hard for many of us with modern sensibilities and "low church" experiences to even imagine, let alone condone. We reiterate the suggestion that, rather than dismiss the seemingly foreign practices of the ancient church, we consider our own humble, discerning and creative approach to baptismal preparation, confirmation and recollection.

Our understandings of baptism. Before discussing how to prepare members for baptism, we need to speak briefly to the matter of what baptism *is* and what it means in the life of a believer and a congregation. The topic is so weighty and church debates about it are so contentious that we must leave it to others to offer a full introduction to the theology and practice of baptism for our times. Here we offer only several points that we consider most critical for evangelicals as we consider our educational and formative practices regarding baptism in our churches today.

In his very helpful book *Christ, Baptism and the Lord's Supper,* Leonard J. Vander Zee offers the following definition (as he calls it) of baptism: "In baptism, God, by water and the Spirit, incorporates us into the new creation in his Son, Jesus Christ, and joins us to Christ's body, the church; to this gift we respond in faith and seek to shape our lives more and more to this new identity we have in Christ."[21] This definition, Vander Zee argues, "highlights six important truths" about baptism as taught in the New Testament:

1. The central action of baptism belongs to God.[22]

2. We are baptized by water and the Spirit.[23]

3. Baptism is the sign and seal of our incorporation into Christ.[24]

---

[21]Leonard J. Vander Zee, *Christ, Baptism and the Lord's Supper: Recovering the Sacraments for Evangelical Worship* (Downers Grove, Ill.: InterVarsity Press, 2004), p. 102.

[22]See, for example, Paul's teaching about baptism in Romans 6 and that of Peter in 1 Peter 3:18-22

[23]Vander Zee, *Christ, Baptism and the Lord's Supper,* p. 106.

[24]Ibid., p. 108. This is clearly Paul's argument in Romans 6.

4. Incorporation into Christ also means incorporation into his body, which is the church.[25]

5. Baptism calls forth and builds up our faith.[26] (Here Vander Zee cites the familiar habit of Martin Luther who, when in the throws of temptation or discouragement, would recall his baptism: "I have been baptized!"[27])

6. Baptism gives us an identity that shapes our lives.

Vander Zee approaches the wonder of baptism from an unapologetically Reformed perspective. But his tone is irenic throughout the book, and he reaches out to Christians from other perspectives in trying to find common ground as he argues for the veracity of the points above. We find his arguments compelling and would add to his six theses the following additional seven suggestions regarding our approach to baptism.[28]

1. Baptism is vitally linked to the doctrine of salvation. Another point of objection that some readers might have to the sketch of ancient practices that we outlined above is that too much weight seems to have been placed on baptism. Many evangelicals will think this unwarranted and unwise. But if the ancients seem to us to have placed too much emphasis on baptism, we should know that they would be scandalized by how *little* emphasis we may place on it. The New Testament writers consistently view baptism in some sense as vitally linked to such matters as salvation, the forgiveness of sins and the reception of the Holy Spirit.

2. There is, as both Scripture and the ancient church make so very clear, only one baptism, and we also ought to be very clear about this. In Ephesians 4:3-6, Paul pleads with believers to "make every effort to keep the unity of the Spirit through the bond of peace." He bases this command on these facts: "There is one body and one Spirit—just as you were called to one hope when you were called—one Lord, one faith, one baptism; one God and Father of all, who is over all and through all and in all." We ought not consider the possibility that

---

[25]"Churchless Christians" has been an issue in contexts such as predominately Muslim or Hindu nations. See Timothy Tennent, "The Challenge of *Churchless* Christianity: An Evangelical Assessment," *International Bulletin of Missionary Research* 29, no. 4 (October 2005): 171-77. But there is also a call for another sort of churchless Christian in contemporary North America as well as other English-speaking countries. Alan Jamieson, *A Churchless Faith: Faith Journeys Beyond the Churches* (London: SPCK, 2002).

[26]G. R. Beasley-Murray, quoted in Vander Zee, *Christ, Baptism and the Lord's Supper,* p. 114.

[27]Vander Zee, *Christ, Baptism and the Lord's Supper,* p. 115.

[28]Much of what we say in the following points is said elsewhere in Vander Zee's book. But we think it helpful to gather these things up into one set of concise points to guide thinking and practice.

there is more than one baptism any more than we should contemplate the possibility that we have more than one Lord or more than one God. Yet we have heard evangelical and charismatic teachers offer detailed explanations about the several baptisms Christians should experience: baptism by the Spirit into the body of Christ, which occurs at conversion; a water baptism to symbolize that baptism, sometime subsequent to conversion; a baptism by Christ into the Holy Spirit, usually at some point later still, and even more. Such teaching seems plainly at odds with the New Testament teaching about our "one baptism."

3. *In the language of our ancient creeds, we ought to "acknowledge one baptism for the remission of sins."*[29] And, in doing so, we acknowledge that there is mystery in all of this that we do not fathom,[30] just as we cannot fathom many other things that we confess by faith. It seems we evangelicals can bow our minds before the doctrines of the Trinity, of the virgin birth of Christ, of Christ's two natures perfectly uniting in his one Person and so much more. But when it comes to the mysterious realities surrounding baptism and the Lord's Supper, we suddenly become so hyperrational that we seem unable to accept, at face value, such biblical language as "This is my body" (Lk 22:19) or "baptism that now saves you" (1 Pet 3:21). We do better to simply confess such language and accept the mysteries to which these words point us, even as we continue seeking to grow in our comprehension of these wonders.

4. *Each of the common modes of baptism practiced by churches today has strengths and limitations in terms of the imagery it presents to us.* It is tragically ironic that our considerations of the "one baptism," which actually unites all believers as the one body of Christ, have been the source of so many fractures within that body. One wonders how many of the denominations in the world today have arisen, at least in part, because of disputes about the meaning or mode of what most of us agree to be the "one baptism." Of all that we might argue about, disputes concerning how much water to use when baptizing seem the most lamentable. We argue about the precise meaning of the Greek word *baptizo* and of how the term was used in the ancient world. We also argue about which mode—sprinkling, pouring, immersing—best comports with biblical imagery. In fact, all these modes have biblical rationale and value.[31]

---

[29]This is the language of the Nicene Creed and is found in numerous other ancient creedal confessions.

[30]The word *sacrament* derives from the Latin *sacramentum,* which means "mystery."

[31]John Castelein, Robert Kolb, Thomas Nettles and Richard Pratt, *Understanding Four Views on Baptism* (Grand Rapids: Zondervan, 2007).

5. Baptism is to be a public celebration in the life of the congregation, for it is a church affair far more than it is a personal affair or a family affair. Vander Zee writes of his growing resolve as a pastor to decline requests from parents to have the baptism of their newborn children "done" by grandparents or some other family members. He reasons, "Innocent as [such a request] may be, it tends to make baptism into a family matter rather than an incorporation into Christ and his church, sending some wrong signals about the meaning of baptism."[32] We saw in the sketch of ancient Christian practices that baptism was often marked by great celebration and that the process leading toward baptism involved participation of the whole community, which included sponsorship of individuals and prayers for all those being baptized.

6. Baptism is the once-in-a-lifetime event[33] of initiation into the life of Christ and is to be followed by the often-to-be-repeated sacrament of the Lord's Supper. It has been to our own diminishment that contemporary Christians have forgotten or simply abandoned this ancient and wise pattern. We may think that the early catechumenal practice was too severe at this point, when those who had not been baptized were actually made to leave the meeting before the celebration of the Lord's Supper. But surely many of our churches have erred in the opposite direction. We do not, in some cases, practice any form of "fencing the table." In other cases, we give little more than lip service to the idea that the Lord's Supper may not be for everyone.

Paul commanded that believers ought to examine themselves before they partake of the Lord's Supper, lest they eat unworthily and thus eat and drink judgment on themselves (see 1 Cor 11:27-34). Although this warning concerned believers who were abusing the Lord's Supper by abusing one another through their exclusivistic and prejudicial practices, the principle of discernment regarding who partakes should be extended to all who may be present in the service, including unbelievers. The meal is, after all, a participation in the blood of Christ and in the body of Christ by those who are themselves the one body (see 1 Cor 10:16-17). The centuries-old practice of reserving participation for those who have been baptized (and have been catechized before their baptism), provided a wise safeguard in this regard. Our once-in-a-

---

[32]Vander Zee, *Christ, Baptism and the Lord's Supper*, p. 111.
[33]Ibid., p. 115. The term *event*, at least in the way Karl Barth has conceptualized, in the event of baptism refers to the inauguration of something that we enter into with eternal consequences as God's elect. "It is the *actus*, the point of contact, the event, from which everything we call nature and condition derives its being." Hans Urs von Balthasar, *The Theology of Karl Barth*, trans. Edward Oakes, SJ (San Francisco: Ignatius, 1992), p. 198.

lifetime baptism marked our new birth. The oft-to-be-repeated Lord's Supper, on the other hand, provides ongoing nourishment for our souls as we grow and mature in faith throughout the entirety of our lives. But as we have said, many among our numbers have moved from this approach or are at least very tempted to do so.

7. *Baptism ought to be preceded by a period of significant instruction.* It has been the practice of the church since New Testament times that baptism be preceded by instruction. In the book of Acts, we have no accounts of lengthy prebaptismal instructional episodes; no three years of "hearing the word" can be found there. Nevertheless, as we noted above, there was always *some* instruction to ensure some level of understanding of the Gospel and the implications of baptism.

In many evangelical churches today, there continues to be some brief and basic teaching of those who are about to be baptized. But that is not always the case. Some will even insist that it should not be so. The pattern of the New Testament *seems* to argue that baptism be performed immediately upon one's confession of faith. For example, we read that three thousand were baptized on the very day of Pentecost after hearing Peter's preaching. Elsewhere in the book of Acts, there is no evidence of lengthy delays between believing the good news and being baptized. All this appears to stand in stark contrast with the practices of the ancient catechumenate.

In light of the above, it might seem difficult to oppose, in some dogmatic fashion, those who would advocate mass baptisms at evangelistic events today. But we do well to ask whether the cultures in which we proclaim the Gospel might not justly call for some hesitation as we proceed. In the book of Acts, most of those who were baptized were either Jews or God-fearing Gentiles who already had some acquaintance with the Hebrew Scriptures.[34] In Acts 2, it is three thousand observant Jews who are baptized into Jesus' name. The Ethiopian official who is later baptized by Philip is a God-fearer, as evidenced by his reading of the scroll of Isaiah. Before being baptized, he receives Philip's Spirit-led instruction from Isaiah 53. Lydia was a God-fearing Gentile who regularly met with others to worship the one true God. Before her baptism, she received apostolic instruction from Paul. So too did the Philippian jailor. He and his family may come closest to an example of truly pagan con-

---

[34]Richard Longenecker, *The Expositor's Bible Commentary: Acts,* ed. Frank Gaebelein (Grand Rapids: Zondervan, 1981), p. 286; I. Howard Marshall, *The Acts of the Apostles,* Tyndale New Testament Commentaries (Downers Grove, Ill.: InterVarsity Press, 1980), p. 82. An exception to this rule might be the Philippian jailor.

verts to Christianity who were baptized very soon after conversion. But we should recall that in the several hours before he and his family were baptized, the jailor had witnessed an amazing miracle from God, been stopped from taking his own life, heard the Gospel from Paul and Apollos, and received further instruction from the apostle (see Acts 16:18-34).

By the time we read of the catechetical developments of the second century and beyond, it was increasingly *not* the case that new believers had such exposure to the things of God before coming to faith. The majority were now coming from pagan, Gentile backgrounds that boasted a radically different ethic, a radically different theology and a radically different spirituality. If our ministry settings are closer to such contexts than to those of Peter or Paul, perhaps we should not discount the notion of extended instruction too hastily. Three years may not be in order, but several weeks, or even several months, may prove a wise investment indeed.

If we are uncomfortable with too long a time of preparation in advance of baptism, then we ought to consider how we might engage as many as possible in post-baptismal catechesis. Surely Paul and Peter both do this in their epistles, which are obviously instructional in general. Beyond this, there are specific passages that can help believers come to grips with the meaning of their baptism, including passages that we cited earlier in this chapter. In our current evangelical Protestant churches, how likely are we to encourage such a looking back on one's baptism? Luther was a champion of this, as we have seen, and we would do well to emulate this emphasis of his.[35]

So then, baptism requires instruction, and those who dislike the notion of putting too much instruction up front—before one's baptism—should resolve to offer, or even require, much significant instruction afterward. The three thousand Jews baptized in Jerusalem on the day of Pentecost "devoted themselves to the apostles' teaching" after being baptized. If we will not provide significant teaching prior to baptism, what mechanisms do we have in place to ensure that there will be suitable teaching afterward?

Do we think we are being "biblical" by baptizing people immediately upon profession of faith? In fact, if we take such an approach to these matters, we may actually be very much out of step with biblical precedents and principles. Tragically, in many of our churches today, people are baptized without significant instruction either before or after. In some cases, the newly baptized actually cease their involvement in the church soon thereafter. Can we really

---

[35]Mark Tranvik, "Luther on Baptism," *Lutheran Quarterly* 13, no. 1 (1999): 75-90.

blame them for this when adequate instruction has been so lacking?

Preparing adults and adolescents for baptism. Drawing on the ideas and examples we have considered in this chapter, we propose the following principles for baptismal preparation of adults and adolescents in evangelical churches.

- *Church leaders ought to urge all believing adults to be baptized in obedience to Jesus Christ.* This is not only the mandate of Jesus in Matthew 28; it is also the clear and consistent practice of the church from the New Testament onward. The examples from the book of Acts and the references to baptism's critical role in the life of the Christian in the Epistles argue strongly for this. Some will point to the thief on the cross to argue that baptism is not strictly "necessary." But as is usually the case, the exception only serves to prove the rule. Believers are to be baptized, and this should be regularly communicated in various ways. Sermons on baptism will occur with some regularity if a pastor is making his way through New Testament texts. Each baptism in the church becomes a great opportunity to highlight the blessings and importance of baptism. A Bible-study series on the sacraments in the life of the church is another helpful idea. From time to time, announcements can be made inviting candidates for baptism and offering instruction to such about how to proceed. Ministry leaders should be attentive enough to the spiritual condition of those whom they are serving to know when someone has come to faith and thus ought to be baptized, or to learn if someone has been in the church for some time but has not yet been baptized.

- *Those wishing to be baptized should be instructed about the church's understanding and* practices *regarding this sacrament.* Having this material in printed form is a good idea. This can be made available as part of a variety of resources for both visitors and members—clear and concise documents on important topics and practices in the life of the congregation. Such resources can be posted online and/or made available in printed form.

- *Following the ancient practice of the church, we strongly recommend that candidates for baptism choose or be assigned a "sponsor."* This sponsor—who ought to be a mature believer of the same gender—can serve as a partner in prayer, study and accountability. He or she becomes a model and mentor in the life of discipleship and can, when appropriate, take part in some aspects of the instruction that precedes or follows the baptism.

- *Preparing for baptism provides the ideal opportunity to clarify and deepen the candidates' understanding of the Gospel and of their place in God's Story.* Taking their place in the Story involves their being joined to the church of Jesus Christ— a key aspect of the meaning of their baptism. Thus preliminary instruction about the church is also vital at this time.

- *Preparing for baptism presents an ideal opportunity for formal catechesis in the three summaries of the Faith—the creed, the Decalogue and the Lord's Prayer—as well as foundational instruction in the sacraments.* A historic catechism, such as the Heidelberg Catechism, may prove to be a helpful guide for this instruction. In contexts where it may be difficult to use one or more of these summaries (for example, the creed) for this sort of instruction, church leaders should prepare some other sort of primer in the three facets of the Faith.

- *The instruction involved to prepare candidates for baptism should be conducted by spiritually mature leaders of the congregation.* Whenever possible, the lead pastor should play a key role in this. The pastor's role is valuable for many reasons. First, it sends the message that this rite of passage is critically important, one of the most important things the church participates in. Second, it permits a great opportunity for the pastor to establish relationships with new members of the community and thus help to enfold those baptized fully into the family of faith. Third, because the instruction involved here is so foundational, the most theologically equipped teachers of the congregation should be part of this task; typically, the pastor is such a person. The pastor may well share the task with mature and gifted lay leaders or fellow staff members, but it is not a task to be wholly delegated to others.

- *The Lenten season is a wonderful time for intensive baptismal training.* This helps the local congregation connect to the historic practices of the church. It also has the advantage of preparation for the actual baptism ceremony to coincide with the celebration of Christ's resurrection at Easter, the best of possible times, both in terms of theological symbolism and historical connectedness. Additional baptisms and the necessary preparation in advance of them can, of course, be scheduled throughout the year as needed.

- *Candidates ought to be engaged in various spiritual disciplines during their season of preparation for baptism.* This also is to tie our own practices to ancient practices in the church. Disciplines that may be of particular value at this point include daily reading of the Scripture, joined with study, meditation and memorization; some form of daily prayer regimen; some form of fasting and repentance. One traditional practice has called for candidates to fast from Good Friday until their baptism during the Great Easter Vigil. All such disciplines will require additional instruction; both prebriefing and debriefing are helpful.

- *The ancient practice of "exorcising" the candidates should not be dismissed as anachronistic.* Surely the enemy of our souls still rages in his work today, and we are as called to spiritual warfare today as were believers in any age. Dismissing from our minds Hollywood imagery about such things, this can be as simple but sober an act as having church leaders and sponsors lay hands on the candidates, asking God to deliver them from the evil one and all his influences. At the same time, we ask God to fill these new believers with the Holy Spirit and direct their lives toward godliness.

- *Church members ought to be very aware of who these candidates are during their weeks of preparation, so that they may cheer them on and pray for their journey.* The particulars of how to recognize these candidates will vary from setting to setting, but this might include a public acknowledgment of the candidates at the outset of the preparation. During the Sunday services of the church, the candidates can be introduced and prayed for with the laying on of hands by church leaders.

- *As they are about to be baptized, some opportunity should be given for candidates to share their stories, their testimonies.* How this is done will depend once again on the culture of the congregation, on the number of candidates and so on. In my family's church, it was formerly our practice to "interview" each candidate just prior to baptism, the pastor asking questions and the candidate replying. As the church has grown in number, we now utilize carefully prepared video presentations introducing each candidate. These videos are presented on a large screen just before the person is baptized. This approach has been very well received in our particular congregational culture, but would not fit in all.

- *The baptisms themselves ought to be events for the whole community of God to experience and celebrate.* Vander Zee argues that baptisms ought to be performed always "in the church" rather than in some other venue. But it can be argued that taking the event into even more public arenas can be appropriate and powerful. In one church I used to serve, we conducted our baptisms outdoors in a lake at a public park. Most, though admittedly not all, of the congregation attended these events. Songs, testimonies, prayers and celebration were all part of the experience. Many passers-by stopped to witness portions of these celebrations. Some of our members found themselves engaged in meaningful conversations with these onlookers.

- *Those who have been baptized should be warmly welcomed and the God of such amazing grace joyously worshiped.* This is a wondrous event that we are experiencing together, and few things we do as a congregation are as worthy of celebrating as this.

- *As part of the celebration, the newly baptized should be invited to participate—for the first time—in the celebration of the Lord's Supper, together with the whole congregation of the faithful.* While we would suggest that this be done on the same day as the baptism, some congregations may prefer to do this on a Sunday soon after.

- *All the rituals surrounding the baptism, including those of preparation and follow-up, should be thought through carefully by church leaders.* We would suggest that these be chosen based on biblical teaching, historical precedents and cultural relevance—in that order. The rituals are themselves powerfully instructive and formative, and their selection is therefore very important.

Preparing for the baptism of infants. We will not here engage the controversy about credo-baptism versus paedo-baptism.[36] For our part, we are committed to the latter position, but we would direct readers elsewhere for full discussions of the challenging issues involved in this long-standing theological debate.[37] In those contexts where the infants of believing parents are received for baptism, we offer the following suggestions.

In general, we would apply most of the principles listed above to the baptism of infants, but with some obvious exceptions and significant adaptations. The principle adaptation, of course, is that it must be parents who receive the instruction in advance of the baptism of their children. The nature of that instruction will also be different, especially if the parents have themselves been baptized and have already received that instructional preparation. Parents should therefore be taught concerning how to raise their children in the fear and instruction of the Lord. For these children, catechesis is to occur in

---

[36]Generally speaking, credo-baptism refers to the conviction that only those old enough to articulate a confession of faith in Christ should be baptized. Paedo-baptists, on the other hand, believe that children of Christian parents are also to be baptized as true members of the covenant community.

[37]See Donald Bridge and David Phypers, *The Waters That Divide: Two Views on Baptism Explored* (Rossshire, U.K.: Christian Focus, 2008).

the years following their baptism. We have addressed this in general terms in chapter six. Beyond general guidance in raising their children, special instruction should be given regarding baptism, its meaning for children, and its implications and obligations for the parents of those children.

There continues to be a significant role for sponsors (in some traditions, such sponsors are called "godparents") to play here. They commit themselves to regular and ongoing prayer for the children to be baptized and to helping the parents raise those children in the fear and instruction of the Lord. At the baptism itself, it is parents who "testify" of the Lord's grace in their lives and confess their commitment to raise their children for the Lord. Grandparents, aunts and uncles, and other close family and friends can stand with the parents in solidarity with them as the infant is being baptized. These too are asked to commit themselves to the godly upbringing of the child. Indeed, the entire congregation is finally called on to play its part in raising this new member of the community.

The celebration of the event should be warm and wholehearted. But participation in the Lord's Supper must obviously be put off for a later date; we suggest a subsequent rite of passage, such as confirmation (see below), as the entryway to that experience. Since Paul plainly commands self-examination before partaking in the Lord's Supper, we cannot add our endorsement to the increasingly familiar practice of paedo-communion. In some church traditions, infants are dedicated to the Lord, rather than baptized. This practice, however, is perhaps as controversial in some credo-baptist circles as the aforementioned practice of paedo-communion is in churches where paedo-baptism is normative.

Preparing for confirmation. In churches where infants are baptized, it is imperative that a follow-up rite of passage, such as confirmation, be observed at a later date. The rite of confirmation developed over the history of the church, but the practice has a very uneven history in terms of its effectiveness. The Jewish practice of the *Bar mitzvah* (and now, in some Jewish traditions, the *Bat mitzvah* as well) involves a similar recognition of the critical juncture in the natural and spiritual development of early adolescents.[38] Tragically, in

---

[38]"Bar mitzvah" means "son of the commandment" and "Bat mitzvah" is "daughter of the commandment." For helpful introductions and overviews, see Eric Kimme, *Bar Mitzvah: A Jewish Boy's Coming of Age* (New York: Puffin, 1997); Robert Schoen, *What I Wish My Christian Friends Knew About Judaism* (Chicago: Loyola University Press, 2004). Some Christian churches now use this language themselves or have otherwise largely adapted practices closely patterned after the Jewish traditions. See, for example, Craig Hill, *Bar Barakah: A Parent's Guide to a Christian Bar Mitzvah* (Littleton, Colo.: Family Foundations International, 1998).

both Jewish and Christian circles, this sort of ritual "coming of age" has often been utterly stripped of its spiritual significance. In some cases, the event is a wholly social affair—another example of a spiritual tradition co-opted by forces of marketing and consumerism. Ironically, these rites of passage, which are intended to mark a new level of maturity and of taking one's place in the faith community, have actually become the exit door for many young persons. Some parents have even affirmed this sort of arrangement: "Just get confirmed, and then you can leave the church if you want."

But this need not be the case. A rite of passage at this stage of early adolescence can be filled with meaning, marking a new commitment and new commencement, if the family and the congregation commit themselves to the thoughtful work that can help to make it so. My daughter was among the first to experience confirmation in our young congregation. Both the process of preparation and the celebration itself were meaningful not only for those being confirmed but also for their parents and the entire congregation.

For the most part, all the principles applied above to preparing for the baptism of adults and adolescents could be applied to preparing for confirmation, but there are certainly differences. Some wonderful resources have been prepared in recent years to help churches think through the rationale and actual practice of confirmation, and these are available online or in print.[39]

Some churches have fixed an age for confirmation, with somewhere between the ages of twelve and fourteen being common choices. However, whether this is the best practice is questionable. We suggest that confirmation be an option open to young people beginning with adolescence, but that no age limit be set on the other side. In my own pastoral ministry, I have had the joy of celebrating confirmation with a number of collegians and young adults for whom the experience of publicly "owning" their faith was very rich indeed. For an individual who was baptized on the basis of his parents' faith, readiness for such an event could come at any point in life, and we should not close this opportunity off as though someone had become "too old."

The emphasis on confirmation is not on individuals confirming their own faith but on the fact that God is confirming his promises to them. Thus confirmation, like baptism, is preeminently a celebration of God's grace. One ritual act that I have found meaningful is to take a handful of water from the

---

[39]Richard Osmer, *Confirmation: Presbyterian Practices in Ecumenical Perspective* (Louisville, Ky.: Geneva Press, 1996). The Evangelical Covenant Church has good resources on confirmation called "The Journey: Discipleship/Confirmation" at <http://www.covchurch.org/forma tion/journey-dc>.

baptismal font (in whatever form that font might take) and, while pouring that water on the head of the individual, say these words: "[Name], remember your baptism, and give thanks to God."

Those being prepared for confirmation can participate in the same sorts of instructional and formative practices that we outlined above regarding preparation for baptism. Separating out adolescents for their own preparation has some value, to be sure. But there may be even greater value in letting them join with adults who are to be baptized or confirmed. In this way the church communicates that God's promises apply equally to the church's members, regardless of their age (see Acts 2:38-39) and seizes the opportunity for bonding generations together in the community of faith.

Even if youth are prepared for this rite separately from others, we strongly encourage that the lead pastor guide this process. The pastor must not miss this opportunity to build relationships with the young people of the church. To delegate this task to others may also send the message that young people in the church are not as important to the pastor as adults. Of course, a pastor may reason that others are more gifted in working with youth than he is and thus argue that it is *because* the adolescents are so important that someone else must be called on to lead the instruction. At the very least, though, we would suggest a partnership in which the lead pastor plays some vital role.

We would add one final note to this rather lengthy section of the chapter. We have titled this commitment "Baptism: Preparation, Confirmation and Recollection." What do we intend by this last word *recollection*? We mean, simply, that those who are members of "the faithful" should always be welcomed to join the training alongside the candidates for baptism and confirmation. Indeed, they should be encouraged to do so, perhaps once every few years. In this way they too can be encouraged to "remember your baptism, and give thanks to God." Congregants should regularly rehearse the truths and practices explored during the preparation. In turn, the candidates can be greatly encouraged by the presence of older brothers and sisters in the Faith. The example of a commitment to lifelong learning will itself be meaningful and instructive. And at the actual celebration of baptism or confirmation, all members should be encouraged to remember their baptisms together and to praise God for the gracious work he has done in all their lives. Just as we often encourage those in attendance at a wedding ceremony to remember their vows, we can and should seize these teachable moments to encourage all members to remember the covenant God has made with them.

HYMN FOR CONTEMPLATION AND WORSHIP

In Token That Thou Shalt Not Fear

In token that thou shalt not fear
Christ crucified to own,
We print the cross upon thee here,
and stamp thee his alone.

In token that thou shalt not blush
to glory in his Name,
We blazon here upon thy front
his glory and his shame.

In token that thou shalt not flinch
Christ's quarrel to maintain,
But 'neath his banner manfully
firm at thy post remain.

In token that thou too shalt tread
the path he traveled by,
Endure the cross, despise the shame,
and sit thee down on high;

Thus outwardly and visibly
we seal thee for his own;
and may the brow that wears his cross
hereafter share his crown.

Text: Dean Henry Alford, 1832
Tune: St. Stephen

QUESTIONS FOR PLANNING AND PRACTICE

1. "The first educational commitment of the church is to ensure that the Gospel is as accessible as possible to as many as possible." Is this the first educational commitment of your church? Why or why not? Do you think there are other goals that should come before this one?

2. This chapter outlines three ways to make sure church services are sensitive to the true Seeker: maintaining our commitment to true worship, practicing hospitality and setting guidelines for explanations at the proper times throughout the service. What would you add to this list, if anything?

3. Do you, or does your church, have a descriptive theology of baptism? Do

you agree with the point made by Leonard Vander Zee that baptism is the sign and seal of our incorporation into Christ? Why or why not? As one in educational ministry, how do you present the doctrine of baptism to new believers in Christ?

4. What are your congregation's current practices for preparing people for baptism and/or confirmation? What would you say are some relative strengths and weaknesses of these practices?

RESOURCES FOR FURTHER STUDY

Castelein, John, Robert Kolb, Thomas Nettles and Richard Pratt. *Understanding Four Views on Baptism*. Grand Rapids: Zondervan, 2007.

Fitch, David. *The Great Giveaway: Reclaiming the Mission of the Church from Big Business, Parachurch Organizations, Psychotherapy, Consumer Capitalism, and Other Modern Maladies*. Grand Rapids: Baker, 2005.

Johnson, Maxwell. *The Rites of Christian Initiation: Their Evolution and Interpretation*. Collegeville, Minn.: Liturgical Press, 1999.

Letham, Robert. *The Lord's Supper: Eternal Word in Broken Bread*. Phillipsburg, N.J.: P & R, 2001.

Osmer, Richard. *Confirmation: Presbyterian Practices in Ecumenical Perspective*. Louisville, Ky.: Geneva Press, 1996.

Vander Zee, Leonard. *Christ, Baptism and the Lord's Supper: Recovering the Sacraments for Evangelical Worship*. Downers Grove, Ill.: InterVarsity Press, 2004.

Webber, Robert. *Journey to Jesus: The Worship, Evangelism, and Nurture Mission of the Church*. Nashville: Abingdon, 2001.

Wilson, Marvin. *Our Father Abraham: Jewish Roots of the Christian Faith*. Grand Rapids: Eerdmans, 1989.

14

Commitments for a Congregational Curriculum

(Part 2)

But grow in the grace and knowledge of our Lord and Savior Jesus Christ.
To him be the glory both now and forever! Amen.

2 PETER 3:18

▼

COMMITMENT TO THE COVENANT COMMUNITY

We looked in the previous chapter at some of the formative practices that could be involved surrounding one's baptism or confirmation. Our focus there was on catechumenal experiences, spread out over a period of several weeks. Baptism, we argued, is the point of entrance into Christian community. The baptized person is now a member of the church of Jesus Christ, the church that spans the ages and extends through the Earth. But it will not do to consider membership of the church only in a cosmic sense. The church of Jesus expresses itself in local congregations. Thus baptism into the body of Christ leads us to consider issues of church membership.

Many regard baptism as having settled once and for all the matter of membership in the church. In other words, if one is a member of the church universal, then we must surely regard him as a member of our local community. To suggest otherwise would be theologically problematic, for some at least. Others feel that there remains a further step to be taken. It is one thing, they reason, to have entered the family of faith in its broad and general expression. But it is another thing to localize that membership in a particular community, for each community embodies, to some extent, particular beliefs, values, policies and commitments. Therefore, it is not unreasonable to expect that additional preparation be required for "membership" in the local church, often with an additional celebratory rite as well.

Depending on how one views the above debate, a process of instruction for church membership may or may not make sense. If baptism concludes the matter of membership in both the universal church and the local congregation, then whatever instruction we have required for baptismal candidates might be regarded as necessarily sufficient. Others will more likely accept the possibility of additional training for membership, since they see local church membership as not directly linked to one's baptism.

It is our conviction that further instruction should be *required* beyond that which we have outlined for baptismal preparation. Later in this chapter, we will make numerous proposals for lifelong learning and formation. At this point, though, we are still arguing that certain instruction must actually be mandated for those who are members of the congregation. Some of this mandated instruction we considered under the heading "Baptism: Preparation, Confirmation and Recollection" in the previous chapter. There we included such topics as clarifying and deepening our understanding of the Gospel and formal catechesis in the three historic summaries of the Faith: the creed, the Lord's Prayer and the Decalogue.

We now suggest that still more instruction is needed, and we will soon turn to consider the actual content we propose. How that is packaged into a model for a particular congregation, however, can vary from one setting to the next, depending on a number of factors, including the church's perspective on the relationship between baptism and membership. Some of the possible ways of "packaging" the material we envision under this heading of Commitment are as follows:

- just as we have proposed: a period of training for baptism followed by a period of training for commitment to the covenant community

- alternatively, an extended period of training for baptism that includes the additional content concerns we are proposing relative to commitment

- or two stages of instruction: the first preceding baptism and preparing a person for membership in the church, beginning with baptism; the second after baptism, ratifying a person's membership in the church

IS CHURCH MEMBERSHIP BIBLICAL?

Although the spiritual reality that becoming Christian means being part of the church of Jesus Christ is biblically and theological irrefutable, it is difficult to build a definitive biblical case for church membership in this secondary sense of joining a local congregation. There are very few proof texts for this to which one can appeal. But it is clear from the New Testament teaching that all believers are to view themselves as vitally linked to their fellow believers and that this envisions participation in an actual community, not merely a theoretical or virtual one.

Most of the New Testament epistles were written to particular congregations or to groups of congregations. So, for example, when Paul told the believers in Colosse to "bear with each other and forgive whatever grievances you may have against one another" (Col 3:13), he was telling these believers how they were to live together in the context of their own community. These were not mere platitudes. In the same way, Paul's letters to the Corinthians make numerous appeals to particular issues and concerns of a particular faith community. Paul "names names" and cites actual situations, problems and questions. He raises issues of discipline, including telling the Corinthians how they ought to respond to particular sinners and particular situations in their midst. The same sort of thinking is clear with regard to most of the New Testament letters; believers take their places as members of living, breathing communities of faith.[1]

Alongside this theological case for church membership are many practical, and even legal, arguments to be made. Congregations must make countless decisions over the years—decisions regarding finances, facilities, personnel, church discipline, ministries and much more. To make those decisions it is essential that some be identified as "members" who are duly empowered to do so. In many contexts, such as churches in the United States, legal obligations actually require congregations to have an official membership for such purposes. There are many who visit a church on occasion, and there are many who attend frequently. But "membership" suggests a deep commitment to the life of the church, a commitment that accords with the emphases of New Testament examples.

---

[1]One of the more helpful arguments for church membership in this localized sense is available on the website for 9Marks, under the headings related to church membership. See, in particular, Mike McKinley, "Separating Insiders and Outsiders: A Biblical Theology of Church Membership—Part 1" at <http://www.9marks.org/CC/article/0,,PTID314526|CHID598016|CIID2238756,00.html>.

In actual practice, there is not a precise, one-to-one correspondence between joining a local congregation and becoming a member of the universal church. There are clearly instances in which people become members of a local church but are not yet members of the true church. They have not heard, believed and obeyed the Gospel of grace. They may have been baptized, but where true faith in the true Christ is absent, one cannot be regarded as a member of the church of the redeemed.

On the other hand, there are an increasing number of Christian believers in the world today who have not identified themselves with a local church.[2] In light of these things, it is critical that we help those in our own church communities be clear about this distinction. We need to teach them well that "joining our church" does not automatically mean that they have become true Christians and thus members of the one, holy, catholic and apostolic church of Jesus Christ. We must also teach that belonging to Christ necessarily involves belonging to his body in a meaningful and tangible way.

OUTLINING A PLAN OF MEMBERSHIP INSTRUCTION

A final point of our rationale for the membership training we envision is that such an approach helps the teaching ministry of the church to be more compelling, in the literal sense of that term. To compel is to force, to induce, to oblige. This may sound to us a strange sort of aspiration for a church's teaching ministry. Especially we who are raised in purportedly democratic societies may stumble over the notion of trying to compel Christian education in the church. But our unease at this point is more a function of our cultural situation than of biblical or historical Christian values.

As we have seen, in the ancient church a kind of compulsion was built into the catechumenate. In nearly all cases, a person was not permitted to the sacrament of the Lord's Supper who had not been baptized. In turn, a person was not permitted to the waters of baptism who had not been catechized, usually in a rigorous and extensive process. How different our approach tends to be in many contemporary evangelical churches. Not only do we permit anyone who has "accepted Jesus as their Savior" to the Table, we may well invite into church leadership anyone who volunteers—member or not, baptized or not, mature believer or not.

Once again, it seems clear to us that we have unwisely removed ourselves

---

[2]See Timothy Tennent, "The Challenge of *Churchless* Christianity: An Evangelical Assessment," *International Bulletin of Missionary Research* 29, no. 4 (2005).

from the precedents of our Christian forebears. The approach taken here would permit neither participation in the Lord's Supper nor formal membership in the congregation to anyone who has not yet been baptized (or confirmed), and no one would be baptized without having been catechized along the lines we proposed earlier. The *compelling* nature of this plan also includes the fact that no one could begin leadership training in the church other than a member. If then, for example, we had a minimum of six weeks of training for baptism and an additional six weeks of training for membership, we would have the benefit of knowing that all members of the church would have had at least twelve weeks of a designated catechesis in a common content and involving common processes.

What sort of content would be appropriate for such membership training? We suggest the following as one example of what a six-session membership training might include. Table 14.1 presents the content emphasis suggestions in an overview fashion; commentary on each of the sessions follows.

Table 14.1. Content Overview for a Six-Session Membership Course

Session	Content Emphasis
1	A review of the Gospel and the Story; an introduction of membership in the local church vis-a-vis the universal church; introduction of the membership covenant
2	Exploring the beliefs of the church, part one: Christian consensus and evangelical essentials
3	The beliefs of the church, part two: Denominational (or other) distinctives
4	Overview of the history, vision and values of the congregation; introduction of the church's bylaws
5	Exploration of the privileges and responsibilities of membership; further look at the membership covenant
6	Focus on how to fully take one's place in the body; matching gifts with opportunities and so on; dealing with questions that remain

The following is a description of what each of the proposed sessions might look like in practice.

Session one—review of the Gospel and the great Story, and discussion of the meaning of membership in the local church vis-à-vis the universal church; introduction of the membership covenant.

The Gospel, once again, has priority of place. Here we rehearse its central features for these would-be members. It is not "new" to them at this point, unless the systems of the church have already failed miserably. Yet the Gospel is ever "new," and we prayerfully seek to cultivate this sense among the congregants. We also rehearse the basic outline of the great redemptive Story and discuss how formally joining the church relates to us taking our places in that Story.

As noted above, there is not a one-to-one correspondence between membership in the church universal and membership in a local congregation. We dispel any mistaken notions along these lines. But we also work to make clear that while there may be some genuine Christian believers who have not joined a local congregation—perhaps for legitimate reasons—this is never the ideal. The universal church is to be expressed in local congregations.

At the close of the membership training, members will sign a covenant. Pastors and/or elders will sign each covenant as well. Why ask members to sign a covenant? First, the seriousness of the matter at hand must be highlighted in many ways, and this is one helpful way to do so. Second, for pragmatic and legal purposes, a covenant can be a very helpful document. Since all members will be expected to sign the covenant, it is best to introduce it at the beginning of the process, so that there will be no surprises later and so participants can begin weighing their commitment with sober judgment.

Session two—consideration of the beliefs of the church along three levels: Christian consensus, evangelical essentials and denominational (or other) distinctives.

It is critical to have participants study the church's statement of faith. It is surprising that some churches have no such statement (this may be part of a trending toward the downplaying of propositional belief systems), but this seems a tragic mistake. Such a statement is both constructive and protective. It is constructive in the sense that it is a positive teaching tool available for all to see, study and consider. It is protective, or preservative, in that it provides a basis for evaluating potential threats in the form of heresy or less severe forms of deviant teaching. Part of the membership covenant should involve affirmation of the teachings of the church; without a statement of those beliefs, any such affirmation will obviously prove difficult.

While some churches are unwise in having no stated summary of their beliefs, others fall into a more common mistake, that of having a statement that makes no distinction between points of greater and lesser import. We have said that there needs to be a distinction between local church membership and what makes one a Christian. Our concern here is an application and extension of that distinction. Good catechesis draws a distinction between primary doctrines and secondary doctrines. Or, to use more traditional lan-

guage, we must distinguish between essentials and non-essentials. The familiar saying "In essentials, unity; in non-essentials, liberty; in all things, charity"[3]
captures this idea well. To fail to make such distinctions is to fail in terms of
both charity and humility; it is to treat our local assembly or our particular
denomination as though we were the *whole* of the Christian community rather
than a *part* of the historical and universal body of Christ. The type of distinction we suggest has three levels, which we label Christian consensus, evangelical essentials and denominational (or other) distinctives.

By "Christian consensus," we refer to those essential doctrines that have
bound together Christians, or all orthodox communions, in all ages and cultures. Some have referred to this body of beliefs as representing "the Great
Tradition."[4] Thinking of the church as falling primarily into three historic
groupings—Orthodox, Catholic and Protestant—this level of the doctrinal
basis speaks of those beliefs shared by those communions. Thus the first part
of the church's doctrinal statement might begin with words such as these: "In
concert with orthodox Christians in all ages and in all cultures, we affirm the
following truths . . ."

The next level of the doctrinal statement is labeled "Evangelical Essentials." Here we refer to the truths that distinguish historic Protestantism[5] from
the Orthodox and Catholic communions. Labeling these "evangelical" suggests a distinction between those Protestants who continue to affirm the basic
tenets of the evangelical Reformation and those who have long since abandoned them (typically, they have also abandoned certain tenets of the Christian consensus as well).

How can we identify the central tenets of the Reformation? One way is by
reference to the historic *solas:*

- *soli Deo gloria* (affirming that God alone is to be praised and glorified for
  our salvation and for all good things)

- *sola gratia* (affirming that it is by grace alone that we are saved)

---

[3]In recent years this saying has been ascribed to Peter Meiderlin, also known as Rupertus Melde-
nius, an irenic Lutheran theologian of the early seventeenth century. The saying, which has
long been popularly attributed to Augustine and sometimes to Melanchthon, became a favorite
of Puritan pastor Richard Baxter, who may be most responsible for popularizing it.

[4]James Cutsinger, ed., *Reclaiming the Great Tradition: Evangelicals, Catholics and Orthodox in Dialogue* (Downers Grove, Ill.: InterVarsity Press, 1997).

[5]We are here using *evangelical* in the historic sense of the term, not in the popular sense of our
own day. See Mark Noll, *American Evangelical Christianity: An Introduction* (Oxford: Blackwell,
2001).

- *solus Christus* (affirming that Christ alone saves)

- *sola fide* (affirming that we are justified freely, by faith alone)

- *sola Scriptura* (affirming that Scripture alone is the authoritative source for our life and doctrine)[6]

We have chosen to call this level "Evangelical Essentials," thus making it clear that from the perspective of an evangelical Christian, these matters are not trivial. Indeed, they are not to be understood as secondary or non-essentials. These are essential matters.

But this assertion will likely raise several objections, and from various quarters. Some may argue that we have drawn an unhelpful distinction between Protestants and other Christians by referring to these beliefs as essentials. But it is surely unhelpful for a Protestant to deny that he holds certain truths to be inconsequential when this is clearly not the case. Honesty about our convictions makes meaningful dialogue possible. Still others will consider it uncharitable of us to exclude more theologically liberal Protestants from our scheme. We reply that those who reject tenets of the faith that have been "believed everywhere, always and by all" have effectively excluded themselves from the body of orthodox believers.

Some who affirm the tenets of the Reformation will, on the other side of the spectrum, feel that our distinctions are overly generous. They will reason that apart from a commitment to these evangelical essentials, one cannot be a Christian at all. Therefore, we need not two levels but one, whether we call it Christian consensus or evangelical essentials. But we consider this to be both a historically problematic and spiritually uncharitable approach.

Next we must acknowledge that a further difficulty presents itself in our discussion. There are many who would self-describe as evangelicals today but who would not affirm all of the *solas* of the Reformation. In particular, the notion of *sola fide* has come under considerable fire in recent decades. We briefly considered this issue earlier in the book and need not revisit it here. We simply reiterate that it is our conviction that all of the Reformation *solas*, properly understood, do represent biblical teaching.

---

[6]While we agree with D. H. Williams and others who have recently questioned popular understandings of *sola Scriptura* that dismiss the contributions of the church fathers as relatively insignificant, we do not follow the lead of some in therefore seeming to dismiss the entire notion of *sola Scriptura*. Rather, we suggest that it is in fact Scripture alone that reveals the truths essential to our salvation and that the fathers of the church both testify to and help to clarify that biblical revelation.

The third level of our proposed statement of faith concerns denominational (or other) distinctives. In practice, a church could label this level by use of its denominational identity or other affiliative identity. Sample headings include "Conservative Baptist Distinctives," "Vineyard Distinctives," "Evangelical Presbyterian Distinctives" and so on. At this point, we are further advancing the view that we must distinguish between primary and secondary doctrines. This is not to diminish the importance of settled convictions about church polity, the meaning of the sacraments, the practice of spiritual gifts and others. These are vital concerns that must be treated with care and respect. But it really is critical to distinguish between what makes one Christian and what makes one Baptist or Presbyterian or Pentecostal. To fail to make this distinction is to teach poorly. Suggesting that the matter of whether or not "the gift of tongues" is still available for believers today is as weighty a matter as the authority of Scripture or the two natures of Christ is simply irresponsible.

Session three—a continuation of session two, with particular focus on denominational (or other) distinctives.

The sorts of distinctions outlined above will very likely take a minimum of two sessions to consider. Some of the items will already have been introduced to participants if they have been part of the baptism or confirmation training explored in the previous chapter. This would especially be true of the Christian consensus and evangelical essentials levels.

Extra attention can be paid in this session to work through denominational (or other) distinctives. Although we suggested above that what makes one Presbyterian (for example) is not as important as what makes one Christian, this in no way is to suggest that what makes one Presbyterian is not critically important. It is disconcerting to hear some pastors say that "most of our folks really don't know the first thing about what it means to be a Baptist" or a Presbyterian, Methodist or whatever the case may be. Some even seem to hold it as a badge of honor that they have so successfully downplayed their denominational affiliation.

Session four—history, vision and values of the local congregation and introduction of the church's "bylaws" and other such documents.

Session five—history, vision and values (continued), with focus on the privileges and responsibilities of church members; further consideration of the membership covenant.

Session six—taking one's place in the body, an introduction to ministry opportunities and gifts assessment.

The final three sessions move us further toward the particulars of the local church. We have discussed the church universal and considered denominational distinctives. We now consider things pertaining to our specific congregation. An overview of the church's history is offered, as is an introduction to the vision and values that the congregation believes God has called it to live out in its community. It is helpful to have documents that address these unique features of the congregation and to make them available to members in training, either in print or online.

Next, attention shifts to helping members understand their place in the life of the congregation. This calls for attention to the privileges and responsibilities of membership, as well as helping members begin the ongoing process of discerning their gifts, talents and other aptitudes for contributing to the vitality of the body. The many concerns we have listed as part of sessions three through six will take a good amount of time to introduce adequately. Thankfully, many denominations offer helpful resources for all these matters, which should be utilized by particular congregations. Helps for churches not linked to any particular denomination are also available and can be useful in the design of the membership training process.[7]

FURTHER CONSIDERATIONS

Aside from the content of the membership training that we have outlined above, we offer two more suggestions. First, as with the preparations for baptism or confirmation, this process should be one of both sobriety and celebration. Consciously and deliberately taking one's place in the life of the body of Christ is a serious matter, and it should be treated as such. Thus the sessions should not be conducted *pro forma*. To the contrary, they should be bathed in prayer. Opening and perhaps also closing each session with a few minutes of intentional worship can help to set this mood well. The reception of the new members into the life of the congregation should be duly celebrated. This could include a formal "ceremony," either during the Sunday-morning worship or during a "congregational meeting" of members.

Second, we must pay attention to the link between membership and church discipline.[8] Once again, we must refer the reader to resources that examine

---

[7]We recommend, for example, Chuck Lawless, *Membership Matters: Insights from Effective Churches on New Member Classes and Assimilation* (Grand Rapids: Zondervan, 2005).

[8]Churches do well to emphasize to new members the place of discipline in the life of the church. Otherwise, when discipline needs to be administered in hopes of restoring the member(s) of the congregation, those who should come under discipline may simply leave and join another

this matter in greater depth.[9] We would simply offer here the observation that discipline should be viewed as both preventive and restorative. Some of our thinking about church discipline is erroneous because we tend to think of the end as punishment. But the end we must always have in view is restoration. Of course, this end is sometimes not achieved, in spite of our best efforts. But it remains the proper aim of all disciplinary efforts. If we would give primary attention to preventive discipline, we would find ourselves having to initiate processes of restorative discipline less often.

From 2 Timothy 3:16-17 we learn that "all Scripture is God-breathed and is useful for teaching, rebuking, correcting and training in righteousness, so that the man of God may be thoroughly equipped for every good work." The four uses of the Scriptures mentioned here suggest both preventive and restorative discipline. Through careful teaching of the Scriptures, we labor to prevent members from falling off the rails, as it were. If they do fall, we use the Scripture for rebuke and correction—restorative forms of discipline. "Training in righteousness," whether done before a failure or after one, suggests another form of preventive discipline.

In view of the above, we suggest that certain commitments for ongoing education be included as part of the process of maintaining membership. Many churches commit themselves to keeping their membership rolls current. One criterion for this could be that members continue to participate in instructional and formational experiences offered by church leaders. Of course, we would fully expect members to attend worship services faithfully and to support the church through the stewardship of time, talents and treasures.

As hinted above, we would further require members to continue to participate in some aspects of the "Christian education" program of the congregation. For example, if the church views its small groups as vital to its ongoing life and health, then participation in a small group may be required to maintain one's membership. If formal instruction is offered in a Sunday school class or in a quarterly seminar format, then the church may require its members to attend at least one or two of these courses each year.

The actual shape of such requirements will obviously vary from congregation to congregation, depending on which ongoing formational practices are most highly valued in the church. Exceptions and accommodations

---

church to avoid the discipline. Compounding the tragedy is that many church leaders do not endeavor to learn about the spiritual background of those who have come to their church from other churches to avoid discipline.

[9]See Lawless, *Membership Matters,* pp. 47-92.

must be made, of course. Issues like health, schedule, age, travel and more will have to be factored into the crafting of any policy. But it is not unreasonably burdensome to ask members to support those ministries that are part of a congregation's heartbeat and to commit themselves to ongoing instruction and formation as disciples of Jesus. In the following section, we offer some suggestions about practices that could be part of such ongoing commitments.

Deepening and Developing in the Gospel

Thus far we have considered some possibilities for the "procatechesis" of "seekers," and formal catechesis for those being baptized, confirmed or becoming members of the church. We now consider the matter of lifelong catechesis, focusing on our ongoing development as disciples of Jesus Christ. Unlike the process related to baptism and membership, what we have in mind here is not restricted to a particular time period. Instead, we are looking toward ongoing, open-ended growth in grace and in the knowledge of our Lord Jesus Christ (2 Pet 3:18).

This commitment is open-ended not only in terms of its length but also in terms of its breadth. There really is no limit to the sorts of activities and experiences, planned and spontaneous, that play into our development as disciples. As we have already noted on several occasions, everything the church does teaches and forms its participants for either good or ill. Our commitment must be to channel as much of these efforts and energies as we possibly can toward the good, for positive formation in Christlikeness.

In chapter five we offered an overview of a CORE content for congregational curriculum, outlined in table 5.2. The third row of that table is especially pertinent for the sort of ongoing development we have in mind (see table 14.2).

Table 14.2. Deeper Immersion in the Gospel and Its Implications

Deeper immersion in the Gospel & its implications	Studying the Gospel: rigorous study of the Scriptures *Lk 24:27, 44*	Retelling & celebrating the Gospel; the sacraments *1 Cor 11:26*	Obeying the Gospel: learning to walk in love *Eph 2:10; 5:2; Tit 2:14; 2 Tim 3:17*

What we are envisioning, in short, is helping to foster a deepening development in the Gospel. As we saw in chapter five, this will sometimes best be cast as a deepening understanding and experience of the great redemptive Story. At other times, this growing in the Gospel will best be cast as deepening our understanding and experience of the Faith.

In chapter four, especially, we considered the Gospel as pointing us toward three facets of the Faith. The sound doctrine that conforms to the glorious Gospel we termed *the Truth*. The godly living that is in line with that sound doctrine we labeled *the Way*. And the life-giving power that flows from the Gospel and enables us to walk in the Way we called *the Life*. In formal catechesis, we focus our energies on grounding believers in all these dimensions. In ongoing catechesis, too, we focus on growing believers in these same facets of the Faith. We will utilize these terms to provide a convenient way of organizing the strategic ministry suggestions that we offer below toward deepening and developing in the Gospel.

Under each of the three categories we will make specific suggestions regarding practices that can aid deepening and developing in that aspect of the Gospel, beginning in each case with a ministry strategy that we believe to be especially important. For many of the practices that we enumerate below, we do not offer further rationale since we have introduced that earlier in the book. In those cases, we direct the reader to the earlier discussion of the topic, noting those chapters in brackets.

DEEPER IN THE TRUTH

The early Christians, after having been baptized, steadfastly devoted themselves to the apostles' teaching *(didachē)*. Too many of us, however, have had the unhappy experience of watching our own congregations lag far behind in this vital commitment. We who have been charged to provide leadership in this area must bear some of the responsibility for such breakdowns in discipleship. Perhaps we have failed to provide in our own lives positive role models of ones who are never satisfied with our present understandings of the deep truths of the Faith. Perhaps we we been too fixated on attracting larger numbers to our churches and insufficiently attentive to the biblical injunctions to teach the Truth and proclaim the whole counsel of God. Perhaps we have been lulled into passivity in this area by forces of culture that we not only have failed to challenge but have even failed to recognize. Perhaps we have unwisely elevated as church leaders people who do not themselves "keep hold of the deep truths of the faith" (1 Tim 3:9) and thus are not in a position to teach such things to others. Perhaps we have uncritically followed trends from churches that had the appearance of success, and in the process, a devotion to serious, sustained, substantive teaching simply fell through the cracks. Perhaps we have failed to adjust some of our structures or venues for teaching to better serve authentic needs of our congregants. Perhaps—like many in the culture that surrounds us and shapes us—we have simply become lazy, negligent, uncritically "tolerant" or unapologetically apathetic when it comes to matters of the Truth.

However we may have gotten into this situation, in many of our evangelical congregations it is hard to deny that we frequently find ourselves ministering in such circumstances.[10] We believe that the sort of commitments we expressed above—access to the glorious Gospel, a refreshed catechetical approach to baptism, and a serious and substantive training toward commitment to the covenant community—can help us move a long way forward in changing our congregational cultures in this area.

But we need more. We need to nurture an ongoing commitment to learning the doctrines of the Faith. As particular and practical expressions of a commitment to deepening and developing in the Truth, we suggest ministries such as the following.

1. Consistent, ongoing teaching of the Scriptures and the Faith to all members, regardless of age. This may involve utilizing a Sunday school format, small group Bible studies, or some other format or setting throughout the week. While there are many informal ways in which we teach the truths of the Faith to our members—including through our times of worship, fellowship and service together—these should be seen as supplementing and supporting, not as supplanting, our commitment to formal and intentional teaching of these truths. We have already noted the fact that many churches no longer feature an intentional ministry of catechesis. Some of those who abandoned that approach to ministry essentially replaced it with a Sunday school model for teaching. More recently, however, many churches have concluded that the Sunday school is no longer reaching a majority or even a sizeable minority of their members—something that is often true for all age groups. In some of these cases, Sunday school has disappeared and small groups or cell groups have become a new locus of much church energy and activity. But as we have seen, this new structure—though very well suited for certain essential minis-

---

[10]Our colleague David Wells's book *No Place for Truth: Or Whatever Happened to Evangelical Theology?* (Grand Rapids: Eerdmans, 1993) well chronicles much of our concern about this very point.

tries—is often not conducive to substantive and sustained teaching of the Scriptures.

Where, then, are the maturing believers in our churches given real opportunity to grow deeper in the truths of the Faith? Are the weekly sermons that they hear typically substantive expositions of the Scripture? Do those sermons regularly feature introduction to and explication of the doctrines of the Faith? Even if they do, is this all the training in the Truth that our members really need for the sake of their personal formation or for the sake of the formation and spiritual health of the congregation?

We would urge church leaders to evaluate their present ministry structures with a view toward reaching as many as possible with as much as possible of the apostles' teaching as recorded in the Scriptures. Where the Sunday school format is proving to still be effective, let it be retained; where it is no longer effective, let it be reinvigorated or replaced with a more culturally appropriate and suitable structure. If it is working for some age groups but not for others, then appropriate adjustments should be undertaken. Similarly, if the small group model is proving to be an effective setting for such teaching, then by all means it should be utilized. If, on the other hand, that setting does not seem to prove effective, then we cannot merely shrug our shoulders at the absence of rigorous teaching, even if other wonderful things have been happening in our church because of our small groups.

The best structures for substantive teaching will vary, depending on the particular cultural realities of each congregation and owing to particular realities of various age and life-stage groups in the church. In my own church's culture, as noted earlier, we have come to believe that a weekend seminar format is likely the best way to proceed for teaching adults, and so we are now planning and preparing accordingly.

One other way that our commitment to ongoing development in the Truth of the Gospel can be demonstrated is, once again, to build a *compelling* feature into this commitment. For example, just as a church may articulate its expectations regarding the commitments of its members to give financially and serve in the church, expectations about ongoing learning of the Faith can also be clearly articulated. This could be made part of a membership covenant and could become one of the factors that is periodically considered when the membership rolls of the church are reviewed. If, for example, the church offers four weekend seminars per year that are dedicated to formal, carefully planned and skillfully led teaching of the Scriptures and of the Faith, perhaps members could be asked to participate in at least one or two of those events each year as a minimum expectation of their continued, active membership. The content of these teaching opportunities could include a balance of CORE and "elective" teachings.

2. Occasional opportunities for extended times of teaching/learning—seminars, retreats, etc.—that focus on specific themes, topics or Bible books. Even where a weekly venue for formal teaching is being effectively utilized, our commitment to teaching the Truth can be further enhanced by adding occasional opportunities to go even deeper. Thoughtful incorporation of guest preachers and teachers can be valuable in these because they introduce congregants to perspectives they might otherwise not have access to.[11] Members could also be encouraged to participate in ministries available outside the local church; creative partnerships with certain parachurch organizations may prove helpful.

3. Teaching of appropriate materials to specific populations—grouped by age, gender, life stage, special needs or interests. In this book, we have largely emphasized biblical principles that can be applied to a wide variety of ages and life stages in the church. We have also advocated intergenerational educative and formative experiences and frequently decried age segmentation in the church. Yet we do believe that parallel efforts to minister in focused ways to particular audiences within the church can be exceedingly helpful. Thus, though it has not been the focus of this book, we consider it essential that churches design intentional ministries for specific populations within the congregation—such as children's ministries, youth ministries, men's and women's ministries, and ministries to the various life stages of adult congregants. Such ministries should be approached and situated in ways that, far from isolating these groups, actually help them find their places within the larger community. We urge, then, a both/and, rather than either-or, approach to these matters.

Attending to the specific realities of people at a given life stage can help to identify the isms, idols and evil practices over against which we teach the Faith. For example, in ministry among the church's youth, the youth ministers and teachers must be attentive to particular cultural forces confronting these adolescents that may not be as significant for younger children, col-

---

[11]The church will want to be careful that such events fit nicely into the rhythm—the formational/educational flow—of the church, rather than merely having them as events that are isolated from the church's overall efforts to form its people.

legians or adults at various life stages.[12] We need to pursue cultural congruence in this regard as surely as we do with regard to issues of nationality and ethnicity.

4. Encouraging memorization of Bible portions, creeds, catechisms, hymns and other teaching tools, coupled with appropriate teaching/explanation. It has been to our great deprivation that we have downplayed memorization, especially the memorizing of Scripture. This seems to be partly due to our increased dependence on technology. But every technological gain has a corresponding loss.[13] We can load Scripture onto our computer hard drives or onto our Blackberry and have it always at hand. But clearly in times of great challenge and difficulty, having God's word in our hearts is far more valuable (Ps 119:11), as Jesus' response to the tempter so powerfully demonstrates (Mt 4:1-11). Young children should especially be helped and encouraged in this area because of their natural capacity for such memorization. As we have seen, failing to urge our children toward this is a form of "dismembering" them [chapter 11].

5. Provision for a variety of teaching/learning experiences in a variety of settings throughout the week and the year. Reckoning with the reality that there are many different learning styles, intelligences and interests represented in the body, we must offer a wide variety of approaches to teaching, learning and formation—in both ongoing ministries of the church and in the occasional experiences planned throughout the course of the year [chapter 9].

6. Ongoing equipping of parents, and of the entire faith community, to help them do their part in raising their children in the Faith. Church leaders challenge and encourage parents to fulfill their biblically mandated duty of raising up their own children in the Faith, modeling this for them, training them, and providing time and resources for them as necessary for the task [chapter 6].

---

[12]Some helpful books dedicated to understanding issues of great import to American adolescents include Walt Mueller's books *Engaging the Soul of Youth Culture: Bridging Teen Wordviews and Christian Faith* (Downers Grove, Ill.: Inter Varsity Press, 2006); *Opie Doesn't Live Here Anymore: Where Faith, Family, and Culture Collide* (Cincinnati: Standard, 2007); and *Youth Culture 101* (Grand Rapids: Zondervan, 2007). See also Dean Borgman, *Hear My Story: Understanding the Cries of Troubled Youth* (Peabody, Mass.: Hendrickson, 2003); Kenda Creasy Dean, *Practicing Passion: Youth and the Quest for a Passionate Church* (Grand Rapids: Zondervan, 2006); Chap Clark and Steve Rabey, *When Kids Hurt: Help for Adults Navigating the Adolescent Maze* (Grand Rapids: Baker, 2009); Fernando Arzola, *Toward a Prophetic Youth Ministry: Theory and Praxis in Urban Context* (Downers Grove, Ill.: Inter Varsity Press, 2008).
[13]Nicholas Carr, "Is Google Making Us Stupid? What the Internet Is Doing to Our Brains" *Atlantic Monthly,* July/August 2008, pp. 56-63.

7. Ongoing training for those engaged in teaching ministries at all levels. All who have stepped into teaching roles in the life of the church need ongoing training and encouragement themselves. Church leaders should provide regular opportunities and quality resources for such equipping [chapter 6].

8. Reading groups and other kinds of discussion groups. Aside from more "traditional" teaching and learning activities in the church, reading groups, film groups and the like can be wonderful opportunities to help members encounter the Truth, especially in assisting them to perceive it more clearly, consider it more critically, embrace it more passionately [chapter 10].

9. Nurturing within all members a teachable spirit, challenging each one to continual growth and progress. This, of course, is largely a matter of encouraging a particular attitude within the life of the church. Apart from this attitude, none of these other suggestions can bear much fruit. The best way to cultivate such teachability is for leaders to model it in their own lives. Further, continual appeal can be made, from the pulpit and in the various interactions we have with our members, to persistently press on in our study of the Scriptures and all the sound doctrine we discern therein [chapters 7-9].

DEEPER IN THE LIFE

Without question, the primary venue in which Christian congregations cultivate and deepen our experience of the Life is in our gatherings of worship. This is an experience of *leitourgia,* literally meaning, "the work of the people."[14] From this Greek term emerge words like "liturgy," "liturgical" and "liturgics." Liturgics is the study of worship, as catechetics is the study of catechesis and homiletics is the study of preaching. An expression like "the liturgical life" of a church could refer to the need to view all of the church's experience as worship, but it more typically refers to those aspects of our life together that focus on congregational worship. With that in mind, we suggest the following formative practices.

---

[14]Some may object to the notion that worship is "the work of the people," wishing instead to focus on worship as God's gracious gift to us. But these two ideas need not contradict each other if we remember that worship always involves the rhythm of revelation and response. The fact is that in gathered worship there are a variety things that we have been biblically commanded to *do* together. Our worship, though, is always responsive to the God who calls us and is enabled by the Spirit of God who indwells us.

10. Services of congregational worship that are focused on worship of God in Spirit and truth, faithfully formative for believers, and sensitive to inquirers. In these settings, which Paul refers to with the language of "when you come together," we engage together in various elements of intentional worship, such as acts of gathering—a call to worship, an opening prayer or invocation, the singing of songs that help to call us toward conscious experience of the presence of God—prayer in the Holy Spirit (Eph 6:18); hearing God's Word read and exposited; praising God in speech or in song;[15] singing songs of various sorts to the Lord and, in doing so, "speak[ing] to one another with psalms, hymns and spiritual songs" (Eph 5:19); confessing our sins, both individually and corporately; greeting one another in obedience to biblical injunctions (see, for example, Rom 16:3-16), especially with a view to "passing the peace" of Christ to one another; affirming our faith, perhaps by use of a historic confession like the Apostles' Creed or the Nicene Creed; celebrating together sacramental ordinances like holy baptism (usually a joyful but occasional part of our worship gatherings) and the Lord's Supper (hopefully a very frequent feature of our gatherings); and various acts of dismissal, such as a word of commissioning (whereby we are charged to continue our worship of God as we disperse to our homes, work and so on) and a word of benediction (a blessing spoken over the people, whereby God graciously and mysteriously puts his name upon his people; see Num 6:22-27).[16]

Whether our worship services include many such elements or few, all of our churches have some sort of a liturgy (in this sense, *liturgy* can simply refer to our selection and organization of the various elements of worship).[17] Our aim should be to make our liturgy biblically faithful, God-honoring and formative for good.

In worship gatherings that are carefully designed and conducted, we celebrate, proclaim and experience God's reconciling work in Jesus Christ. Espe-

---

[15]Suitable words of doxology (that is, "words of glory") are frequently found in the New Testament letters (see, for example, Rom 16:25-27; Eph 3:20-21; 1 Tim 1:17; Jude 24-25).

[16]The New Testament letters often feature a word of benediction at or near their close, all of which are very suitable for Christian worship; for example, Rom 15:33; 2 Cor 13:14; 1 Thess 5:23-24; 2 Thess 3:16; Phil 4:23; Heb 13:20-21.

[17]For a helpful and easily accessible overview of thoughtful, biblically informed liturgical design, see Marva Dawn, *How Then Shall We Worship?* (Wheaton: Tyndale, 2003). We also recommend, again, the body of work from Robert Webber on the subject of worship, especially his *Ancient-Future Worship: Proclaiming and Enacting God's Narrative* (Grand Rapids: Baker, 2008), and his seven-volume The Complete Library of Christian Worship (Peabody, Mass.: Hendrickson, 1995).

cially through regular experience of the sacraments and thoughtful attention to the church year, we rehearse and retell the great redemptive Story, always focused on the Gospel which is the apex and summary of that Story.

We have already said much concerning the design and conduct of public worship, and how worship actually forms God's people [chapters 11-12]. In support of this most fundamental ministry that focuses on deepening and developing our experience of the Life, we suggest the following further practices.

11. Experiences and training in prayer, both individually and corporately. Aside from the prayers that are experienced corporately in congregational worship, the church can and should feature other gatherings—large and small—that focus specifically on cultivating individual and corporate prayer. Exhortations toward and examples of such gatherings are found throughout the Scriptures (for example, 2 Chron 7:14; Acts 1:13-14; 4:23-31; 12:12; Eph 6:18; 1 Thess 5:17).

It can be very helpful to have classes and study groups that focus on understanding the meaning and practice of prayer. But the instruction will need to go beyond talking about prayer and actually involve the practice of prayer. Likewise, prayer should be a vital element in all the ministries and gatherings of the church, and should be encouraged as a key component in family life, one-on-one discipling relationships, and all gatherings of the church, formal and informal, planned or spontaneous.

Jesus often withdrew to lonely places to pray (Lk 5:16), and he frequently taught about prayer (Lk 11:5-13; Jn 14:13-14; 16:23-24). The disciples' curiosity about prayer was clearly piqued by the model that he provided them (as well as by the example of John the Baptizer), and they asked the Lord to teach them how to pray (Lk 11:1). In response, he taught them a particular prayer, which we have come to call the Lord's Prayer. This prayer has been central in both liturgical and catechetical practice through two millennia of the church and should be utilized in the ongoing prayer life of churches and individual believers.

The early church counted prayer among its core commitments, and it was a commitment, we remember, not simply to prayer in general but, literally, to "the prayers" (Acts 2:42). As we suggested earlier in the book, this likely envisions an experience of prayer that was more liturgical and more communal in nature. The earliest Christians were used to set times of prayer, and in Acts we read instances of the apostles attending to these. It was at the ninth hour—the hour of prayer—that Peter and John were going up to the temple to pray when they met the lame man at the gate called Beautiful (Acts 3:1-2). And it was as Peter went up to his rooftop to pray at the sixth hour of the day that he received the visions that would lead him to the house of Cornelius (Acts 10:9). Such practices of prayer at set hours probably became normative for Jews following the destruction of Solomon's temple (see also Old Testament references in Ps 55:17; Dan 6:10).

Especially since we are here concerned with *training* ourselves in prayer, we would be wise to adopt some form of prayer discipline that reflects this biblical pattern. Prayer at set times of the day is still common among observant Jews, and has been a constant for many liturgical Christians through two millennia. Prayer in Christian monastic communities for many centuries, for example, calls for communal prayer seven times a day, the prayers being chiefly the texts of the biblical psalms. If all this seems a bit strange, it is once again likely due to our being inadequately connected to our history and even to our own Scriptures.

But in our day, as part of the return to historical roots that we have noted elsewhere, many Christians' interest in prayer of this sort is being kindled, or rekindled, as the case may be. Numerous resources have recently emerged in print and online for "praying the hours," as this practice is sometimes called. One of the happiest benefits of such prayer is that it teaches the church to pray the Scriptures themselves, especially the psalms. This certainly helps to ensure that we are praying "according to [God's] will" and can thus be confident that God hears our prayers (1 Jn 5:14). It also leads us to imitate Jesus in a meaningful way, for Jesus made use of the psalms in his own praying (see, for example, Mt 27:46, cf. Ps 22:1; and Lk. 23:46, cf. Ps. 31:5).[18]

12. Exhorting believers toward, and involving them in, practices of evangelism. Although ministries of evangelism may be more properly understood as concerned with outreach rather than with formation, we remember that the lines between these aspects of our life are blurry, and that each dimension informs the other. Youth ministers, for example, frequently arrange to send groups of teens to reach out to others with the love of Christ. But while the desire to involve those young people in serving others may be sincere, most youth pastors would readily acknowledge that they are also motivated by the potential power of such experiences to teach and form their own young peo-

---

[18]For a wonderful introduction to the notion of incorporating the psalms into one's prayer life, see Eugene Peterson, *Answering God: The Psalms as a Tool for Prayer* (San Francisco: HarperSanFrancisco, 1991).

ple. When we as believers share the good news about the life found only in Jesus with friends and neighbors who do not yet know the Lord, our own understanding and experience of that Life is deepened as well.

DEEPER IN THE WAY

The church's ongoing formation in the Way is best experienced not in our Lord's Day gatherings but in our dispersal throughout the week, especially through our fellowship *(koinōnia)* with one another and in our acts of service *(diakonia)* toward one another. Of course, we have much that can be intentionally taught about the Way—instruction in the Decalogue, for example, should be frequently revisited. As we do so, we take care that our instruction is culturally sensitive and developmentally appropriate. There are other great ethical texts as well that can serve as the basis for formal instruction in the Way, including the Sermon on the Mount and the wisdom and prophetic books of the Old Testament. During our gatherings of worship, too, faithful preaching of the Scriptures will lead us continually to biblical teaching about the Way of the Lord.

But helpful as such instruction in and preaching about the Way is, the actual learning of the Way doubtless best occurs not in formal settings but in the informal interchanges of daily living. Jesus commanded that in making disciples of all nations we are to teach his followers "to obey everything I have commanded you" (Mt 28:20). While the teaching of what Jesus has commanded can be done when we gather together, teaching people how to obey those commands is another matter altogether, and requires a wide variety of settings.

The Way of the Lord is well summed up by the double commandment to love the Lord with all that we have and to love our neighbors as ourselves. It is in the daily grind of our interactions at home, at work, at play, in service, in mission and in crisis that we truly learn how to walk this Way. Church leaders must be mindful of this reality. Such awareness requires that we have a vision for teaching that goes far beyond those times when we are gathered together on Sunday morning.

Jesus often taught his disciples the Way while they were together on the way—moving from site to site and village to village in service of the Gospel. For us to encourage formation in the Way, we must be intentional about the following.

13. Cultivation of authentic relationships that allow for significant and on-

going life interactions in a wide variety of settings. This could include

- small groups, including, perhaps, groups formed of a few families that are committed not only to study and pray together but also to work, play and serve together.

- one-on-one or other high accountability relationships in which an older, mature believer can teach by example what it means to live for the Lord (such as is envisioned in passages like Tit 2:4-5).

- a wide variety of activities that encourage church members to serve the needy in their midst, just as the early church devoted itself to care for the widows, orphans, strangers and poor who were numbered among the believers.

- a wide variety of activities that call the church outward to serve all its neighbors, Christian or non-Christian, both near and far.

14. Planned and spontaneous experiences—as a community—for genuine fellowship, recreation and work. It is not only formal gatherings that can positively teach and form God's people. In all manner of informal episodes great good can emerge. *Being* together, and being attentive to what God is doing in our midst when we are, can yield much lasting, God-honoring fruit in our lives.

15. Discipline as needed, biblically practiced, including correction of false teaching. Church discipline—whether preventative or restorative—is a potent tool for congregational formation [see "Commitment to the Covenant Community" in this chapter].

16. Training in the area of relationships—for example, marriage and family education. Since the home is a biblically foundational setting for learning and formation, the church should do all in its power to help families function as well as possible. Classes, counseling, mentoring, retreats, seminars and preaching series can all be of great help in keeping these concerns in the consciousness of members [chapters 6, 9].

17. Equipping of members in the areas of their giftedness and other avenues of service through mentoring, workshops, service opportunities and evaluations [see "Engagement in the Ministry of Reconciliation" in this chapter].

18. Outreach activities of various sorts, including mission trips, accompanied by prebriefing and debriefing. We spoke earlier of how such opportunities can deepen our own experience of the Life. They are also vital expressions of the walking in the Way. When we considered the three great tasks of the church, we noted the overlap between worship, formation and outreach.

When unpacking our definition of teaching, we also noted the relationship between our heads, hearts and hands. Engaging together in ministries of outreach is among the most powerfully formative things congregations can ever do [chapters 11, 13].

THREE IN ONE

There are numerous ministry strategies for formation that remind us that we cannot draw too hard a line between the three facets of the Faith. The various practices we have suggested above all affect one another—what we learn of the Way, for example, affects our understanding of the Truth and experience of the Life. Our motivation in drawing these lines is simply to help us intentionally take aim at particular aspects of our formation, lest something be overlooked.

Then, too, we acknowledge that a number of formative ministries actually seem to attend to all three aspects at once. Congregational worship, though we situated it under the heading of the Life, clearly touches matters of the Truth and the Way as well. Small group activities, and one-on-one discipling relationships also do so, though we may initially view such groups as most naturally fitting into one or other of the three dimensions we have outlined.

The following are other practices or strategies that, it seems to us, nearly always touch on all facets of the Faith.

19. Focused intergenerational and coordinated learning experiences. Examples of these could be intergenerational Sunday school classes or coordinated learning experiences across the generations; also working and serving together, playing together, praying together and more [chapters 9, 11-12].

20. Provision of some form of mentoring or discipleship in a one-on-one or other high accountability situation. In addition to small group and large group venues for teaching and formation, the wise church will also encourage and facilitate relationships of high accountability. Many evangelicals have championed this over the years under the heading of "discipleship."[19] More recently, some evangelicals have been drawn to church practices such as spiritual direction.[20] Whatever approach is taken, personal attention to each member

---

[19]Greg Ogden, *Transforming Discipleship: Making Disciples a Few at a Time* (Downers Grove, Ill.: InterVarsity Press, 2003); Randy Frazee, *The Connecting Church* (Grand Rapids: Zondervan, 2001).

[20]Gary Moon and David Benner, eds., *Spiritual Direction and the Care of Souls: A Guide to Christian Approaches and Practices* (Downers Grove, Ill.: InterVarsity Press, 2004); Jeannette Bakke, *Holy Invitations: Exploring Spiritual Direction* (Grand Rapids: Baker, 2000).

of the flock is really nonnegotiable, as we discussed earlier in one of the definitions for teaching [chapter 10].

**21. Provision of a resource center of teaching and formation materials avail-
able for parents, teachers and all members.** Church libraries have long been
helpful in this regard. Today we should direct members not only toward great
books but to quality audio, video and online resources as well.

22. Seizing upon teachable moments for the whole community. Many of
these experiences will be informal and intergenerational. For example, baptisms, confirmations, weddings and funerals can and should be occasions for
significant learning. To maximize the formative potential of such events, the
church must reject the powerful forces of marketing and consumerism that
co-opt and secularize what ought to be truly sacred events. Also, through
casual building of intergenerational relationships the church can naturally
build numerous opportunities for modeling [chapters 11-13].

**23. Timely teaching of individuals and groups, providing a word according
to the need.** The best teachers are always paying attention to the world in
which their fellow learners live. This means being willing and able to set aside
the planned "curriculum" and respond as needed. Jesus was plainly the master
of such teaching [chapters 7-10].

**24. A serious experience of Sabbath together, practiced by individuals, fam-
ilies and the community as a whole.** While some Christian churches, families
or individual believers take seriously a commitment to observing a Sabbath,
many others seem to have very little sense of this. The Sabbath command is
perhaps the most difficult of the Ten Words for Christians to interpret and
apply. Focusing quite correctly on the biblical teaching that suggests that
Christ—through the finished work of the cross—is himself our Sabbath (for
example, Rom 14:5; Col 2:16-17; Heb 4:1-10), perhaps we have sometimes
been guilty of overly spiritualizing this command. In the process we may well
have lost sight of the fact that since the Sabbath actually predates the giving of
the Decalogue (Gen 2:2-3) it cannot be counted as only applying to Jewish
people; God clearly intended Sabbath as a very practical and tangible way of
blessing his people (Mk 2:27).

I have been privileged to enjoy friendships with a number of observant
Jews. Without exception, these friends testify that their experiences of Sabbath are central to their lives. Typically their eyes light up when they begin to
describe their Sabbath practices and proceed to speak about welcoming in the
Sabbath on Friday at sundown with their families as candles are lit, prayers

recited and a rich, unhurried supper is enjoyed. Following the meal and family activities, the children are put down to bed for the evening. The husband and wife, meanwhile, go to their own bedroom and worship the Lord together by enjoying the great gift of marital intimacy. In the morning, the family may rise at their leisure, enjoy another unhurried meal (of food that has been prepared in advance), then walk together to the local synagogue. There they experience congregational worship, prayer and study together. The synagogue service—which can last for several hours—may be followed with a common meal together (once again with food that has been previously prepared) and a recitation of prayers to bless God, who so graciously provides for his people all things good. That afternoon the family will focus on enjoying each other, and perhaps some spiritual reading or other form of sacred study will occur. They will be "unplugged" from the otherwise relentless flood of media and unconcerned with all regular activities related to work. With the arrival of sundown on Saturday, they will have a service together to bid farewell to the Sabbath until the next week, when the wonderful guest is welcomed back once again.

Of course, the above sketch is somewhat idealized, and the actual experience of Sabbath varies from family to family and from week to week. But I am always struck by the fact that my Jewish friends clearly take great delight in their Sabbath observances. They seem to me to be living testimonies to the familiar remark that it is not the Jews who have kept the Sabbath; it is the Sabbath that has kept the Jews.[21] When I hear them I often find myself experiencing—to borrow that word that C. S. Lewis used—*sehnsucht*. A longing grows within me to more deeply experience this for myself, my family and my church.

Thankfully, many Christian authors, especially in recent years, have been calling fellow believers toward genuine experiences of Sabbath on a weekly basis.[22] In our own lives, we have had wonderful but limited experiences with our own families. But it seems clear to us that fuller experiences of Sabbath will require an entire congregation to join in the com-

---

[21]For helpful and significant explanation of the Jewish understanding and practices of Sabbath, see Abraham Joshua Heschel, *The Sabbath* (New York: Farrar, Straus & Giroux, 1951/2005).

[22]See, for example, Marva Dawn, *Keeping Sabbath Wholly: Ceasing, Resting, Embracing, Feasting* (Grand Rapids: Eerdmans, 1989), and *A Sense of the Call: A Sabbath Way of Life for Those Who Serve God, the Church and the World* (Grand Rapids: Eerdmans, 2007), and Lauren Winner, *Mudhouse Sabbath: An Invitation to a Life of Spiritual Disciplines* (Brewster, Mass.: Paraclete, 2007).

mitment. With this in mind, we envision the following and encourage church leaders to consider adapting this, or something similar, in their own congregations.

Church members can begin a Sabbath experience together in their own homes on Saturday evening.[23] This might become the church's primary venue for small group experiences. Families can gather in homes for a potluck meal, together with prayers and Scripture readings. Following the meal, and before the families return to their own homes, time can be devoted to any number of spiritually rich interchanges—testimony, teaching, prayers and so on. Church members can take turns providing special care and ministry that may be required for younger children.

On the following morning, members can continue their joyous experience of Sabbath as they reconvene for congregational worship. The services, too, can be followed by a meal with fellow worshipers—perhaps experienced all together after services or again in one another's homes. For the rest of the day, believers can enjoy fellowship with one another until, as Sunday evening falls, they bid goodbye to their own experience of the Sabbath until the following week.

A communitywide experience of Sabbath such as that which we have outlined can, we are persuaded, be powerfully formative in a multifaceted manner, touching upon each of those domains which we have identified as the Truth, the Life and the Way.

25. Ongoing evaluation of all teaching/learning activities, with particular attention to whether or not life transformation is occurring in individuals, groups and the entire church body. All that we do in our commitment to develop the people of God should be regularly evaluated. Our primary criterion for such evaluation is not perceived excitement or growth in numbers. Rather, we evaluate based on faithfulness to biblical models and mandates, and fruitfulness in terms of the life transformation to which we are called. We return, then, to the biblical aims of teaching we considered early on, and to the overall purposes of the church. In light of these things, we evaluate whether or not we are wise to continue what we have been doing or need to correct our course [chapters 1, 2].

---

[23]We will not here enter the whole discussion of why Christians observe the first day of the week for worship, except to note that this has clear precedents in the New Testament celebration of "the Lord's Day"—the first day being celebrated by believers because on that day Christ arose from the dead (see Acts 20:7; 1 Cor 16:2; Rev 1:10). Note that in biblical thought the day begins with evening. Thus "the first day of the week" begins at sundown on Saturday.

ENGAGEMENT IN THE MINISTRY OF RECONCILIATION

The building up of the body through the ministries that we have been considering is not an end in itself. Rather, we labor toward ongoing formation so that the body might grow in maturity and thus be better able to walk in the good works of reconciliation to which we have been called as the *poiēma* of God. In chapter five we suggested that when we take up three aspects of the Faith—the Truth, the Life and the Way—with an outward orientation, we may conceive of them as, respectively, *apologia* (faithful defense of the Truth), *kerygma* (faithful proclamation of the Life-giving Gospel), and *diakonia* (service) or *prophēitia* (working and speaking in prophetic ways toward justice and mercy). It is such concerns we have in mind as we now consider practices for engaging God's people in ministry. Row four in table 5.2 addresses these concerns.

Table 14.3. Training for Engagement in the Story

Training for engagement in the Story	Ongoing training in the Truth	Ongoing training in the Life	Ongoing training in the Way

The commitment to equip the members of the body for engagement in God's kingdom is the logical culmination of our ministry model in light of our assertions in chapter one that the church exists in time and space in order to walk in good works of reconciliation. Such works involve a serious commitment to intentional evangelism but cannot be limited to evangelistic endeavors. Thus, when we described the "three great tasks of the church," we chose *not* to label the third of these "evangelism." Instead, we have called this task "outreach" or, better, "work and witness in the world."[24] For, taking our lead from Jesus' own "mission statement" in Luke 4:18-19 (quoting from Is 61:1-2), we must commit to "preach good news to the poor" *and* to other forms of holistic ministry to those who are in various forms of bondage and oppression.

The declaration and manifestation of the kingdom of God were central features in the public ministry of Jesus, and they should be vital components of our ministries today. Sadly, there has long been a tendency among Christian churches to choose as their particular emphases *either* declaring the Gos-

---

[24]For a challenging and insightful exploration of how Christians can engage in and indeed create culture, see Andy Crouch, *Culture Making: Recovering Our Creative Calling* (Downers Grove, Ill.: InterVarsity Press, 2008).

pel of the kingdom (a commitment to evangelism) *or* seeking to manifest kingdom values (a commitment to justice and mercy).

In recent history, this division has often closely paralleled the divide between theologically conservative churches, which have tended toward evangelistic ministries, and theologically liberal churches, which have tended toward justice and mercy ministries. We noted earlier in the book that this bifurcation has proven increasingly frustrating to many, particularly younger, evangelicals. Yet we wondered if the reaction of some so-called emerging churches may not lead us yet again to such a division in the house, for some leaders in that movement seem to be calling for a suspension of declaring the Gospel in favor of "living" the Gospel. The almost predictable response is that some churches of more conservative bent will renew their suspicions of a "social Gospel" in order to champion the declaration of the "true Gospel."

We are called to work diligently to keep together all the biblically sanctioned features of outreach to our unbelieving neighbors. The phrase "work and witness in the world" attempts to do this. "Work" reminds us that we are indeed called to love our neighbors holistically, to commit ourselves to justice and mercy in our communities, in our nation and throughout our world. We have been created in Christ to do good works of reconciliation, and we will not reduce this to merely declarative acts. The example of Jesus' ministry makes this clear, as does the plain teaching of many of the New Testament letters and a great deal of Old Testament emphases.

On the other hand, we dare not become so enamored of the idea of walking in good deeds that we lose sight of biblical mandates to evangelism. Thus we employ the word *witness* as part of our commitment to the watching world. We are called to be witnesses of the saving acts of God in Christ Jesus, testifying boldly to the Gospel of God's grace. We dare not become, in any new, faddish way, ashamed of the Gospel. After all, the most critical aspect of Christ's work of reconciliation is the reconciling of men and women to the triune God.

When we commit ourselves to engagement in the ministry of reconciliation, we then have in view both the doing of good works and declaring the good news. Toward both of these ends, we must equip the saints for ministry.

EQUIPPING THE SAINTS FOR MINISTRY

We have emphasized throughout the book that it is as the body of Christ that we engage in the ministry of reconciliation. But for the body to minister well, each member of it must be functioning properly in its unique role within that body. In chapter two, we considered guidance from Ephesians 4 about these matters and saw that one of our chief teaching aims is to equip the saints for the work of ministry. There is a great diversity of spiritual gifts dispersed within the body. All these are "given for the common good," Paul tells the Corinthians (1 Cor 12:7).

This common good involves the building up of the body (see 1 Cor 14:5, 12). All our gifts are to be exercised for mutual edification (see 1 Cor 14:26), but this is not an end in itself. The body is not built up for its own sake, but so that—as the mature body of Christ—we may walk in the good works of reconciliation to which we have been called (see Eph 2:10). This we do that God may be glorified in and through us as the world sees and is impacted by our good deeds (see Mt 5:16; 1 Pet 2:12).

All our gifts have something to do with the ministry of reconciliation to which we are called, though this may not be obvious at first glance. Once we realize, however, that we function only as a body and not as individual parts of the body, it becomes clear that all our gifts matter. Those that are expressed "when you come together"—that is, gifts that help believers serve their fellow believers—are vital for our mutual strengthening and purifying. Those that are primarily expressed in our dispersal throughout the week are likewise vital, as they help the body actually become engaged in the healing of the broken world in which we live.

ECCLESIA AND DIASPORA GIFTS

R. Paul Stevens has, for many years and in many ways, argued that the church must commit itself to equipping *all* its members, not just some, and celebrating *all* the gifts of the body, not just a few. To make the point, Stevens makes a distinction between *ecclesia* gifts and *diaspora* gifts.[25] All members of the body have been endowed with spiritual gifts, but clearly there is a great diversity of gifts. Some of the gifts in the church, such as preaching, teaching, leadership in worship music, public reading of Scripture and so on, are best exercised when the church is gathered. These are ecclesia gifts, gifts that are typically best exercised on Sundays.

There are others who have gifts that are best exercised during the other days of the week, when the body is dispersed. Such gifts may be called diaspora

---

[25]R. Paul Stevens, *Liberating the Laity* (Vancouver: Regent College Publishing, 1977). In building his case, Stevens cites the work of George Williams (p. 22) and Harvey Cox (pp. 100-101).

gifts and include gifts of evangelism, showing mercy, administration, helps and many more. The body is the body all week long, of course. We are no less the church when we are dispersed than when we are gathered. Thus it is clear that all the gifts are critical, and Scripture tells us that these gifts have been assigned by the Spirit, according to his will, not our own (see 1 Cor 12:4-11). Paul goes on to make it clear that none of the members who may be gifted in one way ought to look down on other members with gifts that may *appear* to be of lesser significance.

Tragically, however, our churches often act as though the "Sunday" gifts are the ones that matter most. It is understandable how such an error in attitude and practice could occur. Gifts that are manifested when we come together are typically more "public" in their usage and thus more likely to be glamorized and celebrated. Diaspora gifts, however, are often exercised outside the church's public viewing and thus may seem less significant, less spectacular. We have ordination services for "ministers" who will preach and teach. We have "teachers' appreciation" Sundays and so on. But when do we celebrate those who are particularly gifted in raising and managing large sums of money? When do we celebrate those who have been gifted to teach in public education settings rather than in church settings? Often we simply do not.

By any reasonable calculation, it is the minority of the body whose gifts are likely to be celebrated and the vast majority whose gifting may well be overlooked. It has always been the case, in both Jewish and Christian religious communities, that relatively few members have been charged and gifted for specific ministry leadership at the gatherings of the community. The priests and Levites were a small minority among the Israelites. Likewise, our pastors and other public "worship leaders" in evangelical churches today are a tiny minority. Yet these gifts are the ones we notice and celebrate most often. It is no surprise, then, that many who attain to new levels of faith commitment reach the conclusion that God must be calling them to become pastors or missionaries.[26] Or laypeople may believe that if they really want to "serve God," they must do so by teaching Sunday school or joining the church's worship team.

Each Sunday, the preacher speaks to a congregation of people who are called to good works of reconciliation. It is his task to speak to an assembly of

---

[26]A missionary gifting may seem like the clearest example of a diaspora gifting, but it may sometimes be, in fact, an ecclesia gifting exercised in a setting other than one's own "home church."

ministers. A great many in the congregation, however, have been called and gifted by God to do good works in settings other than the gathered Christian community. Instead, their assigned settings are the workplace, the dormitory, the home, the neighborhood and so on. And their assigned fields include medicine, business, law, education, technology and much more. Many of these members have been raised in churches and have heard countless sermons and Sunday school lessons. Yet tragically, many remain very ill equipped for ministry in the specific settings to which God has called them.

EQUIPPING FOR THE MARKETPLACE

Stevens points out yet another feature of just how tragic our neglect in this area is. He suggests that a typical North American adult Christian between the ages of twenty and sixty is likely to spend about four thousand hours attending church meetings such as worship services, Bible study classes and the like. That same adult, during the same time span, is likely to spend some eighty thousand hours in the workplace. Yet, Stevens queries, how much attention have we paid to equipping that believer for ministry in the setting that is clearly his primary venue for service? The answer, sadly, is often that we have done very little. Many Christian adults have surely wondered about how all the goings-on during the Sunday services at their churches relate to the rest of the week.[27]

How can we become more obedient to this commitment to engagement and the ministry of equipping the saints for such engagement? Many tools have been utilized by churches to help members discern their gifts, their personalities, their SHAPE[28] and so on. Such tools can be very useful, and we do well to employ them. But we must be wary of certain pitfalls as we do so. Four such pitfalls are

1. *Leading members to the conclusion that use of such tools can be a substitute for actual experience.* It is not uncommon to find believers who refuse to serve in areas where they feel they are not gifted. How do they know they are not gifted? They took a spiritual gifts inventory! As helpful as gifts assessment tools may be, the best way to discern our gifts is to serve. We learn best by doing min-

---

[27]See R. Paul Stevens, *The Other Six Days: Vocation, Work, and Ministry in Biblical Perspective* (Grand Rapids: Eerdmans, 2000).
[28]SHAPE is an acronym—Spiritual gifts, Heart, Abilities, Personality, Experiences—that has been popularized by Saddleback Church. See <http://www.purposedriven.com/en-US/aboutUS/Pdinthenews/Archives/shape_Process_Key_to_unlocking_an_army_of_volunteers_in_your_church.htm>.

istry, by reflecting on our experiences, and by receiving the wise and considered feedback of others about our service. Furthermore, we will sometimes be called on to serve in areas where we do not appear to be gifted at all. A quick survey of the great redemptive Story of the Scriptures makes it clear that God often delights to use his people in just such ways, so that it may be abundantly clear that whatever competence we display comes not from ourselves but from God (see 1 Cor 3:5).

2. *Limiting our understanding of gifts and abilities to those gifts that are explicitly identified in the New Testament.* It is very difficult to demonstrate that only those gifts that are mentioned in 1 Corinthians 12 and 14, Romans 12, Ephesians 4 and 1 Peter 4 are truly spiritual gifts or that it is only for the exercise of such that we ought to be equipping the saints. For our part, we do not see these listings as intended to be exhaustive. If we look at both Testaments and survey the lives of the many men and women God has used in his service, it becomes clear that there is truly a vast array of gifts and talents God has distributed among his people for his glory. If, for example, it is true that God has gifted some to preach the Gospel and has declared that "those who preach the gospel should receive their living from the gospel" (1 Cor 9:14), then those preachers should be very grateful that God has gifted other believers to be financially prosperous, so that their generosity may overflow to the glory of God (see 1 Cor 9:11).

3. *Leaving unequipped those whose primary gifting is for life and work outside the gatherings of the saints.* Once again, if we privilege the "Sunday gifts" and overlook those gifts that function best during the rest of the week, we will find ourselves leaving the vast majority of the saints unequipped for the ministries to which God has called them. It is the rare "spiritual gifts inventory" that helps these believers discover and develop their diaspora giftings. Thankfully, there is evidence of recent movement to correct this imbalance.[29]

4. *Giving the impression that God uses only our areas of strength or gifting for ministry and for his glory.* In fact, God's pattern in Scripture was often to ask people to minister in areas in which they felt they had no ability or gifting. Consider, for example, God's call on such Bible characters as Gideon, Moses, Jeremiah and Mary. God's chief concern is to glorify himself, not us, and thus he often demonstrates his power in and through our areas of pain and weakness. Paul is an example of one who plainly discovered this to be true.[30]

We offer the following suggestions for equipping the saints for full engage-

---

[29]Peter Wagner, *Discover Your Spiritual Gifts,* 2nd ed. (Ventura, Calif.: Regal, 2005).
[30]See, for example, 2 Corinthians 4; 12:1-13.

ment in the ministry of reconciliation to which Christ calls his body.

- *The church itself should seek to develop a variety of ministries across the ecclesia/ diaspora spectrum.* If most or all of the church's "official" ministries are "Sunday ministries," we should not be surprised to find many or most of our members feeling themselves reduced to an unhealthy passivity in their "spiritual lives."

- *People ought to be encouraged in discovering and developing their gifts and abilities.* Utilizing some of the countless tools that are available for this—in spite of their inherent limitations as we discussed above—is a good idea. But offering lots of opportunities for service across a wide spectrum of ministries will provide the best opportunity for people to discern, and grow in, their capacity to minister to others.

- *The church should consider unique aspects of its own calling to serve its community by examining the intersection between the gifts that exist in the body and the needs that exist in the community.* In my own church, for example, we have many people working in medical and dental professions. This has already led us to offer medical clinics in our community, and we are now prayerfully preparing to share this ministry in countries where our church has established ongoing relationships.

- *Church leaders should be diligent in learning about the occupations, gifts, talents, interests and experiences of the members of the church.* One powerful way to do this is to spend time with members in the their workplaces. A pastor could, for instance, ask members for permission to "shadow" them in their various workplaces, spending one week with a member who teaches, another with a member who works in construction, another with a CEO and so on.[31]

- *The church could host seminars, small groups, Sunday school classes and other forums—on a somewhat regular basis—about living and ministering in particular vocational settings (for example, Christians in business, Christians in education, Christians in medicine).* Outside guests could be brought in to help with these ventures. The church can connect itself with other congregations or parachurch organizations and resources to accomplish these emphases.

- *The church can "highlight" and celebrate the endeavors of those who minister*

---

[31]Paul Stevens told a group of us at Gordon-Conwell that he had done this sort of thing during one of his sabbaticals.

primarily in "diaspora" settings. In my congregation, we do this in a special way about once each quarter. One of our ministry teams is called Making A Difference (MAD). Each quarter, the MAD ministry team selects one "hero" from among church members to highlight in a very special way before the congregation. What the members have been doing with their diaspora ministries is typically unknown to and thus unnoticed by the majority of church members until we celebrate these persons in this manner.

- *It is also important that the church broaden its range of "Sunday ministries."* Too often only a few of the gifts that could be employed during our gatherings are actually employed. For example, those who play guitar, drums and keyboard may be invited to use their musical gifts in our worship while other gifted instrumentalists are excluded from the mix. Or we may invite a handful of gifted singers to be part of the "praise team" but ignore the possible contributions of many others. Other gifts we may easily overlook concern the public reading of Scripture, graphic design for worship folders or "bulletins," visual arts for banners and tapestries, gifts of welcoming and hospitality, and much more.

- *Regular and ongoing efforts should be made for the development of servant-leaders in the congregation.* This may take many forms but should include both formal and nonformal elements. Classes and seminars should be offered periodically in a venue that makes the best sense in the context of the community. Leaders in the making should be supported in their growth by means of guided, hands-on experiences, with appropriate prebriefing and debriefing. Follow-up is critical, as is correction or redirection when necessary.

- *For all those whose gifts we seek to nurture—whether ecclesia or diaspora gifts—we do well to provide mentoring relationships.* Pastors and mature believers should share this work, depending on their particular areas of giftedness. If necessary, the church can network with mature believers in other congregations as well.

FOLLOW-UP AND GRACE CULTIVATION

As we discussed at the beginning of chapter thirteen, the final two commitments of our congregational model are primarily matters of the ethos of the church. These two commitments—pastoral follow-up and the cultivation of grace within the community—are really intended to be guardians of the process, keeping us from falling into an unhealthy mechanistic or legalistic approach to Christian formation.

Even if a member of the congregation has "walked through" all the above phases or congregational commitments, we can never see ourselves as having "arrived." This side of glory we are all works in progress, we "all stumble in many ways" (Jas 3:2). The biblical writers pull no punches when describing the human frailties of even our favorite Bible heroes. No biblical character—except Christ himself—is presented in Scripture to us as being infallibly formed.

We ought to design and conduct our ministries of formation as carefully and diligently as possible, but we will never escape the need for pastoral care and follow-up. Sheep wander. We all do. Thus we must remain on the watch for straying and stumbling, for sin and brokenness. Like the Servant of the Lord, we must not snuff out the smoldering wick or break the bruised reed among us (see Is 42:3). We are not now concerned with those matters we addressed earlier under the heading of "church discipline." Rather, we are dealing with the simple fact that all the members of the body—even the most mature among us—are fallible, finite and unfinished. Pastoral care is not the concern only of pastors. It is truly a "one another" ministry that must be pervasive throughout the body. "Above all, love each other deeply," writes Peter, "because love covers over a multitude of sins" (1 Pet 4:8).

The sort of love Peter speaks of can also be called grace. We know the grace of our Lord Jesus Christ, who became poor for our sakes that we might be made rich in him (see 2 Cor 8:9). It is precisely such grace that we must show one another. Are there some in the congregation who, despite all our best efforts, refuse to "get on board" and take their own formation seriously? Of course there are; some of us will always be at such a place. What should our posture be toward these? It must be a posture of grace. This is not to suggest that there is no place for rebuke. No indeed! May God help us to increase our capacity to lovingly correct, rebuke and encourage (see 2 Tim 4:2), to speak the truth in love to one another (see Eph 4:15) and to "spur one another on toward love and good deeds" (Heb 10:24). Even as we do all these things, may we do so in a spirit of grace.

It is grace, after all, that God has used to woo and to win our hearts to himself. It is God's kindness that leads to repentance (see Rom 2:4). It is knowing that the Lord forgives sin that provokes us to fear him (see Ps 130:4). So then, let us also be gentle among God's people, "like a mother caring for her little children" (1 Thess 2:7). And like a father dealing with his children, let us encourage, comfort and urge the flock to live worthily of the King who calls us (see 1 Thess 2:12). Even with those who actively oppose us, we must be gentle, knowing that God alone can turn hearts toward truth and repentance (see 2 Tim 2:24-26). It is the privilege of church leaders to model such attitudes in our dealings with members of the flock and to do all we can to help nurture a culture of such values within the congregation as a whole.

HYMN FOR CONTEMPLATION AND WORSHIP

A Heart of Flesh

God gave us life, a heart of flesh,
together with the Spirit's breath.
We turned from God to live alone,
and turned our heart of flesh to stone.

Chorus: A heart of flesh for heart of stone,
none can restore but God alone.
O come with grace and Spirit's breath,
give us again a heart of flesh.

So Jesus came unto his own,
and left the glory of heaven's throne,
and those he called could not have known
the cost of changing hearts of stone.

He set his face like that of stone
to walk the path of death alone.
New hearts could only come by death,
and so he gave his heart of flesh.

In death he lay behind a stone
making his sacrifice our own,
in rising put an end to death,
the first-fruits of redeemed flesh.

Text: Julie Tennent, 2004
Tune: Wexford Carol[32]

---

[32]Julie Tennent, "A Heart of Flesh," 2004. Used by permission. For more of Julie's hymns (and more of Gary's), please see the forthcoming *Psalms, Hymns and Spiritual Songs* by Gary A. Parrett and Julie Tennent (Chicago: MorgenBooks, 2009).

QUESTIONS FOR PLANNING AND PRAXIS

1. Do you believe that membership training is important in educational formation ministry? How does your own church engage in such a practice, either formally or informally? What are the requirements for being a member of your church? Do they reflect those outlined in this chapter? How so? How not?

2. "Many Christian adults have surely wondered about how all the goings-on during the Sunday services at their churches relate to the rest of the week." Have you ever wondered this? How could the church's ministry of educational formation help your congregation to integrate the Sunday worship experience into the rest of the week? How can Sunday communal and individual practices carry over to the workplace, school and home?

3. We invite you to thoughtfully reflect on each of the following points concerning some of the ministry strategies suggested in this chapter for deepening and developing in the Gospel. For each item below, use the continuum to evaluate the current practices of your church's educational formation ministry relative to each ingredient. After evaluating each point, prayerfully reflect on how you can better adapt each of these ingredients into the educational ministry in your church.

1. Consistent, ongoing teaching of the Scriptures and the Faith to all members, regardless of age.

   very strong   moderately strong   rather weak   very weak   nonexistent

2. Occasional opportunities for extended times of teaching/learning that focus on specific themes, topics or Bible books.

   very strong   moderately strong   rather weak   very weak   nonexistent

3. Teaching of appropriate materials to specific populations grouped by age, gender, life stage, special needs or interests.

   very strong   moderately strong   rather weak   very weak   nonexistent

4. Memorization of Bible portions, creeds, catechisms, hymns and other teaching tools coupled with appropriate teaching and explanations.

   very strong   moderately strong   rather weak   very weak   nonexistent

5. Provision for a variety of teaching/learning experiences in a variety of settings throughout the week and the year.

   very strong   moderately strong   rather weak   very weak   nonexistent

6. Ongoing equipping of parents, and of the entire faith community, to help them do their parts in raising children in the Faith.

very strong   moderately strong   rather weak   very weak   nonexistent

7. Ongoing training for those engaged in teaching ministries at any and all levels.

very strong   moderately strong   rather weak   very weak   nonexistent

8. Nurturing within all members a teachable spirit; challenging each one to continual growth and progress.

very strong   moderately strong   rather weak   very weak   nonexistent

9. Cultivation of authentic relationships that allow for significant and ongoing life interactions in a wide variety of settings.

very strong   moderately strong   rather weak   very weak   nonexistent

10. Training in the area of relationships—for example, marriage and family education.

very strong   moderately strong   rather weak   very weak   nonexistent

11. Provision of some form of mentoring or discipleship in a one-on-one or other high accountability situation.

very strong   moderately strong   rather weak   very weak   nonexistent

12. A community experience of Sabbath.

very strong   moderately strong   rather weak   very weak   nonexistent

RESOURCES FOR FURTHER STUDY

Conde-Frazer, Elizabeth, S. Steve Kang and Gary Parrett. *A Many Colored Kingdom*. Grand Rapids: Baker, 2004.

Crouch, Andy. *Culture Making: Recovering Our Creative Calling*. Downers Grove, Ill.: InterVarsity Press, 2008.

Dawn, Marva. *How Then Shall We Worship?* Wheaton: Tyndale, 2003.

Kallenberg, Brad. *Live to Tell: Evangelism for a Postmodern Age*. Grand Rapids: Brazos, 2002.

Lawless, Chuck. *Membership Matters: Insights from Effective Churches on New Member Classes and Assimilation*. Grand Rapids: Zondervan, 2005.

Mouw, Richard. *When the Kings Come Marching In: Isaiah and the New Jerusa-*

lem. Revised edition. Grand Rapids: Eerdmans, 2002.

Ogden, Greg. *Transforming Discipleship: Making Disciples a Few at a Time.* Downers Grove, Ill.: InterVarsity Press, 2003.

Owen, John. *Communion with the Triune God.* Edited by Kelly Kapic and Justin Taylor. Wheaton: Crossway, 2007.

Stevens, R. Paul. *The Other Six Days: Vocation, Work, and Ministry in Biblical Perspective.* Grand Rapids: Eerdmans, 2000.

Wright, Christopher. *The Mission of God: Unlocking the Bible's Grand Narrative.* Downers Grove, Ill.: InterVarsity Press, 2006.

Conclusion

The Beautiful Body of Christ!

Christ loved the church and gave himself up for her to make her holy,

cleansing her by the washing with water through the word,

and to present her to himself as a radiant church,

without stain or wrinkle or any other blemish, but holy and blameless.

EPHESIANS 5:25-27

It is easy to grow discouraged about the church as we see it today. A flurry of recent books has been written to decry the current state of the church in the United States,[1] and many of the authors seem to be advocating that we more or less abandon ship. Few put it quite that way, of course. Mostly authors speak about the need to rewrite the rules, to deconstruct and reconstruct. Everything must change, we are told. A common refrain is the need to move away from "institutional" forms and move toward "true community." This usually includes advocacy of a house-church movement. Some authors suggest that "church" must be significantly redefined in our minds to include almost any gathering of believers and their friends or neighbors. If a few of us meet in a pub and share a few stories over a couple of pints, we will have "had church" together by the time we part.[2]

---

[1]Sarah Cunningham, *Dear Church: Letters from a Disillusioned Generation* (Grand Rapids: Zondervan, 2006); David Fitch, *The Great Giveaway: Reclaiming the Mission of the Church from Big Business, Parachurch Organizations, Psychotherapy, Consumer Capitalism, and Other Modern Maladies* (Grand Rapids: Baker, 2005); David Kinnaman and Gabe Lyons, *unChristian: What a New Generation Really Thinks About Christianity . . . and Why It Matters* (Grand Rapids: Baker, 2007).

[2]For interaction with some contemporary authors who seem to hold views along these lines, see Katie Galli's thoughtful piece "Dear Disillusioned Generation: The 'failed experiment' called the church still looks better than the alternatives," *Christianity Today*, April 2008 <http://www.christianitytoday.com/ct/2008/april/28.69.html>.

Pressing the envelope even further are those who suggest that Christians really do not need "church" at all. All that matters is that we be "Christ-followers." Participation in an institutional "church" is superfluous, perhaps even antithetical to this, our only real calling.

In this book, we trust we have made it clear that we believe in the church. Indeed, as the ancient creed invites us to confess, we "believe in the one holy, catholic and apostolic church." Luther reminds us of the importance of that little word *believe*. Citing his insights on this matter, Finnish Lutheran scholar Tuomo Mannermaa writes, "Only the eye of faith can see what God does in the church in order to sanctify human beings. Therefore . . . , it is vital that in the article of the Creed, 'I believe in a holy church,' 'I believe' is not replaced by 'I see.'"[3]

We do not *see* the church as beautifully holy as we wish it were or as truly catholic in its expression as it ought to be. But we *believe* in the church and *believe* it to be holy. This is not to advocate a strict distinction between the "visible church" and the "invisible church." It is simply to acknowledge that the church as we currently see it is not the church as it shall finally be for all eternity. This also means that the church as *we* see it is not the church as *God* sees it. God sees the church—and all its members—in Christ, our risen and glorious Head. We, in Christ, have been crucified. We were buried with him in baptism. We have risen with him in newness of life. We have ascended with him in glory. Our lives are now hidden, with Christ, in God. We shall soon be unveiled, with Christ, in glory. These truths are not to be applied to individual believers only, or even primarily. These refer, first of all, to the church as the body. All who are part of that body are united with Christ the Head and thus can boldly lay claim to these truths for themselves as individuals.

We need to train ourselves to look with eyes of faith on fellow believers, on ourselves as individuals and on the church in its gathered expressions. In chapter seven, we saw that Christian teachers must minister with such *belief* in their hearts. Like Paul, "from now on we regard no one from a worldly point of view," for we know that "if anyone is in Christ, he is a new creation" (2 Cor 5:16-17). We thus come to see people as Jesus saw Simon, as he saw the woman of Samaria, as he saw Zacchaeus, as he sees *us*. We come to see the church, collectively, with the same sort of vision.

In chapter one, we marveled at Paul's descriptions of the church. The

---

[3]Tuomo Mannermaa, *Christ Present in Faith: Luther's View of Justification* (Philadelphia: Fortress, 2005), p. 85.

church is the fullness of Christ, it is the *poiēma* of God, and it is the bride of Christ. The church is the pillar and foundation of the Truth. God boasts of the church against the cosmic forces of darkness. In the church and in Christ Jesus, God shall be glorified forever. All this we *believe*. It is only with eyes of faith that we *see* it.

As tangibly expressed in time and space, the church has caused much pain to many people. We, the authors, have personally experienced it and have real scars—spiritual, emotional and vocational—to show for it. Few believers have not had their share of hurt. And those unbelievers who have been with us for any extended period have likely suffered as well.

On a flight home from ministry in China several years ago, I was seated next to a young man who became very ill in flight. The young woman who was seated on the other side of him helped me to clean up after our neighbor's discomfort had become too much for him. The man left to go to the washroom, and while he was away, I spoke with the woman for some time.

Our conversation, and her kind actions in our mutual clean-up effort, led me to think she was a fellow believer. She certainly was familiar with the language I was using as I told her about what I "did for a living." Finally, however, she confessed to me that though she had attended church for most of her adolescence, she had "left the Faith." I asked her to tell me her story, and she obliged. She had been hurt repeatedly by the pride, prejudice and pettiness she had seen in her local church. She was finally persuaded that the Faith could not be true, since the believers she had known so long were so unloving. So she opted out.

Her feelings were very understandable, and quite familiar to me. But I was just returning home from a week with church leaders who were laboring faithfully in a context that was very hostile for Christians. During our week together, one of the pastors had played for us a song that he had downloaded onto his computer, Twila Paris's "How Beautiful." He played it over and over again. The song's central message, repeated numerous times on the recording, says simply "how beautiful is the body of Christ." Those words had become emblazoned on my soul by the week's end. The powerful and poignant lyrics had even greater power for me because of what I had seen and heard during that week.

I told this young woman how sorry I was for the pain that she had experienced at the hands of the church. But then I told her about what I had just witnessed during that week and about what I had seen in other places and on other occasions. I know how ugly the church can be. Yet I know that the opposite is true as well. "The church is beautiful," I said to her, surprising myself by the conviction and passion with which I spoke. And I invited my new friend to "try again" and even to offer herself to God as an agent of change.

I have seen the beautiful church at work on many occasions. A couple of years ago I was participating in a worship service in Phnom Penh, Cambodia. I was the guest preacher that morning. Early in the service, a number of young men and women led us in singing praises. As they sang and played instruments, a group of about a dozen young girls danced worshipfully and led the congregation in other movements to accompany the singing. My host explained to me that these girls had been rescued from the sex-trafficking industry. The congregation was particularly invested in this ministry.

Over the course of many visits to Sri Lanka, I have witnessed numerous acts of beauty wrought by the church. The *poiēma* of God, created in Christ Jesus, is walking in wondrous works of reconciliation in the midst of much pain and brokenness. My friend Adrian DeVisser has taught me so much about what the Gospel can look like in action. He is constantly dreaming of new ways for his church network to proclaim and to manifest good news to the poor.

In our own church experiences here in the United States over the several decades of our faith journeys, we have witnessed, received and participated in numerous Gospel works of love and life. There has been much pain and disappointment along the way. But the good and the beautiful that we have experienced have far outweighed the bad and the ugly.

So which church are we? Are we the church ugly or the church beautiful? Are we sinners or are we saints? The answer, of course, is *yes*. As Luther reminded us, we are *simul iustus et peccator* (simultaneously righteous and sinful).

Can the church—as manifested in our own, flesh-and-blood-in-time-and-space congregations—be *more* beautiful than it presently is? Can we grow in godliness and in our experience of holiness? Can we be more *saved*? If the answer to these questions were not affirmative, we would have very little material in our New Testament. Most of the New Testament was written as an appeal toward such growth in grace. What is the appeal based on? It is consistently based on the grace and mercy of God displayed so potently in the glorious Gospel. In the final analysis, we do not evoke Christian formation by hammering congregations with guilt or shame. Rather, it is as John makes so very clear, the lavish love of God and the assured hope we have in Christ that stir us to purify ourselves (see 1 Jn 3:1-3). We ought to diligently remind the flock of God's righteous commands, but it is God's kindness, after all, that leads us to a life of repentance (see Rom 2:4). With the psalmist, we find ourselves in awe of God's mercy: "If you, O LORD, kept a record of our sins, O Lord, who could stand? But with you there is forgiveness; therefore, you are feared" (Ps 130:3-4).

What then makes the difference between our being—in practice—the *church beautiful* or the *church ugly?* We certainly know that if there is any good in us at all, it is all of God's grace. Paul said of himself, "I know that nothing good lives in me, that is, in my sinful nature" (Rom 7:18). But the risen Christ had appeared to him, though he was "the least of the apostles" and not worthy even to be called an apostle. And so "by the grace of God I am what I am, and his grace to me was not without effect" (1 Cor 15:9-10). "Apart from me you can do nothing," Jesus had taught (Jn 15:5). Paul learned, however, that *in Christ,* "I can do everything through him who gives me strength" (Phil 4:13). If we are to grow in godliness, it will always and only be a growth "in the grace and knowledge of our Lord and Savior Jesus Christ" (2 Pet 3:18).

However, our growth in grace is not a passive growth. It is active, as we have sought to demonstrate throughout this book. Peter reminds us to "make every effort to add to your faith goodness; and to goodness, knowledge; . . ." (2 Pet 1:5). As Dallas Willard's writings have been reminding us with such ringing consistency, we actually have something to *do* in the process of becoming like Jesus. Like Timothy, each one of us must train ourselves to be godly (see 1 Tim 4:7). This in no way contradicts the fact that progress in godliness is all of grace and thus all of God. Paul's words remind us to "work out your salvation with fear and trembling, for it is God who works in you to will and to act according to his good purpose" (Phil 2:12-13).

Throughout this book we have sought to draw attention to certain faithful practices that believers and congregations can engage and participate in—that is, to some things we can actually *do*—to help foster personal and corporate formation. But we dare not end our considerations with the emphasis on ourselves. There are means of grace we avail ourselves of. But it is the grace of God, not the means by which we appropriate that grace, that transforms our lives.

In our days, before our very eyes, God is doing glorious things in and through the church. We have been taught to pray, "Thy kingdom come; thy will be done on earth as it is in heaven." The sovereign God—Father, Son and Holy Spirit—is surely answering this prayer, in ways we sometimes recognize and sometimes do not. Jesus Christ has assured us that he is building his church and that none of hell's forces can ever prevail against it. Christ is keeping these promises even now. That church—the *poiēma* of God—is the very body of Christ into which we have been called. Through that body—full of love and good works—Jesus Christ continues the ministry of reconciliation today.

May we who have been charged with leadership roles in the teaching and formation of that body give ourselves anew to these grand purposes of God, delighting in and laboring for the glorious Gospel, diligently teaching the Faith and fully engaging in the unfolding of the great redemptive Story. As we endeavor to do so,

Soli Deo Gloria!

HYMN FOR CONTEMPLATION AND WORSHIP

The Wondrous Cross That Saved My Soul

The wondrous cross that saved my soul,
that bore my sin and bought me whole,
a further wonder did achieve—
uniting all those who believe.
The wondrous cross brought down the wall,
stilling the strife between us all.
Now from all flesh—Gentile and Jew—
God forms one body from the two.
(Eph 2:11-22)

Though we are many, we are one:
each part reflecting God's great Son.
Female and male, servant and free,
bound by one Spirit's unity.
Across the earth, the church expands.
Saints lift God's praise in distant lands,
while many weep and suffer loss,
still clinging to the wondrous cross.
(1 Cor 12:12-27; Gal 3:28; Col 1:6; Rev 7:14-17)

Forgive us, Lord, the harm we do
when we refuse to follow you.
Forsaking love, we grasp at pow'r.
Come, heal our sickness in this hour.
O love amazing, love divine—
transform our hearts. (Lord, start with mine!)
As we've received, teach us to give:
born in your love, in love to live.
(Mk 10:42-45; Rom 12:2; Mt 10:8)

Text: Gary A. Parrett (2004)
Tune: Jerusalem (Parry)
Familiar use of the tune: "Jerusalem"

Name Index

Subject Index

administration of the
sacraments, 112, 113,
324, 331, 345n. 10,
347, 348, 359, 374,
381-82, 408
adolescents 230, 234,
290, 317, 381-84, 385,
386, 387, 406. *See also*
teens, youth
adults, 220, 228, 234,
256, 310, 322n. 25,
366, 421
  adult education, 142,
  165, 173, 243, 280,
  288, 312, 371,
  381-84, 386-87,
  404-7, 427
  adult learner, 156n.
  6, 229-30, 243-44,
  263, 290
Advent, 22-23, 328, 347
affections, affective
domain, 115, 117, 271,
281-82, 292-93,
294-95, 298-99, 300,
301, 349
age appropriateness, 165,
309, 405, 411
age segmentation,
306-7, 313, 405
age-ism, 313, 331
America
  American church, 66,
  104, 141, 142, 197,
  282-83, 306, 312n.
  12, 313, 317, 335,
  374, 376n. 25, 421
  American life, 232n.
  73, 287, 308, 331
  American society,

129, 223, 231, 283,
308
  See also United States
andragogy, 243-44, 263
Anglican *Book of
Common Prayer,* 329,
345n. 10, 356
apostle, 7, 50, 101, 103,
154, 155n. 5, 178,
179, 180, 188, 200,
201, 239n. 4, 434
Apostles' Creed, 79,
92n. 34, 93, 123,
125, 134, 327, 353
apostolic church, 29,
29n. 18, 80, 84, 95,
112-13, 120, 198,
329, 351-52, 353,
359, 374, 393, 431
apostolic ministry,
38, 50, 51, 63, 65,
79, 81, 106, 109,
114n. 26, 153, 187,
375, 380, 409
  See also teaching of
  the apostles
assembly, 114, 120,
242n. 9, 311, 336, 339,
348-49, 352, 369, 396,
420
assimilation, 220, 220n.
43, 282n. 22
attendance, 140-42, 157,
162, 288, 344, 355,
367, 369n. 14, 387,
392, 400
attentiveness, 36, 71, 78,
83, 105, 130, 134,
136, 139, 167, 197,
271, 282, 284, 286,

288, 290, 308, 346,
348, 351, 369, 381,
402, 405, 412. *See
also* perception
authority, 25, 31, 43,
139, 192-98, 216, 223,
225, 240-42, 269,
291-92, 301
  of the church, 50,
  151, 251
  of Jesus, 50, 70,
  192-98, 207
  of rabbinic teachers,
  26, 310
  of Scripture, 135,
  139, 199n. 14, 251,
  263, 397
autonomy, 213n. 16,
214, 223, 228
baby boomers, 288n. 36,
308n. 3, 309n. 7
baptism, 39, 50-51, 64,
83, 113, 179, 199, 237,
324, 330, 353, 370-91,
402, 403, 408, 431
  baptismal rites, 51,
  347, 363, 393, 394
  and confirmation,
  134, 164n. 19, 362,
  398, 401
  of infants, 330,
  384-85
  preparation of,
  79-80, 89, 337, 362,
  393-94
belief, 110-12, 114,
141-42, 177, 178-80,
224, 245, 258, 370,
391, 395-97
belief systems, 135, 138,

Scripture Index